GAIN THE EDGE!

GAIN THE
EDGE!

NEGOTIATING TO
GET WHAT YOU WANT

MARTIN E. LATZ

ST. MARTIN'S PRESS ❧ NEW YORK

www.stmartins.com

Library of Congress Cataloging-in-Publication Data

Latz, Martin E.
    Gain the edge! : negotiating to get what you want / Martin E. Latz.
      p. cm.
    Includes bibliographical references (page 355).
    Includes index (page 365).
    ISBN 0-312-32281-X
    EAN 978-0312-32281-6
    1. Negotiation in business. 2. Negotiation. I. Title.

HD58.6.L38 2004
302.3—dc22   2003070106

First Edition: May 2004

10 9 8 7 6 5 4 3 2 1

To my wife, Linda, whose love motivates and sustains me as I strive to achieve the right balance in life.

To my parents, Bob and Carolyn Latz, who have always provided me with more than enough support, advice, encouragement, and love. They have been incredible role models in my personal and professional life.

And to my sister, Shari, and her husband, Mike Rothman, who have been my informal editors ever since I started writing a column and who have spent countless hours and late nights editing and helping me translate my thoughts into words.

CONTENTS

INTRODUCTION

Adam was nervous as he walked into the managing partner's office. He had lost his job at another architectural firm less than two weeks before. It had been a shock. He had worked hard and performed his job well but still ended up on the street. The weak economy, they said, did him in. So now he was back out there looking for work along with a bunch of other junior architects in San Francisco.

After the usual pleasantries the managing partner asked him what salary he expected. Adam thought this was a good sign. Why would they care if they weren't going to offer him the job?

But now he faced a dilemma: How should he respond?

How would *you* respond?

Would you tell the managing partner what you truly expect? Or would you lowball it, given that you don't have a good alternative? If you lowball it you might leave money on the table.

Of course, you could puff up your initial salary expectations so you have room to concede later. But if you do this and it appears too high they may not offer you the job. That would be disastrous.

Perhaps you could just avoid answering the question; appear noncommittal and change the subject. But that's risky, too. The managing partner may falsely sense you're not really interested, or that you're not a straight shooter.

You could always turn around and ask what the firm is looking to pay. Get your counterpart to throw out the first number.

But what if he or she refuses to answer?

Quick—what would you do? What *should* you do? You've only got a split second to decide—and your compensation and job satisfaction for years may depend on your decision.

The fact is, most of us don't really know what to do in this situation. But we should.

This book will explain what you should do and will help you get what you want in this situation and in many others.

Negotiation Is an Important Part of Life

We negotiate constantly—with everyone. Business professionals and lawyers spend hours every day negotiating. Kids play their parents off against each other. Families even try to reach consensus on where to vacation. Whether you're arguing with your spouse, buying a car, or selling a product or a house, you're negotiating.

Yet few have ever learned the strategies and techniques of effective negotiation. Even fewer have mastered them.

Wait a second, you might say. I know some extremely skilled negotiators who do it instinctively. And I've been able to get a lot of what I want in life. So, why should I read this book?

That's exactly how I felt when I started studying negotiation. Since then I've spent thousands of hours studying and teaching negotiation. Plus, I've negotiated—and helped others negotiate—countless deals. One thing I know beyond a shadow of a doubt: There's always more to learn about negotiation. That one new strategy or tactic you gain from this book may make the difference between your walking away a winner and leaving empty-handed. The margin of difference can be infinitesimal, yet the ramifications are often huge.

I've thus included in this book the lessons I've learned from: the most up-to-date negotiation research; the vast experiences of highly successful businesspeople, lawyers, and expert negotiators; my own legal, business, and negotiation experiences in a variety of settings, including negotiating on the White House Advance Teams; and teaching thousands of businesspeople and lawyers how to negotiate more effectively.

To start, it's critical to understand the guiding principles that permeate the entire negotiation process. Once you understand these you will be able to more effectively apply the lessons in this book to your negotiations. These principles include:

- Negotiate strategically—not instinctively.
- Confidence and success come from knowledge and practice.
- The power of preparation *always* makes a difference.
- Protect your reputation.
- Learn by doing.

Negotiate Strategically—Not Instinctively

Let's say you're at your desk Monday morning looking at your overwhelming "To Do" list, your stacked-up "In" box, and wondering if your bonus for once will reflect your true value. Then Jane, a potential business partner, calls and asks if you have a few minutes to chat about your marketing proposal for her new product.

Because you're mostly up-to-speed on the substance of the proposal and intended to call Jane later in the week anyway, you say, "Sure, I've got a few minutes; just give me a second to find the proposal."

"Not a problem," Jane replies, and asks you some innocuous questions while you search for and finally locate the proposal on your desk. You then jump right into the negotiation.

Thirty minutes later, after Jane has rejected most of the elements in your proposal and offered seemingly reasonable alternatives, you tentatively agree on the major deal points. Jane then suggests she would be happy to draft it and send it over. You readily agree after looking again at your overflowing "In" box.

Two weeks later, despite some misgivings, you ink the deal. You know it's not great, but after discussing it with your boss you conclude it's better than your alternative of no deal.

What happened?

You, like millions of others, made a major error when you agreed to speak with Jane *before* you had strategically prepared for the negotiation. Most individuals negotiate instinctively or intuitively. It's natural. It can also be devastating.

In this instance Jane had a significant advantage. Not only did she set the agenda, but she likely put her negotiation knowledge to work *before* ever picking up the phone, by strategically determining:

- How to create the right atmosphere that would help her achieve her goals
- The questions she needed to ask to improve her leverage

- The strength of her alternatives if the deal started going down the tube
- What options might satisfy her interests
- What independent standards she might use to justify her offers or concessions
- What might be her next offer or concession, and why
- Which issues to discuss first and last, and how to control the agenda

Contrast this with *your* situation. Were you thinking strategically about the negotiation that Monday morning? Unlikely.

Like most people, however, you jumped right in.

Adam, the architect, faced this same problem. The reality is most individuals don't think strategically about the negotiation process. They go with their instincts, and—even if they think strategically—simply use tactics that seem to have worked for them before.

Yet some individuals' instincts are more effective than others. And some instincts have been honed to succeed in certain circumstances, but inevitably fail in other situations. In fact, I'm sure you have instinctively used some of the negotiation strategies in this book. "I remember doing that when I bought my house," you may say. Or, "My boss tried that last time I asked for a raise." Or, "Now I know why I didn't get that big sale last year."

But how certain are you that your instincts led you to the best possible result? And how many times have you walked away from a negotiation wondering how much you left on the table?

This book will help shift your mindset from instinctive to strategic. Next time you face these negotiation situations you will systematically think about which strategies to use. You will have a framework within which to approach specific negotiations and to help you determine what to do in challenging situations. Your strategies and decisions then will be based not only on your own experiences, but on the collective experiences of the best negotiators in the world and on the most up-to-date research.

The bottom line is this: Reading this book will provide you with a more sophisticated, strategic mindset and a comprehensive, practical toolbox to use when facing a variety of negotiation contexts. Overall, you will then have a greater likelihood of getting what you want in the everyday negotiations life invariably throws your way.

Confidence and Success Come from Knowledge and Practice

"I hate to negotiate," some of my seminar participants tell me. "It makes me anxious, and I just don't like horse-trading. How will this help?"

"Treat it like a game," I tell them. "Don't take it personally. And study it so you will be able to recognize what's being done and why. Knowledge of the process will increase your comfort level and your ability to get what you want. Unless you're isolated from all human contact, negotiation is a part of life. Like any life skill, you can improve it with understanding, knowledge, and practice."

Make no mistake: *Everyone* can improve his or her negotiation skills. No negotiation presents exactly the same challenges, because an unlimited number of variables exist in *every* negotiation. So, each negotiation presents unique and challenging situations no matter what your level of experience or expertise: the parties may be different, the issues may vary, your mood that day may be good or bad, and the negotiation dynamic or conversation may ebb and flow in unexpected directions.

Yet, common strategies and tactics underlie success in almost every negotiation. Certain psychological tendencies increase your ability to predict what others will do in many situations. And your attitude and comfort level with the negotiation process affect your ability to succeed.

What does this mean for you? This book will familiarize you with the latest and most common negotiation strategies and tactics. Next time you see them in action you will know how to respond. Your increased confidence will improve your ability to get what you want. That's success.

The Power of Preparation *Always* Makes a Difference

What is the most universally ignored but most effective negotiation tool? *Preparation.* I conclude every one of my seminars with this statement:

"Prepare, Prepare, Prepare. It's guaranteed to succeed. The more you prepare, the better you will do." Most people fail to sufficiently prepare. We have the best of intentions, but we lead busy lives and jump into negotiations without adequately exploring the many avenues down which negotiations may proceed. Renowned UCLA basketball coach John Wooden said: "Failing to prepare is preparing to fail." He's right.

Adequate preparation will not only make a difference, it will make *the* difference.

Negotiation research unmistakably illustrates the concrete value of preparation. Yet, many individuals still inadequately or ineffectively prepare.

Businesspeople comprehensively analyze every substantive element of a deal and engage in weeks of due diligence to ensure they don't miss a substantive point. Trial lawyers spend an enormous amount of time preparing opening statements and cross-examinations. They even map out what they will wear each day in court.

But most lawyers and businesspeople give short shrift to the "process" element of the negotiation. They will know the substance but wing it when it comes to preparing for the actual steps in the negotiation. *To consistently get what you want in negotiations, you must marry the substance to the process.* Adequate preparation—on both substance and process—is essential to success.

This book will provide you with a practical, step-by-step preparation process that will keep you from falling into the inadequate preparation trap. Few strategies are guaranteed to succeed in *every* negotiation. Preparation is one strategy that works *every* time.

Protect Your Reputation

Jealously protect your reputation. Sounds simple and straightforward, right? Of course. But many negotiators apply a different ethical standard to negotiations than to other parts of their lives. Justifications abound. "Everyone lies in negotiations," some will say. Or, "It's just a white lie."

Here's the deal. Even the most competent and professional negotiations involve a certain amount of "salesmanship." In fact, a significant dynamic in many negotiations involves one party attempting to convince the other party that their bottom line is different than what it is in reality. Or that they have more leverage than is actually the case. Or they try to avoid answering certain questions or revealing strategically important information.

But at the end of the day, deal or no deal, everyone will leave the negotiation with an impression of whether their counterparts dealt with them in a professional and honest fashion. If you gain a reputation as an honest and trustworthy negotiator you will be more likely to get what you want in the future. If not, you will lose credibility, fewer opportunities will come your way, and fewer negotiations will conclude with your achieving your goals.

This book will provide you with specific guidance and criteria to use in determining where and how to make the tough ethical decisions common in many negotiations. You will then know what strategies and tactics to use to most effectively achieve your goals *and* protect your reputation.

Learn by Doing

Strategic thinking. Confidence and a comprehensive negotiation toolbox. Preparation. A stellar reputation. Effective negotiators need all of these tools. But they don't help much until you have learned how to apply them in real-life negotiations.

It's one thing to understand the negotiation process. It's another to put this knowledge to use in actual negotiations. The most effective principles, strategies, and tactics can be found in this book, along with a variety of examples and practical stories illustrating how to successfully use these strategies and techniques. These will give you the intellectual base, the tools to succeed, and the context in which to use the tools.

The last step is up to you.

As with any skill, becoming a more effective negotiator takes time, effort, understanding, and practice. Especially practice. My negotiation seminars are heavily interactive and require the participants to practice what I preach. Why? It's in the application of these skills that most participants internalize these strategies. The knowledge you gain from this book is a crucial first step. But it's only the first step. You will still need to apply these strategies in your negotiations.

Remember, most negotiations require split-second strategic decisions and leave little room for error if you inadvertently blurt out critical information. The more you apply these strategies in your daily negotiations, the more effective they will be in helping you get what you want.

With these guiding principles as a baseline, the rest of the book is organized into three parts:

- The Strategic Template: Latz's Five Golden Rules of Negotiation
- Making the Golden Rules Work for You
- Applying these Strategies to Real-Life Situations

Part One—The Strategic Template:
Latz's Five Golden Rules of Negotiation

My Five Golden Rules of Negotiation provide the essential building blocks for every negotiation. They are:

1. Information Is Power—So Get It
2. Maximize Your Leverage
3. Employ "Fair" Objective Criteria
4. Design an Offer-Concession Strategy
5. Control the Agenda

Described in detail in Part One, along with many in-depth examples illustrating their impact, these Five Golden Rules provide the procedural framework for all effective negotiations. It's equally important, however, to know when and where and how to apply these Golden Rules. That's in Part Two.

Part Two—Making the Golden Rules Work for You

Understanding negotiation strategies is one thing. Personalizing these strategies so they work for you in various contexts is another. Effective negotiation requires that you understand how you personally come across and how you interact with others' negotiating styles. And you need to know when and where to open up with more information, in what circumstances to talk frankly about your leverage, and where to simply hint at it. In other words, it's essential that you learn how to apply the Five Golden Rules in various negotiation situations. Most people negotiate differently with children than with car salesmen. They should.

In Part Two, we explore how you should negotiate in different contexts. Then we set up an easy-to-use outline to determine what approach will be most effective. The first step involves examining your own personal negotiating style and approach to conflict. The second involves examining individuals' various approaches to negotiation ethics. Third, we analyze the two most common negotiation strategies and discuss when to use each.

Finally, we address a number of typical negotiation problems and propose solutions and tactics to use in each. Each requires a unique application of the Five Golden Rules. These problems include:

- Foiling common negotiation "games"
- Impasse-breaking strategies
- Dealing with emotional counterparts
- Overcoming a fear of the negotiation process

Part Three: Applying These Strategies to Real-Life Situations

Finally, Part Three provides practical advice on how to apply these strategies to the following common negotiation situations:

- Garden-variety business negotiations
- Salary negotiations
- Family negotiations
- Car negotiations
- House negotiations

Each of these situations presents unique negotiation challenges. Each also requires the application of specialized negotiation strategies and skills. You will find these strategies and skills in this section.

The most effective negotiators think and act strategically. By applying the strategies and tactics in this book to your negotiations, you will improve your success rate—in business and in life. You will, in fact, gain the edge.

PART ONE

THE STRATEGIC TEMPLATE: LATZ'S FIVE GOLDEN RULES

The first five chapters in this book extensively explore my Five Golden Rules. In order for you to begin to synthesize these Golden Rules, let me briefly describe each one. Then, as you study each chapter in depth, you will have some context in which to understand how they work together.

Golden Rule One: Information Is Power—So Get It

The first Golden Rule is essential to success in any negotiation: *Information Is Power—So Get It*. It's critical to ask questions and get as much relevant information as you can throughout the negotiation process. You need sufficient information to set aggressive, realistic goals and to evaluate the other side's goals. With this information in your pocket, you've got the power. Without it you will be scrambling.

Self-described "expert" negotiators often enter negotiations with arguments intended to persuade the other side of the legitimacy of their positions. Unknowingly, they're giving up power from the first time they open their mouths. I will take an effective questioner and listener over a talker in almost any negotiation. *Negotiation power goes to those who listen and learn*.

Golden Rule Two: Maximize Your Leverage

How much do you want or need that item on the table? How much does your counterpart need it? What are your and your counterpart's alternatives if you don't reach agreement? What can you do to strengthen your leverage before and during the negotiation? How can you weaken your counterpart's leverage? What might your counterpart be doing at the same time? Finally, are you exercising your leverage in an appropriate fashion?

Finding the answers to these leverage questions as early as possible in the process can be the key to success. Ignoring them can be a recipe for disaster.

Golden Rule Three: Employ "Fair" Objective Criteria

"I just want what's fair and reasonable," a friend said in the midst of his divorce. "That's not too much to ask, is it?"

"Of course not," I replied. "The key here, though, is *how* to determine what's fair and reasonable. I suspect you have a very different perception of what's 'fair and reasonable' than your soon-to-be-ex-wife. We need to figure out how to get her to accept *your* proposal as fair and reasonable. Not only to you, but to her, too."

The quest for fairness and the perception of fairness serve as central elements in many negotiations. Fairness, in most instances, boils down to a matter of relatively objective standards and/or an independent process that ensures an acceptable, "fair and reasonable" result. If both sides can agree on an independent standard that is fair and reasonable, or on an independent process that inevitably will conclude with a fair outcome, the deal will likely be done. If not, it's far more difficult to reach agreement.

For example, finding and using an independent standard or process that favors your side, like market value—and then negotiating over what's "fair"—will provide you with a distinct advantage. It also will help you keep that "reasonable" hat on your head—an important element for your reputation and success.

Golden Rule Four: Design an Offer-Concession Strategy

The most common question raised in my negotiation seminars is "When, if ever, should I make the first offer?" The second most common question is "How far should I move for my next concession?" This Golden Rule takes the guesswork out of when, where, and how to make offers and concessions. No one wants to leave valuable items on the table gratuitously. The best way to avoid this is to first design the right offer-concession strategy.

Doing this will require you to understand the psychological dynamics underlying concession behavior, as well as improve your ability to evaluate your counterpart's "flinch" point. It's not an exact science, but you can learn to draw out and recognize certain signals. Here I will show you how to make these crucial decisions.

Golden Rule Five: Control the Agenda

The final Golden Rule seems self-explanatory. Of course you want to control the agenda. But it's more complicated than it appears. For instance, trying to dictatorially impose a set agenda at the beginning of a negotiation can create lasting damage. Yet, it may be critical to address Issue A before Issue B. How should you do it?

And what about timing issues and deadlines—real and artificially imposed? Understanding when to use deadlines, how to effectively operate within them, and the psychological tendencies underlying them will give you a leg up in your negotiations. Effectively managing the negotiation process—overtly or covertly—is one of the most challenging elements, even for the most expert negotiators. This Golden Rule will arm you with the knowledge and tools to better navigate and control your negotiation agendas.

Now that you have a basic understanding of my Five Golden Rules, let's explore each in depth.

GOLDEN RULE ONE:

INFORMATION IS POWER—SO GET IT

Tom is in his midforties and has been growing his software company for about fifteen years. He started as its marketing guru, gradually progressed to become a part owner, and took over its helm when its founders decided to become less involved. The company grew steadily for most of its existence and had recently experienced a real growth spurt that showed promise of substantially higher profits. This prompted the industry's leaders to take notice, and several contacted Tom to discuss buying his company.

Tom is married, has two young children under six, and is seriously considering selling. He has been working nonstop for twenty years and recently began to reevaluate his priorities. While he wants to continue working, he also wants to spend more time with his family.

He was thus excited to learn in his preliminary discussions on price and value with the two potential buyers that he could become financially comfortable for the rest of his life if he sold. However, the initial cash portion of the offers varied significantly. Each offer also required him to remain as the CEO for several years and to take a substantial portion of the company's value in relatively risky shares of the new venture. Unsure exactly how to maximize his company's value, he asked for advice as to how he should respond.

After finding out some basics and the status of the negotiations, I suggested the following, which applies to *everyone* engaged in *any* negotiation:

"Tom," I said, "back up. The first thing you must do in any negotiation is gather sufficient information to set your goals. Unless you have thoroughly explored both sides' personal and professional objectives, set your own specific, aggressive and achievable goals, and designed a strategy to accomplish them, you're destined to negotiate in a reactive mode. If you're reacting, you're far less likely to end up with what you want."

Overall, I told him, start by taking these three major steps:

- Get information to set your goals
- Develop an information-bargaining strategy—ways to get and share information
- Reevaluate your goals

Get Information to Set Your Goals

The first step for Tom and for you is to figure out exactly what you want. Define your objectives, set your goals, and take the time to do it right at the start. Otherwise, your whole strategic mindset will be flawed.

Research in a variety of disciplines supports the value of goal-setting. You see it in the field of sports psychology, where studies have shown that setting goals improves performance. You see it in the political field, where some politicians set their sights from grade school on. And you see it in business and negotiation.

In each area, research shows that you increase the likelihood of achieving your goals if you start by systematically setting them. Goal-setting also provides the crucial first step to thinking strategically about the negotiation process. Almost anyone can jump into a negotiation and—if there's a large zone of possible agreement between the parties— reach a result both sides find acceptable. But only a skilled practitioner can go into that same negotiation and reach a result that truly maximizes what he or she wants. This may include creating more value for both sides, the traditional "win-win" scenario. Or it may mean maximizing their share of a pie that must be cut in a "zero-sum" way—where more for one side necessarily means less for the other.

Take the time to set your goals at the outset. It's essential, if you want to become a more effective negotiator.

That's what Tom did. Subsequently, he ended up in semiretirement with a seven-figure nest egg in the bank.

And if you think setting goals is simple, consider the following story about Akio Morita, the longtime leader of Sony Corporation.

In 1955, according to G. Richard Shell in *Bargaining for Advantage,* Akio Morita received an offer from Bulova to purchase 100,000 of Sony's new $29.95 transistor radios. This would have been Sony's biggest deal ever. Morita turned it down. In fact, he later called his tu "best decision" he ever made for his company. He even reject own board's objections.

Why?

Accepting it would have run contrary to one of Morita's fundamental long-term goals. The deal-breaker? The offer would have required Sony's radios to be sold under the *Bulova* name.

At first it seemed like a great deal. A "win-win." Sony had leading-edge technology but was relatively unknown in the United States. Bulova had the reputation and an extensive retail distribution network throughout the United States. While the deal involved some risk—no one knew the marketability of Sony's transistor radios—it seemed like an excellent opportunity that took advantage of Sony's *and* Bulova's strengths.

Critically, Morita focused on his true long-term goal: to make the Sony name synonymous with quality electronics throughout the world. This "great" deal, even though it would have generated substantial short-term profits, was inconsistent with his goal. Morita walked, shocking Bulova and Sony's board. Sony later sold a smaller number of radios to a different distributor and stamped the Sony name on them. The rest is business history.

The lesson? Start by focusing on what you *really* want to achieve. Setting goals sounds simple. It's not. Morita's board recommended that he accept the Bulova deal, even though it contrasted with his long-term branding goal. Defining your true goals takes time, effort, and thought. Spend the time to do it right. Your goals should establish your negotiation behavior, not the other way around.

What kind of goals should you set? Sometimes your goals appear clear-cut. Pay the least amount possible for that new car. Sell the house at the highest offered price. Maintain the long-term relationship with your children.

Other times, it's unclear. Morita gave up a huge deal-in-the-hand for the possibility that he would create a world-class brand. In retrospect, his decision appears obvious and brilliant. In 1955 it was controversial.

While getting the information and appropriately setting your goals may be difficult, it will be much clearer if you use this three-step strategic framework.

1. Set and prioritize your long-term strategic and short-term tactical goals
2. Determine and prioritize your counterpart's goals
3. Evaluate the power of the relationship

Set and Prioritize Your Long-Term Strategic and Short-Term Tactical Goals

Morita focused on Sony's long-term strategic goal. His board focused on its short-term tactical goal. There's a crucial difference. To most effectively get what you want in the long and short term, distinguish between strategic and tactical goals. Then set both.

Strategies focus on your long-term goals and impact how, in a global sense, you should try to accomplish them. Tactics, by contrast, are concerned with immediate, detailed maneuvers designed to accomplish your overall strategic goals.

Recognizing that *Information Is Power,* and focusing on it, is a strategic view. Deciding what kinds of questions to ask, which questions to ask, and when and where to ask them to get that information is tactical. Effective negotiators use strategies *and* tactics to achieve their goals.

In this book, as in real negotiations, we will sometimes move seamlessly between strategies and tactics. At times we will break out a strategy or tactic and discuss it. Other times the interrelationship between the two will be subtle. Overall, you will see the big picture—what you want to strategically achieve—and get practical, tactical advice as to how to achieve it.

Some negotiators excel at strategy. Others maneuver more effectively in a tactical sense. The best use both to achieve their ends.

To summarize, first gather sufficient information to set and prioritize your long-term strategic and short-term tactical goals. This will help you determine at the beginning what success will look like at the end. And while you may not definitively set specific goals at this preliminary stage, it will highlight the information you will need to get later to achieve these goals.

Determine and Prioritize Your Counterpart's Goals

"The most critical thing in a negotiation is to get inside your opponent's head and figure out what he really wants," former White House Office of Management and Budget (OMB) Director Jack Lew told me in August 2000. He should know. He managed the budget negotiations for the Clinton White House in the late 1990s, when they went up against the Republican-dominated congress. Most would agree—regardless of political preference—that President Clinton and his team achieved most of their budget goals during this time.

But what does this mean within the context of goal-setting? And why does it matter what the other side wants, if you know what you want?

It matters because negotiations always involve more than one individual or entity. Your ability to achieve your goals therefore often depends on whether the other side also can achieve *its* goals. Sometimes their goals conflict with yours. Other times their goals are consistent with yours. In all cases find out their goals earlier in the process, not later.

Also guard against the tendency to assume the other side shares your views. Many would naturally assume that a software developer selling the rights to his or her software wants the most possible money for it. This may not be true. Perhaps the developer inherited a great deal of wealth and is more interested in his or her reputation in the software community than any financial reward he or she might reap from the sale. If your company has a unique marketing ability to get this software into the mainstream markets, this may be far more valuable to him or her than the money.

Stepping into your counterparts' shoes and understanding their perspective—in the beginning and throughout the process—is also a critical part of the mindset shift necessary to negotiate strategically, not instinctively. Most of us instinctively focus on what we want and only haphazardly find out what the other side wants. Don't let this happen to you. Until you know what and how much your counterpart wants to achieve certain goals, you can't really know when to hold and when to fold. By contrast, if and when you learn this information you can maximize your ability to achieve *your* goals.

Consider the impact of the following exercise I use in some of my seminars. It's called the $20-Bill Auction, and the idea was devised by Yale Professor Martin Shubik. As you read, think about the goals you might set and the actions you might take in this situation. Then consider the possible goals and actions of others.

The $20-Bill Auction

"Here's a $20 bill," I start by announcing to the seminar participants. "I'm going to auction it off to the highest bidder. You are free to bid or not bid. The bidding will proceed in one-dollar increments until no further bidding occurs. At that time the highest bidder will pay me the amount bid and receive the $20 bill. But there's a catch: The second highest bidder at the end of the auction must *also* pay me the amount he or she bid. So, if Frank bid $5 and Sally bid $4 and the bidding ended, Frank would pay me $5 and I would give Frank the $20 bill. Frank thus "wins" and makes a net profit of $15. Sally, the second highest bidder, would then pay me $4. Sally thus incurs a loss of $4."

I then start the auction. Invariably, the bidding quickly gets up to the

$15 range. Most participants figure any bid up to $19 makes sense. After all, if you're the winning bid at $19, you have made a one-dollar profit. And even if you push and pay $20 for the $20 bill, you probably got some enjoyment value out of the auction, so you might find that acceptable, too.

The rub occurs, however, when bids reach the $15 range. It's here—in the heat of the negotiation—that bidders start to think through how their goal of getting a profit interacts with their *opponent's* apparent goal of getting a profit. *Wait a second,* the bidders say to themselves, *what if I end up second? Then I lose whatever I bid.*

When this thought occurs—and bidders start to explicitly consider *other bidders' actions*—the number of bidders precipitously declines until only two remain. Quite quickly, these two feel stuck. Why? They've fallen into the trap. One will surely lose—and neither wants to lose.

Each remaining bidder's focus then switches from figuring out: a) the amount they would pay for the $20 bill (as noted above, they initially figured they would pay up to $19 and still make a profit); to b) the amount the *other* bidder might pay. In other words, both bidders now increasingly focus on the *other* bidder's goals and actions. Each bidder's goal also appears to subtly change from making a profit to avoiding a loss—which the second-highest bidder will inevitably suffer.

The dynamic has completely changed. Assume Frank bid $17 and Sally bid $16. Sally now can bid $18 and potentially get a $2 profit. Or she can suffer a sure loss of $16. It's logical, isn't it, for her to bid $18? In isolation, it's logical. But now factor in what she believes *Frank* wants and what *he* will do. If it's logical for her to bid up to $19, it's also logical for Frank. And if he will bid up to $19 and so will she, what then?

As you think through *both* sides' goals and potential actions, it becomes clear that Frank and Sally, at around the $19 mark, have moved from an allegedly rational decision-making process to an arguably irrational one. What do I mean?

Let's say Sally bid $18 and then Frank bid $19. Both bids are perfectly rational, right? Wrong. Why? Because they're perfectly rational if one *only* considers one's own goal and actions in deciding whether and what to bid. What happens next explains this.

In most cases, Sally bids $20. *Then Frank bids $21.* Frank figures it's better to possibly suffer a $1 loss than a certain loss of $19. This seems rational. And so it goes on.

True, they're both now acting "irrationally"—bidding more than the $20 bill is worth. But their logic, based only on their individual goals, appears unassailable.

Interestingly, final bids often end up in the $30 to $70 range. A colleague has even reported selling the $20 bill for $204—a tidy profit of $387 for the auctioneer. (He collected $204 from the "winning" bidder and $203 from the second highest bidder. He then subtracted the $20 bill he sold to the "winner" and profited by $387.) My highest sale was in a seminar for about one hundred New York City lawyers. I sold my $20 bill for $83, and the "winning" bidder insisted I sign the $20 bill. He told me he was going to frame it to illustrate to his law partners the importance of thinking through your counterparts' goals along with your own.

What should we learn from this?

First, explicitly evaluating *both* sides' goals and the dynamics of the exercise before this auction began would have highlighted the trap. A simple mock auction would have illustrated the bidders' dilemma. Understanding that the last two bidders will almost always lose leads to the conclusion that it makes little sense to bid in the first place.

Second, the goal "not to lose" only became obvious to most when the bidding reached around $15. Each party's short-term goal appeared clear: make a profit and/or win. But in the longer-term—at the $15-bid mark—their "not to lose" goal became apparent. At that point, when it was likely down to around two bidders, it was probably too late to pull out. This underscores the importance of analyzing and prioritizing the other side's goals—to the extent possible—at the start of the negotiation. Analyzing them for the first time in the middle may be too late.

Third, watch out for egos. Paying $204 for a $20 bill had everything to do with ego and winning, and nothing to do with rationality. Ego can undermine rational decision making. It's okay if your goal is to pump up your ego. But if your true goal is unrelated to ego, beware of ego's often stealthy impact.

To summarize, get into your counterpart's mind and ascertain his or her goals. What does he or she want? Then actively consider what strategies and tactics he or she might use to try to accomplish those goals.

Here's a rule of thumb to help you remember this: *Know thyself and thy counterpart!*

Evaluate the Power of the Relationship

The third and final strategic element in goal-setting involves the value of your relationship with the other side. As we will explore in depth in Part Two, effective negotiation strategies and tactics often revolve around the extent and type of your relationship with your counterpart. And while some say they always value having a relationship with their counterparts, or vice versa, it's usually not an "always-never" proposition. It's a question of degree.

For example, you shouldn't use the same negotiation strategies and tactics with your spouse or longtime friend as with a rug merchant in a foreign open-air market. You care deeply about continuing your long-term relationship with your spouse or longtime friend. By contrast, you're unlikely to ever see the foreign rug merchant again. The nature of your "relationship goal" should impact your entire strategy.

It's this overt focus on relationships as a goal that underlies the rags-to-riches success story of one of sports owners' most respected figures—Arizona Diamondbacks' and Phoenix Suns' CEO Jerry Colangelo.

The Sale of the Suns

The negotiation lasted almost twenty years. Colangelo had a clear goal: ownership of the Phoenix Suns professional basketball team. But in 1968, when the negotiation started, he didn't have "two nickels" in his pocket. In 1987 he had more, but not nearly enough. The cost? $44.5 million.

How did he manage to buy the Suns and join one of the most elite groups of businessmen in the world, professional sports franchise owners?

To learn from this negotiation, we must first recognize that the negotiation didn't simply occur in 1987, when Colangelo rounded up the Suns' purchase price. No, it started in 1968, when a twenty-seven-year-old Colangelo was hired as the Suns' general manager. Even then he had a clear goal and wasn't afraid to ask for what he wanted. What did he do? He asked the Suns' owners for the right to buy if they ever decided to sell. Even though this outcome didn't appear likely at the time, they agreed.

Colangelo's next step took almost twenty years to accomplish and consisted of thousands of telephone calls, business meetings, social outings, and almost every conceivable form of communication with literally hundreds of people. In many ways, this next step reflected one of Colangelo's major strengths as a negotiator: He built strong, trusting relationships with the Phoenix community—business and otherwise—based upon respect, honesty, fairness, mutuality, and a willingness to work hard to achieve his objectives. He built the same relationship with the Suns' owners. In short, he recognized and developed the power of relationships.

"Negotiating," Colangelo told me when we discussed his purchase, is "relational in a very large way." Colangelo paid attention to his reputation and relationships, and in 1987, it paid off. His Phoenix business community colleagues invested almost $20 million toward his effort to buy the Suns. And the Suns' owners sold the team for what Colangelo considered a fair price.

Colangelo anticipated this and factored it in from the beginning. A clear lesson emerges: Strong, trusting relationships have a distinct and significant value in most negotiations. A reputation for honesty, fairness, respect, and hard work will make a bottom line difference.

Colangelo moved to Phoenix in 1968 with little in his pocket and a blank slate in the community. Since then, he has engaged in countless negotiations. A big key to his success: an overt, explicit goal to develop and strengthen his long-term relationships with business and other community leaders.

Different negotiations require varying levels of focus on relationships. One important element at the goal-setting stage is to evaluate the nature and potential power inherent in your current and potential relationship with the other side. Colangelo understands the power of relationships. You should, too.

Two final notes about the power of relationships. One, you never know when a previous relationship may affect a current negotiation. I'm constantly amazed at the small world in which we live and the sometimes-unknown interrelationships between individuals. Marquette Law Professor Andrea Kupfer Schneider's brother Jeff once rented a house in Washington, D.C. for the summer from a United States diplomat stationed in Egypt. Who cares about the relationship, right? Wrong. Several years later that diplomat applied for a job with Northwestern Mutual in Milwaukee. Guess who helped make the hiring decision for Northwestern? Professor Schneider's husband. As Professor Schneider is fond of saying: "You just never know."

Two, some consider relationships to have an intrinsic value, regardless of the potential future practical value associated with them. Keep this in mind. Future relationships almost always have *some* value—the question is how much.

So far we've laid out a three-step strategic framework to effectively set your goals—all within the context of the First Golden Rule: *Information Is Power—So Get It.*

INFORMATION IS POWER—SO GET IT

Get Information to Set Your Goals
1. Set and prioritize your long-term strategic and short-term tactical goals
2. Determine and prioritize your counterpart's goals
3. Evaluate the power of the relationship

This is the overall strategy. Practical tips and tactics to use in accomplishing this strategy come next. Here are five critical tips and tactics you should use in this process.

Practical Tips and Tactics for Goal-Setting

- Brainstorm to set your goals
- Set aggressive and specific goals—don't just "do the best you can"
- Tie your goals to realistic standards
- *Expect* to succeed
- Commit to it

Brainstorm to Set Your Goals

How many times did you hear growing up that "two heads are better than one"? Here it's true. Brainstorming will help you focus on what you fundamentally want, and help you realistically evaluate the likelihood of achieving your goals.

I once spent several hours brainstorming about a religious discrimination lawsuit with a successful lawyer who had been practicing law for over forty years. In this matter the plaintiff allegedly had been fired for refusing to engage in certain religious practices at work. At the end of our session the lawyer reset his expectations of the case's settlement value. The brainstorming process focused his attention on several issues he had largely ignored.

Three major benefits exist to brainstorming about goals, each of which existed in my session with this forty-year lawyer. *First*, brainstorming invariably spawns a more creative dynamic and often generates a valuable discussion of innovative options and insights about your goals. This rarely occurs if you just think through the issues on your own. The truth is, some people think more logically and analytically than others and focus on tangible goals and benefits. Others think more laterally and creatively and tend to emphasize intangible goals. No matter how you think and process information, bringing different types of thinkers together can help you evaluate what's really important.

Second, it's natural to focus on short-term goals in negotiations. What price can I afford for this house? Or, in Sony's case in 1955, how can we sell the most radios and maximize our short-term profits? While it's important to set short-term goals, it's also essential to take a longer-term, more strategic view. Brainstorming helps you focus on the short *and* long term. In buying a house, your long-term goal might be to either sell it in five years or keep it as rental property. This decision will affect your negotiation strategy. Brainstorming helps you incorporate a longer-term focus into your strategy at the beginning of the negotiation, not at the end.

Finally, working collaboratively to set goals will help create in your mind a more realistic expectation of what you can accomplish. If others agree you can achieve X, you're more likely to believe it yourself. Your changed expectations will lead to more confidence, which will increase your likelihood of success.

Set Aggressive and Specific Goals—
Don't Just "Do The Best You Can"

"I believe in always having goals and always setting them high," said Wal-Mart founder Sam Walton. Be ambitious. Adopt aggressive goals. Remember that old saying: "You can't get what you don't ask for." Your goals will set the upper limit to what you can achieve. Set aggressive-enough goals to ensure you don't mentally concede anything before you have even begun. Answer the question: How much is enough? And answer it at the beginning, before you jump into the rest of the negotiation.

As you will see, a direct relationship exists between individuals' goals and what they achieve. The more you expect, the more you will get. The less you expect, the less you will get. Interestingly, however, parties' satisfaction with their result does not change with their goal. In one study of negotiators involved in the *same* negotiation, those with high goals got high settlements, and those who expected less got less. But both groups were *equally* satisfied with their respective outcomes. Everyone felt like they had succeeded to the same degree—but some had done substantially better than others. The lesson: Set aggressive goals.

In another study psychologists Sydney Siegel and Lawrence Fouraker designed a buy-sell negotiation and told the negotiators they could 1) keep all their profits from the negotiation, and 2) qualify for a double-their-money bonus round if they met certain goals in the initial round. They thus built in plenty of incentive to bargain hard.

In the study, two sets of negotiations took place. Each group of negotiators received identical instructions—with one exception. Group One was told their goal was to achieve a $2.10 profit. Group Two was given a much more aggressive goal of $6.10. Each group was told they would go to the bonus round if they achieved their goal. The result? Those with the $6.10 goal achieved a mean profit of $6.25. Those with the $2.10 goal achieved a mean profit of $3.35. *Conclusion: A direct relationship exists between your goal and what you achieve.*

Setting aggressive goals increases your likelihood of achieving them. But limits exist. The goal-setting process should be a continuous exercise that doesn't end when you first pick your goals. The negotiation process inevitably ebbs and flows, depending on a number of nonstatic factors, including leverage, the utilization of different standards, the information you discover, and the interplay between the parties. So, keep your initial goals somewhat flexible.

When you get critical information, adjust your goals. For instance, when your leverage substantially changes (perhaps you're selling your car, a potential buyer pulls out, and you need the cash from the sale for an upcoming trip), adjust your goals accordingly. Of course, keep your goal-changing behavior to a relative minimum. Constantly adjusting your goals dilutes their overall effectiveness.

Along these same lines, also set *specific* goals. Negotiation research tells us we will be more motivated to achieve concrete, specific goals than vague, ambiguous ones like "I will do the best I can." As your motivation increases, so does your likelihood of success. Which do you think would be more effective as a goal: *"Improve cost savings,"* or *"Increase cost savings by 10 percent"*? Obviously, it's *"Increase cost savings by 10 percent."* Specific goals also provide a benchmark you can use throughout the negotiation to keep on track and will help you decide whether, when, and how to much to move in the offer-concession stage (addressed in detail in chapter 4: Design an Offer-Concession Strategy). The more concrete and specific your goal, the higher your likelihood of achieving it.

Setting aggressive, concrete, and specific goals will help you achieve your goals. By contrast, "winging it"—no matter your level of confidence in your abilities—will increase the likelihood you will do worse. Negotiation is an exercise in probabilities. Setting aggressive and specific goals increases the probability that you will achieve your objectives.

Tie Your Goals to Realistic Standards
But don't be *too* aggressive. Instead, be realistic. If you constantly set your goals so high you never achieve them, you will become discouraged over the long term. This attitude will negatively affect your performance and you will start to set your goals too low. No one wants to continually "fail." Likewise, if you consistently set your goals too low you won't have sufficient motivation to achieve all you can.

How can you pick appropriately aggressive, yet realistic, goals? Tie your goals to appropriate standards. Find an objective standard or precedent that provides a "fairness" baseline for your goal. Answer the question: Why would achieving this be "fair and reasonable"? As discussed more fully in chapter 3, this step will provide a reality check on your goals.

Let's see how this might have worked for Adam, the San Francisco–based architect. Before he ever set foot through the architectural firm's door for a job interview he should have researched the salary range in San Francisco for similarly experienced architects, and found out his market value. Let's say he discovers from a trade journal and his colleagues at other firms that it ranges from about $42,500 to $65,000 annually. Another standard he might consider is his own precedent—what his previous firm paid him. Let's say he was paid $47,000 prior to being laid off. He might also find out what the interviewing architectural firm pays other architects at his level, perhaps by asking one of the younger architects at the firm. Let's say he finds out the firm is paying a former classmate of his $55,000.

These standards—market value, his own precedent, and the firm's precedent—will provide Adam with objective standards on which to evaluate his goal. With this information, he should tie his goal to one of these standards. He might, for instance, set a goal of $60,000. While it may be aggressive in relation to what he was previously paid, he can justify it by noting that several similarly experienced San Francisco architects received this the previous year.

(Note: This is Adam's goal, *not* his first offer. First-offerwise, Adam may decide it does not make strategic sense for him to even make the first offer, and let the firm make it. Or, if he thinks he would be better off making the first offer, he might start at $65,000 and note that this represents what one of his colleagues received as a salary in the past year. This builds in room to move, if necessary. More on first offers—whether to make them and, if so, at what level—in chapter 4.)

The critical point? Tie your aggressive goal to a realistic standard. It will be more powerful and effective than picking one out of thin air.

Expect to Succeed

A passionate, positive attitude makes a difference. Those with an optimistic, can-do attitude toward achieving their desired result will be more likely to succeed than those with a lackadaisical approach. So, consciously transform your mindset about goals from theoretical targets to genuine expectations. Goals are one thing, expectations another. If Adam set a goal of $60,000, this represents his target. It's what he *wants* or *desires*. By contrast, if he walks into the negotiation *expecting* to agree to $60,000, he believes he *deserves* this salary.

Expect it. Your mindset and attitude will lead to improved results. Your expectation of success will change how you come across. Your comments will carry more conviction, your body language will exhibit more confidence, and you will be more animated.

Most of us have heard a pep talk at some point in our lives. Maybe it was your high school football coach. Perhaps you recently heard a motivational speaker. Or maybe a sermon by your spiritual leader inspired you to focus on a neglected part of your life. Part of what they were saying was: *Expect it. Don't just try. Do it. Believe you will achieve.* This works equally effectively in negotiations. Expecting success and visualizing it before the negotiation begins will increase your likelihood of achieving it.

How can you transform goals into expectations? Part of it relates to your self-esteem. Some individuals always expect to succeed. Others bring a more pessimistic attitude to the table. Regardless of your tendencies, here are some ways to change your mindset *and* your success rate.

• *Do your homework.* Find an appropriate standard on which to base your expectations. Finding a fair and reasonable basis for your expected result will make you more comfortable in sticking with that expectation throughout the negotiation. Some individuals' tendency to change goals midstream results from starting with an amorphous goal unrelated to any standard. The more justified your standard, the easier it will be to expect to achieve it.

• *Brainstorm to create realistic, achievable expectations.* You will be more confident you can achieve $60,000 if you set that goal with others you respect. If you all agree $60,000 is realistic and achievable, you will be more committed to this result and more likely to get it.

• *Consciously adopt a positive attitude.* Don't walk into a negotiation thinking it's unlikely you will succeed. Or that you're afraid to fail. Give yourself a pep talk. Stride into the negotiation knowing you've got a great chance to get what you deserve. Psych yourself up. And do this consciously. While it may seem hokey, the difference will be noticeable. I once heard a motivational speaker tell us the first thing we should do every morning is look in the mirror and say, à la Tony the Tiger, "This is going to be a *Grrreat* day!" Whether you actually feel this way is not the point. Saying this will help you feel it. And feeling it will help you succeed.

H. Wayne Huizenga, the man who made Blockbuster a household word and the owner of the Miami Dolphins professional football team and Florida Panthers professional hockey team, is known for his aggressive personal commitment to achieving his negotiation goals. As he has said, "I believe in what I'm doing and I go after it." He expects to succeed every time. So can you. Expecting it will help make it happen.

Commit to It

It's a simple proposition with a powerful impact at the goal stage: Once you mentally commit to something—like achieving a specific goal—you're more likely to get it. Social psychologists have understood this commitment principle for years.

As you read the following story, consider how the power of commitment increases your tendency to take actions that will lead to greater success. Likewise, understand how the power of commitment when used against you can increase your tendency to agree to what you might otherwise reject.

The Coat Watcher

In 2001 I went downhill-skiing with a friend who patrols the slopes. On our third day my legs gave out, while my friend's continued to function, so I retired to the lodge to read a book. After taking off my gloves, coat, goggles, hat, and boots, I decided I wanted a drink. But I didn't want to carry all my gear to the drink line. I faced a dilemma: If I left my gear unattended, it might be stolen. Yet, it wasn't practical to carry it all or put it all back on. What did I do?

I checked my immediate area for a responsible-looking person, caught her eye, struck up a conversation to establish some rapport, and asked if she was going to be around for five minutes. When she said yes, I asked her if she would watch my stuff while I got a drink. She said yes, and I then went over to get my drink, confident my stuff would be safe until I returned. It was.

This social negotiation involved four elements: 1) *my goal:* get a drink and not lose my gear while away from the table; 2) *her goal:* be neighborly with a relative minimum of effort; 3) *relationship value:* small, but since I had struck up a short conversation with her, it was higher than if I had just asked her to watch my stuff; and 4) *commitment:* I asked her to orally commit to safeguard my gear. I knew that once she made this commitment my gear would be far less likely to walk away in a stranger's possession.

Psychologist Thomas Moriarty tested this power of commitment by staging a series of thefts on a New York City beach in the summer of 1972. As psychologist Robert Cialdini noted in his classic book, *Influence: Science and Practice,* Moriarty wanted to see if bystanders who had committed to watch a stranger's gear would risk personal harm to halt the crime.

Moriarty thus had an associate randomly pick a spot on the beach next to someone and lay out his beach towel and radio. Moriarty's associate would then listen to his radio for a few minutes, not engage his subject in any conversation, and then get up and walk away from his stuff, including his radio. Several minutes later, another of Moriarty's associates would walk by, grab the towel and radio in a staged theft, and hurry away. Of the twenty times they staged this, only four of the twenty random "neighbors" challenged the "thief" in any way.

Moriarty then staged this same scenario with a twist: His first associate would ask the "neighbor" to "please watch my things." All twenty "neighbors" agreed. Drastically different results occurred. Nineteen of the twenty "neighbors" challenged the "thief." Some even ran after and stopped the purported thief, demanded an explanation, and physically restrained the thief.

This is the power of commitment. If you commit to achieving your specific goal you will be more likely to achieve it. Similarly, if you can get your counterparts to commit to what you want they will be more likely to fulfill that commitment.

"How can I commit to my goal?" you might ask. "Isn't expecting to achieve a goal the same as committing to it?"

No. In fact, while various forms of commitment exist, the following three are most often usefully applied in the negotiation context: the oral commitment, the written commitment, and the public commitment. Keep in mind as we address them that: a) each of these progressively represents a stronger level of commitment; b) the more active the parties' commitment, the greater its impact on their behavior; and c) the more parties understand the reasons underlying the commitment and take personal responsibility for it, the more powerful it becomes.

• *The Oral Commitment*—In personal relationships, the "C word"— commitment—carries a great deal of meaning. If you and your significant other are in a committed relationship it often means you're exclusive. Usually this commitment is made orally. You discuss it. You agree to it. And hopefully you follow it.

Stating you're "committed," or otherwise orally agreeing to a goal, is one form of commitment. Even if you only "tentatively" commit, it's still more powerful than saying nothing.

• *The Written Commitment*—More powerful still is the written commitment. Write down your goals. Once you have decided on a specific goal, pull out some paper or sit at your computer and put it down in black and white. This will help you internalize it. Seeing your goals on paper also will visually remind you of your commitment and minimize the likelihood that you might later subconsciously revise your expectations downward.

Many organizations use this commitment technique to increase their employees' effectiveness in achieving their goals. In the late 1990s I trained several hundred managers in a large company how to more effectively negotiate with their coworkers. We focused on perhaps the most challenging of all internal negotiations—the performance and salary review process. The first stage of this process involved the employee filling out a self-evaluation form. On this form the employee was required to set out in writing his or her professional goals for the following year. The manager, after reviewing the goals, met with the employee to provide input and discuss the achievability of these goals. The final review was written and it required the approval of the manager *and* the employee.

Writing down your goals will make you more committed to achieving them than just thinking about them or even stating them out loud. In this context, it also created a standard by which the employee could be evaluated later. This provided everyone with a greater incentive to achieve their goals.

In one of my seminars I asked a panel of Arizona business, political, and legal leaders to share their most effective negotiation strategies. Mal Jozoff, the former Chairman of the Board and CEO of Dial Corporation, shared the following on the importance of writing down your goals.

> The thing I always try to keep in mind in any negotiation is to know what I want at the end of it. And I always make a practice of writing it down—what is victory for me? And then I set up a series of stages, as the negotiations unfold, and I always try to be sure that the steps and maneuvers and motions and practices are consistent with getting us to that end line. I've seen more bad negotiations simply because the client, or side A or side B, really forget what they're trying to get in the end.

The bottom line: Write down your goals at the beginning of your negotiation. It will increase the likelihood you will achieve them.

• *The Public Commitment*—Have you ever worked harder because you told a friend you were going to achieve something and didn't want to fail? Perhaps you were selling your car and told your brother you felt your car was worth at least $10,000. Then you held firm at $10,000 because you didn't want to be embarrassed when you saw your brother.

If so, you were using an effective form of goal commitment by *publicly* stating what you expected to achieve. In essence, you were putting your credibility on the line. By doing this you increased your internal incentive to achieve that goal. Publicly committing to a specific goal has that impact. You will work harder to achieve it if you tell someone else you will do it.

To summarize, here's an outline of the goal-setting process:

INFORMATION IS POWER—SO GET IT

Get Information to Set Your Goals
1. Set and prioritize your long-term strategic and short-term tactical goals
2. Determine and prioritize your counterpart's goals
3. Evaluate the power of the relationship

Practical Tips and Tactics for Goal-Setting
- Brainstorm to set your goals
- Set aggressive and specific goals—don't just "do the best you can"
- Tie your goals to realistic standards
- *Expect* to succeed
- Commit to it (oral, written, and public)

Develop an Information-Bargaining Strategy—
Ways to Get and Share Information

As you know, the first step in implementing Golden Rule One (Information Is Power—So Get It) is to get a sufficient amount of information to appropriately set your goals. Step two is to develop an information-bargaining strategy to organize a way to get the information you need and to share the information you want your counterpart to receive.

Did you know the United States national intelligence budget was around $38 billion in 2003 for largely one purpose—to get information? Businesses also spend huge sums of money to find out information about their customers and competitors. Why? *The more information you have, the more power you have to get what you want.* It applies to arms-control negotiations, the sale or purchase of a business, or to any negotiation. To maximize your chance of success you must gather as much information as you can.

The more you learn about what both sides have, want, and will agree to, the better you will do.

From 1993 to 1995 I negotiated for and helped organize more than a dozen trips for the president of the United States. Before the president travels anywhere the White House sends out an advance team to coordinate all aspects of the visit, including political, media, logistical, and housing issues. Then, once the president arrives for the visit, the White House Advance Team coordinates the president's on-site activities.

On one trip in 1994 our advance team arrived at a naval air station about a week before President Clinton was due to visit. Our job? Work with the base commander and the other military personnel to ensure President Clinton achieved the objectives of his visit. The first meeting with our military counterparts was in a conference room near the base commander's office. It was our first negotiation session, and we needed everyone on board if we were to accomplish our objectives in such a limited time frame.

This trip was especially important for two reasons. One, President Clinton's relationship with the military early in his presidency was strained, due to a variety of factors, including the circumstances surrounding his lack of military service and the gays in the military controversy. Two, President Clinton was due to select a new Chairman of the Joint Chiefs of Staff shortly after this trip concluded. Several candidates for this position were scheduled to fly in from around the world to attend this event. The military personnel on the base thus appeared on edge from our first meeting.

At this meeting, we sat around a large oval conference table with our lead White House representative at one end. The base commander sat at the other end. The meeting began with the base commander offering his full cooperation and assistance to make the Commander-in-Chief's visit proceed flawlessly.

What occurred during the remainder of the meeting was critical.

Instead of overtly taking charge as the president's lead representative and divvying up assignments to the various military personnel, which he could have done, our lead White House representative started by asking questions and actively listening to the military's responses.

He was trying to get information that was crucial to ensuring a successful presidential visit. He was also implementing a classic negotiation technique that many bright, articulate people overlook. *Asking questions and actively listening is a critical step in almost all negotiations, especially at the beginning.*

Understand, however, that your counterpart—assuming some negotiation sophistication—will likely also want information from you. As such, the beginning stage of many negotiations involves an extensive information-bargaining process. Don't be wary of this stage. Embrace it. Ideally, this "information negotiation" and the relationship you develop with your counterpart here will help you get past the inevitable rough spots you may hit later.

What kind of information do you want? To start, get as much information as you can about the *substantive* issues involved. Equally as important and oftentimes much neglected, get as much *tactical* information as you can about the parties involved. Of course, it's not always easy to obtain this information or to find a way to keep from disclosing it. I will thus share my Top Ten Information Gathering Tactics below, as well as explain some blocking techniques to keep your strategic information to yourself.

To start, here are the steps you should take to organize the critical *substantive* information:

- Get as much **substantive** information as possible
  —Find out facts, issues, and opinions
  —Uncover fundamental interests underlying positions
  —Brainstorm options that might satisfy interests

Get As Much *Substantive* Information As Possible

Find Out Facts, Issues, and Opinions

First find out all the facts, issues, and opinions relating to your negotiation. While this seems obvious, many sophisticated individuals fail to comprehensively explore these issues before crucial negotiations. If you're considering buying a company, find out as much about that company as possible, both what is publicly and privately known. The most effective buyout specialists say that before they make an offer they know more about their target than their target knows about themselves. While this may be hyperbole, knowledge does bring power.

Guess where many get their information? From public sources and sources other than their counterparts. This is critical. Successful negotiators are comprehensive and creative information gatherers.

Sales professionals know this well. "Know Thy Customer" is a frequent and fundamental admonition to those in sales.

Sometimes you will even want to hire an expert to supplement your findings. Experts independently carry power into negotiations, due to: 1) their knowledge and information base; 2) the persuasive power of their opinions based on their expertise; and 3) the high regard and deference accorded them, based on the qualifications that make them experts, be it their academic pedigree or their practical experience. It's no coincidence that experts on all sides of the table play major roles in arms-control negotiations.

Uncover Fundamental Interests Underlying Positions

It's also critical to uncover the fundamental interests underlying parties' positions. What is this? Good question. Roger Fisher, William Ury, and Bruce

Patton, in their classic negotiation book, *Getting to Yes: Negotiating Agreement Without Giving In*, focused on the fundamental difference between interests and positions. Here's how they introduced the subject:

> Consider the story of two men quarreling in a library. One wants the window open and the other wants it closed. They bicker back and forth about how much to leave it open: a crack, halfway, three-quarters of the way. No solution satisfies them both.
>
> Enter the librarian. She asks one why he wants the window open: "To get some fresh air." She asks the other why he wants it closed: "To avoid the draft." After thinking a minute, she opens wide a window in the next room, bringing in fresh air without a draft.

Here, the parties' positions—open the window versus close the window—dominated their negotiation. But their underlying interests—fresh air and no draft—provided the basis for the best solution for both parties.

Interests, according to Fisher, Ury, and Patton, are parties' needs, desires, concerns, and fears. They're the fundamental driving forces that motivate parties. For some it's ego. They want everyone to know they "won." For others it may be security or economic well-being. Still others crave recognition, a sense of belonging, or control over one's life. The number and type of interests at issue in negotiations are many and varied.

Positions, by contrast, are what each side believes will satisfy their interests. Positions are *what* you want. Interests are *why* you want it.

In the information-gathering stage, drill down far enough to discover your and the other side's fundamental interests.

Why? It will help you define success, leave as little as possible on the table, and find the true "win-win." Let's analyze each.

- Fundamental interests determine success or failure
- Don't leave it on the table
- Find the true win-win scenario—and potentially expand the pie—by analyzing shared, conflicting, and compatible interests

Fundamental Interests Determine Success or Failure

Negotiation success or failure is directly tied to the extent that the parties involved satisfy their true interests. If you haven't fully explored your interests you can't really know whether you have succeeded or failed. Success isn't necessarily having your offer accepted. If the deal doesn't satisfy your interests and you sign, you may come to regret your "success."

A lawyer once told me he always buys his cars from a Ford dealership that advertises a no-hassle experience. The dealership sets what it considers a "fair" price for each car and doesn't move. Take it or leave it. General Motors uses a similar selling philosophy for its Saturn division. Set a fair price, and no haggling.

I asked him why he always bought at this dealership, especially as he likely could get the same cars for less money by shopping around. He told me his most important interest is "not to feel taken." Secondarily, he didn't want to spend the time to shop around. His biggest fear? Walking away from a dealership after a day of negotiating and knowing someone else got a better deal for the same car.

His position? Pay a fair price for the car. His interests? Not to feel taken and to spend a minimum of time and stress on the process. Critically, he explored his interests at the start of the negotiation process. He was willing to pay more money for the satisfaction of feeling he was not taken. The result? Success.

Personally, I will never go to this dealership. Why? I love to negotiate, enjoy the time spent in the process, and have a stronger interest in getting a better financial deal on my vehicles. My position: Pay the least possible for a new car. My interest: Enjoy the process and spend the difference I save on something else I enjoy.

Don't Leave It on the Table

Another reason to explore both sides' interests is that you may not be able to *fully* satisfy your interests if you only exchange positions and never uncover each other's true interests. You might partially satisfy your interests, but what about the rest? What if the librarian had not happened upon the discussion of whether to open the window? The parties likely would have compromised and opened the window halfway. Both sides would have received half of what they wanted. This is one place where negotiators who ask probing questions and actively listen come out way ahead. Had either party in the library asked, listened, and really probed the other side's interests, and not simply stated their position, the librarian's intervention likely would have been unnecessary.

Find the True Win-Win Scenario—and Potentially Expand the Pie—By Analyzing Shared, Conflicting, and Compatible Interests

Assume you have figured out your own interests and you think you have determined your counterpart's. Next, prioritize these interests and preliminarily determine which are shared, conflicting and/or compatible.

The easiest negotiations in the world involve parties with *shared interests*. Why? Everyone wants the same end result. Your interests are the same. It thus makes sense to work together to achieve them. Let's say you're a sales executive at a large corporation and the sales force has been divided into teams. Assume your compensation—which is all anyone really cares about here—is tied to the extent your team achieves its goals. Your personal interests and your team's interests are the same. In this situation, negotiations between teammates should be straightforward and tied directly to their ability to help the team achieve its goals. There should be little professional conflict.

Shared interests provide the crucial foundation for many negotiations. As such, always search for shared interests with your counterparts. Often you will also want to highlight them. For example, many companies have a strong interest in maintaining relationships with customers so they keep coming back. In fact, their interest is often so strong they provide financial discounts to repeat customers and provide many other benefits, like special sales, frequent flyer programs, etc. Repeat customers, once they've found a place that provides good quality at a fair price, usually don't want to waste time looking elsewhere. As a result, the parties' shared interest in a long-term relationship benefits both and provides the basis for their ongoing negotiations.

Rule of thumb: *Find the common ground.*

Contrast this to a negotiation between two hungry teenage brothers who go into the kitchen looking for ice cream. Two scoops are left, and each wants both scoops. Their interests: satisfying their immediate hunger for ice cream. Here their interests conflict. More ice cream for one necessarily means less ice cream for the other. Of course, one might just grab it all and run into a room and lock his brother out. But perhaps they will negotiate some way to split the ice cream. No matter how they split it, however, each will leave the table only partially satisfied.

Many straight, one-time purchases involve directly conflicting financial interests. You might want to sell your boat for the most money you can get for it. And a potential buyer may want to pay the least amount for it. Be careful not to overlook, however, situations where the parties' interests initially appear to conflict but actually involve shared or compatible interests. Remember the quarreling parties in the library.

The important point is this: Find out whether your and your counterparts' interests conflict. Then you will know how to proceed and how to define your success.

Of course, in most negotiations parties have differing but compatible interests. Here's where you can expand the pie. The furniture store might need room in the warehouse for new furniture arriving in a week. The student might need furniture for her apartment when school starts next week. The luxury homebuilder might need a quality, stable lumber subcontractor for the new housing community starting construction next month. The lumber subcontractor might want to expand from starter home construction to luxury homes, which provide a larger profit margin. These parties' interests differ but don't conflict. They're compatible. After uncovering interests, evaluate their compatibility. By doing this you will see the additional value you can get in your negotiations.

In the furniture and housing negotiations, both sides' interests can be satisfied without sacrificing either. Understanding this compatibility will make the negotiation more productive for everyone. Here's another example of a negotiation involving compatible interests.

In early 2001 I was in Atlanta for a negotiation seminar. After checking out of my hotel I took my suitcase outside to find a cab to the airport. As I was standing there a businessman in front of me was watching his bags get loaded into the back of a Lincoln Town Car. He turned to me, saw my travel bag, and asked if I was going to the airport. I said yes, and he invited me to share his ride. Since he looked respectable, I agreed and offered to split the fare with him. He declined my offer, saying his company had already hired the car for the day.

As it turned out, we had a fascinating conversation on the way to the airport. He is an international businessman who spends much of his time engaging in cross-cultural negotiations. Here we had compatible interests. He enjoyed meeting new people and wanted company on the ride to the airport. And he had no financial interest at stake. I also enjoy meeting people, and my financial interest was compatible with his. As a result, I had a pleasant ride to the airport and saved my client cab fare in the process.

Of course, many negotiations involve a mix of shared interests, conflicting interests, and/or compatible interests. The challenge is to find out which interests fall into each category and to satisfy your most important interests.

Let's see how this works in the context of negotiating a raise.

Negotiating a Raise

Jack's in the midst of his annual performance review, and his boss, Kelly, says "Jack, you have done a great job this year, but I can't give you more than a $10,000 raise. I would love to give you $20,000, but I just can't. Unfortunately, that's my final decision."

"I'm curious," Jack responds, "what's so magic about $10,000? Why can't you give me $20,000?"

"Well," Kelly says, "we can only afford $10,000 because, at your suggestion, we're hiring a new person to assist you. To get the most qualified person, we needed that extra money. Plus, as you know, we've got a cash-flow issue, given our investment in those new computers."

"That's great you're hiring someone to help," Jack responds. "That will make me more productive and increase the company's long-term profits. It's an excellent investment, and I'm sure it will pay off. I also obviously love the new computers. All this will help me do the best job I can. But I'm a bit disappointed in the raise. I don't think it truly reflects the contributions I've made this past year and gives me the recognition I deserve."

"My hands are tied on the raise," Kelly responds. "But what else can the company do to show its appreciation? We also think you had a great year, and want to keep you satisfied."

"You know what would be nice," Jack replies, "is Joe's old corner office with the river view. I love that view, and even though the office is smaller than my present one, the view more than makes up for it. Plus, while it sounds like we've got some short-term cash flow constraints now, perhaps we could agree on an additional $10,000 bonus in six months if the company's profits increase by five percent due to our division's increased productivity?"

"Interesting ideas," says Kelly. "Since Joe's old office was smaller than yours, we figured you didn't want it. We were going to use it for storage, but if you want it, it's yours. We can use your bigger office for storage. On the bonus issue, that sounds fair, but let me first run it by my boss. I don't think it will be a problem, though, if our profits increase by that much."

In this negotiation Kelly had at least four fundamental interests: short-term cash flow management, long-term profits, efficient use of office space, and keeping Jack satisfied and productive. Jack had at least three fundamental interests: financial, appropriate recognition for his contributions, and staying satisfied and productive. At first glance it appeared Jack's financial interest conflicted with his company's cash-flow and long-term profits interests. More for Jack was less for the company.

But once Jack found out the company wasn't completely averse to paying him more—it was simply constrained by cash flow—a solution that satisfied *both* the company's and Jack's interests became apparent. Jack's solution worked because Jack and Kelly uncovered their shared and compatible interests. Jack and Kelly shared an interest in keeping Jack satisfied and productive. They also had compatible interests regarding Joe's old corner office (more satisfaction for Jack and more efficiency for the company). Jack also found a way to satisfy his financial interest by tying it to the company's long-term profits interest. This was mostly compatible, although it was still somewhat in conflict. His bonus—while compatible with the company's short-term cash flow interest—still lessened the company's long-term profits.

Jack's effort to explore both sides' fundamental interests helped both sides achieve success. Here it was a true win-win. Jack could have pushed harder for a bigger raise. He also could have taken it personally and approached this in an adversarial fashion. If either occurred, it likely would have increased his tension with Kelly and reduced his satisfaction at work. Neither Jack nor Kelly wanted that.

Instead, when faced with a less-than-ideal raise, Jack: 1) explored the basis of the raise and found out the company's fundamental interests, 2) considered his own interests, 3) analyzed the extent to which the interests were shared, compatible, or conflicted, and then 4) suggested ways to largely satisfy everyone's interests. Jack found a win-win solution, in that everyone did better than if Jack had just accepted the $10,000 raise or directly engaged on salary alone.

Research in England in 1978 confirmed the effectiveness of negotiators exploring and finding common ground between the parties. The study found that effective negotiators spent nearly four times *more* time during the planning stages of the negotiation looking for shared or compatible interests than those identified as less-skilled. Overall, less-skilled negotiators only spent about 10 percent of their time focused on shared or compatible interests. The more-skilled spent about 40 percent.

I can't stress this enough: Find out everyone's interests, then evaluate which are shared, which are conflicting, and which are compatible. Take the time to comprehensively explore your and your counterpart's interests. The more interests you uncover, the better you will do.

Brainstorm Options That May Satisfy Interests

The final step in getting as much *substantive* informaion as possible—after finding out the facts, issues, and opinions, and then uncovering the fundamental interests underlying the parties' positions—is to brainstorm possible options that may satisfy the parties' interests.

The Prison Hostage Exercise

In my law school negotiation class, I assign an exercise called the Prison Hostage Negotiation, developed by University of Michigan Law School Professor James J. White. In this exercise forty of a mythical state's leading citizens are touring a state prison when a riot breaks out and they are taken hostage. The hostage-takers, all convicted murderers sentenced to death or life without parole, are angry about overcrowded conditions, lousy food, inadequate recreational facilities, and limited medical care. Once they have the hostages the inmates demand improvements in each of these areas. To start, they impose a two-hour deadline. If it expires without an agreement, they say, they will start killing hostages.

The state's governor, up for reelection that year, sends his top two aides to negotiate with two prisoners' rights advocates who represent the convicts. Two of my students assume the role of the governor's aides, while another two assume the role of the prisoners' rights advocates in the negotiation. The governor's aides have some flexibility on meeting the prisoners' demands, in part because an independent commission had previously recommended implementation of many of the inmates' demands. None of the recommendations, however, had yet been accepted by the state.

In most cases my students start by information-gathering. But often they quickly jump into discussing possible options and solutions. In large part this is due to the tight time constraints and the significant number of issues on the table.

This is typical of many negotiations—and often counterproductive. Why? Most negotiators don't adequately explore the parties' interests. Instead, they too rapidly proceed to discuss what options might be acceptable. My students regularly leave valuable items on the table by exploring options *too soon*.

Don't fall into this trap. You cannot adequately explore what options might satisfy both sides' interests if you don't fully understand both sides' interests. *So hold off on exploring the various options until after you have uncovered all the interests.* Then and only then brainstorm options. This will be more productive and efficient and lead to a more creative array of interest-satisfying options—options that: 1) satisfy shared interests; 2) form the basis for conflicting interests; and 3) create value by satisfying compatible interests. This will increase the likelihood your options will be accepted and will more fully satisfy your interests.

Finally, wait until after you have generated all possible options to evaluate them and their likelihood of success. Once parties start evaluating options, the atmosphere often becomes more tense and can shut off the information flow. Keep that information flowing as you explore the options. Then, once they're all on the table, evaluate them.

Get As Much *Strategic* Information As Possible

After obtaining as much *substantive* information as you can about the negotiation, next focus on discovering as much *strategic* information as possible. Here are the steps you should take to efficiently gather the critical *strategic* information:

- Negotiate with the right person
- Investigate your counterpart's reputation and past tactics

Negotiate with the Right Person

Everyone has spent time in a negotiation, only to find near the end that they've been negotiating with the wrong person. Perhaps that person didn't have the authority to do the deal. Or perhaps you were negotiating with the hotel desk clerk, and his manager had the information.

In 1994, I had an opportunity to help run a gubernatorial campaign. After discussing this opportunity with the candidate and meeting with his campaign cochairs, we decided it was a good fit. The Washington, D.C.–based political campaign consultant then contacted me to negotiate the details of my employment. We met several times and worked out a deal that included my title, responsibilities, compensation, benefits, and the use of a car for my travel around the state with the candidate. Near the end of this process the consultant and I met with the campaign manager. But this meeting was general, and we didn't discuss the specifics of our negotiations. Ultimately, some of this was put in writing and some was not. During this entire time I assumed the consultant had the authority to negotiate for the campaign.

Two days into my new job as deputy campaign manager I found out I was wrong. While the consultant had authority on the major issues, he made some commitments to me he had not discussed with the campaign manager. In the end I had to renegotiate certain elements of my employment with the campaign manager. In retrospect, I should have insisted the campaign manager—at the least—be included in the final negotiation session with the consultant and be copied on all our correspondence.

Here's the critical point: Make sure you're negotiating with the right person. If not, you may have to unexpectedly start over again when the parties on the other side switch.

Investigate Your Counterpart's Reputation and Past Tactics

Knowing your counterpart has acted irrationally in the past as a tactic will help you immeasurably in your negotiations. Knowing your counterpart only responded to power moves in the past will prepare you to effectively approach him. And knowing your counterpart has hidden a competitive nature behind a reasonable façade will help you counter when the competitive issues inevitably arise.

As noted in Roger Dawson's *Secrets of Power Negotiating,* former United Nations Ambassador and current New Mexico Governor Bill Richardson was once asked by *Fortune* magazine to describe the traits of a good negotiator. He responded, "You have to be a good listener. You have to respect the other side's point of view. You have to know what makes your adversary tick." When asked how he prepared for negotiations, he replied, "I talk to people who know the guy I will be negotiating with. I talk to scholars, State Department experts, and journalists. . . . With Castro, I learned that he was always hungry for information about America. Sure enough, he was fascinated with Steve Forbes, fascinated with the congressional budget impasse. He fancies himself an expert on United States politics. With Cedras of Haiti, I learned that he played good cop and that a top general, Philippe Biamby, played bad cop."

Richardson knew that effective negotiators must find out as much strategic and tactical information as possible about their counterparts. So, research your counterpart's reputation and negotiation characteristics. The earlier you do this, the better.

Knowing the reputation of my counterpart, an airline company, comprised a critical element in a highly stressful negotiation on May 11, 2000. At the time airlines, as frequent travelers knew, often approached negotiations with passengers in a competitive fashion and only reluctantly shared information with them about the true status of delayed flights. My experience highlights the importance of knowing your counterparts' reputation *before* the negotiation begins.

On May 11, I was sitting on a Boeing 767 at Phoenix's Sky Harbor International Airport around 4 P.M., waiting for my United Airlines flight to leave for Chicago. Shortly after boarding a flight attendant told us that our weather-delayed 2:31 P.M. flight would experience even more delay, due to a scheduling mix-up.

Since my goal was to be in Chicago that night for a seminar I was leading the next morning, I started by getting as much information as I could about the facts, issues, and opinions underlying our delayed status. By politely asking questions, I learned the flight attendants possessed little information about our status and that their lack of information appeared to be consciously determined by the airline.

The airline's reluctant information-sharing along with my knowledge of airlines' reputations increased my distrust of their statement that we would be leaving shortly.

I thus immediately evaluated my leverage (a point addressed at length in chapter 2) and called my travel agent from the plane to check my travel alternatives. I learned the next Chicago flight, on United, was due to leave at 6 P.M. It was on time.

I then became more aggressive in my effort to get more information. I left the plane—despite the flight attendants' request that I remain—and went to speak with the gate agent. Strategically, I decided to move up the ladder to those with the information or the authority to get me what I wanted. I then was told a captain was on his way to the airport and we should be ready to leave when he arrived, probably within thirty minutes. By this time, however, it was 5 P.M. Still skeptical, due to my knowledge of airlines' reputations, I wanted to ensure if United canceled that flight I would have a seat on the 6 P.M. flight.

Back to my alternative. I asked the gate agent to book me on the 6 P.M. flight.

She refused, telling me United had a policy prohibiting "double booking."

Since she appeared inflexible and told me she didn't even have the authority to double book, I asked to speak to her supervisor.

While waiting for her supervisor I called my travel agent and had her book me on the 6 P.M. flight. Overhearing this, the gate agent returned and told me her supervisor approved the double booking, at no extra financial cost to me. I thus canceled my booking with my travel agent and accepted her effort.

It was a good thing, too. When I left on the 6 P.M. flight, the Boeing 767 was still sitting on the tarmac. While a captain had arrived, the flight's long delay had disqualified several of its flight attendants from working the flight.

Knowing how airlines typically negotiate with their passengers was key. Like the majority of the 767 passengers waiting, I could have watched a movie or read. But I knew that most airlines have a vested financial interest in not transferring you off your scheduled flight. They have traditionally accomplished this by withholding information. Now, however, passengers can get this information far more easily with the proliferation of cell phones and the Internet. Some airlines, not coincidentally, are now sharing more information, too.

Knowing airlines' reputations at the time, I started asking questions, aggressively seeking information and negotiating early enough to book a seat on another flight.

Bottom line: Find out as much strategic and tactical information as you can about your counterparts. Talk to others who have negotiated with your counterpart in the past. Research their reputations. Don't negotiate without investigating your counterparts. If you do, you will regret it.

Here's a summary of the type of information you want to get, all within the context of your information bargaining strategy.

INFORMATION IS POWER—SO GET IT

Get Information to Set Your Goals

Develop an Information-Bargaining Strategy—Ways to Get and Share Information
- Get as much *substantive* information as possible
  - Find out facts, issues, and opinions
  - Uncover fundamental interests underlying positions
  - Brainstorm options that might satisfy interests

- Get as much *strategic* information as possible
  - Negotiate with the right person
  - Investigate your counterpart's reputation and past tactics

---

Top Ten Information-Gathering Tactics

You now know what information to get. Your next step is to effectively and efficiently get it. Here is a list of my Top Ten Information-Gathering Tactics, and then a comprehensive discussion of each. Use them. You won't be disappointed.

1. Leave your ego at the door
2. Be sincere
3. Establish trust
4. List your information needs
5. Do the "big shmooze"
6. Ask questions. Ask questions. Ask questions!
7. Use the Funnel—open- to close-ended questions
8. Actively listen and use the "power of silence"
9. Ask "why"—get to interests, not positions
10. Evaluate and use nonverbals/body language

Information-Gathering Tactic #1:
Leave Your Ego at the Door

One of the best lawyers I know, Chuck Price, is a master information-gatherer. Interestingly, you might never suspect it if you met him. While a top-notch attorney, he's pretty low-key. In fact, he's practically the definition of a "nice guy." And while he can be tough if the situation requires it, he more naturally comes across as everybody's best friend. He has an ego, but he almost always keeps it tucked away.

What makes him a very effective negotiator? He never stops gathering information. And people can't seem to stop telling him information, even when it serves their best interests to keep their mouths shut. Chuck just has an ability to get people to share information. Even in the most adversarial contexts—cross-examining the opposing party in a lawsuit—Chuck gets valuable admissions.

Chuck gets these admissions, in part, by leaving his ego at the door. He's not afraid to admit he doesn't know. Importantly, this works to his advantage. If he admits he doesn't know, he will ask. And when he asks, he gets information. When he gets information, he stores it away until he wants to use it. Then he asks more questions. And more. He will even ask for information he thinks he already knows, just to confirm it. And he's always strategizing what to ask next to help him get the information he needs to succeed.

Information-Gathering Tactic #2: Be Sincere

Some lawyers love to hear the sound of their own voices. They love to talk and argue. Not Chuck. He loves the art of questioning and listening.

This is Chuck's other key to information-gathering success: He *sincerely* wants to find out the information. His sincerity oozes out in a very real way. In conversation he exhibits genuine concern and interest. There's no artificiality there. When he asks you a question you get the sense he really wants to know the answer. It's not just a formality. As a result people open up to Chuck. This gives him an enormous advantage. It also gives him the luxury of deciding when and where to use this information.

Sincerity plus a lack of ego. Both represent keys to success in the art of information-gathering. If you gave me a choice between two lawyers to represent me in a negotiation: One, a world class trial lawyer with a big ego who loves to argue, debate and win, and the other an equally bright and articulate lawyer with a reputation as one of the most effective questioners and listeners in the profession, which would I select? Nine times out of ten the listener. In the negotiation world, listening and asking most often will be more valuable than arguing. It matters little who thinks they won the debate. It matters a lot who walks away with actual success.

Information-Gathering Tactic #3: Establish Trust

Trust is critical in many negotiations and often difficult to establish. Why? Most do not give it freely. It must be earned. It's especially important to establish trust early in the information-gathering stage. If you lose it here, it will be far more difficult to establish later. But if you can establish it early on it will vastly increase your chances of getting the information you need.

Here's an example. In many of my seminars I use an eight-round exercise developed by the Harvard Negotiation Program, in which participants negotiate in teams of four to six with their colleagues. Each team's goal is to maximize its profits. In each of the eight rounds each team has a choice of several options. The option they select, compared with the option selected by the other team, determines their profits for that round.

At several points in the exercise I increase the incentives for each team to lie to their counterparts. In other words, I create a profit incentive for them to *tell* their counterparts that they will select one option, but then turn around and actually select a *different* option. It appears that they will "maximize their profits" if they convince their counterparts they will pick X, but then turn around and pick Y. Of course, both sides have the same incentive to lie, thus creating an environment largely devoid of trust. Invariably, several teams lie to their counterparts. Sometimes, both teams lie to each other. This is predictable, as the teams view this behavior as consistent with their goal.

But there's a catch. If the teams can find a way to ensure the other side does not double-cross them, each team will maximize its profits for all eight rounds to the greatest extent possible. The key is finding a way to develop sufficient trust for the exercise.

How do the teams do it?

Some teams just blindly trust that their counterparts will keep their word, figuring it's not a big deal if they've misplaced their trust. Sometimes their counterparts lie. Other times they keep their word. Often it depends on the level of competitiveness within each team. The more competitive, the more likely they will double-cross.

Other teams try to reach agreement based on some trust, but can't consummate the deal. Since they make greater profits if they *don't* trust the other side, versus trusting them and getting double-crossed, they resign themselves to a less-than-optimal result. They console themselves, however, by noting that at least they didn't "lose." This is true. They could have done worse.

Finally, some teams find a way to develop sufficient trust to ensure everyone sticks with their commitments. They find a way to make sure their counterparts do what they say they're going to do. In doing this, they maximize the profits for each individual team and for the teams collectively.

How do they do it, and what does this have to do with information-gathering?

Let me first explain how they do it. Then I will address its impact on information-gathering.

These teams recognize that few individuals *blindly* trust others when the issue at hand is important. In fact, the more it matters, the less people trust. If my financial security is at risk, I'm not going to just trust the other side to do what they say they will do. It's too risky. If they lie I'm in the poorhouse. Harvard Law Professor Roger Fisher says "trust is a matter of risk analysis." He's right. The more at risk, the less likely you will simply trust your counterpart. The less at risk, the more likely you will simply trust your counterpart. So, how do these "winning" teams ensure their counterparts follow through on their commitments? They make it in the other team's interest to follow through. If my financial security depends upon you taking some action, I will give you sufficient incentive to do it. I will make it in your interest to "be trustworthy." This largely takes trust out of the equation. Instead of depending on a party's trustworthiness, the deal now depends upon each party satisfying its *own* self-interest.

How can you ensure it's in the other party's self-interest to be trustworthy?

Create a reason to trust the other party. Change the incentives in the negotiation. Why do you trust others? Some do it naturally. This is fine when the stakes are low. But as you raise the stakes the risk of being double-crossed increases.

Most people trust others at the most basic level for logical, rational reasons. For example, some people may gain your trust by consistently following through on their commitments. You trust them because their past actions have given you a reason to trust their future actions. Your trust is based on their previous behavior.

Likewise, some may have a reputation for being trustworthy. You trust them because they consistently exhibited trustworthy behavior over time. They kept their word in many instances with a wide variety of individuals. Reputation is based on past behavior.

Another reason we trust others is because something bad will happen to them if they don't follow through on their commitments. If I have never met you before and don't know your reputation, I don't yet have a reason to believe you will do what you say you will do. But if we both sign an enforceable contract stating you will pay me $100,000 if you don't follow through on your commitment, I will be more likely to "trust" you. Of course, this presumes you care about losing $100,000.

For example, in one of my seminars the teams agreed that they would actually pay the other team $10 if they breached their agreement. Each team then gave me—a neutral third party—their respective $10 and instructed me to distribute it per their agreement. In effect, I acted as an escrow agent. This agreement took trust out of the equation and gave each team a $10 incentive to satisfy their commitment. This same concept kept the peace during the Cold War between the United States and the former Soviet Union. Basically, both sides told each other that if one side launched nuclear weapons the other side would immediately launch, too. It was called Mutual Assured Destruction. Horrible consequences would flow if *either* country didn't follow through on its commitment not to engage in a first strike.

It's true, this doesn't address the moral obligation many individuals feel to keep their word. It just evaluates the impact of "trustworthy" behavior in negotiations. Personally, I feel a moral obligation to keep my word and hope others share this feeling. In negotiations, however, the question is what you will risk to find out if your counterpart shares this feeling. In most situations involving large stakes, I'm risk-averse.

How to Develop Trust

How do we develop trust and how does this help us gather information?

First, make minor commitments to the other side early in the negotiation and meticulously follow through. Your commitments might be as minor as telling the other side you will call them at 2:00 P.M., and then calling them promptly at 2:00 P.M. Or you might promise to send them a document. Make sure they receive it in a timely fashion. In short, create a series of instances in which you follow through on your commitments. The more such history you can create, the more likely the other side will trust you. Obviously, avoid the opposite.

Second, explicitly emphasize the importance of your reputation and encourage your counterparts to independently research it. The better your reputation as a trustworthy individual, the more likely they will trust you.

Finally, be clear in your communications and don't purposely make ambiguous commitments. Mistrust in negotiations often results from miscommunications. One side believes the other committed to do X and failed to do it. But the other side believes it never made the commitment. Avoid this by identifying and clarifying your and your counterparts' commitments. Sometimes even put them in writing.

Trust is critical in many negotiations. It's especially important in the information-gathering process. The more your counterparts trust you, the more likely they will open up. The less they trust you, the less likely they will open up. Earn their trust.

Information-Gathering Tactic #4:
List Your Information Needs

Most negotiators start with a vague idea of what information they want to get and what they want to share. Change this vague sense to a concrete, specific list.

In fact, make *three* lists. Each will help you get information.

First, list the information you want to get *before* you meet with your counterpart. As you obtain the information check it off.

Second, list the information you want to get *during* your negotiation. Again, check it off once you get it.

Finally, list the information you want to initially share and the information you want to initially withhold. In every negotiation you want to strategically share and/or hide certain information. Decide which information fits in each category *before* you go into the negotiation. And know how you want to respond before you're asked, not after. If you don't, you may inadvertently disclose critical information just by your facial expression.

Making lists will help you strategically and comprehensively think through the information-gathering process. I'll bet there have been instances shortly after a negotiation where you suddenly realized you forgot to ask about a critical issue. Or you remember asking your counterpart something, but he or she never answered. Often, it's the questions your counterpart did *not* answer that represent the key to your success. Keep track of your questions which have been answered and which blocked.

Of course, sometimes it's impractical to make these three lists and write down all your information needs. Always do it if the stakes are high. But in the day-to-day negotiations with colleagues and family you just may not have time. If so, consider quickly jotting down your most critical information needs. It will be time well spent.

Information-Gathering Tactic #5: Do the "Big Shmooze"

Effective information gathering will not occur unless you create the appropriate atmosphere. If you initially come across in an adversarial fashion, your counterpart will likely respond in kind. Relevant information flow will be largely nonexistent. If you appear friendly, your counterpart will likely do the same. Relevant information flow then will likely take place.

My advice: Do the "big shmooze." Build rapport. Here's an example of rapport building from a sophisticated car salesman.

I bought a Porsche Boxster on December 31, 2001, a time of year when dealerships traditionally have a great incentive to move cars. While at the dealership the previous Friday, I was admiring a Boxster when a salesman named Steve approached and introduced himself. He was roughly my age and looked similarly professional in appearance.

After talking about the Boxster and illustrating his extensive knowledge about the vehicle—our first shared interest—he asked me where I was from. In Phoenix, this is a common question, as many people have moved here from somewhere else. I told him that, while I had lived in Phoenix for about ten years, I had grown up in Minnesota.

"What a coincidence," he said. He then told me that he and his wife had been part owners of a golf resort in northern Minnesota, near Detroit Lakes, and had lived there for a year. Another coincidence! My family had a cabin in Detroit Lakes and we used to spend part of the summer there every year when I was growing up.

What was Steve doing? Finding common interests and building rapport. Steve also—by discovering these common interests—increased the likelihood I would buy a Boxster from him.

How?

Psychologist Robert Cialdini calls it the Liking Rule. "We most prefer to say yes to the requests of someone we know and like," he notes in *Influence: Science and Practice*.

Studies have shown that we like others more when they exhibit similar characteristics. In other words, we tend to like others—and thus be more likely to say yes to them—when they look like us in clothing and appearance, share our beliefs, and display similar attitudes.

Knowing this, some sales professionals will generally mirror prospective customers in their expected appearance and attitude and attempt to find some similarity with them on any of a number of subjects.

Interestingly, this usually works, even when recipients know it's occurring. Individuals still find it more difficult to say no to those with whom some true rapport has been established.

Individuals are also more likely to say yes if they negotiate over lunch, especially if it's at a club where they both belong. Why? They appear to share some interests, since they belong to the same club. And studies since the 1930s show we have more positive feelings toward people and things we experience while eating. Politicians learned this years ago. They rarely ask for money at fund-raisers until *after* food has been served.

What should you do in negotiations to increase your likelihood of getting relevant information?

Start with the "big shmooze," and preferably do it over a meal. Spend time at the beginning of your negotiations establishing some personal or professional rapport with your counterpart. Find common interests, common friends, or a common background or experience. Did you attend the same university, or do you share the same passion for college basketball?

Research possible similarities with your counterpart before *the negotiation starts.* As Richard Shell notes in *Bargaining for Advantage,* when Steve Ross, founder of Warner Communications (now Time Warner), was starting out, he helped a small rental car business negotiate a deal with Caesar Kimmel. Kimmel owned some New York City parking lots that the rental car business wanted to use.

What did Ross do? Before meeting Kimmel he learned that Kimmel owned and raced horses. So did Ross's in-laws. In their first meeting Ross looked around Kimmel's office and saw a photo one of Kimmel's horses in the winner's circle of a big race. Ross examined the photo closely and said "Morty Rosenthal [Ross's in-law] owned the number-two horse in that race." Ross and Kimmel hit it off. This made a difference.

Show a genuine interest in your counterpart. I'm a curious person. When I meet folks I like to find out who they are, where they're from, what they like, what they dislike, what makes them tick, etc. This helps in my negotiations.

Why? Almost everyone likes to talk about themselves. This is not a bad thing. It's natural. Find out about your counterparts. Ask them about themselves. Discover your common elements. There is bound to be something, however remote, that can form the basis for a professional bond between you.

Don't build rapport in a dishonest way. Ross did his homework. But he didn't make anything up. Nor did he use the information he knew under false pretenses. If he had, Kimmel likely would have smoked him out—if not initially, then eventually. Rapport building is one thing, artificially faking a relationship is another. Dishonest negotiators burn bridges. Effective negotiators build them.

Next time you go to buy a car and the salesman says he grew up where you did, ask where he went to high school. I must admit, I was skeptical when Steve told me his connection to Detroit Lakes, Minnesota. Was he telling me the truth, or was he trying to dishonestly build rapport? As it turns out, he really did live in Detroit Lakes. And I did buy the Boxster from him.

Information-Gathering Tactic #6: Ask Questions.
Ask Questions. Ask Questions!
Remember the classic television detective show *Columbo?* In it Detective Columbo was a bumbling cop who investigated high-profile murders. Egos

abounded all around him. Often wealthy businessmen or politicians would be under suspicion, and Columbo would get badgered for results. Invariably, seemingly minor and unrelated clues just didn't seem to add up.

What did Columbo do? Gathered information. How? Asked questions. And everyone answered them. Why? Because Columbo never appeared threatening. In fact, suspects viewed him as slightly dimwitted. Of course, he was clever. Every question he asked had a purpose. And he analyzed every response and nonresponse. Eventually he maneuvered the suspects into giving away information they didn't really want to—and that's when Columbo pieced the puzzle together and pounced.

His key: asking questions and getting everyone to share information.

Columbo was a great detective and an effective negotiator.

Research confirms his approach. First, it shows that effective negotiators ask twice as many questions as average negotiators. *Twice as many.* That's significant. Most effective negotiators also specifically design their questions to elicit strategically valuable information.

Second, effective negotiators don't simply accept the information provided. They probe. They test. They confirm. And they summarize. This is critical. It not only leads to more accurate information, it reduces the likelihood of miscommunication.

Finally, effective negotiators don't just ask questions, they carefully listen to and evaluate the responses.

One study shows effective negotiators spend almost 40 percent of the negotiation getting and clarifying information. Ask questions. Be perceptive. Remember: The more information you get, the more power you will have.

Information-Gathering Tactic #7: Use the Funnel— Open- to Close-Ended Questions

We do an information-gathering exercise in almost all my seminars that illustrates the effectiveness of different questioning techniques. In this exercise I ask how many have ever been involved in an automobile accident or know the facts of an accident in which a friend has been involved. Invariably everyone raises his or her hand. I then ask them to pair up with the person next to them and get as much information as they can about the accident in which that person or their friend was involved. One asks the questions and the other answers them. Their goal: Get as much information as possible about the accident. However, I place two restrictions on them. The exercise will only last two minutes. And the person answering the questions has just two responses—yes or no.

After two minutes I ask them to reverse roles (so the initial questioner now answers questions about his or her accident). This time, while the goal remains the same, I only give them one minute. And I place no restriction on how they can answer the questions. They can answer yes or no, or they can answer as expansively as they want.

After one minute I stop and ask whether more information was shared in the one-minute or two-minute segment. Most feel more information was shared in the *one*-minute segment.

Why?

When your goal is to just get information, it's more *efficient* to ask open-ended questions. Open-ended questions or phrases include what, where, how, why, who, tell me about, describe, and explain. In the two-minute segment, I forced them to ask close-ended questions—questions that necessarily elicit a one-word yes or no response. Close-ended questions include: "Did the accident occur at 2:30 P.M.? Was it raining when the accident took place? Were you injured? Isn't it true that you were speeding? You were talking on your cell phone when you rear-ended that cabbie, right?" Each is asking for a one-word answer.

I conclude the exercise by asking whether anyone in the one-minute segment asked only one question. In other words, did anyone get the respondent to share information during the *entire* one minute? Usually someone did. How? They asked: "What happened in your accident?" or said "Tell me about your accident." They then remained silent and listened. Notice the open-ended question and phrase.

Only once in all the years I've been doing this exercise, however, has someone used the perfect information-gathering statement. What is it? "In the next one minute, please tell me as much information as you possibly can about an accident in which you were involved or someone you know was involved." Imagine how much information you might get with this *strategically* designed question that bears a direct relationship to your goal. Think strategically, not instinctively.

"Wait a second," you might say. "Don't you lose control by asking open-ended questions? When I ask open-ended questions, my counterparts go off on tangents and raise issues I don't care about."

Good question.

In fact, this sometimes occurs. However, you can minimize the likelihood of this by focusing your open-ended questions on relevant issues. For instance, you might initially ask your counterpart, "What happened in a car accident in which you were involved?" If your counterpart goes off on an irrelevant tangent, ask: "What happened to you in your 1999 car accident?" In other words, start with the open-ended part of the question and add a restrictor or more directed focus at the end. This will keep your counterpart on track and you in control of the information flow.

It also forms the basis for the "Funnel Approach," a term coined by David A. Binder and Susan C. Price. What is this? The most effective and efficient way to gather information is to start with general open-ended questions and gradually become more focused and specific. After you have elicited as much relevant information as you can with open-ended questions, and your counterpart starts raising extraneous issues, use more close-ended questions. At the end, use close-ended questions designed to extract the specific answers you need. Start with open-ended questions. End with close-ended questions. That's the Funnel Approach.

Sounds simple, right? Unfortunately, many people understand this yet still instinctively use close-ended questions. In practice it's a difficult pattern of behavior to change.

Lawyers especially seem to love close-ended questions. Probably from all those *Perry Mason* and *L.A. Law* shows. The most dramatic scenes always involved the lawyer cross-examining the witness and using close-ended after close-ended question. "Isn't it true you had four martinis the night Jane Cross was murdered?" Mason might bellow.

What should you do if you find yourself consistently using close-ended questions? Here's what I did early in my career. Before my negotiations began, I would write on the top of my notepad: "What. Where. How. Why. Who. Tell me about. Describe. Explain." Each time I looked down during the negotiation, I was reminded to use open-ended questions. Eventually I changed.

There's another benefit to starting with open-ended questions. Open-ended questions tend to send the message that you're really interested in your counterpart's response. They say: This person genuinely wants this information. Close-ended questions, by contrast, often are perceived in the opposite way. They either make you feel defensive and increase the likelihood you will clam up, or they make you wonder if the questioner really wants the information or is just trying to confirm what he or she already knows. This is the last thing you want when you're interested in gathering information.

Information-Gathering Tactic #8: Actively Listen and Use the "Power of Silence"

Remember the naval air station story where my White House colleague started asking questions instead of telling everyone what to do? That negotiation also illustrated the effectiveness of active listening as an information-gathering technique. Active listening refers to verbal responses in which a listener reflects back a speaker's main ideas or feelings in an effort to obtain more information. Active listening, in effect, lets the speaker know that you're interested in what he or she is saying. The more interest you show, the more speakers will speak.

Active listening, however, takes concentration.

I used to think active listening just meant maintaining eye contact and nodding your head. I was wrong. Active listening requires attention, thought, and practice.

For example, one effective active listening technique—the "Parrot Approach"—involves repeating back the speaker's key thoughts, ideas, or feelings by responding with short phrases and incomplete sentences.

A speaker might say: "It sounds simple to put together a lunch for the president with some enlisted men, but there are many complicated parts."

The active listening response might be "Simple but complicated?" This response will likely get and/or keep the speaker talking and giving you more information.

Another effective active listening technique involves paraphrasing the essence of what the speaker said in less than a complete sentence.

A speaker might say: "I never thought about the fact that every time the president travels, he must have a team of people get to his destination first to negotiate difficult and sometimes highly sensitive issues."

The active listening response might be "Staff always arrives in advance?"

Here are a few more effective listening techniques devised by Professor Ralph Cagle at the University of Wisconsin-Madison Law School, along with some of my thoughts. They work.

• *Want to Listen*—If you don't care what someone is saying, they will know it. Don't "fake listen." Decide why you want to listen and pay undivided attention to that person and what they're saying.

• *Stop Talking*—You can't listen while you're talking. When you talk your counterpart is usually silent. They're getting information, not you. Stop talking. Resist the urge to be the center of attention.

• *Don't Interrupt*—I have a tendency to interrupt. So does my mother-in-law. Put us together and we tend to drive my wife crazy. It got so bad once that my mother-in-law bought me a pillow that says "It's irritating when you talk while I'm interrupting!" Why is interrupting harmful to information gathering? People who have been interrupted often presume the interrupter believes his or her thoughts are more important than theirs. This shuts off the information flow. Plus, the act of interrupting signals that you're not interested in what they were saying and, likely, weren't really listening anyway. (By the way, if you're dealing with someone who just won't shut up and they're talking about irrelevant issues, try this as a polite way to interrupt: "Hold on a second. Let me see if I understand you correctly. You mean that . . ." Then paraphrase what they were saying and switch the subject while you have got the floor. In this way you won't appear rude. After all, how can they refuse to let you clarify what *they* were saying?)

• *Pay attention*—Listen with all your senses and focus on your counterparts' words, ideas, and what they're not saying. Intensely listen.

• *Eliminate distractions*—The fewer distractions, the better. Effective listeners don't constantly get interrupted by phone calls. Mute your calls. Don't check your e-mail. Get rid of physical barriers between you, like large desks or tables. Don't multitask and listen while you're doing something else. The only exception might be some limited note-taking, which I consider a form of active listening, because note-taking physically validates what your counterpart is saying. (Of course, I also recommend you say at the start that you're taking notes to ensure you accurately get down what they're saying. I do not, by the way, consider typing notes into a laptop the equivalent of taking notes on paper. Laptops serve as more of a physical barrier.)

• *Encourage Your Counterpart to Tell You More*—Encourage your counterpart to tell you more by using phrases such as "that's a good point," or "interesting," or "tell me more." This overt receptiveness will help them open up.

• *Don't Mentally Argue When Someone Is Speaking*—If you're mentally planning your response while they're talking you will miss information.

• *Defer Judgment*—Be patient and tolerant. Don't prejudge what they're saying before you have heard everything. If you do, you will likely do everyone a disservice. Reacting and responding too early is often counterproductive.

I've got one final piece of advice on the listening front. *Use the power of silence.* Americans tend to be uncomfortable with silence. So we fill it by talking. Who's getting information while we're talking? Our counterparts. Don't let this happen. Train yourself to be comfortable with silence. And if you spend a significant amount of time negotiating on the telephone, be especially aware of this tendency. People hate silence on the phone.

Sales people sometimes use a variation of this Power of Silence called the "Silent Close." They make an offer and remain silent. The ensuing uncomfortable silence is designed to exert pressure on the potential purchaser to sign on the dotted line.

Of course, be careful in using this power. If the pregnant pause extends too long, it can create an unnecessarily competitive atmosphere. But usually someone will fill the silence before this occurs. Try being silent next time. See who fills the silence with important information.

I once had a boss who used this power all the time. You would finish an assignment, like a research memo, and then you would meet to discuss it. Only the discussion was largely one way. You would explain your conclusion in the memo and he would just remain silent, with a questioning look on his face. In our first few meetings I felt an overwhelming urge to just keep talking—so I did. Unfortunately, I tended to ramble a bit after I had explained my conclusions and the reasons underlying them. Later, I realized he was just using this silence tactic to emphasize his control position as my boss and to get me to keep talking. I subsequently taught myself to patiently wait for his next question. Our working relationship improved as a result.

Information-Gathering Tactic #9: Ask "Why"—
Get to Interests, Not Positions

As discussed above, it's critical to move beyond parties' positions to find out their fundamental interests. The challenge, often, is how. Try these magic words, suggested by Roger Fisher and William Ury in *Getting to Yes*. Using them will help you focus on interests.

• *Why?* "Why" is the magic question in negotiations. "Why do you want to wait until July 31 to close on our house" you might ask. The answer—"because the sale of our condo closes on July 30 and we need the cash from it to close with you"—reveals your counterpart's critical cash-flow and timing interests.

One cautionary note, however, about the question "why?" Be sensitive to how you ask it and the tone of your voice. It's especially important to be or appear to be sincere in asking this question, because some people will react defensively to this kind of a direct probe about what they want.

If you sense this reluctance, soften up your question, as in: "I'm not sure I understand you completely. Tell me a little bit more about what you want here." Or, "I'm curious about that," and then ask why. Personally, I generally like the softer approach and transitioning into the "why" question, as transition phrases often help others open up more freely than just asking directly.

• *Why not?* This is a good question to use if your counterpart rejects or counters an offer you thought they would find appealing. "Why didn't you appear interested in investing in my software company?" you might ask a venture capitalist. The response? "Actually, I thought it was a great proposal. And I am interested in exploring a possible investment personally. But our firm already has a sizable investment in a similar company, and we need to diversify more."

Alternatively, consider suggesting options you believe the other side will reject and then ask the "why not" question. It's a more subtle way to get to their interests.

• *What else?* "What else" is a great information-gathering question. In fact, I used this phrase so often in my law school class when I started teaching that several students called me "What else Latz." I now vary it more, but it's still a very effective information-gathering phrase.

And don't be afraid to use it more than once, even in a row. It's a great follow-up question.

• *What is important to you?* The most direct question can be the best. You will be amazed at how much critical information you can get just from asking "what is important to you" and later asking "what else." While some negotiators will try to mislead you about what's important, many will be forthcoming. Of course, always probe the truthfulness of their responses by asking confirming questions later.

• *What is wrong with . . . ?* Use this question after you have suggested an option that might satisfy your counterpart's interests. "What's wrong with this office space?" the broker might ask. "Well, for starters," you might respond, "most of our employees live about an hour away, and that's a long commute for the Phoenix area. I also hate that orange carpet, and it would cost a bundle to replace it." What interests have you communicated? 1) Convenience and a short commute for your employees; 2) tasteful carpet and surroundings; and 3) price sensitivity.

Using these questions, often more than once, will help you probe parties' interests. And don't forget to use these questions throughout a negotiation. Interests can change.

Information-Gathering Tactic #10: Evaluate and Use Nonverbals/Body Language

Researchers estimate that more than half a person's feelings and attitudes are communicated through nonverbal signals. Consider how Judy is communicating in the following example:

Judy was dressed smartly and professionally, with an obviously expensive dark blue business suit and a brown leather briefcase.

She walked purposefully into the room, surveyed it, sat down and placed her briefcase on the table. She took out a pad of paper, some neatly typed notes, a Mont Blanc pen, and a calculator. Her movements were direct and precise.

She then looked up, leaned forward, made eye contact with her adversary and they were off. The negotiation began.

Or did it?

In fact, the negotiation began the moment Judy walked in. That's when everyone started picking up her nonverbal signals. They also started sending nonverbal signals to her.

Some were conscious, others unconscious. Each had meaning and affected the negotiation dynamic.

In many cases our ability to send and perceive nonverbal cues may be the difference between success and failure. Unfortunately, though, analyzing nonverbal messages and picking up body language cues is not an exact science. And misinterpreting signals can have disastrous consequences. This "science" is further complicated by the intercultural differences attributed to various nonverbal communications. In the United States, nodding your head usually means agreement. In Japan, nodding means only that the message was received. In Bulgaria, nodding illustrates disagreement.

We must thus carefully engage in this analysis and, at the least, recognize that individual nonverbal cues rarely signal any one message with absolute certainty. Therefore, always evaluate the *overall* picture and analyze changes in behavior and patterns of behavior.

So what has Judy communicated to us without saying a word?

Overall she appears to be a confident, no-nonsense, logical, and organized person who pays attention to detail and is not afraid to mix it up.

What are some nonverbal signals, and how should we interpret them? Analyze the following cues:

• *Facial expressions and eye contact*—Researchers estimate the human face can project more than 250,000 different expressions. The face also is responsible for most of the meaning in nonverbal messages.

For example, in the United States we generally expect those to whom we're speaking to look at us. Lack of eye contact often is interpreted as disinterest or even disrespect.

Shifting or darting eyes often communicate discomfort or even dishonesty. Intense staring may be an effort to intimidate. Warm eye contact may reflect sincerity or openness.

Facial expressions and eye contact also can control the flow of communication, a critical negotiation skill.

Next time you're seeking important information from your counterpart, ask a question, listen and, if you're dissatisfied with the answer, initiate eye contact and put a questioning look on your face. Then remain silent. Chances are your counterpart will fill the silence.

• *Body movements and gestures*—Body movements and gestures are especially difficult to interpret, given different cultures' norms and habits. Despite this, others likely will interpret certain movements in the following ways regardless of your intentions.

In meetings poor posture or slouching likely will be viewed as signaling a lack of enthusiasm. Leaning forward will be perceived as an expression of interest and eagerness.

Nervous habits or movements may be viewed as signals of ineptness. And many draw conclusions about others based upon the firmness of their handshake.

• *Clothing and personal appearance*—Finally, don't underestimate the impact of clothing and appearance. Research has shown people use these factors to draw conclusions about your status, credibility, and persuasiveness.

For instance, studies have found that people perceived as more attractive come across as more persuasive, and clothing indicates your status—especially with strangers. People have more influence with others when wearing high-status clothing.

Next time you're about to sit down and negotiate, look around and read the nonverbal signals floating around. And if you're across the table from Judy, smile (reflecting optimism), look her in the eye (telling her you're engaged and ready to start), and steeple your hands (signaling confidence).

Here's a summary of our steps so far to gain the informational power.

INFORMATION IS POWER—SO GET IT

Get Information to Set Your Goals

Develop an Information-Bargaining Strategy—Ways to Get and Share Information
  • Get as much *substantive* information as possible
  • Get as much *strategic* information as possible

Top Ten Information-Gathering Tactics

1. Leave your ego at the door
2. Be sincere
3. Establish trust
4. List your information needs
5. Do the "big shmooze"
6. Ask questions. Ask questions. Ask questions!
7. Use the Funnel—move from open- to close-ended questions
8. Actively listen and use the "power of silence"
9. Ask "why"—get to interests, not positions
10. Evaluate and use nonverbals/body language

Prepare Blocking Techniques: Avoiding Those Tough Questions

These tactics will help you achieve your goals. But what if your counterpart asks *you* these questions and you don't want to share *your* strategically important information. How can you avoid it?

In one of my seminars, the following example came up: "What should I do if he asks if I have the authority to agree to his figure?" a participant asked me. "If I truthfully answer yes, then he will probably just stick to that amount and not move. If I answer no, it would be a lie."

"Excellent question," I responded. "It raises one of the most sensitive and challenging areas in many negotiations—how to effectively block and avoid answering strategically critical questions and still be truthful."

At the outset, recognize that it's perfectly legitimate, expected, and strategically crucial to avoid answering certain questions in negotiations. In every negotiation, parties seek information that will give them a strategic advantage and try to avoid sharing harmful information. I call it the "information exchange game."

Assume I want to hire a new marketing manager and advertise in several trade publications seeking qualified applicants. Despite receiving one hundred applications and interviewing four applicants, assume I only found one, Laura, with the requisite skills and qualifications.

How should I respond if Laura asks me if she's the only one qualified and interested in this position? Deflect her question, because sharing this information will weaken my leverage and allow Laura to hold me hostage in negotiating her compensation.

Instead, I want Laura to believe that, while she is extremely qualified and I'm interested, other applicants could also do this job well. How can you do this?

First, I would never recommend that a person lie in a negotiation. Lying is morally wrong, and you will be far less effective if you are caught and your credibility takes a hit.

However, this does not mean you cannot or should not honestly respond in a way that still protects your crucial information.

In fact, parties in negotiations often evade or misdirect in response to certain questions.

The key is to do this in a way that protects the information *and* your credibility.

Of course, it's tough to effectively and credibly avoid sharing strategically harmful information, if you have not both anticipated the questions and considered how to strategically block them.

So, start by preparing a list of information you do not want to share and questions you want to block. Preparing this way will also help you refocus on issues beneficial to you after you block.

Then, consider using one the following blocking tactics, each of which can minimize the likelihood your counterpart will perceive it as an effort to cover up harmful information:

- *Change the subject and/or delay answering.*

Question: "Marty, am I the only one qualified and interested in this marketing position?"

Block: "Good question, Laura. I can certainly appreciate where you're coming from. But it's critical to first address my overall marketing needs and your ability to satisfy them. I'm also interested in what other opportunities you're exploring, if any. It's tough out there now for those looking for marketing positions. . . ."

- *Answer a different question.*

"Funny you should ask that. Just the other day, another applicant asked me how many we were interviewing, and I told her four."

- *Respond with your own question.*

"You know, that reminds me of an issue I forgot to raise earlier. Why don't you tell me about your references?"

- *Discount the question's relevance, or ask for clarification.*

"I'm not sure I understand how that makes a difference to you and to your interest in the position? If we're a good fit, this will work. That's more important than anything. Right?"

- *Answer a specific question by focusing on the general, or vice versa.*

"Excellent question. Let's take a look at the market. After advertising this position in three trade magazines, we received one hundred resumes. My assistant narrowed these down to four, each of whom has excellent credentials and experience. I interviewed each and have been generally impressed."

Alternatively, you can also block a general question by responding with such specificity that the answer has little value to the questioner.

• ***Refuse to answer due to policy, tradition, lack of authority, etc.***

"I would be happy to tell you, but our policy prevents me from sharing that information." (Of course, this response requires that you have such a policy or implement one prior to this conversation.)

Next time you're about to start an important negotiation consider what information you don't want to share and prepare a few blocking techniques. Remember, inadvertent disclosure of critical information may destroy your best deal.

I want to end this section by repeating my earlier point: *Do not lie*. Do not answer Laura's question by saying "you are not the only one qualified and interested." As we explore in depth in chapter 7, the damage to your credibility will be just too great if your lie ever comes to light.

Reevaluate Your Goals

There's one final step to the information-gathering process. Reevaluate your written goals. Based on the information you have gathered, you may need to slightly revise your goals. As discussed above, maintain some flexibility in your goalsetting. At this point it may make sense to reset them.

Let's now summarize chapter 1. Here's an outline of what we've learned:

CHAPTER 1 REVIEW

Golden Rule One: Information Is Power—So Get It

Get Information to Set Your Goals
1. Set and prioritize your long-term strategic and short-term tactical goals
2. Determine and prioritize your counterpart's goals
3. Evaluate the power of the relationship

Practical Tips and Tactics for Goal-Setting
- Brainstorm to set your goals
- Set aggressive and specific goals—don't just "do the best you can"
- Tie your goals to realistic standards

- *Expect* to succeed
- Commit to it (oral, written, and public)

Develop an Information-Bargaining Strategy—Ways to Get and Share Information

- Get as much *substantive* information as possible
  — Find out facts, issues, and opinions
  — Uncover fundamental interests underlying positions
  — Brainstorm options that might satisfy interests

- Get as much *strategic* information as possible
  — Negotiate with the right person
  — Investigate your counterpart's reputation and past tactics

- Top Ten Information-Gathering Tactics
  1. Leave your ego at the door
  2. Be sincere
  3. Establish trust
  4. List your information needs
  5. Do the "big shmooze"
  6. Ask questions. Ask questions. Ask questions!
  7. Use the Funnel—open- to close-ended questions
  8. Actively listen and use the "power of silence"
  9. Ask "why"—get to interests, not positions
  10. Evaluate and use nonverbals/body language

- Prepare Blocking Techniques: Avoiding Those Tough Questions
  — Change the subject and/or delay answering
  — Answer a different question
  — Respond with your own question
  — Discount the question's relevance, or ask for clarification
  — Answer a specific question by focusing on the general, or vice versa
  — Refuse to answer due to policy, tradition, lack of authority, etc.

Reevaluate Your Goals

GOLDEN RULE TWO:

MAXIMIZE YOUR LEVERAGE

love leverage. Leverage, above all else, will improve my ability to get what I want. Yet many individuals, including experienced negotiators, don't understand how to evaluate their leverage, what steps to take to improve it, or when and how to most effectively exercise it. Everyone wants leverage. Many people, however, inadvertently give it away.

So, what is leverage, and how can we maximize it and increase our chances of getting what we want?

Assume you're the CEO of a company employing a quarter of the city's employees. Your company provides a significant portion of the city's tax revenue, but neither you nor your company is active in the community's political affairs. Recently you decided to expand your physical plant. You need the city council to approve a zoning change.

Unfortunately, you have met with resistance from a twenty-three-year-old neighborhood activist with political ambitions. He appears to have stirred up enough concern about your expansion to make the city council deny you the permit.

Who has more leverage—the powerful CEO or the twenty-three-year-old activist? The twenty-three-year-old. Why? Leverage often is not about conventional social or economic power. It's about who has, or can gain, a perceived situational advantage in a particular circumstance. At this point, the twenty-three-year-old doesn't have much to lose. The CEO does.

So, how should we analyze and use leverage to help us succeed?

Overall, take these four steps:

- Evaluate parties' initial leverage
- Strengthen your leverage—it's fluid
- Strike while your leverage is hot
- Implement five leverage-enhancing tactics

Evaluate Parties' Initial Leverage

Begin by evaluating each party's leverage at the start. Leverage consists of two elements:

- How much each party needs or wants an agreement relative to the other
- The consequences to each side if no agreement is reached—that is, each side's alternative to a negotiated agreement

Overall, leverage fundamentally relates to how easy it is for you to walk away, relative to how easy it is for the other side to walk away. *The easier it is for you to walk away and the harder for the other side, the stronger your leverage.*

Find Each Side's Need Level

How much do you really need or want an agreement? Are you desperate? The CEO above *really* wants to expand in that city. The twenty-three-year-old doesn't want the company to expand, but doesn't care that much. He just wants the publicity to advance his political ambitions. Knowing how much a party needs an agreement underlies the first aspect of leverage. The greater your need, the weaker your leverage. And vice versa.

New York City real estate magnate Donald Trump said "Leverage is having something the other guy wants. Or, better yet, needs. Or, best of all, simply cannot do without."

Focusing on a party's needs or wants should remind you of our discussion in chapter 1 about getting information on parties' needs and interests. One reason you want this information is for the leverage it provides. Leveragewise, however, go beyond just finding out *what* the parties' want and need and find *how much* they want and need it.

This is more difficult. Such information is often crucial and strategic, and will only be reluctantly shared. Plus, parties will and often should attempt to misdirect their counterparts regarding their level of need.

To get this information then, it's vital to explore the needs issue as early as possible in negotiations. The earlier you find out how much your counterpart needs or wants an agreement, the less likely your counterpart will be prepared to misdirect you about it.

Let's say I was selling my house and, as I was showing my newly renovated kitchen to a couple, the wife told her husband she "loved the kitchen and the house."

The couple's leverage appears weak. The wife indicated within my earshot how much she wanted my house. And she did it early on, in the information-gathering stage. Critically, I just received important information about this couple's needs and wants. The more they want it, the weaker their leverage, right?

Right, except for two critical factors. One, we haven't yet explored how much *I* need or want to sell. If I'm more desperate to sell than they are to buy, their leverage would appear stronger than mine. Perhaps I just bought another house and need to close on my old house within thirty-five days to get the cash for my new house. If true, this would significantly change the leverage situation. Two, they may not know how motivated I am to sell. If they don't know it, they can't take advantage of it.

This underscores two often-overlooked elements of leverage and what you should do about them: analyze parties' *relative* situations and focus on the parties' *perception*.

Analyze Parties' *Relative* Situations

Leverage is only strong or weak *in comparison to* the other side's needs and wants. Most of us naturally focus on how much we need or want what the other side has to offer. Don't. Focus instead on the *relative* needs of *all* the parties. In leverage terms, your needs and wants don't mean much independently. They only gain relevance when analyzed relative to the other parties' needs and wants.

Let's say it's Friday afternoon at 4:30 P.M. and Steve and his wife and family just returned from their summer vacation to find their house flooded due to a water leak. It's uninhabitable. Their kids start school Monday, and they need a place to stay. Unfortunately, a huge convention is in town and no hotel rooms are available. They're driving along the street when they see an apartment complex near their house advertising "vacancy." They drive in, park their SUV in front of the rental office, ask their children to wait in the truck, and Steve and his wife walk in to negotiate the best rate they can get on a three-bedroom apartment.

Do you think Steve and his wife have weak leverage? In my seminars, almost every participant answers yes. They're wrong. At this point, no one knows whether Steve and his wife have weak or strong leverage. While they may be desperate, the apartment complex may be *more* desperate. If so, and they discover this, they have fairly strong leverage.

It's natural to focus on what we need. Ignore the urge. Focus instead on the parties' *relative* needs.

Focus on the Parties' *Perception*

In the house-selling example above, I still have stronger leverage than the couple, even after the wife said she loved my kitchen. Why? They don't yet know I am more desperate to sell than they are to buy. In other words, parties' *perceptions* of the other side's needs and wants impacts the negotiation, not some "true" level of desperation. If I know the couple really wants my house and they don't know I'm more motivated to sell, my leverage is stronger than if they knew.

I thus want to mask my level of desperation from the couple looking at my house. And they should have been more careful about what they said in my presence. Perception trumps reality here. It especially impacts leverage.

Determine Each Side's Best Alternative to a Negotiated Agreement (BATNA)

In addition to the parties' relative level of need, your leverage also depends on what will happen to each party if you can't reach agreement. If you have sold your house, must be out in five days, have teenagers in public high school, have no place to live next week, and are negotiating to purchase and move into a vacant house nearby owned by a multimillionaire, your leverage is weak. If you're negotiating for a raise, have a unique expertise, and just got an attractive job offer from a competitor, your leverage is strong.

Roger Fisher, William Ury and Bruce Patton in *Getting to Yes* call this your Best Alternative to a Negotiated Agreement, or BATNA. It reflects what you will do if you do not or cannot reach agreement with your counterpart. The better your alternative, the stronger your leverage. The worse your alternative, the weaker your leverage.

This element of leverage is also relative. In other words, your leverage is dependent upon your BATNA *and* its relationship to your counterpart's best alternative to a negotiated agreement with you, or its BATNA. What will your counterpart do if he or she does not or cannot reach agreement with you? If you have a horrible BATNA, but the other side's BATNA is worse, you have decent leverage. It also depends, of course, on what you know about your counterpart's BATNA. Perception, once again, makes a difference.

Know your BATNA, not your bottom line. "I always have a tough time figuring out my bottom line," many of my clients tell me. "I'm just not ever sure when to walk or when to give just a little more and hope for the best. After all, I want the best deal I can get. And I don't want to leave anything on the table."

When to hold and when to fold? That is the question.

Here's my "bottom line" answer: Use a BATNA analysis. If you accurately determine your Best Alternative to a Negotiated Agreement, it will tell you when to sign and when to walk. It will prevent you from making agreements you should reject and ensure you only accept agreements that are in your best interest. How?

Assume you work in the procurement department of a Fortune 500 manufacturing company and are working with your information technology (IT) department to purchase five hundred new laptop computers to replace the nearly obsolete models currently in use. So you contacted three well-known computer manufacturers and asked each to send a proposal to provide you with five hundred new laptops that satisfy your needs. Computer manufacturer A's proposal came in at $500,000. Computer manufacturer B's came in at $395,000. And computer manufacturer C's came in at $350,000. Price is the only significant difference. Each includes similar-quality laptops with the same power, speed, weight, warranties, service levels, and other essential characteristics. Each company has an excellent reputation.

However, your IT department has requested—all else being relatively equal—that you choose B. B manufactured your current laptops, and your colleagues generally like them. You tell your IT colleague you will honor his wish, but only if B's offer price is at or below the other bids. In other words, a nonmonetary interest exists, but it's relatively minor. Your monetary interest largely trumps your nonmonetary interest. As a result, you want to negotiate with B to get the lowest price you can. Regarding your authority, you have $400,000 in your budget for the new laptops. However, each procurement employee gets a small portion of the difference if your department comes in under budget. So you also have an internal incentive to spend the least amount possible.

Here's where your BATNA analysis comes in. First, contact A and C and try to get each to lower its bid. With A—initially the high bidder at $500,000—indicate its bid is high compared with the other bidders, and is over your budget. With C—initially the low bidder at $350,000—share that some of your colleagues would like to stick with B, so it would be really helpful if C lowered its bid and provided you with a significant financial incentive to choose it. Overall, start by trying to get even lower bids from A and C. At this point, assume neither A nor C moves.

Then contact B's national sales vice president, or whoever put together its bid. Tell him or her you're currently inclined to go with B, as you've heard great things about its new laptops and B has a great reputation. Then build some rapport and ask how things are generally going with its laptop sales. Let's say the VP says things are going well. Your research suggests, however, that B's not doing nearly as well as last year. And you know that volume and profits are down throughout the industry. So you make a comment about this, and the VP generally agrees.

It's natural to assume, based on your research and the VP's comments, B has a significant need for your contract. And it's likely, you believe, that B will provide an additional discount to get it. Your leverage appears fairly strong. After all, you have several quality bidders—alternatives—at relatively reasonable prices.

At this point, I would tell B's sales VP again you'd like to go with them, but the price is high. Ask him or her to crunch the numbers again, reevaluate the bid, and give you his or her absolute best price. Also tell the VP that C "significantly" beat B's original bid. Be specific that it was C, so he or she knows you're dealing in an upfront fashion. But, don't reveal by how much C beat B's original bid. Only hint at it. You want the VP to give you the *best* price, not just a lower price than C's. If you reveal C's bid, the VP may just beat it by $1,000. Without that knowledge, the VP's offer might beat it by much more.

Let's say B came back with an additional 5 percent discount and its "final" bid is $375,000. Should you walk? Yes. Why? Your BATNA—buying from C at $350,000—is better than buying from B at $375,000. Choosing C saves you $25,000. Given your price sensitivity, you walk.

But if B came back with a "final" bid of $345,000 and you can't get A or C to beat it, grab it. Why? Your BATNA—buying from C at $350,000—is a worse alternative than buying from B.

The BATNA concept is critical, so here's another example. This one comes from the legal field and involves the leverage in many company mergers. Often in mergers, a company's senior deal team will negotiate the major deal points, including price, corporate structure, name, and so forth. (The senior deal team often includes the CEO, CFO, corporate development officer, and an investment banker.) After the senior deal team has finished this portion of the negotiation, a due diligence period often exists during which the parties analyze each other's books and operations and agree to exclusivity. In other words, they agree not to talk with other potential partners. At the beginning of this period, the senior deal team will often direct their lawyers to go ahead and "paper the deal." It's also often made clear to the lawyers that they should not mess it up.

This can be incredibly frustrating for their lawyers, and weaken the company's leverage. Why? The senior deal team has just taken away much of the company's leverage on the remaining issues. First, the senior deal team has effectively told their lawyers that the company really wants and needs the deal. In many cases, a nonbinding letter of intent has already been signed and a commitment has been made to the other company, sometimes even publicly. The senior deal team's credibility is on the line.

Second, the senior deal team has removed the second critical piece of leverage—a good alternative to the deal. Instead of having another suitor lined up and ready to go in case your counterpart doesn't give you what you want in terms of employee security—or other unresolved issues—you can't even look for another one. A weak BATNA all around.

Of course, many negotiators will mitigate this situation by inserting a termination clause into the deal. Termination clauses generally state that if one or the other company pulls out of the deal from that point on, it owes a "breakup fee" to the other. The higher the breakup fee, the worse both sides' BATNAs, and the greater the incentive to agree on the deal point on the table.

Plus, since leverage is relative, if both senior deal teams instruct their lawyers in the same way, both sets of lawyers will appear to have similar leverage. This may equalize the situation. But if just one of the senior deal teams tells their lawyers to close the deal, but indicates it's not that critical, as the business is doing great without it, that side has stronger leverage. They will likely get the minor deal points in their favor. Added up, these could be significant.

One final note on the subject of BATNAs and alternatives. Sometimes it's not clear what will happen if you walk away from the table. Let's say you're negotiating to sell your company to Buyer A and believe you have a 50 percent likelihood of doing a slightly better deal with Buyer B if you walk. But you also believe you have a 50 percent chance that a deal with Buyer B will not happen at all and you won't be able to sell to anyone, a very poor alternative for you. This is called your Worst Alternative to a Negotiated Agreement (WATNA) with Buyer A. How should you factor this into your decision-making process? In the context of your negotiations with Buyer A take into consideration the relative likelihood of your various alternatives. Still determine your BATNA. But in calculating your BATNA's overall value and evaluating whether Buyer A's offer is better than it, factor in the likelihood that worse alternatives may also come to pass. In short, your evaluation of your BATNA should also take into consideration the relative likelihood that other alternatives—some worse—may occur.

To summarize, leverage consists of: 1) the level of both parties' needs and wants, along with 2) each party's Best Alternative to a Negotiated Agreement. And leverage does not exist independently. It can only be strong or weak *relative* to your counterpart's situation. Plus, both parties' leverage is dependent upon the other side's *perception* of their leverage. There is no "real" leverage. It only exists as a form of influence and thus can only be exercised if the other side perceives it as you present it.

Parties' need levels and BATNAs are the two strategic building blocks of leverage. But there's much more involved to maximizing your leverage than just understanding and evaluating these elements. Next, you should:

- Strengthen your leverage—it's fluid
- Strike while your leverage is hot

Strengthen Your Leverage—It's Fluid

Many negotiators have a basic sense of leverage. They understand that the more they want something, the weaker they appear. Or that if they absolutely need what only a monopoly provides, they have a very weak BATNA.

Understanding this is critical. But the most effective negotiators also know that everyone has the ability to change their leverage. Leverage is not static. Everyone's level of need likely will change during the negotiation. At the least, a party's perception of its level of need may change. This changes its leverage. Likewise, you may be able to improve your BATNA. Or you might be able to make your counterpart's alternative less attractive. In short, you can change your leverage and improve your ability to get what you want even when it appears you have weak leverage. The lesson: Analyze your leverage—then strategize ways to strengthen it. Take charge of your leverage.

Let me give you an example that illustrates the fluid nature of leverage and that answers a fairly common question I'm asked: "What should I do if I have really weak leverage?"

The No-Leverage Dilemma

"We're going to court," Ellen told me during a break in my seminar. "What else can we do? We really want to sell, but my brother-in-law's 'best offer' for our share of the family business will only give us ten percent of what it's really worth. Plus, the relationship is over. What have we got to lose?"

"Well, what's your leverage?" I responded.

"We don't have any," she said.

Here's what I advised:

First, evaluate the parties' initial leverage—their level of needs and BATNAs. Since Ellen "really wanted to sell," her leverage was weaker than if she didn't care. It also didn't appear as if her brother-in-law needed to buy.

Ellen also had a poor BATNA; she didn't have a good alternative to selling to her brother-in-law, largely because she hadn't looked for one. Her BATNA, at that point in time, was asking a court to split up the company. Few would have been satisfied with this. Her relative lack of leverage was even worse when compared to her brother-in-law's BATNA. Given his ownership share, he retained control of the business either way.

What did I suggest she do? *Strengthen her leverage by soliciting other potential buyers for her share.* Create an auctionlike, competitive environment. Collect bids. And do this even though she wanted to keep it a family business.

Why? The probable reason Ellen was only offered ten cents on the dollar was because she had weak leverage *at that point*. She really wanted to sell and had no good alternatives. By creating decent alternatives and strengthening her leverage, she would increase the likelihood her brother-in-law would make a serious offer.

I also suggested she try to change her brother-in-law's perception of the value of *his* alternative. If you can show your counterpart that his or her likely alternative is worse than your offer you have strengthened your leverage. For example, Ellen might emphasize to her brother-in-law the downside to having a nonfamily minority shareholder of the business. Minority shareholders can present major problems.

Many negotiators ignore this step. A client once asked me to help sell his public relations and Internet consulting business. He wanted out and had a good offer on the table from a serious potential buyer. I asked him if there were other buyers on the horizon. He told me he had spoken with another potential buyer six months prior, but nothing since. He said he didn't think it likely this previous company would match his current offer. I told him he might be right, but he should still contact that company and find out. If nothing else, this would allow him to truthfully tell the current potential buyer someone else was interested. This statement alone would strengthen his leverage. Thinking about calling, however, wouldn't do it. He needed to make that alternative a more real possibility.

Here's another example of how you can take concrete steps to improve your leverage. Watch how my leverage changes.

The Car Repair Story

In 1996 I was driving south on Route 51 in Phoenix around 9:30 A.M. when my engine started making a very strange noise. Despite my mechanical ignorance, I knew something was wrong. My only question— could I get it to the shop without destroying the engine? I gambled, and five minutes later drove in to the nearest Nissan dealership.

I explained the problem to John, the guy who usually writes up my repair tickets, and got a ride back to work. I left with a bad taste in my mouth, sensing big dollar signs on the horizon.

I was right. John called around 10:30 A.M. to tell me the damage. Nineteen hundred dollars. Yikes! Interestingly, John said this was a very good price, as it reflected our previous relationship. He also said he would need the "go/no go" sign by noon if I wanted the car that day. They had room in the shop to do it that day, but needed five hours to get it done.

Stage One: John Has My Car and Told Me It Would Cost $1,900 to Fix

What's my leverage?

My level of need? I need a car. Going without one in Phoenix is not an option for even a day. And I only had the Nissan. John knows this, based on our previous dealings.

John's/Nissan's level of need? They have room in their shop to fix it today. Many dealerships' repair facilities are profit centers, so there's probably a decent profit margin in the $1,900 estimate. John's personal level of need is based on how much his compensation is tied to the business he generates. I don't know if he is on commission, but I presume he gets more, based on the work he generates.

My BATNA? I have a weak short-term and long-term BATNA. Short-term, if I don't reach an agreement with John, I'm stranded at my office without transportation. My long-term alternatives are better. But I don't yet know how realistic or cost-effective they might be. My alternatives include: buying another car; getting this car repaired elsewhere; or borrowing or renting a car.

John's/Nissan's BATNA: If I don't do the deal with John/Nissan, they will lose the profit they would have made on me. Of course, this assumes they have an empty slot in their repair facility and cannot fill it with another $1,900 customer. For a large dealership this is not a big deal. For John personally, it's probably more significant.

Overall leverage at this stage? Advantage John/Nissan. I have a stronger need than John/Nissan and have poor alternatives. They also know my need and my lack of good alternatives.

Let's go back to my negotiation.

After giving it some thought, I set three goals: 1) evaluate whether the work truly needed to be done (how much did I trust John?); 2) ensure I received quality work; and 3) see how far down I could negotiate the price.

My next step was to gather more information. So I asked John what exactly needed to be fixed. What parts needed to be replaced? What did each cost? What was their labor charge, and what other charges were included? Finally, what options did I have, other than fixing everything?

Armed with this information, I glanced at the clock: It was approaching noon, so I evaluated the flexibility of John's deadline (deadlines will be discussed in more detail in chapter 6). Often negotiators impose artificial deadlines to increase pressure on the other side. Some feel the pressure more acutely than others and cave too quickly. Deadlines also may prevent the other side from gaining sufficient information and leverage to get the best deal.

The counter strategy? Evaluate whether the deadline can be changed and, if so, determine its cost. In this case, given John's time estimates for the repair, I knew the deadline was real. Yet I ignored it. I figured I would save more than the fifty-dollar rental car cost per day with an hour or so shopping around.

Stage Two: After Information Gathering—But Before Shopping Around

My level of need? No real change yet. I still really needed a car.

John's/Nissan's level of need? Probably no real change, but I'm not sure. I did not gather sufficient information to adequately determine how busy they were.

My BATNA? No real change. Still poor, with just theoretical alternatives.

John's/Nissan's BATNA? Probably no real change.

Overall leverage? Still advantage John/Nissan.

Time to shop around. I called four other dealerships and an independent repair shop.

As discussed above, the value of any agreement should be judged based on its alternatives. The better my alternatives, the stronger my leverage. I dialed other repair shops to try to strengthen my leverage.

In each call I described my car's problems and John's proposed solution, and asked if the work appeared necessary, given the car's symptoms, age, and mileage. I then told each I was calling five different shops, would go with the lowest estimate, other things being equal, and wanted their absolute best price. I also told each I would not likely call back after I got their initial estimate unless it was the lowest.

Interestingly, while the diagnosis appeared accurate, the estimates ranged all across the board. Labor rates ranged from $55 to $72 per hour. Even the parts costs varied substantially.

The best price? $1,450, including tax. And remember, John told me his $1,900 price was very good, due to our previous relationship. Some relationship!

Stage Three: After Shopping Other Repair Shops

My level of need? No change.

John's/Nissan's level of need? No change.

My BATNA? Major improvement. I now have much better alternatives. Several other quality shops will do it less expensively. (I'm assuming the other dealerships do similar quality work, or at the least will back up their work to the same extent as John. Quality goal accomplished.) My new BATNA: another dealer doing the work for $1,450, including tax, plus $50 to get my car towed there, plus $50 to rent a car, plus my additional time to arrange for the tow and a rental car.

John's/Nissan's BATNA? No real change.

Overall leverage? My leverage has significantly improved relative to John's, but he doesn't know it yet.

Time to call John. After all, my car still sat in his shop, and I trusted the work they had previously done. After shmoozing a bit, I told John what I had done, what I had found, where I had found it, and asked him to beat $1,450. He said he didn't think he could—he didn't have the authority—but he would check with his boss.

A short time later John called and said they would match it, but that was their best price.

Done? Nope. I then asked for a free rental car, having previously found out John's dealership had an on-site rental agency. John hemmed and hawed but then agreed. Apparently it was their "policy" to provide free rental cars if a repair bill exceeded one thousand dollars. Interestingly, John didn't tell me this until *after* I asked.

The lessons? Gather information, set goals, evaluate deadlines' flexibility, evaluate parties' initial leverage, and strengthen your leverage—it's fluid—by researching and taking steps to improve your alternatives. And don't forget one of the principal negotiation lessons in life: You will never get what you don't ask for.

Final leverage situation? I ended up with a *better* deal at the end than my final leverage suggested I could get. In fact, I beat my last best alternative by about a hundred dollars, not including my time to arrange the tow. And I would have gotten the work done at a new place where I didn't have any experience with the people.

Why did I get such a good deal? Because: a) John/Nissan didn't want to lose my future business and their future profits; b) they still made a profit; c) they didn't want anyone saying another dealership beat their price; and d) I got their competitive juices flowing, and they didn't want to lose.

Remember, leverage is fluid. Don't accept weak leverage. Take concrete steps to strengthen it.

Strike While Your Leverage Is Hot

There's one final leverage element to address: timing. Given the fluid nature of leverage, you will always want to complete your agreements when your leverage reaches its peak. Strike while your leverage is hot. How?

First, *constantly* strive to maximize your leverage. Don't assume it will stay the same. In fact, time alone often strengthens one of the parties' leverage. Time may work for you or against you. Keep this in mind.

A plaintiff's personal injury lawyer named Bob once asked me for advice about a case he wanted to settle with the defendant's insurance company. Bob had filed the lawsuit about six months before our conversation and had previously written a letter offering to settle the case. The insurance company lawyer, after receiving the lawsuit, asked if Bob would delay the formal litigation proceedings for about a month while they tried to settle. Bob agreed, figuring a short delay would not make a big difference.

Several weeks later the insurance company lawyer countered with a totally inadequate response. Bob, while disappointed, met with his client and countered. The insurance company lawyer then asked Bob for an *additional* month's delay, saying he needed even more time to consider the plaintiff's counter and to respond before incurring the litigation expenses. The amount the insurance company spent on the litigation defense, he said, would mean less available for the plaintiff in settlement.

Bob asked me what he should do. Aggressively push forward, I said. No more delays. While I understood the initial grant of the delay (lawyers often do this as a matter of professional courtesy), subsequent delays would send the wrong strategic message.

I recommended that Bob set an aggressive schedule to depose the defendants' key individuals and get information from them to bolster his case at trial. At the same time, he should be open to settlement negotiations. But he shouldn't settle until he has sufficient information to adequately judge his likelihood of success at trial. At that point his leverage will be strong enough to provide a true benchmark for the settlement discussions.

According to Danny Ortega, one of Arizona's most successful plaintiff's trial lawyers, "The most effective negotiation tactic is to be ready to go to trial, plain and simple. You have to show the other side that you have your ducks in order, that you have your witnesses, that you have your evidence, and that you have your experts. And until the other side knows that you're ready to go to trial, they're not going to want to talk business."

Timing also played a central role in the 1998 signing of then Arizona Cardinals' quarterback Jake Plummer to a contract that made him the second-highest-paid quarterback in the National Football League. This occurred even though Plummer had relatively average quarterback-performance statistics at the time. Guided by agent Leigh Steinberg, Plummer smartly signed a $27.8-million, four-year contract (with a $15-million signing bonus) with his leverage at its peak. At signing he was leading the Cardinals to their first playoff appearance in twenty-three years, despite an 8–7 win-loss record. And his local popularity was sky-high, due to his Arizona State University quarterback days and the way he led the Cardinals—engineering numerous fourth-quarter heroics to snatch victory from seeming defeat. And most important, according to Steinberg, the Arizona Cardinals were not far from asking Phoenix voters to spend hundreds of millions of dollars to build a new football stadium. In short, the Cardinals felt they needed to show the community they would spend their own money to build a winner. Signing Plummer to a very rich, long-term contract was intended to send this message. (Unfortunately for the Cardinals, they lost that public vote—although they won a later one—and Plummer did not play up to their expectations during his remaining time in Phoenix.)

Timing also matters, as factors out of your control can impact your leverage. So don't delay accepting an offer when your leverage is strong and the offer beats your best alternative.

In 2000 I was on the board of the Herberger Theater Center, a non-profit theater that, like most live theaters, must raise private funds to operate. During the fall of that year the theater's then-CEO was negotiating with a local corporation to sponsor a season of programming by contributing $75,000. In return the corporation would get advertising signage around the theater and prominent recognition in programs given to the theater's attendees. The corporation liked the idea, as theater patrons fit its target market.

The theater's CEO, after negotiating for several months and losing leverage when another possible sponsor pulled out (thus weakening the theater's BATNA), finally signed up the corporation to a season sponsorship package for $50,000. The CEO told our board the deal just needed final approval by the corporation's board.

Shortly after our board meeting the deal fell through. The corporation, just before its board met, found out its revenues fell short of expectations. It thus allocated much of its marketing dollars, including "our" $50,000, to a customer rebate program.

The reason the deal submarined? Timing. If the deal had been presented to the board one month before, it would have been signed, sealed, and delivered. In retrospect, could our CEO have done anything differently? It's hard to say. Few predicted the dramatic change in the economy during the fall of 2000. And it can be extremely difficult to anticipate future changes in leverage. But the lesson is clear: To the extent you can, strike while your leverage is hot. When you have strong leverage, exercise it and get the deal done. *When* you sign the deal may determine *if* you even have one.

Implement Five Leverage-Enhancing Tactics

Of course, to put yourself in a position of strength to even make this decision, you will need to take some concrete leverage-enhancing steps. Use these five tactics to put yourself into this position:

- Assess and quantify all sides' initial leverage
- Improve your alternatives and limit the attractiveness of your counterparts' alternatives
- Tactically share your leverage-related information
- Communicate your leverage credibly and confidently
- Selectively use risky leverage tactics like walkouts and threats

Assess and Quantify All Sides' Initial Leverage

Assess all sides' leverage, everyone's needs and BATNAs, and do this early on. The sooner you get this information, the more likely you will get honest and straightforward answers. Discover the parties' weaknesses *before* they've got their guard up. How? Ask general leverage-related questions ("How busy are you these days?" or "What are you looking for here?") and then get more specific.

Then quantify it to the extent possible. Understanding leverage intuitively is one thing. Quantifying it strategically is another. Quantifying the parties' need levels and BATNAs will force you to analytically, logically, and systematically evaluate the relative strengths and weaknesses of everyone's leverage. While the quantification process recommended below is not an exact science, following the process alone will ensure you strategically evaluate and consider, in *all* your negotiations, your level of need, your counterpart's level of need, your BATNA, and your counterpart's BATNA.

And to the extent you regularly reevaluate and quantify your leverage, it will also ensure you keep strategic track of the changes in your leverage.

Finally, quantifying your leverage will provide a mechanism with which you or your boss or subordinates can evaluate your negotiation behavior. It will provide you with a fairly objective procedure by which you can consistently evaluate how your leverage may differ in different negotiations. Let's say you're the vice president of sales for computer manufacturer B and have proposed to sell five hundred new laptops to company Y and also proposed to sell five hundred similar new laptops to company Z. Quantifying your leverage, which may be different with company Y than company Z, will provide you with a consistent and rational basis to determine why you might sell the laptops for different prices.

How does this work?

Assess and Quantify Both Sides' Needs

If you're negotiating to purchase some customized software for your company, and find out the seller *really* wants a foothold in your industry, you have strengthened your leverage. Here's how you should quantify your and the seller's needs. Remember, while the numerical element of this process may be somewhat imprecise, the real value in this process lies in forcing you to sit down, strategically assess your leverage situation, and reach certain conclusions about what you're willing to do in any given negotiation situation. To start, it's a three-step process:

First, determine your need level as reflected in the following Need Level Chart. For each negotiation, categorize your need level from Very High (−2) to Very Low (+2). The higher and more desperate your need level, the weaker your leverage. The lower your need level, the stronger your leverage. Place this numerical value in the box labeled "Your Need Level."

Second, determine your counterpart's need level. Your counterpart's need level will range from Very High (+2) to Very Low (−2). The higher and more desperate your *counterpart's* need level, the stronger *your* leverage. The lower your counterpart's need level, the weaker your leverage. Place this numerical value in the box labeled "Counterpart's Need Level."

Finally, add Your Need Level and Counterpart's Need Level. The resulting figure, Your Need Score, reflects the overall strength or weakness of the first element of your leverage, your need. A score of +4 is your

NEED LEVEL CHART

	Need Level		**Your Need Level**
Yours	Very High	= −2	
	High	= −1	
	Medium	= 0	
	Low	= +1	
	Very Low	= +2	
	Need Level		**Counterpart's Need Level**
Counterpart's	Very High	= +2	
	High	= +1	
	Medium	= 0	
	Low	= −1	
	Very Low	= −2	
			Your Need Score
Your Need Level + **Counterpart's Need Level**		=	

Your Need Score: _____

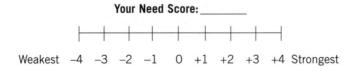

Weakest −4 −3 −2 −1 0 +1 +2 +3 +4 Strongest

strongest point. A score of –4 is your weakest point. Circle your Overall Need Score on the graph below the Need Level Chart.

Since parties' levels of need often change during negotiations, continuously reevaluate this score when appropriate.

Assess and Quantify Both Sides' BATNAs

As you know, understanding the parties' BATNAs also will help enormously by giving you the rational ability to judge any offer and decide when to hold and when to fold. Remember, think BATNA. Here, just as you quantified the parties' need level, you can also quantify the parties' BATNA:

First, determine the strength of your BATNA as reflected in the BATNA Chart on the next page. For each negotiation categorize your BATNA Value as Excellent (+3) to Very Poor (–3). The higher your BATNA Value, the stronger your leverage. The lower your BATNA Value, the weaker your leverage. Place this numerical value in the box labeled "Your BATNA Value."

Second, determine the strength of your counterpart's BATNA. For each negotiation categorize your counterpart's BATNA Value as Excellent (–3) to Very Poor (+3). The higher your counterpart's BATNA Value, the weaker your leverage. The lower your counterpart's BATNA Value, the stronger your leverage. Place this numerical value in the box labeled "Counterpart's BATNA Value."

Finally, add Your BATNA Value and Counterpart's BATNA Value. The resulting figure, Your BATNA Score, reflects the overall strength or weakness of the BATNA element of leverage. A score of +6 is your strongest point. A score of –6 is your weakest point. Circle your Overall BATNA Score on the graph below the BATNA Chart.

BATNA CHART

	BATNA Value	Your BATNA Value
Yours	Excellent = +3 Very Good = +2 Good = +1 Okay = 0 Fair = −1 Poor = −2 Very Poor = −3	
	BATNA Value	**Counterpart's BATNA Value**
Counterpart's	Excellent = −3 Very Good = −2 Good = −1 Okay = 0 Fair = +1 Poor = +2 Very Poor = +3	
		Your BATNA Score
Your BATNA Value + **Counterpart's BATNA Value**	=	

Your BATNA Score: _____

```
|--+--+--+--+--+--+--+--+--+--+--+--|
Weakest −6  −5  −4  −3  −2  −1   0  +1  +2  +3  +4  +5  +6 Strongest
```

Keep on top of the parties' BATNAs, too. While your target company might have another buyer lined up when you start, that other buyer may pull out later. If that happens, and you learn of it, your leverage has strengthened.

Quantify Your Overall Leverage

In the final step to quantifying your leverage, add Your Need Score to Your BATNA Score. The resulting number will reflect Your Overall Leverage at that moment of the negotiation. The leverage graph on the next page illustrates this, from −10, reflecting your weakest possible leverage situation, to +10, reflecting your strongest possible leverage situation.

OVERALL LEVERAGE GRAPH

Your Need Score + Your BATNA Score = Your Overall Leverage

Your Overall Leverage: _____

```
├──┼──┼──┼──┼──┼──┼──┼──┼──┼──┼──┼──┼──┼──┼──┼──┼──┼──┼──┼──┤
```
Weakest –10 –9 –8 –7 –6 –5 –4 –3 –2 –1   0 +1   +2 +3 +4 +5 +6 +7 +8 +9 +10 Strongest

As noted above, the process of quantifying your leverage is not an exact science. But its value largely lies in making sure that you systematically and strategically consider the major elements of leverage.

Here's an example of how this assessment and quantification process can help you strategically evaluate and keep track of the changes that can occur in the leverage arena.

The Software Sale

They offered him $15 million for his software company, and he said "no." So they offered him $25 million, and he said "no" again. Finally they asked him what it would take.

"My board will not accept anything less than three million shares [worth about $45 million]," he responded. In the end the buyer largely agreed.

According to Pat Sullivan, the creator and founder of the best-selling contact-management software ACT!, this is how he sold ACT! to Symantec in 1993.

"Why sell in 1993," I asked Sullivan, "and, did your 2001 sale of Interact Commerce to Sage for over $260 million proceed in the same way?"

Sullivan's answers provide a perfect illustration of how to assess and evaluate the ongoing nature of leverage and timing in the business-sale context.

"The best time to sell is when everything is going really well," Sullivan told me. When he sold ACT! it was coming off a great year. It had received industry recognition as the market leader, and rumors were starting that Microsoft would soon enter as a competitor in that market space.

From a leverage standpoint Sullivan was right. As discussed above, the less you need to sell and the better your situation, the stronger your leverage. And the more you need to sell and the more desperate your situation, the weaker your leverage.

But that's only part of the leverage equation. Another critical factor was Symantec's need to buy.

Sullivan described Symantec's situation as relatively desperate, noting that it had failed to complete its own Windows product on time, and thus had "One hundred twenty sales folks with nothing to sell." The timing for ACT!'s sale was ripe. Let's quantify this.

On Sullivan's Need Level Chart he was at a Low Need Level (+1), as ACT! was coming off a strong, profitable year as the market leader. Symantec, by contrast, was at a High Need Level (+1). Overall, Sullivan's Need Score was +2 (Sullivan's Low Need Level of +1 added to Symantec's High Need Level of +1). This placed Sullivan and ACT! at the following relatively strong leverage position on the Need Level Chart:

Sullivan's Need Score: +2

Weakest −4 −3 −2 −1 0 +1 **+2** +3 +4 Strongest

What about his and Symantec's BATNA Values? Sullivan indicated that ACT! was coming off a great year. But it didn't have any other offers to buy. Thus, its BATNA at that point—not selling—was probably around a BATNA Value of Okay (0). And it might soon become even worse if Microsoft entered its market space. Symantec's BATNA, not buying ACT!, was likely at a BATNA Value of Poor (+2). After all, it had those sales folks with nothing to sell.

On Sullivan's BATNA Chart, this places his BATNA Score at +2 (Sullivan's BATNA Value of 0 plus Symantec's BATNA Value of +2).

Sullivan's BATNA Score: +2

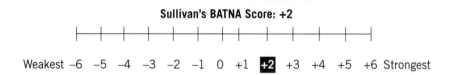

Weakest −6 −5 −4 −3 −2 −1 0 +1 **+2** +3 +4 +5 +6 Strongest

The combination of ACT!'s strong situation and Symantec's weak position gave Sullivan the leverage to get Symantec to bet against itself and, basically, agree to Sullivan's price.

Quantified, Sullivan's Overall Leverage came out at +4 (Sullivan's Need Score of +2 added to Sullivan's BATNA Score of +2). Sullivan and ACT! were definitely on the stronger side of the Leverage Chart. It was a good time for Sullivan to sell.

Sullivan's Overall Leverage: +4

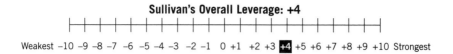

Weakest –10 –9 –8 –7 –6 –5 –4 –3 –2 –1 0 +1 +2 +3 **+4** +5 +6 +7 +8 +9 +10 Strongest

The situation was different in 2001 when Sullivan sold Interact to Sage, a British-based company. At that time the dot-com bubble had burst and the technology industry was reeling.

But Sullivan still felt the "time was right to sell." Why? In part, he wanted to sell before things got worse and Interact's need to sell became even greater. At this time Sullivan's Need Level was probably High (–1), while Sage's Need Level was unknown (suggesting that we use a neutral default Need Level of Medium [0]). Sullivan's Need Score is thus –1 on the Need Level Chart.

Sullivan's Need Score: –1

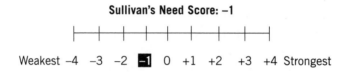

Weakest –4 –3 –2 **–1** 0 +1 +2 +3 +4 Strongest

What did Sullivan do? He analyzed the market and determined that four or five companies might be interested in purchasing Interact. Sullivan also felt Interact was "not only the prettiest girl at the dance, [it was] the only girl at the dance."

How? Despite the weakening industry, Interact owned two market-leading software products, and no other similar company was up for sale. Plus, Microsoft appeared interested in buying, as did Sage.

Sullivan next hired an investment banker to solicit bids from other potential buyers and sought to create an auction-type environment.

Sullivan was attempting to strengthen his leverage by increasing the value of his alternatives to an agreement with either Microsoft or Sage.

Interestingly, Sage knew that time might work against it. So it made a $350 million offer due to expire in three days. In other words, it didn't want to give Sullivan a chance to solicit more bids from Microsoft or others.

What about the parties' BATNAs at this time? Sullivan's BATNA at this time—not selling to anyone while in a weakening industry—was Fair (–1). Sage, by contrast, could easily walk away from the deal, but saw it had a significant benefit from the deal. It had an Okay BATNA Value (0). Overall, Sullivan's BATNA Score was –1.

Sullivan's BATNA Score: –1

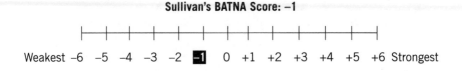

Weakest –6 –5 –4 –3 –2 **–1** 0 +1 +2 +3 +4 +5 +6 Strongest

Regarding Sullivan's Overall Leverage, he was at a –2 (Need Score of –1 plus BATNA Score of –1). While this Leverage Score puts Sullivan on the weaker end of the scale, remember that this was in the context of a weakening industry. He felt his leverage was likely to get even weaker.

Sullivan's Overall Leverage: –2

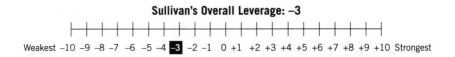

Weakest –10 –9 –8 –7 –6 –5 –4 –3 **–2** –1 0 +1 +2 +3 +4 +5 +6 +7 +8 +9 +10 Strongest

Sullivan and his board thus accepted Sage's offer. Sullivan told me he just didn't have the time to allow Microsoft to do its homework and make an educated offer. Plus, he didn't feel he would get as good a deal from Microsoft, given its history of lowballing and unresolved antitrust issues.

And $350 million is not insignificant.

End of negotiation, right? Wrong. The deal was set to close in May. But the market took a dive before then. And when Sage realized its stock value would also drop if it went through with the deal it pulled out.

In other words, Sage's best alternative to a deal with Interact—not buying Interact—became more valuable, due to the market change. Quantified, Sage's BATNA Value changed from an Okay Alternative (0) to a Good Alternative (–1). And as the value of Sage's alternative increased, Sullivan's Overall Leverage got weaker (from a –2 to a –3).

Sullivan's Overall Leverage: –3

Weakest –10 –9 –8 –7 –6 –5 –4 **–3** –2 –1 0 +1 +2 +3 +4 +5 +6 +7 +8 +9 +10 Strongest

Back to the table. They reopened the negotiations, but now Sage had *stronger* leverage. The final deal came in at around $260 million. Sullivan, I'm sure, wished he had insisted on an earlier close date. A few months cost Interact about $90 million.

That's ninety million good reasons to continually assess your leverage. And quantifying these two negotiations illustrates the four variables in the leverage equation and how the changes in any of them impact the parties' leverage.

Improve Your Alternatives and Limit the Attractiveness of Your Counterparts' Alternatives

Knowing your BATNA will help. Taking concrete steps to create more alternatives and turning them into practical possibilities will make an even bigger difference. Doing this will *improve* the value of your alternative and strengthen your leverage. How can you do this? If you're the CEO negotiating with the city council over the zoning for your plant expansion, explore other cities in which to expand. Then take practical steps to make those alternatives more viable. The better your alternatives, the stronger your leverage. Ultimately, of course, measure the other side's "final" offer compared to your BATNA. If your BATNA is better, reject the deal. If the deal's better, accept.

Because leverage is relative you also can strengthen it by limiting the attractiveness of your counterpart's BATNA. In other words, doing the BATNA works both ways. Both sides thus often try to negatively impact the other side's BATNA, while at the same time improving their own. "I made him an offer he couldn't refuse," said Marlon Brando in *The Godfather*. What was the recipient's likely alternative, his BATNA, to accepting the offer? Death. Because the recipient valued his life, the Godfather strengthened his leverage with his "offer." It made the recipient's BATNA as weak as it could possibly get. While I obviously don't recommend threatening your opponent with death, brainstorm ways to limit the attractiveness of your counterpart's alternatives. Then follow through. Of course, also take defensive measures, as your counterpart might be trying to do the same to you.

Here's an example. Let's say you work in a large corporation and its biggest division does a lot of business in Mexico. You currently are one of two executives under consideration to run the division next year. Assume things now are fairly equal between you and Harry, the other candidate. The CEO will be making the decision.

What can you do to limit the attractiveness of the CEO's BATNA, i.e., picking Harry? Learn Spanish. If Harry does not know Spanish and is unwilling to learn, you just made the CEO's choice of Harry substantially less attractive.

As noted in Shell's *Bargaining for Advantage,* Donald Trump used this tactic while negotiating for the air rights for Trump Tower in New York City. To build the tower he wanted, he needed the air rights over the neighboring land occupied by Tiffany & Company. Tiffany occupied a small, classic building adjacent to Trump's proposed tower. Trump was willing to pay $5 million for the air rights, but didn't want to. He also was afraid Walter Hoving, who ran Tiffany, would balk, as Trump's proposed design was radically different from the architectural style in that area.

What did Trump do? Before meeting with Hoving, Trump had his architect construct two different models of his tower. One was a graceful, fifty-story building. The other was an ugly building that Trump could argue would be what New York's zoning folks would require if he didn't have Tiffany's air rights. Trump showed Hoving both models, implicitly suggesting Hoving's best alternative to an agreement with Trump for his air rights (Hoving's BATNA) would be a very ugly neighbor. Trump limited the attractiveness of Hoving's perceived BATNA. Hoving sold Trump his air rights.

Tactically Share Your Leverage-Related Information

Tactically Share Your Level of Need

How much information should you share regarding your need for a deal? Here's the dilemma. You want your counterpart to know you're serious, but you usually don't want him or her to know how much you truly need it—especially if you're desperate. If your counterpart knows you're desperate, he or she will hold out for a better deal. But if you don't express a sufficient level of need, your counterpart may prematurely walk.

The solution? Learn as much as possible about *your counterparts'* level of need and BATNA and *then* evaluate the risk in sharing your needs or BATNA. If they really need a deal and have no good alternative, you should feel more comfortable sharing your strategically valuable information.

Let's say you want to rent a lake cabin in Wisconsin for two weeks for a family vacation. You discuss this with your family and conclude that only August 1–14 works with all your schedules. So you do some Internet research, ask around, and find the perfect cabin. But its listed price is high. If necessary you're prepared to pay full price, but you want to pay the least amount possible. It's now mid-April and you figure most good places will be taken soon, so you're feeling slightly desperate. On our need scale, your Need Level is High (−1).

What should you do? First find out how much demand exists for cabins on this lake and get a sense of this cabin's overall availability. So you call up the area's tourism office and learn they're experiencing slower-than-normal bookings for this summer. Then you contact the company managing the cabin and inquire about its availability for August 1–14. It's available. In fact, it's also available August 15–28 and July 1–10. Plus, you learn the cabin's owner, who used to live there, took a job in Milwaukee in January and had tried to sell the cabin all spring. However, apparently he never received any decent offers, so he's renting it this summer instead.

At this point you're feeling good about your leverage. While you want the cabin badly, it appears the cabin's owner needs to rent it, too. His Need Level also appears High (+1), putting your Need Score at 0. The owner may even need the cash flow, since it's been vacant awhile. Critically, the owner doesn't yet know how much *you* want it. As a result, you can now be more comfortable telling the management company you're interested in this cabin but find the price high. (Of course, you also should be contacting other possible cabins, your alternatives, in case this doesn't work out.)

Alternatively, let's say you started by sharing how much you needed the cabin, instead of getting information about the cabin owner's needs. "Boy, am I relieved that cabin's available," you tell the management company representative. "I just spent hours on the Internet researching lake cabins in that area, and this cabin is perfect. Plus, the first two weeks of August is the only time we can make it. How much did you say it cost?" The management company person at this point will be unlikely to give you any discount.

Why? You just gave away leverage. And you provided the owner with too much information and no incentive to lower his price. Instead, find out your counterparts' level of needs *before* sharing your own.

Of course, strike a balance in this information-sharing context. Few people will just answer your questions without asking their own, especially if your counterpart understands the strategic value of leverage-related information. And, if required, share your level of need in small chunks. Build up, if necessary, to your true level of need.

Finally, also evaluate how much leverage-related information to share, especially when you don't care that much. If you're desperate, as noted above, be very careful about sharing this level of need. However, if you don't care much, feel free to share your relative lack of interest after you've ascertained your counterpart's need level. Don't hold back your lack of interest as it strengthens your leverage to share it.

Tactically Share Your BATNA

Your leverage also depends on your counterparts' *perception* of your BATNA. Thus, evaluate whether, what, and when to share your BATNA. And determine how much to emphasize it. Remember, perception is king. Manage this perception dynamic by emphasizing your BATNA only when and if it makes strategic sense.

If you're negotiating with the management company for the lake cabin and have no alternative, avoid talking about it. If you have a great alternative cabin at a less expensive price, share it.

Communicate Your Leverage Credibly and Confidently

How you communicate about leverage also makes a substantial difference. If you don't need a deal and have an excellent BATNA, but your counterpart doesn't believe you when you share this, you're worse off than if you said nothing. Likewise, if you're desperate and have a poor BATNA, but can convey the opposite impression without lying, you're better off.

Of course, it's easy to suggest you should be confident and credible. It's more difficult to do it. Here are some tips to help you convey this impression.

- Be truthful about your leverage—don't make it up
- Be detailed
- Provide independently verifiable alternatives
- Explain the rationale underlying your best alternative

Be Truthful About Your Leverage—Don't Make It Up

James Freund, the lawyer who negotiated many of the major corporate takeover battles of the 1980s, wrote in *Smart Negotiating: How to Make Good Deals in the Real World*, "When you take a strong bargaining stance or convey information that appears to increase your leverage, your effectiveness depends on whether the other side believes you. Your strongest weapon in providing information is the truth. With it, you may still have trouble convincing your counterpart, but at least you've got a firm platform for support." He's right.

Don't tell the other side you have an excellent alternative if you don't. Aside from the morality and ethics of it (addressed extensively in chapter 7), too often such lies become obvious upon investigation. If that happens you have lost your credibility, a critical factor in every negotiation.

Plus, most of us are not good enough actors to convince the other side that something exists when it doesn't. Don't try. You will give yourself away in subtle ways and harm yourself in the long run. And even if you *are* a great actor, expert negotiators don't just accept statements about leverage. They research them. When they do, you will likely be found out. This means, of course, always check out your counterpart's statements on their level of need and their alternatives.

This does not mean, however, you should just offer up your desperation and poor BATNA on a platter. That would be negotiation suicide.

If these are poor, you still want the other side to perceive them as decent.

How can you do this—especially when you're desperate, have a very poor BATNA, and your counterpart doesn't appear to need a deal and has excellent alternatives?

Avoid talking about leverage. Remember our blocking techniques? Prepare to block leverage-related questions. Change the subject. Emphasize instead your strengths, which might include the objective criteria—like market value—underlying your offer. Discuss how this standard supports a "fair and reasonable" result.

And if forced to address leverage, focus on *your counterpart's* level of need and alternatives. While your counterpart's alternatives may be better than yours, the critical question is: How do they *appear* to your counterpart. See if you can change your counterpart's perception of the value of his or her alternatives. There is a reason both of you are at the table. It's because you both have evaluated your alternatives and decided it makes sense to explore a deal. Emphasize the relative weakness of *their* alternatives; then change the subject.

Don't do this in a defensive way, either. There's nothing wrong with changing the subject and/or focusing on your strengths. It's a normal and expected part of the negotiation process.

To see how this works, let's reexamine the Prison Hostage negotiation. As you will recall, this involves a situation where forty leading citizens are taken hostage by prisoners serving life sentences without parole and those on death row. The governor, facing reelection, knows he will not get reelected if any of these leading citizens get killed or if he deals lightly with the hostage-takers. He must get the citizens out unharmed at practically any cost. Since he desperately needs a deal (Very High Need Level: −2) and his best alternative, dead hostages, is defeat at the polls and a horrible legacy (Very Poor BATNA Value: −3), his leverage appears extremely weak.

The hostage-takers, however, *also* desperately need a deal (Very High Need Level: +2). Their alternatives to an agreement are either worse conditions than they currently face or death (Very Poor BATNA Value: +3). Since they don't want either, their leverage also appears extremely weak.

Overall, both parties' Overall Leverage is 0, the middle of the chart.

What should you do?

If you represent the governor, avoid talking about *your* poor alternative and emphasize how much the *hostage-takers* need a deal to end up better off.

If you represent the hostage-takers, avoid talking about *your* poor alternative and emphasize how much the *governor* needs a deal to get reelected.

And neither side should make up a better alternative than what exists. Neither side could, and still maintain its credibility. Unless they're irrational (a negotiation strategy addressed in chapter 9) the hostage-takers won't believe the governor doesn't care about reelection or his legacy. And the governor likely won't believe the prisoners don't value their lives or their conditions, especially as the prison's conditions prompted the hostage taking in the first place.

I can't emphasize enough: *Don't lie about your leverage.* It doesn't pay.

Be Detailed

The more detailed your statements about your need and your alternatives, the more credible they appear. Vague language communicates uncertainty and suggests, regardless of the truth, that you're making up facts to bolster your leverage. Of course, this presumes it's strategically beneficial to share your alternatives.

Remember my car repair negotiation? In my seminars this story often generates a lively debate concerning how specific I should be in my conversation with John after I have shopped around for other estimates. John, you will recall, is the service consultant at the dealership with my car. The debate surrounds whether I should tell John the name of the alternative dealer that quoted me the $1,450 repair price. Some participants suggest I name the dealer and the price. Other participants suggest I just tell John the amount of my alternative offer and say I got it from "another repair facility." Some participants even suggest I lie (they call it "puffery" or "bluffing") and tell him I got an offer of $1,000 to fix my car.

In the actual negotiation I told John the other dealer's name and the exact other price offered. Why? Sharing this detailed information enhanced my credibility and raised John's competitive instincts. Plus, if I had not shared it John probably would have asked for it. And, while I could have avoided his question, expert negotiators would read my blocks as signaling that my leverage-enhancing statement was less than credible. If John doubted the veracity of my statement about the other offer he would have been less likely to match it.

Finally, I have little to lose and much to gain by providing a detailed description of my strong alternative.

I must note, however, that revealing the name of your alternative(s) in some industries is considered inappropriate and sometimes even unethical. If this is the case don't name your alternatives. Your reputation as an ethical negotiator is crucial. Understand, though, that this prohibition increases the likelihood that unscrupulous negotiators will make up strong alternatives in an effort to gain a competitive advantage.

Provide Independently Verifiable Alternatives

Because leverage is so critical there's a great incentive to lie about it. In discussing strong leverage you thus want your counterpart to know you're telling the truth. Bolster your credibility and your leverage by providing your counterpart with a way to independently verify your leverage-related statements. And press for independent verification of your counterpart's leverage-related statements.

In my car repair negotiation, I told John the name of the service consultant at the dealership that gave me the $1,450 estimate. That way, my credibility and my leverage increased, as John could independently verify my alternative.

Some retail stores have even institutionalized a verification process to ensure they don't fall victim to unethical negotiators. They first promise not to be undersold by any competitor. But they worry that a consumer may falsely claim a competitor is offering an extremely low price. To protect themselves, they require that consumers either tell them the name of the store offering the lower price or show them the competitor's advertisement including the lower price. They are independently verifying the consumer's leverage statement.

Some shops counter this by refusing to quote prices over the phone. They don't want to be your verification. They want your business. Of course, they also don't want you to maximize your leverage. That would eat into their profits.

Explain the Rationale Underlying Your Best Alternative

Finally, your credibility will improve if you explain the rationale underlying your best alternative. Tell your counterpart *why* you may have to choose your BATNA. Get your counterpart's competitive juices flowing. Give him or her some incentive to provide you with a better deal. Explain the logic underlying your choices. By showing your logical thought process and strategic analysis you will improve your chances of getting a better deal.

Selectively Use Risky Leverage Tactics Like Walkouts and Threats

The final leverage-enhancing tactic relates to when, where, and how you should use risky leverage tactics like walkouts and threats.

Donald Trump has walked out of so many negotiations purely as a tactic that his "Trump walkout" has become fairly well known.

And who hasn't experienced butterflies in their stomach near the end of a long-drawn-out negotiation when the other side walks or signals serious doubts about the deal?

What should you do if the other side walks near the end? And when should you walk as a tactic, even when you want the deal?

First, Shell in *Bargaining for Advantage* suggests that walkouts can either be: a party's sincere signal that they have reached the end of the line; a theatrical effort designed purely to extract a concession and play off a party's fear of not reaching agreement; or a signal that the issue under discussion is especially important to that party.

Knowing this, start your analysis by evaluating which of these is likely happening. (Or, if you're considering walking out yourself, determine which you want to accomplish.)

How?

Find out what negotiation strategies your counterpart has used in previous negotiations. Then evaluate the sincerity of your counterpart's promises and actions on other items in your negotiation. As in poker, determine who has a history of bluffing.

Next, analyze your leverage at the time of the walkout. As Shell notes in *Bargaining for Advantage*, Wayne Huizenga, the founder of Blockbuster, was once negotiating to buy a company owned by a New Orleans family. The deal was virtually done at $4 million.

The last issue was $100,000 in cash in the company account. Both sides emphatically stated they wanted the cash.

So Huizenga closed his briefcase, told his lawyers to pack up, and walked out. His partner grabbed him in the hall, and said, "Wayne, are you crazy? Over $100,000?"

Huizenga replied, "They're never going to let us get to the elevator." He was right, and he got the $100,000. Why? Stronger leverage. The New Orleans family had more to lose, and Huizenga knew it.

Huizenga also didn't appear to care that much about a future relationship with the sellers. The stronger and more important the relationship, the less likely you should use brinksmanship tactics like walkouts. Such tactics can create adversarial dynamics. When was the last time you walked out on a coworker with whom you needed to continue to work closely?

Parties also become more psychologically committed to a result—any result—the longer negotiations last. Taking a firm stand on issues near the end of negotiations can be effective in certain circumstances. Of course, this requires that you can sweat it out and maintain a certain comfort level with the risk of an exploding deal. Walkouts and other brinksmanship tactics are thus more effective near the end of negotiations than near the beginning.

The leverage tables were different when Huizenga sold Blockbuster to Viacom for billions. In late 1993, Huizenga walked from those negotiations, and even checked out of his New York hotel. He then, however, checked into another New York hotel. Knowing he really wanted that deal, and that his leverage wasn't that strong, he called to restart the bargaining.

Why did he walk? To send a signal about the importance of the issue on the table and gauge his counterparts' reaction.

Finally, humans tend to want something more when the likelihood of getting it appears to be diminishing. The scarcer an item, the more we want it. The more we communicate we want it, the weaker our leverage.

Ever played "hard to get" in a budding relationship? You're using what psychologist Robert Cialdini calls the Scarcity Principle. Walking out of a negotiation or convincing your partner you're relatively unavailable is likely to make them want it, or you, more.

The next time your counterpart walks, stop and analyze the situation. They may be bluffing and may come back on their own. If they do you're probably better off.

And if they don't, and your alternative doesn't look good vis-à-vis their last offer, consider a concession. While you may lose face, it will be better than flushing the deal down the drain.

But what if *you* want to communicate that you're at the "take-it-or-leave-it" stage? Or want to emphasize, but not threaten, that you can make the other side's alternative worse. How should you accomplish this?

Let's say you're negotiating with your boss for a promotion. You're fairly satisfied, but you want more money and a bigger office. And your boss is stonewalling. You've received a good offer from a competitor, but you would prefer to stay. How do you present that offer in a nonthreatening way, especially as you know your boss responds negatively to threats?

Simply share the information with your boss that you recently received a call from a competitor about a job. Subtly pointing out or hinting at the negative consequences to the other side if no agreement is reached often will be more effective than threats, especially if you value the relationship. (By the way, a threat is simply a very aggressive way of telling the other side you can make its best alternative, or BATNA, very, very bad.) In certain highly competitive contexts where you have strong leverage a credible threat can be an effective tactic. It is relatively risky, however, and should only be used when you don't particularly value a future relationship. Often it will create an overtly adversarial context.

Be matter-of-fact about your leverage, too. Don't raise your voice, dramatically push back your chair, or pound the table. Expert negotiators will view these as theatrical efforts to cover up your lack of leverage. Instead, lower your voice, look your counterpart directly in the eyes, and calmly lay out the facts and your and their alternatives.

Don't gloat, either, especially if you have strong leverage. You want the other side to calmly and rationally analyze the leverage equation and see that you hold the better cards. Then give them a graceful way to accept. Help them to recognize—not resent—your leverage.

Conclusion

Leverage is crucial in every negotiation. By strengthening it and using it wisely you will increase the likelihood you can get what you want. Used unwisely, you may inadvertently destroy a great deal.

Let's see how all this works together:

Remember the movie *Jerry Maguire* with Tom Cruise and Cuba Gooding Jr.? In it, Jerry Maguire (Cruise) was a sports agent who represented Arizona Cardinals wide receiver Rod Tidwell (Gooding) in his negotiations for a new contract. Tidwell, who was to become a free agent at the end of the season, told Maguire early on he had no interest in signing with any team other than the Cardinals. He had played football at Arizona State University, and he and his family loved Arizona.

At the beginning of the negotiations Maguire received a three-year, $1.7 million offer for Tidwell. Tidwell rejected it, as he considered it well below his worth. At that point his leverage was at its low point. He had a young child, a pregnant wife, and debts piling up. He thus badly needed the income and a deal—with somebody. His Need Level was Very High (−2).

He also had a weak alternative, and consequently a poor BATNA (BATNA Level: Poor (−2)). Few other teams wanted him. His reputation around the league was poor, due to his lackadaisical, arrogant attitude and its negative impact on his performance. While many recognized his physical potential, his attitude prevented them from believing he could capitalize on it.

Understanding this, Jerry Maguire challenged him to change his attitude. Maguire did this knowing that leverage—like Tidwell's attitude—is fluid. By changing his attitude, Tidwell strengthened his leverage. But that alone wasn't enough. He still needed to effectively communicate the change to the Cardinals and the other team owners.

Of course Maguire tried to *tell* his counterparts that Tidwell was a new man. But they didn't believe him. He didn't have sufficient credibility to pull it off. Tidwell himself had to physically demonstrate his attitude and change the team owners' perception of him.

He did this by making several spectacular catches that demonstrated his full physical and emotional commitment to winning and to his team. Critically, he did this during a Monday Night Football game, which all the NFL owners and general managers—his alternatives to a deal with the Cardinals—were likely watching.

After the game, with his leverage at its peak, he received a four-year, $11.2 million offer from the Cardinals.

Jerry Maguire was all about leverage: needs; BATNA; fluidity and improving one's leverage; perception; timing; and credibility. All these elements apply to your negotiations too.

One final point on leverage. If you are in doubt as to your leverage, and you have no impending deadline, say "no" and see what happens. Test it. In *Swim with the Sharks Without Being Eaten Alive,* businessman Harvey Mackay titled the first chapter of his short course on negotiations "Smile and Say No Until Your Tongue Bleeds." He's right. Here's how he starts the chapter: "No. No. No. No. . . ." Mackay then writes "You will be amazed how the terms of your deals will improve when you learn to say *no.*"

What will happen when you say "no"? If you have strong leverage the other side will offer a better deal. And if you have weak leverage, while you might have to swallow some ego and go back to the table, you will have confirmed the leverage situation and will be more comfortable you're near or at the other side's endpoint.

Here's a summary of how to most effectively maximize your leverage:

CHAPTER 2 REVIEW

Golden Rule Two: Maximize Your Leverage

Evaluate Parties' Initial Leverage
- Find each side's need level
- Determine each side's Best Alternative to a Negotiated Agreement (BATNA)

Strengthen Your Leverage—It's Fluid

Strike While Your Leverage Is Hot

Implement Five Leverage-Enhancing Tactics
- Assess and quantify all sides' initial leverage
- Improve your alternatives and limit the attractiveness of your counterparts' alternatives
- Tactically share your leverage-related information
- Communicate your leverage credibly and confidently
- Selectively use risky leverage tactics like walkouts and threats

GOLDEN RULE THREE:

EMPLOY "FAIR" OBJECTIVE CRITERIA

The insurance adjuster practically laughed out loud. My 1981 Datsun 280ZX had seen better days. Bought in Minnesota, it had rust around its wheel rims and even a rust hole where the rear bumper once attached to its right rear quarter.

It also had two ugly-looking gashes on its front hood where the four-wheel-drive pickup with the lift kit and chrome bumper had backed straight into it. These gashes explained the insurance adjuster's presence.

He took a few notes, snapped some pictures, and said he would get back to me. He eventually offered me several hundred bucks. He said it reflected the value of a used front hood.

I didn't believe it.

At this point many people would just reject his offer and demand more. The conversation might go like this.

Insurance adjuster: We will give you $300 to pay for the damage that occurred when our insured backed into your car. This will fully compensate you for replacing the hood on your car with another used hood.

Marty/car owner: I don't think $300 fairly reflects the actual damage. In fact [pulling a number out of the hat], I think $1,000 would more accurately compensate me for the damage.

Insurance adjuster: That's ridiculous. What basis do you have for your conclusion that a used hood is worth $1,000? Frankly, your entire car is probably worth just over $1,000. Tell me how you arrived at the $1,000 figure? And what makes you such an expert?

Marty/car owner: Well, I just think $1,000 would be fair.

Insurance adjuster: I disagree. But if you change your mind, here's my card. Give me a call when you're ready to accept $300.

At this point the negotiation has come down to a question of wills. Who will be more stubborn—the adjuster or the car owner? Leverage-wise, it doesn't make sense for either of us to pursue our alternative of going to court. The amount of money is just not worth it, and both sides know it. We've reached an impasse.

Here's my problem: I have no good response to the adjuster's question of how I arrived at $1,000. He can justify his offer based on his expertise. I'm at a disadvantage, however, because I have no such expertise. At this point I have no legitimate, objective basis for my conclusion that $1,000 is fair and reasonable.

In a nutshell, that's what Golden Rule Three is all about. It's about using and examining the underlying basis for a person's conclusion that his offer is "fair and reasonable." The term "fair and reasonable" means little in a negotiation. It's just a conclusion people use to justify their positions.

The critical question to ask, then, whenever you hear the term "fair" or "fair and reasonable," is *why*. Why does your counterpart believe his offer is "fair and reasonable"? What is the objective basis for the amount of damage to my car? How did I or the adjuster reach the conclusion that our respective numbers were "fair and reasonable"? Why is $1,000 more "fair and reasonable" than $300? Or $600? Or even $2,000?

What should I have done instead of countering at $1,000 and creating a contest of wills? How can I add a principled basis into the negotiation, and not just try to use pressure tactics?

Consider the following response:

Instead of immediately countering with $1,000, I said I would get back to him after I had done some research. After all, I only *felt* $300 wasn't "fair and reasonable." I needed evidence to support my feeling. So I took the car to some auto collision shops and confirmed my suspicion. The adjuster had lowballed me.

How did I know? Auto experts' opinions—a type of objective criteria—told me. I then contacted the insurance adjuster, rejected his offer, and told him about the repair shop that had given me the highest estimate for the damage. This was *my* objective criterion.

At this point it wasn't Marty Latz the layperson suggesting $300 was not "fair and reasonable." It was, in essence, the repair shop. They were the experts, not me. *Now* I had a substantive basis to demand more money. I also had a specific, detailed justification in the form of a written estimate for the exact amount I demanded.

Eventually, after some haggling, the adjuster coughed up significantly more money. Our end point was somewhere in the middle of my demand (based on *my* objective criteria) and the adjuster's first offer (based on *his* objective criteria).

This dance occurs in almost all negotiations, including some of the most adversarial and high-stakes negotiations in the world, labor negotiations.

The America West Airlines Standards Dispute

In 1999 America West Airlines flight attendants were using a variation of this standards strategy as they approached their strike deadline (the strike was their BATNA). America West was countering with its own variation.

The biggest issue in the America West dispute appeared to be the flight attendants' salaries. America West's offer at the time was around $16.5 million less than what the flight attendants were seeking over five years. At that point the union and the airline were attempting to convince each other and the flying public that each had the most "fair and reasonable" request. How? By using objective criteria such as independent standards. Each used these standards—like the auto experts' opinions about the value of my Datsun's damage—to suggest they had the most legitimate basis for their demand.

Exhibit A for the union was the industry average for flight attendants' salaries. This was how they defined "market value," a concept most consider a "fair" estimation of an item's worth. The industry average strongly supported their position. According to the union, United Airlines—which was then considering purchasing America West—paid its flight attendants $18,000–$46,000 a year. Compare this to the $15,000–$22,000 paid by America West, the union argued.

Of course, America West defined "market value" differently. Its salary and benefits must already be "fair" and market value, it appeared to argue, because it enjoyed low turnover among its attendants and because five applicants were applying for every attendant opening.

Plus, it argued, it should be entitled to a certain level of profitability, another type of objective standard justifying its "fair" offer. America West said it would run in the red to the tune of $250 million annually if its labor costs were on par with the six largest airlines.

America West's flight attendants then countered with another type of objective criteria—reciprocity. They pointed out that many of them took salary cuts when America West went through bankruptcy in the early 1990s. They argued it's time for some payback. The carrier made record profits in 1998. That's only "fair," right?

The battle over the appropriateness of various types of objective criteria and the fairness of different independent standards is a common negotiation dynamic. It reflects a legitimate and often effective attempt to independently assess the value of a disputed item to each party's benefit.

In the America West negotiation, the alleged "market value" of the flight attendants' salary competed for legitimacy against the principle of reciprocity. Each standard was used to try to convince the public, an important constituency for both parties, that their respective positions were "fair." In short, the legitimacy of the parties' objective criteria formed the crux of this negotiation.

To most effectively employ "fair" objective criteria, then, take these steps:

- Understand the power of "fair and reasonable" standards and procedures
- Find your most powerful independent standards
- Consider mutually powerful procedures
- Harness the full power of objective criteria by using four critical tactics

Understand the Power of "Fair and Reasonable" Standards and Procedures

Creates the Perception of Independence and Objectivity

Why does it help to use objective criteria to support your position? Because we derive power and legitimacy from the perception that standards and criteria are based on objective, independent factors. Standards and criteria are usually not simply tied to what any individual negotiator wants. As a result, since our position appears to be based on objective, independent factors, our counterparts will more likely conclude our position is truly "fair and reasonable."

Focusing on independent, objective standards also depersonalizes negotiations by appearing to remove parties' subjectivity from the process. The more objective and independent and the less subjective the negotiation, the less overt emotion is usually involved.

If I say "I believe my house is worth $262,500," a potential buyer might naturally respond, "You're wrong. It's only worth $250,000."

I might interpret this as a personal attack. "You're wrong" is strong language.

By contrast, if I said, "My house is worth $262,500 because the pretty much identical house across the street sold last year for $250,000. And a recent survey by the local real estate association indicates that housing values in this area have increased this past year by an average of five percent."

Your response, in all likelihood, will not focus on me. Instead, it will probably focus on the factors forming the basis for my conclusion. In other words, you will focus on the standards, not me.

This benefit—depersonalizing the negotiation dynamic—can be a huge element in a deal.

Objective criteria also provide a good-faith basis for your offers and concessions and increases the likelihood they will be accepted.

So how can you use objective criteria to increase your ability to get what you want?

First, understand that two forms of objective criteria exist: independent standards and independent procedures. Standards, like market value or an expert's opinion, provide parties in a negotiation with an independent basis on which to justify the "fairness or reasonableness" of their position. Procedures provide an independent mechanism parties can choose to resolve their negotiation, e.g., if the parties agree to have a neutral third party decide the dispute. The parties, in effect, determine that using the agreed-upon procedure will lead to a result *both* will accept as "fair and reasonable."

Second, keep in mind that while these provide a legitimate basis for what objectively might be viewed as fair and reasonable, each negotiation is ultimately still a subjective exercise. It's what you believe is "fair" versus what your counterpart believes is "fair." Thus, use standards to support your position. But don't forget that they're often being used in an advocacy context. In many cases, no truly "objective" standard exists that everyone will view as legitimate. Of course, in some cases truly objective and independent standards *do* exist that both parties will rely upon to form the basis for an agreement.

Finally, assess the true independence of the standards or procedures suggested by your counterparts. In some legal cases the experts involved have little independence or objectivity. The less objectivity and independence, the less power. In other situations the chosen standards or procedures have a great deal of objectivity and independence. In these situations they carry the most power.

Find Your Most Powerful Independent Standards

How should you put this power to work for you? Try using one or more of the following ten independent standards, each of which you will see used in a wide variety of negotiations:

- Market-Value Power
- Precedent Power
- Tradition Power
- Expert- and Scientific-Judgment Power
- Efficiency Power
- Costs and Profits Power
- Policy Power
- Reciprocity Power
- Status Power: Title and Position
- Professional or Industry Standards Power

Here's a "how to" template for using them and some effective counter-measures if your counterparts use them too.

Market-Value Power

Because market value is generally understood to reflect an objective value assigned by the laws of free market economics and supply and demand, it is perhaps the most common and powerful independent standard. In lay terms, we commonly understand "market value" to be shorthand for what all buyers and sellers through their collective buying and selling behavior have determined is a particular value for an item at a certain time.

Why is this important in a negotiation? If every other interested person (collectively, the market) will pay or accept X dollars for an item, X must then by definition be "fair and reasonable," right? If you disagree, the rationale continues, you're rejecting the collective standard and want *more* than what everyone else will accept. Since most consider this greedy and somehow "unfair," you should thus accept "market value."

Of course, some economists would point out that market value simply reflects what a buyer is willing to pay and what a seller is willing to accept for an item at any given time. The end *result* of your negotiation, then, reflects its real market value. While true in purely economic terms, "market value" as an independent standard in negotiations usually does not refer to this end result. Instead, parties most often refer to an existing market value to support their position as "fair and reasonable."

Ways to Use Market-Value Power to Your Advantage

There are three keys to most effectively using market value power in your negotiations:

First, find out what market, if any, exists for the items on the table. How many other parties in the past have reached agreements and assigned values to those items? Under what circumstances were those agreements reached? Compare their item to yours—is it the same or similar? Comprehensively research the market so you have a full appreciation of what's out there and how it compares with your negotiation.

Second, obtain any documents, studies, reports, or statistical analyses that purport to collect such market information. Then prepare to use the most favorable documents and studies you find. Saying the market is X is one thing; showing some independently objective written report that reaches the same conclusion is far more powerful.

Finally, evaluate whether the end result of this analysis provides you with an objective "market value" you consider legitimate. Then determine how, if at all, to use this in your negotiation.

As a business owner, I regularly hire individuals and companies to perform various services. Sometimes I negotiate their rates.

What role does market value play in these cases?

First, I research whether a significant market exists for the service I need. When I hired my current executive assistant I knew a substantial market existed in Phoenix for executive assistants. As one of the largest cities in the United States, Phoenix has a thriving job market. And thousands of individuals in Phoenix have executive assistants. Knowing this, I called several friends in the job-placement arena and asked them to send me whatever information they had concerning the market rate for executive assistants' compensation. I also could have researched this on the Internet.

One friend sent me a recent study by a reputable firm detailing the market rates in Phoenix for executive assistants and other support staff. Another friend who regularly negotiated salaries on behalf of those seeking similar positions told me the range of salaries she had negotiated for her clients.

Since I considered this market-value information legitimate, I offered my prospective executive assistant slightly less than the current year's average market rate. I justified it by describing my market research. (One reason I offered less than market was due to her lack of experience in this type of position.) Critically, using market value to provide an objective basis for my offer fostered a principled atmosphere and increased the likelihood she would view my offer as "fair and reasonable." She then considered this offer and countered with a slightly higher rate, based on what she had been paid by a previous employer (precedent—another independent standard).

Since her counter was well within what I considered the market value for her services, based on my research, I accepted. Using market value as an independent standard turned what could have been a difficult negotiation into a straightforward one that both sides considered principled.

Countermeasures to Market-Value Power

What should you do, though, when your counterpart's market-value analysis leads to a significantly different value than what you want? How can you decrease its legitimacy and power?

Challenge the Definition of "Market Value"

In the America West Airlines flight attendant dispute, both sides argued that market value supported their position. But each defined market value differently. The airline argued, in effect, that it already paid its flight attendants market value, given their low turnover, and because five applicants applied for every open position at the *current* salary and benefits level. Since many willing sellers (flight attendants) existed for every willing buyer (the airline) at that compensation level, it said it paid market value.

The flight attendants, by contrast, suggested the market value for their services would be more accurately estimated by evaluating the salary and benefits at comparable airlines, such as United Airlines. United, not coincidentally, paid its flight attendants significantly more than America West.

This "fairness" debate revolved around how to most accurately define market value. If your counterparts' definition of the market leads to a value you dispute, challenge the basis for their evaluation. Then find a way of evaluating market value that more closely aligns with what you consider "fair and reasonable."

Challenge the Validity of the Underlying Market

The power of market value depends on the validity of the market on which it is based. If that market is flawed, its validity diminishes. A market value analysis can be flawed in a number of ways, including the size of the market and the area on which the market is based.

Let's say I lived in a small rural town in Georgia and wanted to determine the market value for an executive assistant's compensation. This isn't easy, because the size of the market is so small. If there are only five executive assistants in town, my market value analysis could be challenged, due to the market's small size. The market size just may not be statistically significant. There may not be enough buyers (demand) or enough sellers (supply) to reach a fair conclusion as to market value.

Knowing this, and also knowing any compensation based on values in that town would be comparatively low, let's say my potential executive assistant based her salary request on the market value for executive assistants in Atlanta.

What should I do? Challenge her analysis and suggest it's not appropriate to use these comparisons because they are based on *different* markets.

What if I represent a quarterback just selected with the number-two overall pick in the National Football League draft? How do I or the owner of the team that drafted my client select the most appropriate market value analysis and/or challenge its validity? If the number-one selection was a defensive end, and he has already signed with another team for an amount less than my client's goal, the team owner will likely use this "market value" as a benchmark. By contrast, I would suggest one cannot compare the market for defensive ends to the market for quarterbacks. The market value for quarterbacks is higher, on the quarterback position is the most difficult and important position to fill on the team. Therefore, I would argue, this quarterback is more valuable than the defensive end selected ahead of him in the draft and should receive a more lucrative contract.

Find out the sample size and area for your counterparts' market value estimation. Then, if appropriate, challenge it as inapplicable in area or insufficient in size to be valid.

Distinguish Your Item from the Market

"I am unique," said my potential executive assistant. "I bring qualities to this position you cannot find elsewhere. I know the corporate and legal training business extremely well, as I've worked in it for over ten years. I can also design marketing brochures and edit your book. I did a substantial amount of this type of work in my previous position. You would be hard-pressed to find these skills in another executive assistant."

She was right. And her uniqueness, which distinguished her from the rest of the market for executive assistants in Phoenix, diminished the applicability and power of my market value research.

This tactic also works well in negotiations for housing. "Sure, the other houses in this neighborhood have sold for an average of $100 per square foot, but I just put $10,000 into resurfacing the pool. None of the other neighborhood houses have a newly resurfaced pool. Plus, the layout and interior changes I made to my house are unique. This is not reflected in the other recently sold houses."

Market value represents a general estimate. Therefore, you can almost always distinguish your item from the market. The more distinguishable and unique, the less relevant and powerful the alleged market value.

"Circumstances Have Changed"

Market value rests on circumstances that occurred in the past. The survey of executive assistant compensation I received from my friend was published in 1998. I hired my executive assistant in 2001. The comparable houses in my neighborhood were sold in the last two years. I'm selling now.

Why do you care? Market values constantly change. In the three years since the executive assistant compensation survey was published, there may have been a significant change in the supply and/or demand for executive assistants in Phoenix. Such changes impact the current market value. Let's say you live in a company town and the company just closed its plant and transferred most of its employees out of state, thus prompting a flood of homes for sale. Houses that sold six months ago, which made up the seller's market value analysis, will be largely irrelevant.

Highlighting market changes calls into question the validity of your counterpart's market value analysis.

Focus on the Market of One—Individual Leverage

I vacationed in Big Bear, California, during the summer of 2001. One weekend there was a hotrod convention in town featuring around 400 fascinating cars, including 1923 Ford T-Buckets, 1934 Ford Coupes, and 1957 Chevy Corvettes. Some were for sale. One day I was speaking with some of the owners of these cars, most of whom love to talk about their vehicles. I asked them about the market for such cars. They told me it's extremely difficult to define such a market. Some sell for $120,000. Others sell for $20,000. Many are truly unique, making a market analysis almost impossible.

More important than any market analysis, however, is the leverage for each particular seller and potential buyer. How much does Joe Seller need to sell, and what is his BATNA, relative to how much Linda Buyer needs to buy, and what is her BATNA? As was pointed out to me by Mike, who was selling his 1938 Ford (he was asking $26,500) so he could buy a Chevy Nomad Station Wagon, "It only takes one."

If the market value is unclear, uncertain, or represents a value you would like to ignore, focus on leverage. Strong leverage trumps market value any day of the week.

Switch to More Favorable Independent Standards

Finally, you might also refocus the negotiation from market value to another independent standard that helps you more. This will be an especially good move if none of the above countermeasures appears helpful.

These last two countermeasures—focusing on the market of one, that is, your individual leverage, and switching to more favorable independent standards—also apply as countermeasures to *all* independent standards. *Individual leverage always trumps independent standards.* And finding a standard more supportive of your position also will often counter the other side's standard. Keep these in mind as we explore the other standards.

Precedent Power

Historians suggest that the past often represents the best evidence of what might occur in the future. In the negotiation world past negotiation history represents powerful independent evidence of what may happen in future negotiations. Historic vehicles generally appreciate in value, so if Mike paid $20,000 for his 1938 Ford in 1996, it's unlikely he will accept less than $20,000 in 2001. Likewise, if Mike knows a similar 1938 Ford sold for $23,000 last week, it's unlikely that he will accept less than $23,000 for his vehicle today.

Precedent—what has happened in the past in similar negotiations— forms another powerful independent standard for determining what now might be "fair and reasonable." In fact, it's so powerful that some companies insist on a confidentiality provision in certain negotiation agreements just to prevent that agreement from being used as precedent in future negotiations against themselves. This is often the case in product-defect cases where the defendant may face many cases involving different plaintiffs.

Ways to Use Precedent Power to Your Advantage

How can you put precedent power to work for you? Research all the applicable precedents, then evaluate whether and how to use each as an independent standard in your negotiation. If you find enough similar precedents, you might even suggest that they collectively represent the market. Combining independent standards can double your power.

Prior to the events of September 11, 2001, I regularly stayed at the Marriott World Trade Center when in New York City, in part because I got an excellent rate when I *first* stayed there (my leverage then was strong, given the season and the market). After my first stay I often invoked the deal I originally received as precedent for receiving an equally good deal during subsequent stays. Of course, Marriott still made a "fair" profit, just not as much as it might have otherwise. During the holiday season, though, I had to pay higher rates because Marriott had stronger leverage, given the high demand for hotel space during that time period.

Or consider my executive assistant's use of precedent in our salary negotiation. She used her previous salary for another employer as precedent for what I should pay her.

Countermeasures to Precedent Power

What can you do when your counterpart calls upon precedent power to suggest he or she is the "fair and reasonable" one?

Challenge the Validity of the Precedent

Find out whether the negotiation issues surrounding the precedent accurately reflect the factors in your negotiation. Are the circumstances sufficiently similar to form a powerful precedent? Suppose Mike's friend, Rick, had weak leverage when he sold his 1938 Ford for $23,000. Assume Rick desperately needed the cash to prevent the bank from foreclosing on his house. Plus, the purchaser was buying it on a whim. Now suppose an interested buyer for *Mike's* car found out about Rick and this previous sale price.

The interested buyer might say, "Mike, I will offer you $23,000 for your 1938 Ford. As you know, this is fair, as Rick recently sold his 1938 Ford for this exact price."

If Mike's leverage is stronger than Rick's, Mike should attack the validity of this precedent, given the different leverage situations. "That sale doesn't really apply here," Mike might respond. "It took place under different circumstances. Rick had to sell it to keep his house, so he sold it for less than it was worth. By contrast, I have the luxury of being able to wait for a fair and reasonable offer."

Distinguish Your Facts

Every negotiation is a unique negotiation in a unique environment. So ask yourself: Are the parties or issues the same? Do both 1938 Fords have original parts? What about the mileage? Are they both in pristine condition?

The more you can distinguish your negotiation from the precedent, the less powerful the precedent.

"Circumstances Have Changed"

Time has passed and what else has changed with it? The more relevant changes you can identify since the precedent occurred, the easier to distinguish your negotiation from the precedent.

Or use one of the universal countermeasures we already discussed above (your leverage, or another independent standard).

Tradition Power

"We've always done it this way," your counterpart might state. Or, "We've always paid this rate in the past, with annual inflation adjustments. It's always been fair before, so why change now?" This is the power of tradition.

Like precedent and market value, this standard derives its power from the fact that others in the past have considered it "fair and reasonable."

But there's a twist. The most powerful examples of precedent and market value took place in the *recent* past. Usually, the most recent equals the most powerful. You want to determine the most current market value. And if I find a similar negotiation result last week that supports my position it will be a more powerful precedent than one from ten years ago.

The opposite, however, provides tradition with its power. The longer and more consistently it has been done a certain way, the stronger the rationale needed to change it. This is especially true if it has been consistently applied for years and individuals have developed a strong set of expectations regarding it.

This standard is often effectively used within large bureaucracies, especially government entities or large educational institutions. "We just don't do things that way around here. Never have, never will." Ever heard that when you started a negotiation?

A lawyer friend had this exact experience many years ago while negotiating with the Internal Revenue Service. His client, a trade association, requested an opinion letter from the IRS detailing the circumstances under which individuals employed by its members would be classified as employees or independent contractors. This classification has important tax ramifications, and the association's members wanted to treat some of its workers in a particular way and did not want to run afoul of the IRS and the law. Unfortunately, the laws and regulations on that issue did not clearly address this question.

The IRS response? We will not issue such a letter to a trade association because we have never done such a thing. If one of the trade association's member companies wants to request a private letter ruling based on its individual facts and circumstances, the IRS would consider issuing it. But it would not issue a letter to a trade association.

There was no IRS policy or regulation prohibiting such a letter. It just had never issued such a letter to a trade association in the past (tradition), and so refused to do it.

Stability and resistance to change are hallmarks of those using tradition to define what is "fair and reasonable."

Ways to Use Tradition Power to Your Advantage

Using tradition as an independent standard sounds simple. Just point out the tradition and suggest that its very existence illustrates its inherent fairness and reasonableness. That's a good start, but there's more. It will be more powerful if you can also:

- Show how long it has been a tradition (the longer the tradition, the more power);
- Provide evidence of consistent application, and that few, if any, exceptions exist (the more consistent and fewer exceptions, the more power);
- Illustrate the problems experienced when exceptions have been made; and
- Explain the rationale for the tradition in the first place, and point out how it continues to apply now.

Countermeasures to Tradition Power

"Circumstances Have Changed"

Tradition falls victim to "the circumstances have changed" counter, just like precedent and market value. The older the tradition, the more likely you can show that its original justification no longer makes sense. How? Find the original justification underlying the tradition, then determine if it applies with equal force today.

Explore the Exceptions

Exceptions to a tradition also undercut its validity by providing a precedent for the exception you want. The more exceptions, the better. Of course, determine before you use certain precedents that they resulted in positive results for the party in your position. Otherwise you undercut your own effort for change.

In the IRS example, my friend could have made a persuasive case for the IRS to issue a letter to his association client if he had found an example where the IRS had previously issued a similar letter to another association. Without such evidence, however, his only alternative was to focus on his leverage or another standard. Unfortunately for him, he had weak leverage and the IRS knew it.

Expert- and Scientific-Judgment Power

Have you ever negotiated with an expert when the issues fall within the expert's realm of knowledge? It's tough because the expert has a great deal more information and knowledge about the issue than you do. Remember Golden Rule One: Information Is Power—So Get It? Here the expert starts with information power. In my negotiation with the insurance adjuster over the value of the damage to my Datsun he was the expert in damage to cars. That's what he did for a living. What did I know? Not much at first.

This same advantage goes to those who use experts and scientific evidence as independent standards.

"Don't take my word for the value of this 1938 Ford," Mike might say. "The world's foremost expert in Ford hotrods just appraised it at $26,500." The assumption is that the $26,500 value must be "fair and reasonable" *because an expert said it.*

Experts' power derives from both their actual expertise and knowledge, and their perceived knowledge. If your counterpart considers you a trustworthy expert, your opinion will be valued and your persuasive power substantial regardless of your actual expertise. Of course, the more you know, the better you will be able to use this knowledge to your advantage.

The use of experts and scientific knowledge is common in legal negotiations. Consider the use of medical specialists in personal injury lawsuits. Expert physicians are asked to opine on what caused the injuries and the appropriate treatment. In the divorce context, lawyers commonly rely on experts to value parties' business assets. Experts enhance the credibility and "reasonableness" of their side's position in settlement negotiations.

In fact, experts provide power to parties in negotiations in almost every field. Businesses use the opinions of stock market experts to help predict companies' stock prices in merger-and-acquisition negotiations. Banks use real estate appraisers to provide independent opinions supporting home and commercial real estate loans, which they use in negotiating rates and loan amounts with customers. Even consumers use expert studies (like those in *Consumer Reports*) to determine the quality and value of goods they want to purchase. Many use these studies to determine what to buy and how much is "fair and reasonable" to spend.

Ways to Use Expert- and Scientific-Judgment Power to Your Advantage

Find an expert or an expert's opinion on the issue in your negotiations. If your car has been damaged and you want to negotiate a settlement with the insurance company, ask several repair shops to provide their expert opinions on what needs to be done and the cost. If you need to lay off an employee, ask your human relations department or a human resources consultant to determine what, if any, severance package might be "fair and reasonable." Or, if you're looking to sell your business, hire a business valuation expert or an investment banker to provide you with an independent opinion as to what might be a "fair and reasonable" value to expect.

And if you are leading a team of negotiators, make sure everyone knows your team's expertise, accomplishments, knowledge, and special qualifications as you start the negotiation—not at the end. In this way you will enhance the other side's perception of your team's expertise, a critical factor.

Experts and scientific judgment play a prominent role in many negotiations. Use them.

Countermeasures to Expert- and Scientific-Judgment Power

What should you do if your counterpart has an expert or an expert opinion?

Counter with Your Own Expert

Find an expert to provide you with an opinion that supports your side. A battle of experts occurs in many negotiations. It should. It gives both sides more credibility and a greater ability to justify their positions.

Undermine the Credibility of Your Counterpart's Expert

Closely examine the other side's expert or expert opinion. Then undermine that expert's credibility by attacking the expert's credentials, qualifications, independence, and/or objectivity. Many experts charge large fees for providing their opinions. This undercuts their perceived independence and objectivity.

Make Yourself an Expert

Gain the knowledge that forms the basis for the experts' opinions. Many lawyers have become virtual experts in certain medical specialties by reading all the literature on those subjects and examining and cross-examining the world's foremost experts in those areas. While these lawyers may not have the M.D. after their name or the perceived status as an expert, their substantive knowledge provides them with the ability to poke logical holes in the opinions of experts adverse to their clients.

Finally, of course, counter by switching to a more favorable independent standard. Try, for instance, efficiency power.

Efficiency Power

I've trained a substantial number of commercial general contractors. In this field, a company's negotiation effectiveness bears a direct relationship to its profits. Commercial general contractors negotiate with the owners that hire them to build a commercial structure like a shopping center, hotel, or commercial building. They also negotiate with the subcontractors they hire to perform the various building tasks, including the concrete work, framing, plumbing, etc. Commercial general contractors' profits are largely based on the difference between what the owners pay them for the project and what they pay their subcontractors.

Their ability to efficiently manage the project thus often takes on an almost mystical importance. The more efficiently and effectively they can complete a project and bring it in on time and "under budget," the more satisfied the owner and the higher the profits for themselves and the owner. And satisfied owners will keep using the same commercial general contractor as long as their track record holds.

Commercial general contractors and others in similar industries use the term "value engineering" to describe efficiency power. Here's how they use it and how you can use it in similar negotiations.

In 2000 I advised a commercial general contractor's project manager on his negotiations with three potential electrical subcontractors. The general contractor had been hired to build a shopping center complex for a set price. It thus solicited competitive bids for the electrical work. After the bids were submitted the project manager generally would contact the potential subcontractors to ensure their bids included everything noted on the specification sheets and the architect's plans. During these conversations he also would negotiate to get the subcontractors to increase the scope of their work and/or lower their price. The more effective his negotiations, the higher his profits.

One goal in each of these negotiations was to find a way for the subcontractor to more efficiently complete its work. The project manager would do this by "value engineering" the project. In effect, he would brainstorm with the subcontractor to find ways the subcontractor might do its work more efficiently. In one of his negotiations, he and the subcontractor found a way to significantly increase efficiency by using a different route for the electrical cabling. In another negotiation with a heating, ventilation and air conditioning (HVAC) subcontractor, he awarded it a related subcontract as, by doing so, he avoided duplicating some work on the facility. This saved him money and increased his profits.

Ways to Use Efficiency Power to Your Advantage

Always explore ways you and/or the other parties can increase efficiency. Then structure the negotiated result so you, and possibly also the other side, benefit from the increased efficiency. This sounds simple. But many negotiators do not explore ways to "value-engineer" their deals. Systematically approach this process. It will increase your efficiency and possibly add great value to your negotiations.

Also find ways your proposal efficiently satisfies *both* parties' interests. Then highlight its efficiency. Efficiency adds credibility and power to the "fairness and reasonableness" of your offer.

Countermeasures to Efficiency Power

Since efficiency often benefits everyone, there is little downside to pursuing it. My only caveat relates to negotiations involving parties paid on a time basis, like lawyers and some consultants. From their financial standpoint, there is a short-term disadvantage to operating efficiently. It is thus even more important that you aggressively explore more efficient ways of achieving your stated goals when dealing with these types of entities.

Costs and Profit Power

Almost every negotiation involving the transfer of business or consumer goods or services involves costs and profit power. It doesn't matter if you want to purchase or sell a car, refrigerator, television, business, restaurant meal, software program, building, furniture, or business suit. In each of these negotiations, both the seller and the buyer will benefit from knowing the item or service's cost and/or profit margin.

Why? The item's cost provides you with a benchmark idea of what profit might be "fair and reasonable" on the transaction. How many advertisements have we seen highlighting the sale of an item "below cost"? This is designed to tap into our desire to "get a deal." Since many of us are price-sensitive and want the most product or service for the least price, advertisers try to hook us by emphasizing that the item is being sold—at least temporarily—at a loss.

My former neighbor Pam sold her house in 2000 for $190,000 after listing it for $210,000. She had bought it in 1996 for $155,000. Shortly after she listed the house Pam received the $190,000 offer. She asked me if she should accept it. After asking her about her house and doing some research on the market value of comparable homes nearby, I told Pam that selling it for $190,000 would be below market.

However, Pam didn't have strong leverage, as she had already bought a new house and wanted to sell her old one before she moved. Plus, she kept telling me she had bought the house "five years ago for $155,000." Even though she likely could have received more for her house, based on its market value, Pam focused on the $35,000 profit figure. She accepted the $190,000 offer because, based on her original cost, the offer appeared eminently "fair and reasonable."

Pam's bottom line? Given her weak leverage, she focused on a good standard for her. And $35,000 is not an insignificant profit for four years.

Ways to Use Costs and Profit Power to Your Advantage

Find out the item or service's cost *before* the negotiation. If you can't find it before, ask for it during the negotiation. Then emphasize it if it makes your position appear more fair and reasonable. Deemphasize it if it does not.

If you're a buyer and the profit margin seems high in relation to what others in the industry charge, highlight it. If it seems low, find another standard to reduce it even more.

And if you're a seller and the profit margin seems reasonable, lead with it. But if you bought it in bulk at a very low cost, and marked it up significantly, avoid talking about its cost.

Remember Mike and his 1938 Ford? He was asking $26,500 for it. As a disinterested observer, I asked him how much he had paid for it several years before. He refused to answer, even though I promised this book likely would not be published until after he had sold his car.

Why did he refuse? Probably because it would have shown that his profit was so substantial it could be used against him in the future. He didn't want to become known as someone who was "unreasonably" profiting on his car. If he had that reputation in the relatively tight-knit community of hotrod owners, it would make it more difficult for him to maximize his profits on future sales. Plus, who wants to be known as "unreasonable"?

Countermeasures to Costs and Profit Power

Many people have an intuitive sense as to what constitutes a reasonable profit margin. But some hotels have a significant markup, relative to their costs, on telephone calls from your room. What can you do? How should you respond if your counterpart suggests your profit margin is "unreasonable"?

Research the Average Profit Margin and Compare

Research the profit margins of others in the industry. Show how in your market you're only making average profits. Or emphasize how your counterpart will still be able to increase *its* profits even at your price/its cost. Show how it's a good investment.

And if you're in a hotel and the phone charges appear excessively profitable for the hotel, exercise your leverage and use your cell phone. That's your BATNA, and it's usually less expensive.

Policy Power

"Sorry, our newspaper has a policy against that. Our vice president for sales two months ago gathered all our advertising salespeople together and told us we could no longer provide free color in our advertisements. It costs too much. Since then we've charged extra for color. I would love to help you out, but my hands are tied."

How many of us have run up against the "policy" standard? "Just can't do it. It's our policy." It's common.

Why use policy as a standard, and under what circumstances should you or your company implement certain policies?

First, companies use policies in the negotiation context to promote uniformity and consistency. Without a policy on what negotiators can offer, concede, or even discuss, negotiators will be lone rangers in negotiating deals. While this might maximize the completion of deals in the short-run, it can cause long-term problems, as the deals will result in varying levels of profitability. Inconsistency of result will also create future negotiation problems. Each deal sets a precedent. If you have expert counterparts, they will smoke out these precedents—especially the less-profitable ones. Then they will use this precedent power against you in future negotiations.

"You gave ABC Trucking free color in its advertisements a month ago," XYZ Trucking's representative might note in negotiating with the newspaper. "Why are you treating me differently? That's not fair."

Second, setting and following certain policies effectively insulates the individual negotiator from possible ill feelings from his or her counterpart. "It's not me. It's company policy." The presumption? The negotiator has no ability to affect the policy. It may be true, too. That depends on the policy.

You often see policy power used in the consumer goods arena. While growing up in Minnesota I sold children's shoes at a large department store. It had a policy about returns—take everything back, no questions asked. I remember a woman once brought back her child's tennis shoes six months after buying them. The shoes were in horrible shape. We took them back.

Why? The department store had determined that it would gain more with repeat customers due to this policy than with the occasional loss suffered when customers abused it.

Policy power works because it taps into your counterparts' interest in being treated the same as everyone else. If you treat me the same as everyone else, I will feel it is more "fair and reasonable" than if you treat me differently than other similarly situated individuals. Policies help achieve this goal.

Ways to Use Policy Power to Your Advantage

Evaluate the benefits of adopting policies regarding your negotiations by determining the relative importance of:

- Uniformity and consistency;
- Insulating your negotiators from potentially emotional counterparts; and
- Ensuring your counterparts feel fairly treated by the process.

Keep in mind, though, the costs involved. There's a greater likelihood a counterpart will just walk if he or she comes up against a policy he or she dislikes. Policies also limit the flexibility of negotiators and can prevent valuable give-and-take in the process. Plus, implementing policies and ensuring a consistent application takes time and effort. Of course, these factors impact the process from a negotiation standpoint, and do not address the advantages and disadvantages of any particular policy.

In making this decision you should also consider: a) who, or what entity, should make the policy; b) how such policies should be made; c) the form of the policy, be it written, oral, or in some other form; d) the level of specificity and flexibility to adopt within the policy; e) who, if anyone, should be able to create policy exceptions; and f) whether, how, and under what circumstances exceptions may be made. Each of these factors will impact the policy's power and effectiveness in negotiations.

Countermeasures to Policy Power

Learn About the Policy and Find a Principled Way Around It

Your initial response to a seemingly adverse policy should be: "Tell me about it." Find out as much as you can about the policy. What exactly is the policy? How specific is it? Does it directly apply to your situation or not? Is it written, or is it just your counterpart's understanding? Who made it? When and how was it made? Why? Who has the ability and/or authority to change it or make exceptions? What, if any, exceptions have been made in the past? How flexible is it? To whom does it apply? Why does it apply to some and not others? You get the drift.

Answers to these questions will provide you with a road map to your most effective countermeasures. If it's a long-standing policy set by the board and only the board can make exceptions, take it to the board. If your counterpart just created the policy last week in anticipation of your negotiation, simply consider it another issue on the table. If many exceptions to the policy exist, and you can find some precedent for an exception similar to what you want, ask for it.

The key? Get information about the policy and find a principled way around it.

Reciprocity Power

"Fair is fair," Congresswoman A told Congressman B. "Remember six months ago when you asked me to vote for your farm aid legislation? Since my urban district includes few farmers, I didn't care much about it. But you told me then if I supported you on farm aid you would support me on one of my pet issues where your district didn't have strong feelings one way or the other. I need your support now. I strongly support campaign finance reform, and so do my constituents. You owe me."

The "reciprocity" standard—it is "fair and reasonable" for you to do this for me because I did something for you in the past—can be powerful. Political negotiations involving the same players again and again use it, despite the fact that it's bad form in some contexts to explicitly mention the return of favor. Individuals also use this when involved in long-term relationships, and where they depend in part on their reputations for their success.

The power of reciprocity often applies when there are ongoing negotiations between parties involving disparate issues. There's no substantive connection between farm aid and campaign finance. Instead, Congressman B will likely support campaign finance reform because of the power of reciprocity. If he doesn't support Congresswoman A here his reputation will suffer. He will then have a more difficult time rounding up support for his pet issues in the future. Politicians have long memories. They need to in order to survive and thrive.

Former President Lyndon B. Johnson was a master at horse trading and using the power of reciprocity to get legislation passed. Members of Congress knew if they crossed him or broke their promises to him they would pay.

In a business context, imagine that you ask your boss if you can leave early Friday, as your son is coming home from college for an extended weekend and you're taking him fishing. Your boss says fine. Three weeks later your boss asks if you can stay late two nights that week as *his* boss just asked him to finish the year-end report early. He needs your data for the report. In all likelihood you will agree. This is how the power of reciprocity works. Two separate negotiations, but one independent standard determining a "fair and reasonable" result. Fair is fair.

Ways to Use Reciprocity Power to Your Advantage

Look for opportunities to "give things away" to those with whom you may be negotiating in the future, especially if what you're giving away doesn't cost you much. Keep a mental note of those for whom you do favors, and be careful how you ask for return favors. Subtlety and silence can be effective tactics in this context. Individuals will likely be offended if they believe an explicit *quid pro quo* exists, especially between friends. But it's important to keep a mental sense of what's going back and forth. Maintain a decent balance. If it gets too far out of whack in the long run, relationships often suffer.

Of course, it's appropriate in some business contexts to be more open about this than in others. In politics there are even some legal restrictions on the process, especially in fund-raising. Be careful how you use this.

Finally, reciprocity power also impacts parties' offer-concession behavior. If I concede on one issue, I will expect you to reciprocate with a somewhat equivalent concession either on that or another issue. Why? It seems fair. I extensively address reciprocity in the after-concession context in chapter 4.

Countermeasures to Reciprocity Power

If you don't want to owe someone a future favor, pay for it now. Do not accept gifts or favors from individuals to whom you do not want to feel a reciprocal obligation. Labor union negotiators must be very sensitive to the perceptions involved in accepting favors from management. They don't want to appear to their fellow union members to be unfairly influenced by management. As a result, they will often either refuse "favors" or insist on paying for any benefit received.

Alternatively, explicitly state that your acceptance of the "gift" does not create a future obligation. I once presented a seminar at a conference in Texas that also featured a communication skills presenter. After our respective presentations, the other presenter told me he would be interested in helping with my seminars if I had more clients than I could handle. I told him I would certainly consider it. He then gave me his book on communications skills and insisted on not charging me. I thanked him for the book. I then jokingly noted that, of course, he understood this did not obligate me in any way to hire him. He smiled and said, "Of course not." He knew what he was doing in giving me his book for free. He also knew why I accepted it with my caveat.

Importantly, stating how you intend to reciprocate the favor also tends to set a relative value on the original gift. Since small favors often tend to beget larger favors, explicitly noting how you will return the favor will help limit your future obligations. Congressman B told Congresswoman A, after he originally asked for her support on his farm aid bill, that he would be happy to return the favor on an issue *where his district didn't have strong feelings*. He thus limited the openness of his return favor and implicitly put an equivalent value on his return obligation. He could also have noted a specific concurrent issue on which he would be happy to return the favor, such as another pending bill. This would help nail down the value of the favor.

Finally, don't feel obligated if you feel the gift or favor is being offered to manipulate you. Everyone receives "free offers" in the mail or from telephone solicitations. These almost always come from strangers. Don't feel any obligation to return them. They are offered purely to manipulate your purchasing behavior. Treat these favors differently from those that come into play when the parties have an ongoing relationship.

How should you treat favors from those with whom you have a relationship? Consider whether it is being offered strategically (to create a possible future reciprocal obligation) or sincerely (out of the goodness of their heart). The more strategic favors I evaluate more cynically from a cost-benefit perspective. With sincere favors I always feel a reciprocal obligation.

How can you tell if the offer is more strategic than sincere? Ask yourself if the predominant reason the other party is giving you the gift or favor is because he or she will later expect a reciprocal—but likely larger—gift or favor? If your answer is yes, it's probably more strategic than sincere. If the answer is no, it's more likely sincere.

With friends and family, I assume a favor is sincere, unless the person's history of behavior suggests otherwise. With business colleagues I tend to assume the motive is more strategic than sincere. Not necessarily in a bad way, however. But I do keep my guard up and fairly explicitly keep mental note of the favor ledger.

Status Power

"I couldn't believe it," the businessman told me. "While I was an outside consultant this company followed all my recommendations. Then I went full-time with them and my success rate plummeted to fifty percent. What happened?"

"Excellent question," I responded. The answer? Status power.

In short, as discussed in Dawson's *Secrets of Power Negotiating*, an individual's status affects the negotiation dynamic and that individual's ability to achieve his or her negotiation goals.

Webster's defines "status" as a "position or rank in relation to others." In the negotiation context, the higher you sit on the status totem pole, the greater your credibility, or at least appearance of credibility. Many people use another's perceived status as shorthand in determining how much influence and credibility to afford the holder. That, in turn, can increase your ability to influence the parties' belief of what is "fair and reasonable."

Status power exists in several forms, including title status and position status. Your title and/or position can provide an independent standard and power in and of itself. Let's examine how this works.

Title Status

I used to be impressed when I found myself across from a "Corporate Vice President." A corporate VP, I figured, was usually the number-two person.

No longer. Why not? Because I learned that some companies have a large number of vice presidents. The reason? Title status. Corporations know most people consider vice presidents, by definition, to be high-ranking and influential.

Thus, if we have a lesser title, or one perceived to be lesser, we will likely feel somewhat intimidated. At the least we will perceive that our counterpart, the vice president, will have a high level of knowledge, credibility, and influence.

If I'm the Southwest regional sales manager of a software company and I'm negotiating with the chief operating officer of a large insurance company, I will likely assign more credibility to the COO's opinion of the "fairness and reasonableness" of the software price than if the COO's title were "office manager."

Understanding this, what should you do?

Ways to Use Title Status Power to Your Advantage

If you have a good title, use it. Otherwise, get a good title. Add a better title to the options on the table for your next salary negotiation. Titles by themselves generally don't cost much, and titles that sound higher ranking can positively impact your negotiations. It may be in your company's best interest to bump you up.

Of course, don't overdo it. Many people now know which companies hand out vice-president titles liberally. The impact of these companies' titles thus diminishes. Plus, you can lose credibility if your title oversells, and bears little relationship to your responsibilities. Don't call yourself the chairman and CEO if you only have a one-person shop.

Countermeasures to Title Status Power

Test the other side's titles against reality. Find out your counterparts' job responsibilities and where they fit within their corporate structure. Then you will know how to truly assess their legitimate influence in the negotiation. Remember this next time you negotiate with a VP. Find out how many other VPs exist in his or her organization. You never know, you may outrank them.

Position Status

An individual's substantive position—or others' perception of it—can also provide power, influence, and credibility, and provide parties with a better assessment of what's "fair and reasonable." The most powerful individual in the world is the President of the United States. This is not due to his title or individual qualities, however, although they're part of it. No, the president has negotiation power because of his institutional position and what can be done as president.

Position status also partially explains the difference in success rate my friend experienced when he was hired by the company that formerly used him as a consultant. While a consultant, his position power derived from: a) his perceived independence and ability to control his own destiny; b) his reliance on multiple clients; and c) his clients' perception that he held at least an equivalent position to theirs.

When he became an employee he lost a portion of his independence and ability to control his own destiny, became formally dependent on his employer for his livelihood, and became corporately subservient to his former equal. He lost negotiation power and lost a portion of his ability to influence his employer.

Ways to Use Position Status Power to Your Advantage

If you have an inherently influential position that provides you with position power, make sure your counterpart knows it. Not that you should tell them. Often it's more credible if someone else shares this information. But make sure your counterpart knows. If he or she doesn't, it won't do you much good.

Likewise, find out the position and responsibilities of your counterparts. Don't be intimidated by them, but find out so you can independently evaluate their impact.

Countermeasures to Position Status Power

Investigating the position of your counterpart and independently determining the influence that position deserves can be a countermeasure to Position Status Power. And while you want to be sensitive to the influence afforded by individuals' positions, don't solely judge issues based on another's position or opinion. Use additional independent standards to evaluate them, too.

Status power is critical. So find it, evaluate it, and use it to your advantage.

Professional or Industry Standards Power

"This is our standard commercial lease," the shopping center's leasing agent said to the potential retail tenant after they had negotiated a two-year lease and agreed on a monthly rate for the space. "I've put in our agreed-upon terms, and here are two originals. Please review and sign both. I will then have the owner sign them and send you an executed original for your files. If you have any questions give me a call."

Ever faced a similar "standard" agreement? If you have ever bought or sold a house you have probably signed a ton of standard agreements. Or your accountant or lawyer might have said to you, "This is my standard hourly rate, and these are the firm's standard charges for photocopies. If you will just sign our standard fee agreement we can get started."

Of course, if you object to any of the "standard" terms the response often is "I'm sorry. I would love to help you out. But this is what all our [tenants/customers/guests/clients] sign."

Interestingly, most people agree to such standard rates, or sign standard agreements with few, if any, changes. And we do so even though such agreements most often favor the individuals proposing them. In effect, we presume every other similarly situated person has agreed to it and, as a result, it *must* be "fair and reasonable," right?

In some cases this is true. Many professionals have standard hourly rates. Others have different "standard" rates, based on their leverage with different clients. The bigger clients get the most preferred "standard" rate, while smaller clients pay the regular "standard" rate. Often, these professionals have spent a great deal of time researching other independent standards—like market value, expert opinions, efficiency, costs, tradition, reciprocity, and status power—and have concluded their services are worth a certain amount. They then present this amount to potential clients as a developed "standard." Industry standards are often derived from similar industry-wide investigations.

For instance, I regularly provide potential clients with my standard fees for seminars and my standard consulting rate. I have spent a significant amount of time researching various independent standards and, based on them, determined "fair and reasonable" rates. I also send new clients my standard agreement and ask them to review and sign it. In about 95 percent of the cases they sign my standard agreement. Why? I've taken the time to research and evaluate what makes sense for everyone and have incorporated these terms in the agreement. My clients know this. Plus, it's usually not worth their time or mine to negotiate every minor detail when the agreement already includes balanced terms.

In the less than 5 percent of the cases where my clients have an issue with one or more of my standard terms (or their legal staff wants to use *their* "standard" language), we negotiate. Sometimes I concede certain points. Other times they relent. This is normal and expected.

Ways to Use Professional or Industry Standards
Power to Your Advantage

If you provide professional services or products, and tradition dictates that you make the first offer, develop your own standard rates, terms, and an agreement. Then present it to the other side. In many cases your new clients will simply accept your proposal. Even if they don't, your language and terms will likely become the baseline agreement and you can negotiate from there.

In developing your standard rate or terms, however, research and select rates and terms based on the independent standards described above. Don't pick a number out of thin air. If you do, and the other side does its research, you will lose credibility.

Be wary also of how others can misuse allegedly "standard" terms or agreements. Some might present a standard wage or industry standard agreement just to get you to sign on the dotted line. The "standard" may not be the industry or professional standard at all. Parties also sometimes bury critical terms within mind-numbingly detailed boilerplate paragraphs.

If you suspect this, or want to confirm the standards being presented, take the following steps.

Countermeasures to Professional or Industry Standards Power

First research what true professional or industry standard exists, if any. Check the market for legal services and find what other law firms charge for photocopies. Speak with an industry expert to determine if the agreement's terms are truly "standard."

Second, generally assume that most "standard" rates and terms are negotiable. Then, request a better rate or more favorable terms if it makes sense timewise and the issues are sufficiently important. *It doesn't cost anything to ask,* and you will likely ferret out helpful information, like what other standards were involved in setting the rate.

Third, develop your own "standard" agreement or terms and prepare to counter with it. In 2001 a state attorney general's office asked me to present a customized negotiation seminar to about one hundred of its lawyers. After we agreed on the major terms I said I would be happy to send over my standard two-page agreement. My client said not to bother, as the state had its own detailed "standard" agreement it used in contracting with all outside vendors. I subsequently received six original copies of an eight-page agreement with small print, accompanied by a four-page exhibit with "General Terms & Conditions." While I was tempted to just sign it, I resisted the urge. I'm glad I did. After reviewing it in detail, I found six issues critical enough to raise and negotiate. Here the state countered my standard agreement with its own standard agreement. Then we negotiated from it.

Fourth, consider the standard to be a first offer and probe it. Be especially wary of overly detailed standard agreements that are presented as a done deal. While practicing law I paid strict attention to footnotes in legal documents reflecting parties' agreements. Some lawyers bury important terms in the small print, assuming lazy lawyers will never read everything. Business people do the same thing. Read the fine print.

Finding and using appropriate independent standards is a powerful way to justify "fair and reasonable" positions. Put these standards into your negotiation toolbox and use them. Here's a summary of the most powerful independent standards and the ways to most effectively counter them.

GOLDEN RULE THREE: EMPLOY "FAIR" OBJECTIVE CRITERIA

Understand the Power of "Fair and Reasonable" Standards and Procedures

Find Your Most Powerful Independent Standards
- Market-Value Power
  Countermeasures
  — Challenge their definition of "market value"
  — Challenge the validity of the underlying market
  — Distinguish your item from the market
  — "Circumstances have changed"
  — Focus on the market of one—individual leverage (*universal*)
  — Switch to a more favorable standard (*universal*)

- Precedent Power
  Countermeasures
  — Challenge the validity of the precedent
  — Distinguish your facts
  — "Circumstances have changed"

- Tradition Power
  Countermeasures
  — "Circumstances have changed"
  — Explore the exceptions

- Expert- and Scientific-Judgment Power
  Countermeasures
  — Counter with your own expert
  — Undermine the credibility of your counterpart's expert
  — Make yourself an expert

- Efficiency Power

- Costs and Profit Power
  Countermeasures
  — Research the average profit margin and compare

- Policy Power
  Countermeasures
  — Learn about the policy and find a principled way around it

- Reciprocity Power
  Countermeasures
  — Don't accept favors if you don't want to owe an obligation
  — State the "gift" doesn't create a future obligation
  — Set a relative value on the favor
  — Don't feel obligated if its intent was manipulative

- Status Power: Title and Position
  Countermeasures
  — Investigate counterparts' titles/positions and determine their true influence

- Professional or Industry Standards Power
  Countermeasures
  — Research if true professional or industry standards exist
  — Assume such "standards" are negotiable
  — Develop your own "standard" agreement
  — Consider the standard offered to be a "first offer"

Consider Mutually Powerful Procedures

What if you just can't find a standard that everyone agrees will result in a "fair and reasonable" agreement? You have tried market value, you have looked up applicable precedents, you can't find an expert, there's no policy or costs involved, and reciprocity didn't work. In short, the other parties just won't accept any standards. What can you do?

Consider a powerful procedure the parties believe will lead to a "fair and reasonable" result. If the parties can agree on a *process* they believe will lead to a better result than their BATNAs, everyone will walk away satisfied.

Here are some examples of powerful procedures that work in various contexts:

- One cut, the other choose
- Take turns, draw lots, or flip a coin
- Use an independent third party, such as arbitration or mediation

One Cut, the Other Choose

I have a brother named Ron. He's fifteen months older than I am. While growing up we were extremely competitive. In fact, we're still competitive. Imagine Ron and I are thirteen and twelve years old and we're hungry. So we go into the kitchen, and there's one piece of apple pie left. I love apple pie more than Ron and Ron knows it. On the need side of the leverage equation Ron has the leg up. But even though I'm younger, I'm a little bigger and more aggressive than Ron. I can probably beat up Ron and grab the pie for myself. However, if we fight Mom will punish both of us. Neither of us wants that. Leveragewise, we both have weak BATNAs.

Here's what might occur as a result:

Marty: Hey, Ron, looks like only one piece of apple pie left. I think I will take it.

Ron: No way. I want that piece too. How about if I take this one, and next time I will let you have the piece? (Reciprocity standard)

Marty: No way. I'm hungry now. (*I give Ron a shove.*)

Ron: Cut it out, jerk. (*He shoves me back.*)

Marty: Wait a second. We both know I could beat you up and take the pie, but you might get in a lucky shot and actually hurt me. And then Mom will punish us both. Why don't you cut the pie in half and I will pick my half. That's fair, right?

Ron: I don't know. It sounds fair, but I'm sure you've got some angle. (*So he thinks about it for a minute or so and can't figure out how I might get more than him.*) Okay, where's the knife?

Ron then picks up the knife and spends two minutes choosing the *exact* spot to cut the pie in half. I then choose my half and he takes the other. We both walk away satisfied we got as much as we could—in a fair way—without physically fighting.

Unrealistic for competitive teenage siblings? Probably. In all likelihood we would have fought. But that would have been a horrible negotiation story.

Seriously, this "one cut, the other choose" process works equally well in business and other situations.

Many use a variation of it in the real estate context. A couple of friends of mine jointly bought a condominium in Manhattan Beach in the early 1990s. It was a beautiful condo right on the Pacific Ocean. They paid around $500,000 for it and split it fifty-fifty. For the first few years the condo appreciated in value. But then the housing market started to slide and the condo's value slid with it. Around this time one of the friends became seriously involved with a woman and decided to live with her. While there was enough space for three in the condo, my friends decided that the arrangement wouldn't make sense. But they couldn't decide who would move and how much the remaining person would pay for the "mover's" share. Neither cared too much about who stayed or left.

Here's what they did. They agreed that one of them would decide the amount each share was worth. The other would then decide whether to a) stay and pay that share to the person moving out, or b) move and have that amount paid to him. Both agreed this process would lead to a "fair and reasonable" result.

Take Turns, Draw Lots, or Flip a Coin

How many of us have reached an impasse near the end of a negotiation where there's only a little bit left on the table, and we flip a coin to determine who gets the last bit? Both sides consider the process fair, so why not? Or say five parties desperately want to go fishing but there's only one boat left, and it seats four. What can you do? Draw straws, with the person who drew the short straw staying home. The beauty of this process is that everyone accepts it as "fair and reasonable."

Or try taking turns? Divorce lawyers often use this procedure in determining how to "fairly and reasonably" split up the household belongings from a marriage. First they make a list of all the household belongings to be split, then flip a coin to determine who gets first choice. The spouses then choose alternately until all the items on the list are gone. In this way each spouse can decide how much he or she wants an item and assign a relative value to it, according to his or her needs. This is especially effective when dealing with items that have far more emotional value to an individual (e.g., a furniture piece carved by the person's grandfather) than can be captured by an independent appraiser.

Many professional sports also use a variation of this, the draft, to allow their member teams to select the top amateur players wishing to move up to their level. The NBA, for instance, starts with a lottery among the teams with the worst records to determine who gets the top picks. Then the rest of the teams take turns to select the rest, with the best team choosing last.

Use an Independent Third Party, Such as Arbitration or Mediation

A growing number of lawyers and business professionals these days are resolving lawsuits and other disputes by bringing in an independent third party to either decide the issue (arbitration) or just to help them negotiate with each other in a more effective way (mediation).

Arbitration

Arbitration—where the parties select an independent third party to hear the evidence and render a final decision—is often more cost-effective than litigation. There are many variations of arbitration. Traditionally, the parties would simply hire an independent third party to serve as the arbitrator and then present their best cases to him or her. The arbitrator then would make the decision, like a judge. Many other forms of arbitration, however, now exist. Final-offer arbitration is used in baseball salary disputes where the parties have reached a negotiation impasse. There, each party provides the arbitrator with its recommended salary and the arbitrator can only select one. Each party thus has a great incentive to present a figure within a relatively reasonable and objectively supportable range. This weeds out outrageous demands and minimalist offers and leads to a result that both parties usually consider within a "fair and reasonable" range.

Another form of arbitration exists in disputes between securities brokers and their customers. Here, the National Association of Securities Dealers (NASD) sends the parties a list of fifteen possible arbitrators, ten with a securities industry background and five with a public-customer-oriented background. Each party then ranks these arbitrators according to their respective preferences and sends their preferred list back to the NASD. Each party also may strike, or eliminate, any of the possible arbitrators from the list. Upon receiving the parties' respective lists, the NASD compares the lists and selects the two highest "public" arbitrators according to both parties' rankings and the highest "industry" arbitrator. These three arbitrators then serve as the arbitration panel for the parties' dispute.

Often parties will institutionalize this process by agreeing to use arbitration to resolve any disputes even *before* such disputes arise. They do this by inserting a clause into their "standard" written agreements stating that they will use arbitration to resolve any disputes that arise on the issues in the agreement. This helps both parties, because their alternative would be to go to court, and litigation is often more expensive for *both* sides than arbitration.

Mediation

Mediation—where the parties ask an independent third party to help them communicate and negotiate, but not make the decision—is another process that can help parties achieve a "fair and reasonable" result. While mediators have no decision-making power, they operate as walking, talking independent standards that can help parties resolve difficult issues by independently and often expertly controlling the agenda and the negotiation process. Mediators also often provide parties with independent evaluations of what they consider "fair and reasonable." Sometimes they're experts in the field, other times not.

Mediation can be particularly effective in many situations. It's especially helpful in disputes involving high emotions and potential future relationships between the parties. Overall advantages to mediation include the following, many of which were described in Howard Raiffa's classic *The Art and Science of Negotiation: How to Resolve Conflicts and Get the Best Out of Bargaining*:

- Providing a potentially face-saving way for the parties to sit down in the first place
- Establishing the appropriate atmosphere and environment in which to negotiate
- Helping parties skillfully navigate through difficult issues that might otherwise cause an impasse, and breaking through impasses that do occur
- Efficiently helping parties explore their fundamental values and interests and how they define "success"
- Helping determine where the parties have shared, compatible, and conflicting interests and selectively, where useful, sharing such information with the other party or parties
- Systematically exploring mutually beneficial solutions and ways to "expand the pie" by focusing on the parties' shared, compatible, and conflicting interests
- Providing a largely independent, realistic, and possibly expert assessment of all the parties' needs and alternatives (their leverage) and assisting the parties in determining when to walk and when to fold
- Managing the offer-concession dynamic (discussed at length in chapter 4) in a way that may reduce the role of the parties' egos and increase the parties' chances of reaching agreement

In short, skilled mediators can help parties successfully engage in almost all aspects of the negotiation process. Of course, all of this may prove crucial to the parties reaching *any* agreement.

One potential downside to mediation, however, is that the parties give up some ability to control the agenda—a subject we explore in depth in chapter 5. Of course, this has advantages and disadvantages, and should be explicitly evaluated prior to deciding to enter mediation.

Overall, keep in mind that two crucial factors should be evaluated *before* parties agree to use *any* independent procedure to resolve a negotiation. One, the parties must agree *before* they consent to the procedure that it likely will lead to a "fair and reasonable" result. Or, in mediation, substantially increase the likelihood of getting there. And two, each party must believe that using the procedure will ensure a better result than its BATNA. If the parties do not agree on these points, the procedure's effectiveness will be called into doubt. No one wants this to occur.

Here's a review of mutually powerful procedures to consider.

GOLDEN RULE THREE: EMPLOY "FAIR" OBJECTIVE CRITERIA

Understand the Power of "Fair and Reasonable" Standards and Procedures

Find Your Most Powerful Independent Standards

Consider Mutually Powerful Procedures
- One cut, the other choose
- Take turns, draw lots, or flip a coin
- Use an independent third party, e.g., arbitrator or mediator

---

Harness the Full Power of Objective Criteria by Using These Four Critical Tactics

Using these powers will help you achieve your goals and place a "fair and reasonable" hat on your head. But to achieve the best possible result you can you must do more. Try these four tactics.

- Find your most powerful standards and procedures *at the start*
- Research standards and procedures your counterpart *previously* used
- Do the "standards dance"
- Never forget: Leverage trumps objective criteria

Find Your Most Powerful Standards and Procedures *at the Start*

Don't get caught in a negotiation without doing your homework on applicable independent standards and procedures. Watch Bill show us how *not* to do it.

> *Bill at an estate sale*: I'm interested in that 24" x 36" painting over there of a desert landscape by Jean Artiste. I've heard of him and I really like him. And that particular painting would look great over our couch in our family room. I notice there's no price tag on it. Why don't you tell me what you want for it and the basis for its price?
>
> *Kate, estate sale manager*: Let me first introduce myself. My name is Kate, and I'm the manager of this estate sale *[position status]*. And let me say, you've got excellent taste. Jean Artiste is very well-known regionally. In fact, I'm particularly familiar with him, as I used to manage the Scottsdale gallery that represented him. I even studied his work while an art student *[sets herself up here as an*

expert]. Regarding its value, we sold another Artiste yesterday for $4,000, and it was pretty much the same size *[precedent]*. There's also a fairly active market for Artiste's works, and a painting this size usually gets around $4,000 *[market value]*. Of course, he's hot these days, and you'd likely have to pay at least $5,000 for that, or a similar painting, if it were in a gallery *[effort to convince him his alternative to buying from her—his BATNA—is relatively weak]*. You know, overhead and all *[a variation of the cost standard]*. I tell you what. It's the next-to-last day of the sale, so I would let it go for $3,500. At that price it's a deal.

Bill: You know, I really didn't intend to spend more than $3,000 for a painting today. But I really like it. How about $3,000?

Kate: Bill, I would love to sell it to you. But $3,000 is well below its market value, and even significantly below what we sold a similar painting for yesterday. $3,500 really is a good price. Trust me, I know this artist. You'll love it.

Bill: Well, okay. $3,500 it is. What about having it shipped to my home?

Kate: No problem. We'll be happy to ship it to you for an additional $50. That's our standard shipping charge for a painting this size *[industry standard]*.

Bill: Great. Thanks.

Game, set, and match to Kate. Why?

Bill entered this negotiation without doing his homework. He didn't know the painting's market value. He didn't know any precedents. He hadn't investigated the artist and had to trust Kate's expertise. Kate, of course, had a vested interest in selling it for the highest price possible. Bill also didn't know how much the painting had cost the owner or when or where it had been purchased. In short, he was negotiating with both hands tied behind his back. He failed to investigate the standards prior to negotiating the deal.

But he still got a "fair" price, right?

I don't know. What if Kate was lying about one of her standards? Or just slightly misrepresenting it? More likely, she was cherry-picking the standards that helped her the most. For instance, she told Bill she sold an Artiste painting for $4,000 yesterday that was "pretty much the same size." It's likely that painting was larger. By how much we don't know. Nor does Bill. He didn't ask.

Kate also might have sold an Artiste painting that morning for $3,000, but she chose not to share this precedent with Bill. It might have been the exact same size. It's also possible—if not likely—Kate's evaluation of the painting's market value was high. Not unreasonably so. But its true market value may have been closer to $3,000 than $4,000.

What should Bill have done as a price-sensitive purchaser? Obtained information about these standards *before* the negotiation. He also should have asked Kate more questions about these standards. For instance, he should have asked about other precedents and about the seller's cost. While she might have refused to answer, the *way* she answered likely would have provided him with relevant information. Why might she have refused to tell him its cost or about other precedents? Because sharing this likely would have been to his strategic advantage. The painting's cost was probably well below her asking price. And other precedents might have been evidence of a market value well below $4,000.

Bill also should have done some additional research before concluding the deal. At the least he should have made a couple phone calls, perhaps to the gallery that represents Artiste. He should have generally confirmed Kate's evaluation of the market value. He also could have found out what a "standard" shipping rate might be for a similar-size painting and the "standard" commission for the sale of art like this in a gallery and at estate sales. How much "profit" is Kate getting on this $3,500 sale?

Bottom line: Research the standards and procedures *before* you start the negotiation.

Research Standards and Procedures
Your Counterpart Has Previously Used

Let's say I represent plaintiff John Businessman in a medical malpractice lawsuit against Dr. Cutter Sawbones. Dr. Sawbones allegedly fell below the medical standard of care when he operated on John Businessman to repair a torn rotator cuff. John, since the surgery, has continued to experience problems with his shoulder and has had additional surgery to repair the problems allegedly created by Dr. Sawbones.

Larry Litigator, a well-known lawyer who previously practiced exclusively on behalf of plaintiffs in medical malpractice actions, represents Dr. Sawbones.

If I'm looking for an orthopedic medical expert that will testify that Dr. Sawbones's actions fell below the medical standard of care, I would be well served to find an expert who Larry Litigator has used in the past. Why? It will be difficult for Larry to undermine the credibility of an expert he is on record as finding credible and well-qualified. To do so, he would appear inconsistent—which doesn't look good.

In other words, find a powerful standard or procedure your counterpart has previously used. Then rely on the individual's interest in appearing consistent and apply it to your negotiation.

Alternatively, you might find that your negotiation counterpart has relied on a certain methodology to value businesses in the past. If this methodology supports your position, use it to suggest it must be "fair and reasonable." After all, your counterpart considered it "fair and reasonable" in the past.

This works equally effectively when applied to powerful procedures. Let's say you want to use a particular mediator, as you believe that mediator's style favors you. If you find your counterpart has used that mediator several times in the past, especially in similar matters, you will be more likely to get your counterpart's agreement if you suggest that mediator.

Understanding this dynamic, Bill at the estate sale did do something right: he avoided the "consistency trap." This trap is based on what psychologist Robert Cialdini calls the Consistency Principle. In some cases, a party will try to get his or her counterpart to commit to the fairness of a standard *before* that counterpart knows the end result of using that standard. Let's say Kate had initially asked Bill if he would be willing to pay "market value" for the painting. "That's fair, right?" she might ask. If Bill agrees, he's just fallen into her consistency trap, as Kate already knows she can justify a "market value" of at least $3,500. Given her BATNA—the estate sale ends the following day and she may not have any other interest in the painting—she just significantly improved the likelihood of a sale that's better than her BATNA.

Of course, Bill has not yet committed to paying $3,500. But he has agreed on a fair principle to determine the painting's value and expressed his willingness to abide by that principle. Since we have a strong psychological tendency to act and appear to act consistently, it will be difficult for Bill to appear consistent if he backs out later. Most view consistency, after all, as a positive personality trait.

Overall, keep track of the independent standards used by your counterparts, especially if you regularly negotiate with the same individuals. This will provide you with strategically critical information for your future negotiations with them.

Do the "Standards Dance"

In many sophisticated negotiations, everyone will have found the standards that favor their side and will use their most favorable standards to independently justify the "fairness" of their positions. But what next? What happens when one side suggests "market value" to justify their position and the other side suggests "precedent" and "cost" as more powerful justifications for *their* position? We get the "standards dance."

The parties negotiate over which standard represents the most fair and applicable justification. Remember the America West Airlines flight attendants' negotiation? Each side had its own evaluation of market value, and then negotiated over which was most compelling and applicable. This same dance occurs in many negotiations. A wide variety of different independent standards and procedures end up on the table.

But you can't dance well if you don't do your homework. So, research the applicable standards *before* the negotiation. Then come prepared to use the most favorable ones and discredit the most unfavorable ones. Negotiate over the most appropriate objective criteria.

This dance occurred in 2001 after I sent my standard agreement to a Fortune 500 company for a customized training program for some of its international lawyers and business professionals. After I had e-mailed my agreement I received back a redlined copy of it with a number of minor changes to my "standard" terms. One change involved the arbitration clause in my agreement. This clause stated that if any dispute arises concerning the agreement, it will go to arbitration instead of to the courts. As noted earlier, arbitration often makes sense in contract matters as it's almost always cheaper and more efficient than the courts. Up to this point no one had ever questioned this clause. This client, however, deleted my arbitration clause and substituted a clause stating that any dispute would be litigated in the courts.

When I contacted my client to discuss this and several other changes, I asked her why she made the change. She told me her company has a "policy" precluding it from entering into agreements with arbitration clauses. It prefers the court system to arbitration, at least for agreements with other United States–based companies. Why? It has the internal resources to aggressively prosecute disputes in the court system, and most of its counterparts, including me, have substantially less resources. Thus, it figures to make my future BATNA—going to court in a dispute—more expensive, and thus weaker relative to its own BATNA. Its policy against arbitration is based on an evaluation of its leverage. Here, the "standards dance" was between my "professional standard" arbitration clause and my client's "policy."

Interestingly, my client's policy does not apply to its agreements with non–United States companies. This makes sense. My client's leverage changes overseas. An arbitration clause is generally better for its disputes in other countries, as it's considered risky for a large United States–based corporation to litigate in foreign courts.

Never Forget: Leverage Trumps Objective Criteria

In the mid-1990s I represented a client who wished to buy out her part-ner's share in a building they co-owned. The building was worth several million dollars and they couldn't agree on a fair price for the departing partner's share. Unfortunately, the partners' relationship had gone sour for a variety of unrelated reasons.

To start, we researched the market value of the building, and my client offered to buy her partner out at a price based on this research. Her part-ner rejected this offer.

My client then offered to settle the dispute by using what most con-sider to be a fair procedure to determine the objective value of a piece of real estate. My client would choose an appraiser. Her partner would choose an appraiser. These two appraisers would choose a third appraiser. The parties then would agree to a value collectively determined by the three appraisers.

My client's partner rejected this offer. When asked why, his lawyer gave a nonsensical response.

How could this procedure result in anything but a fair and reasonable result for both sides? But the parties' actions did make sense. You just had to set aside the objective criteria and analyze the leverage. You see, my client badly wanted to buy out her partner *and her partner knew it*. He, however, didn't appear to care much whether he sold his share or kept it. The problem was, my client's partner felt that he had enough leverage to get my client to pay *more* than fair market value at the time. He was right.

He thus rejected our "fair and reasonable" offer and held out for more. He got it. My client ultimately paid a premium over what might be objec-tively considered to be the building's fair market value.

Of course, my client still ended up with an excellent deal. She was a very astute businesswoman who closely followed the real estate market in this part of town, and she believed this building would appreciate at a higher rate than its appraised value reflected. She was right.

My point? Leverage trumps objective criteria in almost all circum-stances. Always evaluate your objective criteria within the context of your leverage.

CHAPTER 3 REVIEW

Golden Rule Three: Employ "Fair" Objective Criteria

Understand the Power of "Fair and Reasonable" Standards and Procedures
- Creates the perception of independence and objectivity
- The more independent and objective, the more power

Find Your Most Powerful Independent Standards
- Market-Value Power
  Countermeasures
  — Challenge their definition of "market value"
  — Challenge the validity of the underlying market
  — Distinguish your item from the market
  — "Circumstances have changed"
  — Focus on the market of one—individual leverage (*universal*)
  — Switch to a more favorable standard (*universal*)

- Precedent Power
  Countermeasures
  — Challenge the validity of the precedent
  — Distinguish your facts
  — "Circumstances have changed"

- Tradition Power
  Countermeasures
  — "Circumstances have changed"
  — Explore the exceptions

- Expert- and Scientific-Judgment Power
  Countermeasures
  — Counter with your own expert
  — Undermine the credibility of your counterpart's expert
  — Make yourself an expert

- Efficiency Power

- Costs and Profit Power
  Countermeasures
  — Research the average profit margin and compare

- Policy Power
  Countermeasures
  — Learn about the policy and find a principled way around it

- Reciprocity Power
  Countermeasures
  — Don't accept favors if you don't want to owe an obligation
  — State the "gift" doesn't create a future obligation
  — Set a relative value on the favor
  — Don't feel obligated if its intent was manipulative

- Status Power: Title and Position
  Countermeasures
  — Investigate counterparts' titles/positions and determine their true influence

- Professional or Industry Standards Power
  Countermeasures
  — Research if true professional or industry standards exist
  — Assume such "standards" are negotiable
  — Develop your own "standard" agreement
  — Consider the standard offered to be a "first offer"

Consider Mutually Powerful Procedures
- One cut, the other choose
- Take turns, draw lots, or flip a coin
- Use an independent third party, e.g., arbitrator or mediator

Harness the Full Power of Objective Criteria by Using These Four Critical Tactics
- Find your most powerful standards and procedures *at the start*
- Research standards and procedures your counterpart *previously* used
- Do the "standards dance"
- Never forget: Leverage trumps objective criteria

GOLDEN RULE FOUR:
DESIGN AN OFFER-CONCESSION STRATEGY

As San Francisco architect Adam sat down for the interview with his potential boss, he wondered: *Should I make the first offer? If I do, what should it be? Then, how much should I move, if at all? And when and how should I make my moves?* In short, he thought, *what should I do regarding the timing, speed, and size of my offers and concessions?* These offer and concession decisions can make or break your negotiations, and they deserve a great deal of strategic consideration and preparation.

Let's say Roger just filed for divorce and decided to represent himself in negotiations with the attorney for his soon-to-be ex-wife. In preparing, Roger first analyzed their property and comprehensively researched the standards. Based on all the standards, he concluded a "fair" property settlement would be for him to pay his wife $500,000. He had an expert's valuation that suggested he pay $100,000, and his wife had one that suggested he pay $1 million. The property involved tough valuation issues, putting the standards all over the map.

What did he do?

After receiving a one-million-dollar settlement offer from his wife's attorney, whom he didn't know, he decided to "cut to the chase." Efficiency was one of his goals. Roger thus countered by stating to his wife, "I could start at $100,000, based on *my* expert's opinion, similar to you starting at $1 million. We could then go back and forth for the next year, paying our lawyers a lot of money. Neither one of us wants that. Instead, I will offer you, today, $450,000. We both know that's where we would end up in a year if we both played the game."

His wife's attorney countered at $900,000, calling it "reasonable, too," based on *her* expert's opinion. Roger then offered $460,000, at which point his wife and her attorney walked. In walking, they accused Roger of negotiating in "bad faith." After all, they said, he only moved $10,000 after they moved $100,000. That's not "good faith," right? One year later, after they had both paid their lawyers a lot of money to litigate it, Roger and his ex settled for $540,000.

This story highlights several key issues you must understand to effectively design successful offer-concession strategies, including:

- Know your offer-concession patterns
- Whether and where to start (first offer issues)
- Psychological tendencies underlying offer-concession behavior
- The nuts and bolts of making offers and concessions

Know Your Offer-Concession Patterns

The best way to predict future offer-concession behavior is to research the offer-concession patterns that exist in similar situations in the past. By identifying these patterns of acting and reacting in general negotiation circumstances, you will increase your ability to predict what similarly situated negotiators will do in the future. These patterns shape your expectations.

Knowing these patterns, you can then more logically determine what offer to make, when and how to make it, how much to concede, if at all, and whether and how much of a response to expect from your counterparts. Understanding offer-concession patterns forms a crucial element in the negotiation process.

Keep in mind, though, two caveats. First, patterns represent general conclusions that do not apply in every instance. I'm sure you can point to at least one exception, based on your experiences, to the following patterns. But in terms of your ability to predict future actions, relying on patterns of past behavior is a good general rule of thumb.

Second, different patterns may exist in your industry or in your own typical negotiation context. Offer-concession patterns in personal injury negotiations differ from those in salary negotiations. Patterns in new car negotiations may not be the same as those in commercial real estate negotiations. And patterns in negotiations in the Middle East are different from those in negotiations in the Far East. So, find the patterns that apply in your industry or your context. The more specific the context in which the pattern appears, the more it will help you determine what to expect and how to act and react with your own offers and concessions.

So, what general offer-concession patterns generally exist in the American culture?

- Most negotiators enter the offer-concession stage too soon—so beware of the premature offer
- The longer you wait, the less eager you appear, and vice versa—the timing pattern
- Early concessions include relatively larger moves—the size pattern

Most Negotiators Enter the Offer-Concession Stage Too Soon— So Beware of the Premature Offer

Information, leverage, and objective criteria. These Golden Rules represent the strategic building blocks of every negotiation. Don't give them short shrift. Comprehensively explore them. Dig deep. And do it *before* you start with your offers and concessions. Unfortunately, many in the United States jump too quickly into the offer-concession stage. Resist the urge. Our country's "get to the point" and "cut to the chase" attitude has many benefits. This attitude in the negotiation context is not one of them. Wait to make your offer or concession until *after* you have set appropriately aggressive goals and sufficiently explored the critical information underlying the parties' interests, maximized your leverage, and thoroughly prepared to use the "most fair" independent standards.

Next time you feel ready to make an offer or a concession, ask these questions.

- Have I received sufficient information about the parties' interests to really know what everyone wants and to specifically set my own aggressive goals and realistic expectations?
- Have I done everything I could up to this point to maximize my leverage, and is my leverage relatively strong right now?
- Have I evaluated all the applicable independent standards and procedures so I know where to do the "standards dance" and understand what procedures might benefit me the most?

If you can't answer yes to these questions, wait. Of course, don't wait forever. You will never have *all* the information you want. Your leverage may never be optimal. And independent standards like market value constantly change. But if in doubt err on the side of waiting and digging deeper. Unless you have a deadline approaching (a dynamic discussed in the next chapter), it's always better to enter the offer-concession stage with more information than less.

Why is this? The atmosphere often changes once the offer-concession process begins. Sometimes it's a subtle change. Other times it's overt. In most cases the negotiation becomes more competitive and tense, and the parties start eyeing each other more warily. It thus becomes much more difficult to gather information, especially strategically helpful information. A friend says he goes on "yellow alert" when the parties first engage with an offer. Once this occurs a line has been crossed. Make sure you're ready to cross that line.

When you're ready, then, stick out your antenna and read the signals going back and forth. Each offer and concession sends and is expected to send information to the other side, especially about goals and leverage, and this will affect your counterpart's offer and concession decisions, and vice versa.

Assume I own a successful software company with gross annual revenue around $1 million and proprietary technology with proven market acceptance and significant potential, and I want to retire. I decide to sell if I can get at least $5 million. Assume two software companies express interest: Bigsoft and Smallsoft. Assume it's traditional in this industry for the seller to set an asking price, and because I want to control the offer-concession agenda, I start on January 2 by asking $7.5 million cash.

This $7.5 million offer will impact both Bigsoft's and Smallsoft's counteroffers. Both will try to get into my head to determine what factors formed the basis for my asking price. Assuming they want to pay the least amount, their main offer-concession goal is to figure out the minimum I will accept. Here that's $5 million. But I'm certainly not going to tell them this, at least not yet.

What factors will they analyze, and how will they decide when to counter and with what? Expert negotiators initially will analyze the offer and their future counter in terms of the issues discussed in Golden Rules One through Three. They will especially focus, however, on leverage and the parties' needs. Neither company will want to signal with its counter that it desperately wants my company. They will want to express serious interest, but not too much. Finding the right balance can be tough. If Bigsoft's or Smallsoft's counter signals too much interest it appears desperate, and its leverage weakens. But if it doesn't signal sufficient interest, I may consider its competition more strongly. How do most parties send this signal and try to maximize their leverage? Traditionally, parties send this signal in two ways: time and size.

The Longer You Wait, the Less Eager You Appear, and Vice Versa—the Timing Pattern

The timing of your offer or concession makes a difference. For instance, you generally don't want to send your first counter too soon, because immediately responding to an initial offer likely will be perceived as expressing too much interest, perhaps even a touch of desperation. On the other hand, you don't want to wait too long. This would send the "I don't care enough" signal. (Of course, this changes if external or internal deadlines exist, a dynamic addressed in chapter 5.)

Factors to consider when responding include: the traditional time lapse between offers within a particular industry or context, the time needed to substantively analyze the offer, and the leverage-related signal being sent.

Overall, the longer you wait to start or respond, the less eager you appear. The quicker you move, the more desperate.

Based on these factors, assume Bigsoft countered my $7.5-million cash sales price with $3 million on February 2. A week later, on February 9, Smallsoft countered at $3.5 million.

Now it's my turn. I will consider similar factors in determining when to respond to their first counters, including the signal I want to send regarding how much I want to sell.

Knowing this, it becomes obvious why a relatively substantial amount of time usually passes between offers and concessions near the beginning of negotiations. No one wants to appear too eager, especially at the start.

Another element of the timing pattern is that the time that lapses between offers and concessions often tends to get smaller and smaller as negotiations proceed. Near the end the time between offers and concessions may be just seconds, as they come fast and furious. Factor this into your offer-concession strategy.

What should you do regarding the timing of your offers and concessions? Manage the time between your moves so you send the appropriate signals. And analyze the time between your counterparts' moves so you correctly interpret the signals they're sending you.

Early Concessions Include Relatively Larger Moves—the Size Pattern

Another pattern concerns the size of the moves at the beginning of the negotiation relative to the end. As with the time between moves, parties know that their counterparts will carefully analyze where they start and how much they move. The pattern? The size of concessions tend to be larger near the start of the negotiations than near the end. Concessions tend to get smaller as the difference between the parties narrows.

Let's analyze this in the Bigsoft-Smallsoft sale context. After receiving Bigsoft's and Smallsoft's counters (at $3 million and $3.5 million respectively), say I counter both at $7 million. I've made a $500,000 jump from $7.5 million to $7 million. This $500,000 move will be significantly larger than my and my counterpart's final moves. Sizewise, at the end we will likely move in increments of tens of thousands, not hundreds of thousands. Our final move also will likely be our smallest. Not always, but most often. That's the size pattern.

Take time and size into account in deciding when and how much to move. Analyze these factors when your counterpart moves, too.

Here's a summary of offer-concession patterns, so you can easily evaluate these in your negotiations.

GOLDEN RULE FOUR: DESIGN AN OFFER-CONCESSION STRATEGY

Know Your Offer-Concession Patterns
- Most negotiators enter the offer-concession stage too soon—so beware of the premature offer
- The longer you wait, the less eager you appear, and vice versa—the timing pattern
- Early concessions include relatively larger moves—the size pattern

---

Whether and Where to Start (First-Offer Issues)

Should you make the first offer, or get your counterpart to take the first step? In many negotiations this can be the most critical strategic decision you make.

Early in my career I heard that you should never make the first offer. Frankly, this is unrealistic. Sometimes this decision is out of your control. If you're selling your house tradition dictates that sellers make the first offer. If you decide not to make it you might be waiting a long time to sell. Likewise, if you get in a car accident caused by someone else and hire a lawyer to sue, tradition dictates that your attorney start the negotiations by sending the defendant a demand letter with an explanation of the accident's facts, your injuries, course of treatment, medical damages, and costs. This letter almost always concludes with a settlement offer.

Tradition often plays a major role in who starts. If tradition doesn't dictate this decision, however, or if you believe you might gain by bucking the trend, evaluate how you might achieve a strategic advantage by making the first offer. In other words, analyze the advantages and disadvantages of making first offers.

After analyzing the factors underlying whether you should make a first offer, we will then consider several situations where, as a general rule, you should or should not make a first offer.

Here's a preview of the advantages and disadvantages of making first offers. It should give you some additional context as you read.

Advantages to Making First Offers

- Set expectations
- Elicit genuine reaction
- Strategic advantages, i.e., leverage timing, information, etc.

Disadvantages to Making First Offers

- Lack of information to appropriately set it
- Other side gains important information
- Bracketing

First Offers—to Start or Not to Start?

Advantages to Making First Offers

Set Expectations

Longtime Wall Street lawyer James Freund, who was involved in many of the 1980s takeover battles, says he often likes to make the first offer on price matters, because it allows him to take control of the issue. If you are a knowledgeable buyer, he writes in *Smart Negotiating: How to Make Good Deals in the Real World,* you want the seller "negotiating off *your* opening number, not his own. Your bid sends a message to your counterpart: If he wants to play ball, here's the ballpark where the action will occur. Or, to change (and mix) metaphors, think of this as a first-strike deterrent against the seller shooting for the moon."

Freund makes an important point. Jumping out front with a first offer provides parties with the opportunity to set the initial offer-concession tone, and sends an important message to the other side about your range of acceptable numbers and the value you place on the item. You set the tone, mindset, and range for concessions. This has important strategic benefits.

When I was a college freshman I traveled to Jamaica for spring break. A short walk from our hotel was an outdoor market with a variety of items for sale, from cheap trinkets to intricate pieces of art. Prices varied hugely. While walking around one day a three-foot tall carved wooden bird of prey caught my eye. I thought it would look great guarding the entrance to my dorm room. (No accounting for taste, is there?) I approached the individual selling the sculpture and asked him what he wanted for it. He said, for me, he would sell it for $85 (U.S.). I laughed. I had no idea what it was worth or what any standards might justify. But I figured it was his first offer, and there was plenty of room to move. I also wanted him to know I was aware that haggling was expected in markets like this. I offered him $10.

A week later, just before flying back to Wisconsin, I paid $20 for the bird. I had visited him half a dozen times by then. Each day I dickered over the bird. In the end I figured I got a "fair" price. Why? Not because of any independent standard. For all I knew, he paid $1 for the bird. No, I thought $20 was fair because he moved down $65 and I moved up $10.

Critically, he controlled my understanding of the bird's value by making the first offer. His $85 first offer became the baseline by which I determined my $20 price was fair. If he had asked $150 to start and we ended up at $50, I probably would have felt just as satisfied—even though I would have paid $2\frac{1}{2}$ times more.

Controlling the negotiation dynamic and setting expectations is the major reason why most retail stores mark their products with a price tag. It's a first offer. They want you to just look at the product and accept their price as "fair."

Most customers, of course, accept these prices as nonnegotiable. Yet, many retail stores will at least match other's prices. Some negotiation room exists, dependent on your leverage (your BATNA is buying from the other store). Most stores also will negotiate over floor models and items with nicks or visual defects in them. Yet, many people don't even think to negotiate with retail stores. The retail industry has controlled and set our expectations in this venue.

For this same reason you also regularly see first offers for rates in many professional areas, like lawyers, accountants, doctors, and business consultants. When I practiced law I had a client who needed specialized help with some securities issues. Because I had no securities expertise I suggested he find a lawyer who focused on securities law. He found a securities lawyer who charged $475 per hour, probably the highest hourly rate in Phoenix at the time. My client hired him and told me he figured he was getting the best lawyer, due to the high rate charged. You get what you pay for, right? This lawyer's regular rate, his "first offer," set his clients' expectations as to his worth.

Elicit Genuine Reaction

Let's say you were looking to purchase a local bar and, in an effort to set expectations, made a first offer of $250,000. The seller then genuinely replied, "That's reasonable." How would you respond? Hopefully, you wouldn't move. Why not? You gained crucial strategic information solely from the seller's reaction to your offer. This is another advantage to making first offers—eliciting strategically critical information from your counterpart's genuine reaction.

Of course, it's not easy to evaluate the genuineness of parties' reactions. Sometimes, in fact, you must be especially wary. Roger Dawson, author of *Secrets of Power Negotiating,* suggests that everyone react to their counterparts' first offers by doing "The Flinch." Visibly flinch at their proposal, he suggests, by reacting "with shock and surprise." He recommends this because most people believe what they see more than what they hear. And if you *don't* visibly flinch, he believes, they will presume their first offer is reasonable.

I generally disagree with Dawson's suggestion. Expert negotiators will see through most individuals' renditions of "The Flinch." It thus will create an unnecessarily adversarial atmosphere. But Dawson's underlying rationale is correct: Parties send important messages about offers and concessions with their reactions. As a result, you want to: a) evaluate your counterpart's reactions to your offers and concessions, especially your first offers; and b) be ready to react (or not react) when responding to your counterpart's moves.

But how can you determine if your counterpart's reaction is genuine? Here are some tips. *One,* research your counterpart's reputation for "slippery" moves like the flinch and consider their credibility, or lack of credibility, during the negotiation. If I'm negotiating with someone I don't trust, I initially will assume his reaction is fake.

Two, evaluate if their reaction is consistent with your expectations and probe it. If your first offer, based on several independent standards, falls well within the reasonable range and they physically flinch when you state your offer, find out why. Ask them why they don't consider it "fair and reasonable." Get more information on which to determine the genuineness of their reaction. Then draw your conclusion. Don't just accept their reaction as genuine or presume it's fake.

Finally, go with your hunches. We consciously and unconsciously perceive an almost unlimited number of verbal and nonverbal signals from our counterparts. Our conclusions, based on these factors, often come in the form of hunches. Go with them. At the least you will feel better about your conclusions than if you fight them and they prove right.

Strategic Advantages—Leverage Timing, Information, Etc.

You also gain by making the first offer in certain strategic situations. For instance, you may have an upcoming deadline that will weaken your leverage if you have not reached an agreement by then (perhaps your BATNA will disappear). If you can't get your counterpart to make the first offer, you may need to make it to speed up the pace.

Sales people in many industries work on quotas that conclude at the end of their companies' fiscal year. Companies also regularly report earnings and profits at particular times of the year. Companies' need to conclude certain negotiations can be driven by their changing leverage situations during these times. This may prompt them to make first offers in situations where they might otherwise wish to wait.

Another situation where companies find it advantageous to make first offers is when they possess significantly more strategically important information than their counterparts *and* they may be forced to disclose that information in the future. Often they couple their first offer with trying to quickly reach agreement. This is especially true where the information they possess, when shared, will weaken their leverage. Insurance companies in certain accident cases often will make first offers to injured parties shortly after the accident has occurred, where it's clear that the company's insured was the one who caused the accident. Why? The insurance company has investigated the accident quickly and determined that its leverage may weaken if the injured party retains an attorney. Interestingly, the injured party may also prefer to settle early, before retaining an attorney. This depends on the fee charged by the attorney.

Various parties in lawsuits may also want to settle early and make a first offer if they have smoking-gun-type documents they want to keep confidential. If the other side ultimately obtains those documents it will weaken their leverage by making an adverse trial result more likely.

In other circumstances your counterpart may just refuse to make the first offer. Depending on your leverage, you may have to make the first offer or walk. In that case it's logical to make the first offer, even though it may not be ideal.

In determining whether to make a first offer, consider such advantages as: 1) setting expectations and controlling the offer-concession dynamic;

2) eliciting and judging your counterpart's genuine reaction; and 3) strategically determining whether and when your leverage or information has reached a vital stage.

Of course, it's equally critical to consider the disadvantages to making a first offer. If the disadvantages appear greater than the advantages, try to get your counterpart to make the first offer.

Disadvantages to Making First Offers

Lack of Information to Appropriately Set It
The biggest disadvantage to making a first offer occurs when parties lack sufficient information or independent standards to determine an appropriate starting point. If this happens you just may lose a great deal, and you may never even know it. The following story, as described in Donald Gifford's *Legal Negotiations*, vividly makes this point.

Thomas Edison invented the "Universal" stock ticker, a device used for many years by brokerage houses. When Edison first offered this device for sale he added up the time and effort he had put into inventing it and concluded he was entitled to $5,000 for it. That's what he decided to ask for it. Ultimately, though, he figured he would accept $3,000.

When General Lefferts, the president of the Gold & Stock Telegraph Company, came to negotiate, Edison was going to name his price. But he couldn't, Edison said, because he "hadn't the nerve to name such a large sum." Instead, Edison asked General Lefferts to make him an offer.

Lefferts offered $40,000. Edison said he thought that was "fair." *Edison would have lost $35,000 just by making the first offer.*

In a free market the price of an invention, a house, or any item depends upon many factors. Most important, however, is what someone Is willing to pay for it. If you're selling something, how do you maximize its value and get the most you can?

One thing you *don't* do is make the first offer without sufficient information or standards to reasonably evaluate its worth to a potential buyer. Edison would have thrown away $35,000, just by naming his price first.

In fact, Edison appeared to make two fundamental negotiation mistakes in selling his stock ticker.

First, he didn't adequately prepare. He figured the stock ticker was worth $3,000–$5,000, based on the effort he had put into creating it. But what about the stock ticker's worth to General Lefferts, the potential buyer? Or to other potential buyers? Both Edison's effort *and* potential buyers' need for it should have been researched *before* the negotiation started.

Second, Edison likely didn't engage in enough information gathering *during* the negotiation. Remember Golden Rule One: Information Is Power—So Get It. If he had asked, Edison might have found out important information about the stock ticker's use and value to Lefferts, or learned other critical factors impacting its value. You can't find out if you don't ask. In short, Edison likely didn't sufficiently evaluate the parties' interests, leverage, or objective criteria.

Fortunately for Edison, he made up for these mistakes by getting Lefferts to make the first offer. The lesson? If unsure about an item's value, don't make the first offer.

Edison said General Leffert's $40,000 offer was "fair." Perhaps. But I bet he could have gotten more. After all, it was Leffert's "first offer."

If you don't have enough information, especially about your leverage and the independent standards, don't make the first offer.

Rule of thumb: *When in doubt don't start out.*

Other Side Gains Important Information

As you know, information is power. When making a first offer you inevitably provide your counterpart with information about your evaluation of the matter. By doing this you're giving away power. In some cases the advantages outweigh this disadvantage. In others they don't.

What information are you providing that may be to your disadvantage? It depends on your offer and how you communicate it. At the least you will likely share information about your priorities and what you consider an acceptable result.

Assume you don't have sufficient cash to close a deal until November 1, so your first offer sets November 5 as the closing date. If this is unusual by industry standards, you just communicated important information about your cash-flow needs. Or perhaps you ask for a promotion and a new title from your boss and initially don't raise the salary issue. Your boss may infer that you don't care much about your salary, just because you didn't initially raise the issue.

The important point? Evaluate the advantages and disadvantages of providing information in your first offer. Beware of giving up too much power in making a first offer. It may come back to haunt you.

Bracketing

Another disadvantage to making a first offer results from "bracketing." In bracketing, the party responding to a first offer selects its counter so that the center of the two parties' starting points is its desired end point. In effect, the party going second picks the center. This provides them with an advantage, as parties generally expect the center of both sides' initial offers to be an inherently "fair" result. After all, both parties moved the same amount to get there, right?

Assume you offer $200 for my skis, and I ultimately want to sell them for $250. I can bracket your $200 first offer by initially countering at $300. It then appears more natural and fair to end up at $250. This operates to the disadvantage of the party making the first offer.

In short, remember my rule of thumb: When in doubt don't start out.

Situations Where You Should Make the First Offer

So, where do the advantages of making the first offer usually outweigh the disadvantages? Here are a few general examples:

- Situations involving sophisticated parties with substantial access to information
- Situations involving complex nonprice issues and technically detailed agreements
- Situations where you have more information, defined standards, and strong leverage

Situations Involving Sophisticated Parties with Substantial Access to Information

It often makes sense to make first offers in situations with equally knowledgeable sophisticated parties on both sides who have thoroughly researched each side's goals, interests, expectations, leverage, and standards. When both sides fully understand the leverage equation and the independent standards involved, the range of mutually beneficial options tends to be more limited. The downside of making a first offer here—lack of information and providing information to the other side—is relatively minimal. The upside—setting expectations and controlling the offer-concession dynamic—often outweighs it.

One example might be a merger where each company has already thoroughly investigated the other's financial and strategic position. Another might involve equally sophisticated parties in service industries, like in law or accounting, where industry or professional standards dominate the fee-setting situation.

Situations Involving Complex Nonprice Issues and Technically Detailed Agreements

Parties often find it advantageous to make first offers when negotiating complex nonprice issues in which the initial offer includes a detailed written document or proposal. If you lease commercial office space, you will benefit by making a first offer that includes your "standard" lease. You want your document, not the lessee's, to be the working draft of the agreement.

This is true whenever a negotiation begins with detailed written agreements or provisions. Get your agreement out there first and maintain control of the document and the changes. Make the other side convince you to change the document. While this is more evenhanded now than it used to be, since e-mailed documents make revisions easier for both parties, it still makes strategic sense.

Situations Where You Have More Information, Defined Standards, and Strong Leverage

Finally, seriously consider making the first offer when you have substantially more information than the other side, enjoy strong leverage, and want to signal intransigence on certain issues, based on specific standards. This is especially true when your policies limit your flexibility. The earlier and more consistently your counterpart understands certain issues are off the table, the better.

Prices listed by retail stores and hotels fall into this category. In effect, they are making first offers. Disney did this when it bought the land for Walt Disney World. While house sellers traditionally make the first offer, there Disney did it. It set up dummy corporations to make first offers to property owners in the area. It did this to maximize its leverage, as it didn't want anyone to know its plans for Walt Disney World. It had a significant need for the land, but didn't want any sellers to know it. Disney then made first offers to the property owners and used comps (market value and precedent) on previously purchased properties as independent standards. Commercial real estate developers often do the same thing when buying land for shopping centers or other developments. It makes sense to make the first offer in these situations.

Where to Start

Once you have decided whether to make the first offer you still must determine where to start. This can be difficult. You don't want to be like Edison and risk leaving a lot on the table. Yet, you don't want to poison the atmosphere by appearing unrealistic. You also need to give yourself enough room to move, so everyone ultimately feels comfortable they reached a "fair" result. Remember Roger's divorce? His first offer didn't provide him with sufficient room to move. It would have been difficult for his wife to ever consider a result "fair" if she moved considerably more than him.

How can you strike the right balance? There are five main factors to evaluate in making this decision:

- First-offer expectations peculiar to your industry or context
- Your original goal
- Your most aggressive, yet reasonable, independent standard
- The "room to move" psychological gamesmanship dynamic
- Special factors underlying first counters

Let's see how these factors work in the context of buying a small business.

Henry is a successful businessman in his midforties who was just laid off as vice president of sales of a large computer manufacturer. Fortunately, Henry received a decent severance package, and he and his wife (an elementary school teacher) had saved $1 million for their retirement. Most of this came in stock options he received while moving up the corporate ladder. He and his wife and two teenage kids, after a great deal of discussion, have decided to change their lifestyle and move from Los Angeles to Mountainside. Mountainside is a small resort town where the economy revolves around seasonal vacationers. In the winter there's skiing at a resort that's regionally well-known. In the summer a large public lake draws thousands of families wishing to escape the heat of the nearby desert. Both teenage kids love to snow and water ski, and Henry and his wife want to experience a more laid-back lifestyle. This move, however, is contingent on Henry finding a reasonable source of income in Mountainside.

Importantly, Henry has always wanted to own a bar and pizza restaurant. His parents owned a pizza place while he was growing up, and he has fond memories of it. Mountainside also is experiencing a significant growth spurt, due largely to an aggressive advertising campaign started two years ago by the area's chamber of commerce. Lakefront homes, to Henry's surprise, generally cost around $500,000, and the residential real estate market has been appreciating by about 20 percent annually. Henry thinks this move will be economically profitable, and prudent long-term, too.

Henry would like to buy Bill's Pizza and Bar. Its location is great—right on Main Street in the middle of town. While it's not listed for sale, Henry spoke with its owner, Bill Johnson, and believes Bill would sell at the right price. Bill is sixty years old and has run the restaurant and bar his entire life. He inherited it from his parents, original residents in the area. Bill is married with kids and grandkids, but all his kids and grandkids have moved away. In short, Henry believes Bill is ready to retire if the right opportunity arises.

Should Henry start with a first offer? If so, where should he start?

Here Henry wants Bill to set the opening price. Bill likely knows the bar and pizza market in Mountainside better than anyone. Henry, despite thoroughly researching the market, may never obtain Bill's breadth of information about the local market and trends.

Henry thus talks at length with Bill about the possibility of selling. In these conversations, it becomes clear Bill will not make the first offer. In fact, Henry asks Bill to name a price, and Bill refuses. In part, this reflects Bill's strong leverage: He is happy, has a successful business, and has no need to sell. While he might sell, his alternative—continuing to run the business—is perfectly acceptable.

In asking Bill to make a first offer, however, Henry found out important information. Bill owns the land and building free and clear. Bill thus told Henry not to include the land and building in his offer. Bill wants to lease it so he has some continuing income.

Largely due to Bill's leverage, Henry must make the first move. The timing of the negotiation, however, is also hurting Henry. It's June, and Henry wants to move during the summer so his wife and kids can start school in the fall.

Let's examine the factors Henry should consider in deciding what to initially offer. Consider these in your negotiations, too.

First-Offer Expectations Peculiar to Your Industry or Context

Expectations exist in various industries and contexts as to who makes the first offer. Similar expectations often exist regarding the nature of the offer or first counter. As noted earlier, in the personal injury field plaintiffs' lawyers customarily make the first offer. It's also almost always extremely high. Insurance companies usually respond with lowball counters. Then the more realistic "negotiating" begins.

In the hospitality industry hotels' first offers to potential conventions often include very reasonable room and facility charges. This is accompanied, however, with relatively high food and beverage charges. Food and beverage have a large profit margin in the industry. Knowing this provides convention organizers with critical information in determining where to start.

Find out what first offer or first counter expectations exist in your industry. If you don't, you risk sending the wrong signal concerning what you ultimately will find acceptable. The messages you send at the start have a disproportionate impact, just like first impressions when you meet someone. Make this move count.

Back to Henry and Bill. Assume Henry researches the expectations of those in the retail bar and restaurant business in mountain resort towns. Unfortunately, he finds that few expectations exist concerning who makes the first offer, especially given Bill's personal circumstances.

What's Henry's next step? Evaluate his original goal and the objective basis underlying it.

Your Original Goal

In chapter 1 we addressed how to set aggressive, realistic goals and expectations. Here we apply this to the offer-concession context. At the onset of the offer-concession stage you should have an excellent idea of your leverage and your most favorable independent standards. Based on these reassess your goals and, if necessary, reset them. Make these goals your touchstone. In other words, where you start and how far you move each time should be evaluated relative to your goals. Your goals should drive your offer-concession strategy.

In reassessing Henry's goal, let's first analyze his leverage.

The Parties' Level of Needs

Henry's leverage initially does not appear strong. While he and his family have sufficient funds for the near future, their retirement and children's college funds will rapidly deplete with no steady income. They also have already mentally committed to moving to Mountainside, further weakening their leverage. Time also is working against them. It's now June, and school starts in September. In short, Henry has a strong need to move forward quickly. On our need scale, Henry has a High Need Level (−1).

On the plus side, Henry's wife has found out there's a substantial demand for elementary school teachers in Mountainside. Her job prospects appear excellent, even as late as August.

Bill's need, by comparison, is low. He isn't looking to sell, but will if the right opportunity arises. This element of his leverage is strong. On the need scale, he has a Low Need Level (−1).

The parties' level of needs: Advantage Bill. Henry's Need Score is −2.

Henry's Need Score: −2

Weakest −4   −3   **−2**   −1   0   +1   +2   +3   +4 Strongest

The Parties' BATNAs

Few alternatives exist for Henry in Mountainside. He has looked around the area for another computer-related job or for an alternative bar/restaurant to purchase, but nothing is currently available. Of course, he could always buy some land or lease a storefront and start from scratch. But that would require a level of risk he and his family consider too high. If Henry stopped with only these alternatives, he would have a Poor BATNA Value (−2).

However, let's say Henry understood the weakness of these alternatives and took specific steps to improve these by looking for work in the Los Angeles area. While not ideal, a Los Angeles–based job offer would strengthen his leverage in his negotiations with Bill. Fortunately, his efforts paid off, as he has been offered a midlevel management position with a start-up computer company near their present home. While his initial income would be less than at his previous job, it could potentially provide excellent long-term compensation. Henry's BATNA Value would thus move from Poor (−2) to Okay (0).

Bill's BATNA, by comparison, is to continue to run his pizza place. And let's say he has tried to improve his BATNA by locating other potential buyers, but has been unsuccessful. Overall, though, his BATNA Value is Good (−1).

Again, Advantage Bill. Henry's BATNA Score is −1.

Henry's BATNA Score: -1

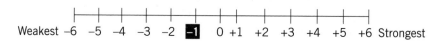

Henry's Overall Leverage: −3

This puts Henry's Overall Leverage at a −3 position, fairly weak. Bill is definitely in the driver's seat from a leverage perspective.

Henry's Overall Leverage: −3

Possible Independent Standards

In reevaluating his original goal, Henry has also thoroughly researched the pizza/bar/restaurant business around Mountainside and found the following independent standards:

Market value: Given Mountainside's small size, there appears to be no substantial market in the sale of bars and restaurants. However, Henry found several restaurants and bars that changed hands in the last five years. Two blocks from Bill's, just off Main Street, an Italian bar and restaurant named Giovanni's sold three years ago for $350,000. In talking with the current owner (an older Italian gentleman who bought it after selling a similar-size bar/restaurant in Boston's North End), Henry found that Giovanni's grossed about $150,000 annually the year before it sold, with profits around $75,000. It currently grosses around $300,000 annually.

Henry also found that Rick's Bar and Pizza, located on the outskirts of Mountainside near the ski resort, sold two years ago for $200,000. Its new owner told Henry that it grossed $100,000 annually the year before it sold, with profits around $50,000. Most of its business is delivery. The owner refused to share her current level of business or profits.

Finally, Henry found a biker bar (Harley's) on Main Street a block from Bill's that sold a year ago for $800,000. While it doesn't offer food, it does a significant bar business year-round. Henry estimates it annually grosses about $250,000.

Each of these bar/restaurants is about the same physical size as Bill's. However, the location and nature of each obviously differs. Each also leases its facilities from others.

Precedent: Other than the sale of the businesses noted above, Henry was unable to find any recent relevant precedent.

Industry standards/expertise: Henry's investment banker friend tells him that, generally speaking, bar/restaurants in small vacation towns usually sell for between two and three times gross revenues, depending on the area and nature of the business. The biggest variables involve location and customer base. But this is also very difficult to predict, given the relative lack of a market in these areas.

Costs/profits: Bill's grosses $400,000 a year with annual profits around $150,000. Its gross has doubled in the last four years due to the increased volume of vacationers in the summer and skiers and snowboarders in the winter.

Efficiency: Henry has reviewed a summary of Bill's books and operations, under a confidentiality agreement, and believes he can increase Bill's efficiency by updating the ovens, decreasing its energy use, lowering its food costs through bulk buying from a large distributor in a nearby metropolitan area (Bill buys from a longtime family friend in Mountainside), and utilizing more modern business practices. Bill also has never focused on pizza delivery, and Henry believes he can build a significant delivery business, especially given the area's growth. Overall, he thinks he can increase Bill's efficiency by 15 percent by the end of his first year, increasing his profits by about $25,000 annually.

Based on his leverage and these standards, what should be Henry's aggressive yet realistic goal?

I would set Henry's financial goal—where he wants the negotiation to end—at $975,000. Twice gross would be $800,000 and three times gross would be $1.2 million. Marketwise, Giovanni's sold three years ago for 2.33 times gross, and it's off Main Street. Rick's, on the outskirts of town, sold two years ago for twice gross. And Harley's on Main Street sold last year for what Henry estimates at 3.2 times gross (assuming it did about $250,000 gross last year). This goal also takes into account Bill's location with a steady customer base, significant walk-in business, plus Henry's potential to increase the restaurant's profits by increasing its efficiency and building a delivery business. Finally, Henry's relatively weak leverage must be factored into this calculation, as should his interest in a future relationship with Bill.

Based on these factors, Henry might realistically expect to pay closer to $1 million. One million would be exactly 2.5 times Bill's gross, and that's the center point of Henry's expert's industry-standard range of values. However, this does not take into account the inevitable intangible factors that may impact the negotiation process. I would be more aggressive and set Henry's expectation at $975,000.

Knowing this goal, however, is only one part of the decision-making process in determining your first offer. You should also rely on your most aggressive, yet still reasonable, independent standard.

Your Most Aggressive, Yet Reasonable, Independent Standard

What is Henry's most favorable independent standard, and why do we care? In making an initial offer, parties should usually start with their most aggressive realistic expectation *that can be justified in some objective way with an independent standard*. If Henry first offers $600,000, which has no objective basis and cannot be justified by any independent standard, Bill will likely walk and potentially feel personally offended. It's not even close to the ballpark by any standard. Since Bill probably has as much, if not more, information about the market value and independent standards as Henry, this first offer must pass the straight face test. It should have a high likelihood of generating a serious counter.

If Bill's leverage were extremely weak—perhaps he was desperate and Henry had an excellent BATNA—a $600,000 lowball offer might make sense. Here $600,000 would be a slap in the face.

What's the lowest independently justifiable offer Henry might select? Henry's most favorable independent standard is the market value sale of Rick's two years ago for twice gross. Henry's twice gross calculation is $800,000. This also is consistent with the lowest end of the industry standard and his expert's opinion.

But we're not yet done. There's still a significant factor yet to be evaluated—the psychological gamesmanship element that impacts every offer-concession dynamic.

The "Room to Move" Psychological Gamesmanship Dynamic

In determining where to start, as we've discussed, you should consider: the first-offer expectations peculiar to your industry or context; your original goal; and your most aggressive, yet reasonable, independent standard. The final factor in determining where to start involves making sure that you build into your starting point sufficient "room to move," so your counterpart feels that he or she psychologically achieved success. Here are four steps to take to ensure you adequately take this into consideration:

- Get into your counterpart's head
- Game it out
- Use round numbers
- Throw an anchor

Get into Your Counterpart's Head

To build in sufficient room to move, you must get into your counterpart's head and evaluate his or her goals and responses throughout the offer-concession stage. What are Bill's goals and expectations? What might Bill consider a "fair and reasonable" first offer? What is Bill's reputation for bargaining, if any? Does he appear to be reasonable? How might Bill perceive a lowball offer? How well does Bill know Henry? Does Bill have an interest in selling to someone whose family was in the pizza business? Might he accept less as a result? If Bill keeps the building and land, how might Henry incorporate the lease payments, if any, into the negotiation?

Explore these issues *before* making a first offer. In fact, many of these issues should be explored before engaging in any serious discussions with Bill.

Game It Out

Henry also should play out several possible offer-concession scenarios in a brainstorming session with a friend, keeping in mind that parties tend to move toward the center of the two opening offers.

The starting point of these scenarios should be his goal. How can he structure the offer-concession process so he ends up at $975,000 or better? Let's examine several scenarios. If Henry offers $800,000, based on the twice gross justification and Rick's Pizza's selling price, and Bill counters by bracketing him at $1.2 million, based on the three-times-gross justification and Harley's selling price, what's the center? It's $1 million—which might be Bill's goal. Individuals tend to think in round numbers, and $1 million has a ring to it. Plus, as noted above, $1 million would be exactly $2\frac{1}{2}$ times Bill's gross. That's the center of Henry's expert's industry standard range of values. But this is $25,000 higher than Henry's expectation. So, assuming Bill likely will start at $1.2 million, strike the $800,000 initial offer.

What if Henry starts at $750,000 and justifies it by noting that he anticipates spending a significant sum to update Bill's facilities? Then the center of $750,000 and $1.2 million is $975,000. Starting at $750,000 also gives Henry plenty of room to move up to his goal, yet appears serious enough to generate a reasonable response.

Use Round Numbers

Pick a round number to start, even if your rationale justifies a more specific figure. If Henry were to decide his best starting point, taking into consideration the above factors, is $747,000, he should still start at $750,000. He should accompany this offer by explaining that his justification suggests a $747,000 starting point, but as a gesture of good faith, he will offer $750,000. By doing this, Henry will gain equity with Bill that likely will pay off in the end. Of course, Bill should lower his starting counter if it's not a round figure so he will gain the same equity with Henry. Small "favors" can often make large impressions.

Of course, reasonable minds differ on where to start. James Freund generally recommends that parties in sales transactions start not less than 10 percent or more than 33 percent away from where they want to end up. His preferred starting point is around 15–25 percent from the desired end point. In the Henry-Bill situation, taking $975,000 as Henry's goal, Freund would recommend Henry start between $650,000 and $877,500. Freund's preferred starting point falls between $731,250 and $828,750. Our $750,000 start lands squarely in this range.

Throw an Anchor

In determining your first offer also consider the "anchoring" effect. This refers to the extent that your starting point will impact your counterpart's expectation of what is reasonable. Research has found that negotiators have fairly changeable expectations early on in the negotiation process.

Thus, your first move, like first impressions, tends to have a disproportionate impact on your counterpart's expectations. In effect, it anchors their expectations of what they consider fair and reasonable moves throughout the offer-concession stage. Harvard Law School Professor Robert Mnookin in *Beyond Winning: Negotiating to Create Value in Deals and Disputes* describes a fascinating experiment that illustrates this:

> [A] group of subjects was asked to estimate the percentage of the United Nations member states that are in Africa. Before giving their estimates, the subjects were shown a spinning wheel of fortune that was marked with numbers from 1 to 100. For one set of subjects, the wheel stopped at 10; for another set the wheel stopped at 65. Even though the subjects knew that the result of the spin was random and completely unrelated to the estimate they were about to make, the median number in the first group [was] 25 and was 45 for the second. A similar pattern has been observed in negotiation settings.

Your first offer or first concession disproportionately impacts your counterpart's expectations, regardless of the standards involved. So throw an anchor, and then carefully evaluate its impact.

Critically, though, this anchoring process backfires if your first offer appears unreasonable. If your first offer is so exaggerated that your counterpart views you as bargaining in bad faith, any subsequent concessions lose their value, given your illegitimate starting point. According to psychologist Robert Cialdini, the "truly gifted negotiator is one whose initial position is exaggerated enough to allow for a series of reciprocal concessions that will yield a desirable final offer from the opponent, yet is not so outlandish as to be seen as illegitimate from the start." I agree.

Your starting point—either as a first offer or a first counter—should be your highest realistic expectation, based on legitimate independent standards and justifications.

Take this into consideration when you make these strategic decisions.

Special Factors Underlying First Counters

A quick note on first counteroffers, since they differ from first offers in two critical ways: 1) the countering party has already evaluated the messages sent by the other side's first offer; and 2) the countering party can bracket the first offer. The above first offer factors still apply to counters. But you should also evaluate these additional two factors.

Let's say Henry starts at $750,000 and justifies it as "fair and reasonable" by noting its market value as defined by Rick's sale, the industry standard per his expert, and his need to invest in new equipment. Bill's response should take into account: a) first-counter expectations peculiar to his industry or context; b) his original goal, based on his expectations and leverage; c) his most aggressive, yet reasonable, independent standard; d) the "room to move" psychological gamesmanship dynamic; *plus* e) Henry's first offer and accompanying message; and f) his ability to bracket if he wants.

Bill, largely due to his leverage and his superior knowledge of the Mountainside market, has a strategic advantage. He likely knows the individual who sold Rick's Pizza and can find a way to distinguish that "fair" standard from this transaction. He also might know the more intimate details of Harley's.

His major advantage, however, lies in his leverage and his evaluation of Henry's starting point. If I were advising Bill, I would first suggest he not respond immediately. Henry has time working against him (a fact likely known by Bill), and Bill has all the time in the world. A slight delay in responding will focus Henry on his weak leverage. I can just imagine Henry's kids pestering him with questions about whether and when they will be moving to Mountainside.

Regardless, Bill's major consideration in determining how to respond will revolve around Henry's first offer. If Henry started out unreasonably low Bill might not even respond. The idea there is to force Henry to "bet against himself." While no one wants to do this, sometimes your leverage is so weak that you either do it or walk. If walking is worse than betting against yourself, you should bet.

Alternatively, if Henry started at $850,000—a very "fair and reasonable" figure according to all the independent standards—Bill might respond with an equally "fair and reasonable" counter. As we will see later in this chapter, the principle of reciprocity governs much of the offer-concession process. If Henry starts out with a reasonable offer it's more likely Bill will respond with a reasonable counter. If Henry lowballs, Bill will be more likely to respond in kind on the high end. And so on. Reciprocal behavior doesn't always occur, but many feel a psychological tendency to reciprocate. In deciding how to counter a party's first offer, then, parties will often seek to send a similar message with their first counter.

Before we examine the rest of the offer-concession process, the chart on the next page shows a summary of the points we've addressed in determining whether and where to start. These issues are absolutely crucial, as Thomas Edison would tell you. Take these steps to heart as you make your own first-offer decisions.

GOLDEN RULE FOUR: DESIGN AN OFFER-CONCESSION STRATEGY

Know Your Offer-Concession Patterns

Whether and Where to Start (First-Offer Issues)
- First offers—to start or not to start
  - Advantages to making first offers
    - Set expectations
    - Elicit genuine reaction
    - Strategic advantages, i.e., leverage timing, information, etc.
  - Disadvantages to making first offers
    - Lack of information to appropriately set it
    - Other side gains important information
    - Bracketing

- Situations where you should make the first offer
  - Situations involving sophisticated parties with substantial access to information
  - Situations involving complex nonprice issues and technically detailed agreements
  - Situations where you have more information, defined standards, and strong leverage

- Where to start
  - First-offer expectations peculiar to your industry or context
  - Your original goal
  - Your most aggressive, yet reasonable, independent standard
  - The "room to move" psychological gamesmanship dynamic
    - Get into your counterpart's head
    - Game it out
    - Use round numbers
    - Throw an anchor
  - Special factors underlying first counters

What about the rest of the offer-concession process? After the first offer and counter, what next? How far should the parties' move and when? What if your counterpart doesn't reciprocate with an equally reasonable and independently justifiable counter? What if Henry starts at $750,000, and Bill counters by bracketing Henry with a highly aggressive counter at $1.5 million, a figure no independent standard can justify? The center then becomes $1.125 million. What does Henry do? Here are some thoughts on this next stage. Often these psychological dynamics dominate the entire offer-concession stage.

Psychological Expectations Underlying Offer-Concession Behavior

Let's say I want to buy the house at 123 Negotiation Lane and it's listed at $300,000. I do my research, analyze comparable sales in the neighborhood, find out how long it's been on the market, evaluate its renovations, and conclude it's worth $290,000. Figuring I will pay $290,000, I offer $270,000. It's my first offer, right? To my shock the seller accepts. My response? Do I jump with joy I got such a great deal? No. I feel I could have done better.

Why? The seller defied my expectations. In doing this she caused me to question my analysis. It's natural to feel this way, even though this reaction may be unjustified, based on my standards and leverage.

People evaluate offers and concessions based on their expectations. They ask: To what extent is my counterpart's behavior consistent with my own expectations and why? Here are the most critical psychological elements impacting parties' behavior during the offer-concession stage. Study them. Then put them into practice in your negotiations.

- Play the negotiation expectation game
- Ways to counter expectations
- The reciprocity principle
- The contrast principle
- The commitment and consistency principle

Play the Negotiation Expectation Game

I call this the "Negotiation Expectation Game," and it's a critical psychological element underlying offer-concession behavior. In short, it means we must understand parties' expectations and make our offers and concessions accordingly.

Here are five common offer-concession expectations and a rule of thumb for each. For maximum effectiveness use these in conjunction with the standards discussed in chapter 3. Plus, these expectations and rules of thumb, similar to general concession patterns, may not exist in certain industries or contexts. Exceptions exist. So evaluate each negotiation context according to its parties' own expectations.

Finally, tactics exist to overcome some of these expectations. We will discuss these. But start with the presumption that these expectations exist.

Expectation: First offers and first counteroffers always have negotiating room built into them.

Rule of Thumb: Almost never say yes to the first offer or counter.

While exceptions apply to practically every rule, this one is pretty sacrosanct. In most contexts, almost everyone includes substantial flexibility in their first offer and anticipates making significant concessions. So, don't accept right away. Counter it. Even if you're accurate according to your analysis of the objective standards, you still may leave items on the table. Consider *their* expectations in your counter.

Expectation: Parties tend to gravitate toward the center of two starting points.

Rule of Thumb: If you make the first offer, build in sufficient room to move, as the "center" will be determined by your counterpart. If you make the first counteroffer, "bracket" the first offer so the "center" becomes your reasonably expected result, assuming you can justify your counter by some standard.

If I've listed an antique clock for $100, and you offer me $60, we will likely gravitate toward $80—regardless of the clock's true market value. If I offer you $2 for your pet rock, and you counter by requesting $10, where do you think we will end up? Around $6, right?

Remember Roger's presumption in his divorce that they would end up at around $500,000 if his soon-to-be ex-wife started at $1 million and he started at $100,000? While he ignored other elements of the offer-concession dynamic, he was right about this. Of course, he tried to "cut to the chase" by suggesting that this dynamic existed and then starting at $450,000 instead of at $100,000. This was not prudent. He ignored the fact that in the adversarial atmosphere of his divorce negotiation his attempt to discount the center-moving dynamic's relevance would likely be viewed solely as a tactical statement intended to gain an advantage. He ignored his counterpart's expectations. As such, his wife and her attorney—understanding this center-moving dynamic—changed their expectations of a $500,000 agreement (near the center of $100,000 and $1 million) to one closer to $750,000 (near the center of $450,000 and $1 million).

Why do we gravitate toward the center? In part we believe that if you move the same amount I move, it must be inherently "fair." This is not based on any independent standard, but on our general expectations, intuition, and ego. Interestingly, it also tends to be self-fulfilling. If we assume each side will move about the same amount and consider "fair" the midpoint of each side's starting position, we will account for this in our offers and concessions.

Knowing this, build in sufficient room to move if you make the first offer, given that the center will be determined by your counterpart bracketing you.

Expectation: Parties' offers and concessions follow a consistent pattern. Equal-size concessions create the perception of unending concessions, and consecutively smaller concessions suggest parties are nearing their end point.

Rule of Thumb: Taper your concessions so they become smaller and smaller and make your last concession a particularly small one.

In 2002 I listed my 1991 Nissan 300ZX for $9,500. Let's say you offer me $5,000 to buy it. I then move $1,000, to $8,500. You counter at $5,500 and I subsequently move another $1,000 (down to $7,500). What have I communicated with my concession behavior? Every time you push I concede an additional $1,000. If I were you I would just keep on pushing.

Alternatively, let's say I first conceded $1,000 to $8,500, then conceded $500 to $8,000, and then conceded $100 to $7,900. I just communicated to you, more powerfully than stating it, that I was right near the end.

Figure out where you want to go, how you want to get there, and be aware of patterns including the size pattern here. Consecutively tapering your offers and concessions sends the appropriate message. Analyze your counterparts' patterns, too. They're also sending signals.

But don't be predictable. Mix it up. If each time you move by half the amount of your last move, your counterpart likely will do the math and figure where you want to end. Don't forecast this message.

Expectation: You rarely get something for nothing.

Rule of Thumb: Always ask for a reciprocal concession.

This sounds basic. Yet many people don't do it, especially near the end. Perhaps you sell computers to large corporations and a new customer recently ordered 500 laptops. After the contract is signed your customer asks if you can deliver two weeks earlier than expected. If the laptops will be ready, you might be inclined to say "no problem."

Resist the urge. Instead, ask for something in return, a trade-off, even if it's just a future IOU. You might half-jokingly state, "Sure. No problem. Happy to do it. Just remember this next time I ask you for a favor." Let them know it's costing you something, if only your time. You don't want your customer to get the impression you give value away for nothing. If they do, many will just keep grinding until there's nothing left to give.

Of course, don't respond in a demanding or confrontational way. That would be counterproductive.

Expectation: Splitting the difference appears to be a fair way to end, when little divides the parties.

Rule of Thumb: Get the other side to offer to split the difference first, then either bracket it or accept it if the difference is minimal.

"Let's just split the difference," he suggested after we had negotiated all day over my client's lawsuit. Our last offer was $320,000; his last was $300,000.

Sounds fair, right? Almost everyone has used this technique when negotiations drag on. After all, splitting the difference means both parties compromise and give an equal amount. What's wrong with that?

The following response in the above negotiation illustrates its problems.

"Let's see," I responded. "You're saying you will come up to $310,000, right?"

"Right," he responded. "But only if you come down to $310,000."

"Tell you what I will do," I said. "I will take your $310,000 offer to my client and see what he says, okay?"

"Uhhh, okay," he responded.

What just happened? My counterpart's split-the-difference offer just turned into a $10,000 concession. He's now mentally and orally committed to $310,000, and we're still at $320,000. We have yet to concede a dime.

I then spoke to my client and returned. "My client wanted to stick at $320,000," I said, "but I convinced him that would lead to an impasse. He ultimately agreed to $315,000." I then said how it would be a shame to leave after negotiating all day with only $5,000 separating us.

My counterpart then offered to split the difference again, and we settled at $312,500.

This negotiation illustrates the problems with offering to split the difference. First, the party making the split-the-difference offer often loses proportionately more at the end. In the above case my client—the recipient of the offer—ended up with $2,500 more than the split-the-difference amount at $310,000.

This resulted from bracketing. When you offer to split the difference you're effectively making a first offer. In doing so you're giving the other side the opportunity to bracket the offer to its benefit. Each time the other side does this, and you concede by more than your proposed "split the difference" amount, you lose more proportionately.

Second, the recipient of the split-the-difference offer always benefits because the person offering to split the difference inevitably feels he won. Why? In the end the recipient most likely had to be "convinced" to make the final concession and to ultimately accept the offerer's last proposal. This is psychologically important, as most parties want to leave negotiations with good relationships.

So, what should you do regarding "splitting the difference"? Roger Dawson in *Secrets of Power Negotiating* makes some useful suggestions:

Don't offer to split the difference. Get the other side to suggest it. You can often prompt a split-the-difference offer near the end of negotiations by lamenting the small amount between the parties' offers and the significant time everyone has spent negotiating.

Don't accept the notion that splitting the difference is "fair." It's not. Conceding the same amount doesn't make it fair. Fairness depends on the standards or principled basis underlying your offer or concession.

If you're selling a used car for its Blue Book value of $15,000, and a potential buyer offers $10,000, splitting the difference at $12,500 makes no sense. The Blue Book value reflects an objective basis for your used car's market value. Splitting the difference means, in that context, simply giving up $2,500.

Of course, you might argue that the amounts at issue near the end of many negotiations don't make a big difference. That may be true. It may also cost you.

Ignoring these expectations will also cost you, in part because they play an integral role in negotiations. They have an independent value that must be strategically considered. Roger in his divorce tried to "cut to the chase." It didn't work. In fact, it made the negotiation *more* contentious and lengthy.

The process of give-and-take makes an independent difference and must be considered and valued, not viewed as a waste of time. Often, regardless of an item's objective value, both sides need to feel the other side gave up something significant. This is a critical psychological dynamic. Only when both sides *feel* the other moved enough will they accept the result as "fair."

Ways to Counter Expectations

Roger tried to counter the center-moving expectation by saying he was going to save everybody time and money by starting and ending near the middle. It didn't work because:

a) This would not have given his soon-to-be ex-wife the feeling that he had sacrificed (or conceded) enough for her to be comfortable with the end result.
b) He wrongly assumed that his soon-to-be ex-wife shared his goal of resolving the conflict efficiently (she may have needed a more protracted negotiation process to accomplish her goal of causing him some pain).
c) He didn't sufficiently consider the increased expectations his statement would cause.
d) His counterpart viewed his statement that he could "short-circuit" the process purely as a tactical ploy designed to gain an advantage.

But he was generally correct about where they would end up. So, is there a way Roger could have truly short-circuited the process and moved there more efficiently? Given all the other factors involved, especially his soon-to-be ex-wife's goal, I don't think he could have credibly accomplished this here.

There are circumstances and tactics, though, that can mitigate the impact of these expectations and the "games" that go along with them. Understand, however, that you will generally face an uphill battle if you try. Most individuals start with these expectations, and it's risky to seek to counter them. Of course, it may be worth the risk.

What are these counter-expectation tactics?

A Well-Known Reputation May Counter Expectations

Roger failed to convince his counterparts of his sincerity because he lacked credibility in making his "cut to the chase" statement. Roger could not overcome their expectations that his statement was solely self-serving. They just didn't believe him. The most effective way to counter the above expectations is by developing a credible reputation that overcomes the expectation. If Roger had a reputation in the business community for consistently using this tactic, *and his soon-to-be ex-wife and her lawyer knew and/or could independently confirm it*, it might have worked.

For instance, there is a negotiation tactic called "Boulwarism." It's named after a General Electric labor negotiator in the 1950s, Lemuel R. Boulware. In short, individuals using this tactic initially present an offer that they explicitly characterize as a first offer, a fair offer, a firm offer, and a final offer. First, fair, firm, and final. That's it. This tactic runs counter to many of the expectations described above. There's no movement from the starting point. There's no request for a counter. There's no center-moving or split the difference. Boulwarism condenses the entire offer-concession stage into one offer. By doing so it attempts to achieve a degree of efficiency that the usual negotiation process lacks.

Is it effective? Sometimes. It depends on who does it and how it's received. For Boulwarism to work, the entity must consistently use it *and* have a reputation for it. In other words, it *only* works if your counterparts believe your offer is truly firm and final. If ACME, for example, tries to use this tactic with Supplier A but not with Supplier B, it will get burned. Supplier A likely will find out about Supplier B and will assume, like Roger's ex-wife, that ACME's offer is not really firm and final. There ACME will only have succeeded in creating a more adversarial and protracted negotiation with Supplier A. However, if all of ACME's suppliers know ACME does business this way and never makes exceptions they will find it more acceptable.

Some insurance companies use this with plaintiffs' personal injury lawyers in cases with clear liability and relatively minimal damages. They do this effectively because, even though many plaintiffs' lawyers don't consider their offers "fair," the lawyers' only alternative (BATNA) is to try the case. Since that would be expensive and time-consuming, especially in small-dollar cases, many lawyers simply recommend that their clients accept the offer. This works sometimes because plaintiffs' personal injury lawyers are usually paid a percentage of what they collect, so taking small cases through trial is rarely cost-effective or profitable for the lawyer.

Of course, Boulwarism does not completely overcome parties' expectations. In fact, its biggest problem is that the recipients of this strategy often don't feel particularly satisfied, regardless of the deal's "fairness" being based on independent standards. They had no control over the process and did not perceive the other side as moving in "good faith" toward their position.

By the way, the most effective counters to Boulwarism are: (a) provide the individual using Boulwarism all the information and standards favoring your side early enough, so they can use it in calculating their "first, fair, firm, and final" offer; and b) assuming you have ongoing negotiations with the individual, change their evaluation of a "fair" offer by exercising your leverage often enough and walking. In the insurance context, plaintiffs' attorneys have done this by taking many of the "Boulwaristic" insurance companies' cases to trial. In effect, they try to create a new "market value" for the cases and a new definition of "fair" from the company's standpoint. In the short run this can be expensive and time-consuming. In the long run it can impact the overall dynamic and change Boulwaristic behavior.

A negotiator's credible, consistent, and well-known reputation for engaging in strategies that counter the above expectations can be effectively used in some contexts.

Aggressively Stick to Independent Standards

Aggressive, consistent use of certain independent standards can also lessen the impact of expectations. The use of tradition and "we've always done it this way" tends to reduce the influence of the normal give-and-take expectation. In many industries negotiators have more flexibility on some issues than others. Where they have little flexibility, they often cite long-standing policy, tradition, or specific precedents for not moving— perhaps even sticking to their first and "final" offer. In these contexts they buttress their inflexibility, which defies your general expectations, by returning again and again to their standard. Unless you can undermine that standard—which can be difficult—they can change your expectations regarding that issue.

The Reciprocity Principle

The next psychological element that underlies offer-concession dynamics is the Reciprocity Principle. Psychologist Robert Cialdini introduces it in the following way:

> A university professor [once] . . . sent Christmas cards to a sample of perfect strangers. . . . [H]oliday cards addressed to him came pouring back from people who had never met nor heard of him. The great majority of those who returned a card never inquired into the identity of the unknown professor. They received his holiday greeting card . . . and automatically sent one in return. [This study illustrated the power of] the rule for reciprocation. The rule says that we should try to repay, in kind, what another person has provided us.

We saw this implemented in chapter 3 as a powerful independent standard. If I do something for you, it will increase the likelihood you will do something for me—even if it's not an equivalent favor. You still feel an obligation—you *owe* me—and if you don't respond in kind society will view you as a selfish person. Nobody wants this label or reputation.

How does this impact offers and concessions?

The Rejection-Then-Retreat Technique

In 2000 I stopped into my favorite men's store after having lunch with a colleague. The store was near the restaurant and, while I didn't really need anything, I'm always looking for good deals. I walked into the store and the owner, an older gentleman with gray hair and a nice low-key manner, welcomed me by saying "good to see you again, Marty." I asked him what was new and what he had that might interest me. He showed me some swatches of beautiful material and told me he just sold a gentleman like me a gorgeous double-breasted suit with this material. The material felt great, and I could envision myself in such a suit, so I asked him its cost. He said he would charge me $950 for the suit.

Now, I have never bought a suit from a swatch, nor have I ever spent $950 for a suit. I visibly flinched—involuntarily! He saw this and, instead of trying to sell the suit to me, walked me over to a rack of suits in my size. Eventually I found a beautiful sports jacket I bought for $350. The owner then sold me a pair of slacks, two shirts, a tie and a belt to go with it. And I had no real intention of buying anything when I walked in. What happened?

The owner was using a technique Cialdini calls reject-then-retreat. It's based on the principle of reciprocity. Here's how it worked on me:

As you know, we often feel we owe someone if they give us a gift or do us a favor. They trigger our sense of obligation with their gift or favor. In a negotiation if you concede something to me I will be more likely to reciprocate with a concession to you. This same sense of obligation—I owe you—also can be triggered when we *reject* an offer. By rejecting an offer, we psychologically feel we hurt the other. We thus feel a need to make it up, and so "owe" them.

In the clothing store, my rejecting the $950 custom suit triggered my subtle sense of obligation to the owner. Thus, when he "retreated" and made me another offer—if you won't buy my $950 suit, what about a $350 jacket—I felt an increased interest in buying the jacket.

Similarly, expert negotiators often will concede on an issue of minor importance to them, in the hopes that their concession will invoke a reciprocal concession from their counterparts on a more important issue. And they will set up their offer-concession strategy so this occurs.

Again, Cialdini explains how this psychological tendency was used in negotiations in the 1970s between successful television producers Grant Tinker and Garry Marshall and network censors. Here's a quote from *TV*

Guide writer Dick Russell, where Marshall admits to "deliberately inserting lines into scripts that a censor's sure to ax" so they could then "retreat" to the lines they really wanted:

> Marshall . . . not only admits his tricks . . . he seems to revel in them. On one episode of his [then] top-rated *Laverne and Shirley* series, for example, he says, "We had a situation where Squiggy's in a rush to get out of his apartment and meet some girls upstairs. He says: 'Will you hurry up before I lose my lust?' But in the script we put something even stronger, knowing the censors would cut it. They did; so we asked innocently, well, how about 'lose my lust'? 'That's good,' they said. Sometimes you gotta go at 'em backward." On the *Happy Days* series the biggest censorship fight was over the word "virgin." That time, says Marshall, "I knew we'd have trouble, so we put the word in seven times, hoping they would cut six and keep one. It worked. We used the same pattern again with the word 'pregnant.'"

Be aware of this psychological tendency, understand its impact, and factor it into your offer-concession strategy. Recognize, however, that using this psychologically powerful technique has a potentially significant downside. If your counterpart considers your concession artificially manufactured, simply to manipulate their sense of obligation, you will suffer a damaging loss of credibility.

The Contrast Principle

Have you ever wondered why car dealers often offer lower-cost accessories like tinted windows and special trim *after* you have negotiated the vehicle price? Several hundred dollars here and there at that point seems minimal, after you have agreed to pay $25,000 for a new car.

It's called the Contrast Principle, and it relates to how we perceive things presented one after the other. Many studies in a variety of contexts confirm that, as psychologist Cialdini notes, "If the second item is fairly different from the first, we will tend to see it as *more different* than it actually is" (emphasis added).

When I bought the jacket, shirts, tie, and belt, it was no coincidence that the store's owner presented the most expensive item first. The shirts, tie, and belt seemed distinctly less expensive in comparison with the suit. This also works the other way around. If you first look at a relatively inexpensive belt, then look at a suit next, the suit will, by contrast, seem that much more expensive.

The Contrast Principle has many applications in the negotiation context. Cialdini notes that a real estate agent once, to show him the ropes, took him through several relatively run-down houses the real estate company kept on the market at artificially inflated prices. They did this so their agents could first show these run-down houses, and then show potential buyers the houses they might really like. After seeing the run-down houses first, the next houses seemed fantastic by comparison—quality and pricewise.

As a result, parties should *separately* value everything they and their counterparts want. Take the time to independently assess each item. Then and only then, determine when and how to introduce each item.

In the first offer, or first counter context, create the largest contrast you reasonably can between where you start and your next move. Your subsequent moves will then appear more reasonable in contrast to your first. Likewise, if you introduce and agree on the larger-value items early on, this will improve your ability to achieve agreement on the smaller items later.

On the other hand, sometimes it's important to create a sense of momentum early in the negotiation process. This can be accomplished by introducing items early on that will be more likely to generate agreement. There it may make sense to wait, if the larger issues are also the most contentious. Of course, the larger issues will then appear even more important in contrast to the earlier, less significant issues.

While there's no fast or easy rule here, it's critical to understand the Contrast Principle. Recognize the impact when it's used by your counterpart, and evaluate when and where to use it yourself.

The Commitment and Consistency Principle

In chapter 1 we learned how the Commitment Principle helps us to more effectively commit to achieving our goals. Here we analyze its application to offers and concessions. In this context it operates in concert with another psychological tendency, the Consistency Principle. Commitment strategies, according to Cialdini, are "intended to get us to take some action or make some statement that will trap us into later compliance through consistency pressures."

For example, Cialdini notes that social psychologist Steven J. Sherman engineered a *700 percent increase* in the number of Indiana residents volunteering for the American Cancer Society by using the following technique: Sherman first called the residents and asked, as part of a survey, if they would be willing to spend three hours canvassing their neighborhood for the American Cancer Society. Many said, as part of the survey, they would. Several days later a representative of the American Cancer Society actually called and, because of their earlier "commitment" in the context of the survey, 700 percent more of them agreed to volunteer than in a group that had *not* first been called as part of the "survey."

Businesses regularly employ this "foot-in-the-door" technique as a sales tactic. Their strategy is to get a customer to make a commitment, any commitment, with the company. In most cases the company tries to get a commitment to a small sale with the knowledge that, once the commitment has been made, larger purchases will more likely follow. This tactic is based on the Commitment and Consistency principles.

In negotiations, if you can get your counterparts to commit early on to a relatively small item or principle that would be consistent with their later actions on larger items or principles, it will increase your success rate on the larger items. To be even more powerful, get an active commitment, in writing or in public, to the first item or principle.

Say you go to buy a new car and find one offered at an incredible price. You tell the sales person you want to purchase the car (oral commitment). You then sign a whole raft of papers signifying your decision (written commitment). Finally, before the final deal is done, the dealer even lets you take the car for a day to "test it out" (a public commitment, as you show it to your family and friends). Inevitably, something falls through and the dealer suddenly can't give you that amazing deal. You have been lowballed. But by that time, you're so committed to the car that you still want to buy it, even at an inflated price.

Alternatively, say you want to trade in your car for a new one and the used car sales person offers you a fantastic *above* market price for your trade-in. You immediately agree, and then agree to purchase a new car from that dealer at a fairly good price. Inevitably, before you sign the final trade-in papers, the sales manager reviews the contract and "notices" your trade-in's above market price. He nixes that deal, but then offers you Blue Book—an objective estimation of market value—for your trade-in. Most people will agree and also buy the new car. It's another form of lowballing, based on the Commitment and Consistency principles.

While I find these car sales tactics unethical because the dealers *intend* to renege later, the underlying psychological principle applies in ethical as well as unethical contexts.

What does this mean for your offers and concessions?

- The earlier you get commitments the better. In chapter 3 we discussed getting a commitment to an independent standard early on.

If your counterpart agrees to that standard, he or she will be more likely to agree to its translation into dollar or other terms later.

- Written or public commitments help more than oral commitments. Get early written commitments, even though the written document may not be comprehensive or legally enforceable. If nothing else, write a confirming e-mail listing the commitments and progress already made. Also consider public commitments in high-profile negotiations. Going public with a commitment—assuming both sides agree—can have a significant impact.

- If you can't get firm commitments, get tentative commitments. Tentative commitments are better than no commitments at all. Psychologically, your counterparts will be less likely to go back on them.

Of course, do *not* use unethical techniques to gain your counterparts' commitment, as in the car examples above. Your reputation and credibility is just too important to risk in this way. But you should understand and be able to recognize this psychological tendency at work, as it underlies much of the offer-concession stage.

The Nuts and Bolts of Making Offers and Concessions

I'm often asked about the actual nuts and bolts of making an offer or a concession. For instance, how do you phrase an offer or concession so that even though you're willing to move your counterpart receives the impression you probably won't? Yet, you still want the opportunity, if needed, to make a further move.

In what order should you introduce your issues? How detailed should you make them? What about hiring someone to negotiate for you, especially when it comes to the offer-concession stage? When, why, and under what circumstances should you hire an agent? To what extent should you plan all your offers and concessions, and how much flexibility do you want to keep? What about offering to settle a dispute within a range of numbers?

What should you do if it appears you have an agreement and, at the end, your counterpart introduces a new, albeit minor, issue? What should you do with such "nibblers?"

How you tackle these issues makes a significant difference. Here are five tips and tactics to maximize your offer and concession effectiveness:

- Language to use in making offers and concessions
- Carefully communicate your priorities and order of issues

- Learn when, how, and under what circumstances to use agents
- To bluff or not to bluff
- Closing strategies

Language to Use in Making Offers and Concessions

The language you use in making your offers and concessions and the signals they send can single-handedly determine whether your offers or concessions will be accepted. In general, you should:

- Be specific and detailed
- Explain the offer's rationale and tie it to standards before introducing numbers
- Promote an air of finality and increasing rigidity
- Point out consequences (leverage)
- Put it in writing
- Avoid ranges
- Be ready to react

Be Specific and Detailed

"Oh, I don't know, Bill. My first offer? Boy, I hate this. Would you accept something around—maybe—in the range of $750,000 for the pizza joint?"

This offer sends all the wrong messages. It is vague, and it communicates:

- Uncertainty and lack of preparation ("I don't know" combined with wiggle words like "something around—maybe—in the range of")
- Discomfort with the process ("I hate this" signifies weak leverage)
- An explicit recognition that this is only the start, and there's more where this came from ("my first offer?")
- A possible incorrect assumption that price is the only issue
- Lack of respect for Bill's longtime family business (calling it a "pizza joint"). No one, I hope, would start like this.

Yet, offers come in all levels of specificity and detail. In general, the more specific and detailed, the better. Specific and detailed offers appear more thoughtful, reasoned, serious, and thorough. This increases the likelihood that your counterpart will give your offer the significance it deserves. It also increases its chances, based on the reciprocity principle, of generating an equally specific and detailed response. This helps everyone.

Explain the Offer's Rationale and Tie It to Standards
Before Introducing Numbers

The more you discuss your offers and concessions within the context of appropriate independent standards, the more they will appear "fair and reasonable." Explain upfront why your counterpart should accept your offer. Illustrate the "fairness and reasonableness" of your offer by tying it to a specific independent standard or combination of standards.

In the summer of 2001 one of my bar association clients asked me if they could videotape my live seminar and replay the video around the state to lawyers who couldn't attend it live. Here was their offer and my counter (via e-mail). Note our use of independent standards, indicated in brackets.

> *Latz Negotiation Institute (LNI) client*: We could try to videotape the program for replay in the spring. Would that interest you for a lower per-head fee? The reason the fee would have to be lower is that we have to pay the local bar associations that sponsor the replays a per-head fee as well *[costs]*. The numbers for replays are not huge, but could be a nice supplement for you *[profits]*.
>
> *Me*: Let me first say that I'm very interested in coming to an agreement on video replays. This can be profitable for both of us. Regarding a fee for the video replays, I've given a lot of thought to this, so let me share with you my thought process and some general research I've found. As far as I can tell, most of the bar associations that do video replays generally charge the same amount for a live program as for video replays *[market]*. Thus, they generate the same amount per person as if it were live *[profit]*. Plus, their costs are lower (less staff time to organize and no speaker travel expenses, etc.) *[costs]*. This suggests their per-head take home is actually *higher* for video replays than for live programs. I thus charge other state and local bars my same standard per-head fee for video replays as for my live programs. In fact, given these bar associations' costs, I believe I would actually take a smaller proportion of their net income from video replays than I would take from a live program. If you want, we can discuss video replays more extensively on the phone or when we see each other this fall. While it's probably not a big income earner, everything helps.

Notice four points: *First,* I discuss my strong interest in reaching agreement on this issue *before* addressing the fee issue. I also emphasize how it's *mutually* beneficial to reach an agreement by restating the "profits" standard my client raised.

Second, I then discuss my reasoning and the standards underlying my evaluation of a "fair and reasonable" fee (market price, industry standard as reflected in my agreements with other bar associations, costs, and profits). I discuss these standards *before* stating my fee.

Third, I indicate the standard fee I charge similar clients *after* laying out my reasoning and standards. I follow this with another explanation of its fairness by pointing out the proportion of the program's net income I receive. It's critical to state my number *after* I have explained my reasoning and standards. In my experience, those receiving offers or concessions sometimes tune out after hearing the actual offer. So don't lead with your offer, or your rationale and standards may not strike with the same force. Lay out your reasoning and standards *first*—hopefully eliciting some kind of "that makes sense" response—and *then* present your offer.

Finally, I conclude by reiterating my desire to reach an agreement, as it would benefit both of us.

Of course, I could have just replied with my standard video replay rate. However, this would have increased the likelihood of a short-term impasse and would not have provided a rational basis for my fee. (By the way, we did eventually agree on my standard fee for video replays.)

Overall, tie your offers and concessions to thorough reasoning and independent standards. This is especially critical with initial offers and concessions, because you want to set the initial expectation and tone. Plus, as you go back and forth it often becomes more difficult to tie your moves to independent standards. The gamesmanship element and the offer-concession expectations tend to rise to the fore. And your leverage will become an increasingly prominent factor.

Bottom line: The longer and stronger you can connect your moves to independent standards, the more likely your moves will generate a positive and principled response.

Promote an Air of Finality and Increasing Rigidity

It's easy to say you want to promote an air of finality and increasing rigidity in your moves. And we've already discussed the actions that communicate increasing inflexibility, like tapering your offers and concessions and decreasing the time period between your moves. But what phrases and language also send these signals?

Here are some phrases that communicate decreasing flexibility. Understand, though, you will be bucking up against parties' expectations early in the negotiation that significant flexibility exists. At the end, most will expect you to become more rigid and reluctant. Don't forget, either, to apply these phrases to specific elements within your offer. Many offers contain multiple items, and you often want to send separate flexibility signals regarding each. Finally, you implicitly send a message of some rigidity and finality when you tie your moves to independent standards. Couple the following language with the liberal use of the standards and rationales underlying your moves.

Message to send	Phrases/language to use	Phrases/language to avoid
Significant flexibility, often at the beginning of negotiations.	*"My asking price is . . ."* or *"I'm looking to get . . ."* Be serious, straight-forward, and confident. Remember, your expec-tation of achievement will change how you come across, including during the offer-concession stage.	Any explicit mention of the phrase *"first offer."* That phrase undermines the validity of your offer. Also avoid initially using words like *"non-negotiable," "best offer," "final offer," "bottom line,"* or other words signaling no room to move. Your credibility will take a hit if you use this language and then move. And don't disparage your offer by apologizing for it or appearing embarrassed.
Middle flexibility. Some room, but approaching the rigid point. Here, communicate reasoned inflexibility. In many ways, this is the riskiest point. If no one moves here, the deal may blow up. Yet, if you move after communicating too much inflexibility, you lose credibility. And if you communicate too much	Use words or phrases that appear to communicate inflexibility but still leave you an out. *"I'm willing to accept . . . because . . ."* *"This is fair and reasonable because. . . ."* Be straightforward, factual, and tie yourself to standards. Don't overtly signal flexibility or inflexibility. Instead, send a strong, reasoned	Stay away from words signaling total inflexi-bility—like *"bottom line," "final offer,"* etc. Unless you are one hundred percent sure you have reached your end point, don't risk your credibility here.

flexibility the other side may dig in—accurately figuring you will concede.	rationale by focusing on standards, and implicitly state, "I'm not going to move unless you give me a reason to move. If you can convince me it makes sense to move, I will consider it."	
Total inflexibility. This is it. No more. Firm but not stubborn.	*"I've given this a great deal of thought, and it's the best I can do. Any more, and it's not worth it for me to do the deal."* Be more explicit here about your leverage and why it doesn't make sense for you to move.	*"Take it or leave it. "* These words often create unnecessary resistance and put your counterpart on the defensive. This is usually counter-productive. Also avoid the word "frankly," especially near the end. This word draws attention to the possibility that your previous statements—which were not preceded by the word "frankly" — may not have been credible.

Point Out Consequences (Leverage)

Your moves will be more effective if you show near the end of your offer how both parties will benefit from an agreement. Show why your counterpart should accept your offer.

This means focusing on leverage and, to the extent possible, your counterpart's BATNA. If their alternative to accepting your offer is worse than what you offered, point it out. Be careful how you do this, though. You don't want it perceived as a threat. Be matter-of-fact here. Your body language and tone of voice also will make a difference. Don't appear overly aggressive, but make your point. Focus your counterpart on this element, especially as you get closer to the end.

Put It in Writing

DELAWARE CLOSED, read the large sign over the highway at the Delaware border. And for an hour and a half it appeared true. As Herb Cohen described in his book, *You Can Negotiate Anything*, "Lines of cars squealed to a halt. Vehicles pulled off the highway. Confused drivers stepped out and approached [the *Candid Camera* representative], who stood beneath the sign as hidden movie cameras recorded the event. Scores blurted variations of 'Hey, what's the story on Delaware?' [The *Candid Camera* representative] merely pointed overhead and replied, 'Read the sign!' The drivers frowned, scratched their heads, then tugged their lower lips. One asked: 'When do you think it will reopen? I live there, and my family is in there.'"

The power of the written word can be awesome. So when, where, and how can you effectively harness this power, especially in the offer-concession stage?

First, understand that written documents provide parties with more credibility, legitimacy, and the appearance of being more definite and inflexible than equivalent oral statements. We believe what we read and see more than what we hear.

Second, strategically determine how to use documents to accomplish your goals. Sometimes putting an offer in writing can be counterproductive. In some negotiations you want an air of informality and flexibility. The use of written documents can counteract this. You also might know that your counterpart does not think well on his or her feet. If this is true, and you have good skills in this environment, meet in person. (Of course, you could meet and share written documents in that meeting.)

Third, jotting down notes can be productive, even if you don't use them. Writing helps me organize my ideas in a logical way and helps me fine-tune exactly what I want to communicate.

Fourth, using written documents reduces the chance of a miscommunication destroying your negotiation and/or the trust you have developed. Writing confirmation letters to your counterpart after oral commitments have been made often makes sense.

Finally, certain written documents provide more power than others. Here are three common written documents used in negotiations, especially during the offer-concession stage, and how and where to effectively use them.

The Written Offer or Counter

I'm a big fan of written offers and counters. How you make an offer will impact its likelihood of acceptance. It's also easier, in a written versus an oral offer, to be clear, specific, organized, detailed, and to include persuasive justifications and standards underlying your offer.

Plus you can carefully choose the exact message you want to convey. This is especially critical if you want to point out certain leverage elements in your offer, including what might happen if your counterpart rejects it. I've spent many hours crafting written offers or counters. In fact, I regularly send potential clients a proposal for my services, even if I've already provided them with the information orally.

Isn't this a waste of time? Absolutely not. Written proposals confirm the legitimacy of my offer, reiterate its elements so my potential clients have no misunderstanding about what I propose, and lay out in a comprehensive and detailed way what I tried to communicate orally.

The Written Standard

Lawyers and business people regularly use written standards such as experts' opinions to assist in their negotiations. Written appraisals or business valuations, written market-value research, written policies, and the list of written standards goes on. Each has more force in writing than if shared orally. Often it makes sense to attach a written standard to an offer.

Leverage-Related Documents

You can improve your leverage by sharing, in certain instances, a written document that describes your BATNA. In late 2002 I was negotiating with several hotels who wanted to host our Spring 2003 wedding. After getting several bids from relatively comparable hotels, I sent a copy of one hotel's bid to another hotel. I wanted to show the second hotel the details of what I wanted it to beat pricewise. I also wanted to underscore the seriousness with which I viewed the first hotel, and to get my counterpart's competitive juices flowing. Plus I wanted to give her some ammunition to get more authority and room to move from her boss. She subsequently came down over 20 percent.

Overall, many advantages exist to using written documents in negotiations. In significant negotiations, put most of your offers and concessions in writing, especially at the beginning of the negotiation, and possibly include your written standards and maybe even your leverage. It will help you analyze your position and increase the likelihood your offer will be accepted. And if it makes sense to make your offer in person or on the phone, consider following it up with a letter (or e-mail) in which you reiterate it in writing.

Most people believe what they read. Remember that next time you drive through Delaware.

Avoid Ranges

"I will sell you this painting for between $800 and $1,000. Sound fair?"

"Sure," you respond. "Here's my check for $800."

"Wait a second," I reply, "I was thinking closer to $1,000."

That's the problem with ranges. If someone proposes a range, most focus on the value closest to their desired result. It's natural. Ranges also communicate an implicit acceptance of any value within the range. By doing so, they suggest that the offer has not been seriously put together.

What should you do?

Avoid ranges. If you're willing to offer an item for $800, say it straight and get the full benefit of that figure. Don't fudge. Be clear and definite. If you don't, you risk creating ambiguities and miscommunications that create trouble for everyone. Plus, ranges often undermine the legitimacy of your standards.

I once said this in a seminar and a lawyer jumped up to disagree. "Wait a second," he said. "I use ranges all the time in offers and I've found them to be extremely effective."

"Interesting," I responded, "tell me how you have used them."

"Well, last week I offered to settle a case for between $100,000 and $125,000, depending on the amount of property that would accompany the cash portion of the settlement. The more property, the less cash."

"Excellent point," I noted. "But I wouldn't characterize your offer as a range. It was really a series of separate, *equivalent value* offers. You have given your counterpart a number of options, each of which you value the same. One option is to settle for $100,000 cash plus property valued at $25,000. Another option is to settle for $110,000 cash plus property valued at $15,000. This is a great technique if you value all the options the same, especially if your counterpart values them differently."

Ranges differ from options. Presenting various acceptable options can be a very effective offer technique, assuming you value them equivalently. Ranges are ineffective, so avoid them.

Be Ready to React

As you know, your reactions to offers or concessions, especially first offers or first counters, communicate important information about your flexibility and affect your counterpart's expectations. What should you do?

Prepare. Don't get caught by surprise and blurt out unthinking responses. Instead, send verbal and nonverbal messages designed to impact your counterpart's expectations. If it's their first offer, don't sigh with relief and call it "reasonable." They will interpret this as acceptance and be extremely reluctant to move.

Instead, consider challenging the offer's rationale or a particular element in the offer. And don't use Dawson's "Flinch." It's a tactic many find transparent and one that can easily backfire (unless, of course, it's genuine). Dig deeper: If their offer lacks an underlying independent standard, point it out. "I just don't understand how you can offer that? The house next door just sold for 20 percent *less*, and it was 500 square feet *larger*."

If it's way out of line, express your disappointment. "Sally, I'm disappointed you're starting with such an unreasonable position. Your offer builds in a 30 percent profit margin. That's out of line in this market."

In short, find something constructively critical to say about their offer. And put it together with whatever facial and body language expressions might naturally accompany it. If you don't, they may interpret your silence to mean you find it reasonable.

While your reactions to your counterpart's first offer or counter carry disproportionate weight, don't make light of your *later* reactions to *subsequent* offers and concessions. These reactions also should communicate appropriate messages. Sometimes you will want to positively react and give your counterpart credit for making concessions. In these instances, call their move "constructive, but . . ." This suggests you appreciate their move, but expect more. Other times you will want to express disappointment in their lack of progress. Avoid overly predictable reactions, too. Predictability undermines credibility.

Overall, prepare to react to offers and concessions. Reactions send important messages. Be strategic with them.

Carefully Communicate Your Priorities and Order of Issues

Now you know what specific language to use in your offers and concessions. But every offer or concession should also send a message about leverage by communicating what and how much the parties want and need something. In short, you want to carefully communicate what you want the most—your highest priority—and what you want the least—your lowest priority. A party may openly send such a signal. Or he may try to mislead and confuse. Whichever you're trying to do, *consciously* send this signal. And analyze how your counterparts present their offers and how strongly they defend various components within them.

Remember the prison hostage situation that my law school students negotiate? Two students represent the governor and seek the release of forty community leaders taken hostage by inmates upset over "unacceptable" prison conditions. On the other side, two students represent the inmates and seek to improve the prisoners' conditions. About ten issues must be resolved within two hours, ranging from food quality to medical treatment. If no agreement is reached, the hostages will be killed (a very poor BATNA for *both* sides).

Most students begin by asking questions and trying to determine how important their counterparts feel about each issue. They're seeking information and leverage by exploring the other side's priorities. In this hostile situation, however, with no previous relationship between the negotiators, this probing often quickly breaks down. Neither side wants to give up strategic information. And even when information is shared, the other side often views it with skepticism. This occurs despite the fact that both sides want the *same solution* on some issues, like better and more efficient health care. Given the competitive dynamic and mistrust, it's difficult, for each side to acknowledge shared interests and goals.

How do they finally determine the other side's *true* priorities? Through their counterparts' offers and concessions and the sometimes-unwilling reactions that accompany them.

About an hour into the negotiation, both sides start to panic. They look at their watches, think about all the unresolved issues, and wonder if they have time to settle all of them. Up to that point most parties address each issue one by one, sequentially, in the order presented in their instructions. This usually changes around the halfway point. Suddenly both sides realize they must speed up to have any hope of a deal. The proposals then start flowing back and forth in packages. Sometimes related issues get packaged together, like recreation time and recreational facilities. Other times packages include unrelated items, like immunity from prosecution for the inmates' actions and the frequency of conjugal visits. With each new proposal the parties analyze the changes from previous proposals. This way they ascertain the other side's true priorities.

How else might the parties uncover their counterparts' true priorities? Present several offers and evaluate which is most acceptable. Or directly ask: "Would you prefer X or Y?" Or say: "If we agree to X, will you agree to Y?"

These methods will help you to efficiently and accurately elicit information about parties' priorities. But what happens when parties consistently mislead about their priorities? Three possibilities exist, none favorable. The deal will either: a) break down after it becomes "clear" no mutually beneficial solution exists, given the parties' stated—though inaccurate—needs; b) reach a point where it becomes obvious that one party is trying to mislead, given that its positions make no sense (how can you rationally argue that prisoners don't care much about limited immunity for their hostage-taking actions?); or c) reach a point where the misleading party backs off on the allegedly critical issues and loses credibility.

So, how should you effectively, efficiently, and credibly communicate your priorities, especially with multiple items on the table?

Prioritize the Issues Before the Offer-Concession Stage

Divide your issues into two categories: what James Freund calls Blue Chips (most critical); and Bargaining Chips (medium-to-low importance). Depending on the number and importance of the issues, prioritize them for your internal use. Then prepare to send different signals regarding each type of issue. In deciding how to send your signals and how to accurately evaluate the other side's signals, keep in mind:

- Credibility is constantly at stake, especially during this stage. Protect yours and evaluate the other side's.
- Don't indicate that *all* your issues are "critical." Send a variety of signals regarding the importance of your issues. You will lose credibility and diminish the perceived value of your true Blue Chips if you constantly overstate. As James Freund says, "You gain credence for your inflexibility on a few choice issues by your willingness to give ground on the rest."
- Hint at flexibility—yet hold off on moving. I will often say something like "You know, I have no doubt we will ultimately be able to agree on my fee, so why don't we address this other issue first?"
- Look for value-creating opportunities—where both parties appear to want the same thing and your interests align (the shared and compatible interests discussed in chapter 1).

Put a Numerical Value on Your Nonmonetary Issues

In 2001 a friend signed a contract to purchase a condominium in Phoenix for $135,000. During the inspection period they found termites. Her real estate agent told her it was no big deal, as the termites could be exterminated, likely at the seller's cost. This worried my friend, though. It gave her the creeps to know that termites might be in her bedroom wall and might have caused structural damage. I told her to quantify in her mind the decreased value of the condominium due to the termites. She subsequently withdrew from the contract. The decreased amount was just too much.

We all know not to compare apples to oranges. But in a negotiation it's important to prioritize nonmonetary issues and compare them to monetary issues. As James Freund recommends in *Smart Negotiating,* putting nonmonetary issues in monetary terms will help. While it will be subjective, it will help you evaluate their relative importance.

Tips for Determining the Order of Issues

Which issues should you raise first—the most or least critical? Do you want to start with the easier ones and build momentum, or with a blue chip and leave the least important to the end? Which issues logically might be traded for each other? Which appear to have roughly the same value to each side? Do you want to confirm how the other side values an issue by direct questioning, or do you want to try to determine its priorities by putting together multiple packages and logrolling (if you give me this, I will give you that)? On which issues do you want to send false signals, if any?

A huge number of variables impact this offer-concession element. Here are some general rules of thumb to help you orchestrate the best game plan.

- Expect, plan, and insist on reciprocity of movement. Be prepared to give to get. But don't give more, unless you're getting more.
- Don't hesitate to start out by using what Dawson calls "The Vise." Simply put, Dawson suggests you respond to whatever offer the other side initially makes by saying, "I'm sorry. You will have to do better than that." Then keep responding this way until you have no choice but to counter. Expert negotiators will see through this and get you to counter by asking, "How much better do I need to do?" You will be surprised, however, by how many just keep on giving.
- Consider starting with Blue Chip issues on which both sides likely will agree.
- Don't underestimate the value of momentum. The longer the negotiation lasts, the more committed both sides psychologically feel to reaching an agreement.
- Initial moves less than 5 percent rarely generate meaningful moves from the other side.
- Rarely make a larger concession than your counterpart.
- If you're a buyer dealing with monetary issues, understand that a $100 increase in your offer is *proportionately more, percentwise,* than a $100 decrease by the seller. If a buyer offers $1,000 and increases it $100, he's increased his offer by 10 percent. But if a seller starts at $2,000 and decreases it $100, she's only decreased her offer by 5 percent. Buyers start with a lower base amount from which to determine the percent move. As a buyer, then, talk in terms of reciprocal *percentage* moves, not in dollar terms. Sellers should express their moves in dollar terms and insist on reciprocal *dollar* moves, not percentage moves.

- The earlier and more consistently you raise an issue, the more it's perceived as a Blue Chip. Likewise, if you raise an issue near the end for the first time, it will be perceived as relatively unimportant.
- Consider limiting your authority on the bluest of the Blue Chip issues, at least initially. There's almost always an entity to which you can make yourself accountable. Even corporate CEOs must answer to a board of directors. Don't overuse this tactic; but maintaining the ability to say, "I have to check with my [board, partner, boss, client, etc.] before I can agree to that," can be very useful. Your truthful accountability to someone else, even if you expressly create it *before* the negotiation for this purpose, will increase your reluctance to concede.
- Remain somewhat flexible. You will invariably learn a great deal about your counterparts' values and priorities during the offer-concession stage. Maintaining sufficient flexibility allows you to take advantage of new strategically important information and unanticipated opportunities.

Learn When, How, and Under What Circumstances to Use Agents

You want a new house and you're considering whether to hire a real estate agent or go it alone. Or perhaps you're selling your business and an investment banker wants to represent you in lining up potential buyers.

You might even manage a sales force and are uncertain whether to negotiate that potentially huge contract or let your sales person handle it.

These instances present you, as the decision-maker, with a dilemma. Should you use an agent to represent you, especially in the offer-concession stage, or would it be more effective to negotiate for yourself?

Here is what should you do.

Consider Your Ability to Objectively Negotiate for Yourself and Factor in the Value of Your Future Relationship with the Other Side

I'm often a more effective negotiator for others than for myself. It's true for most of us. We tend to be more objective, relaxed, patient, and even more creative when our own property or interests are not at stake. The more we're personally at risk and stressed, and the more our ego gets involved, the less effective our negotiation abilities.

Thus, as your objectivity goes down, the value of using an agent goes up. And as the value of your future relationship with the other side increases, the importance of using an agent decreases.

For instance, many will hire a divorce lawyer to represent them if they know their emotions will cloud their judgment and likely lead to a highly adversarial atmosphere. Objective agents can help ease the tension.

Alternatively, if you're a successful CEO and negotiator and want a long-term strategic partnership with another company, avoid using agents—at least in the beginning. This way you can personally develop the type of working relationship that will lead to a successful partnership.

Consider Your and Your Potential Agent's Substantive Issue-Related Expertise

The less knowledge you have on the relevant issues, the more likely you should hire an agent. Vice versa, too. In real estate, many sellers hire agents to help them sell their homes, because agents should know how to promote a house to maximize its value to potential buyers. Agents should also intimately know your housing market, a significant negotiation advantage.

Likewise, many sports agents bring a wealth of experience, expertise, and contacts in their specialized sports fields. Going this alone, regardless of negotiation ability, is risky.

Personally, I was unwilling to take this risk, as I considered how to get the best publishing deal for this book. As a result, I hired a literary agent to help me sell this book to potential publishers. I'm glad I did.

Evaluate Your Own Negotiation Ability Vis-À-Vis Your Potential Agent's

Some individuals know they're ineffective negotiators. In these instances it's almost always helpful to hire an agent. Always research your potential agent's negotiation reputation, too, by getting references from principals he or she has represented and from the opposing parties in the agent's negotiations.

Plus, don't equate negotiation experience with effectiveness. Some extremely experienced negotiators consistently leave value on the table.

Assess the Strategic and Structural Advantages and Disadvantages of the Principal-Agent Relationship

Strategic and structural *advantages* also exist to using an agent, as noted by James Freund in *Smart Negotiating,* including:

- Agents depersonalize the negotiation
- Principals can maintain the ability to avoid sharing important information
- Principals can retain additional strategic flexibility and options with the process

- Agents can float trial balloons without any real commitment
- Agents in my experience have a tendency to concede less than principals largely because they are accountable to someone else for their performance

Plus, principals may gain a significant strategic advantage by limiting their agents' authority, within reason, while the other side negotiates for himself or sends out an agent with too much authority. I have found that agents with authority tend to use most of it up.

Disadvantages to using agents, on the other hand, include:

- Possible miscommunication between the principal and agent
- Agents who may primarily look out for themselves or who may stray from their instructions. (This disadvantage, however, is lessened in situations like sports agenting, where the agent receives a percentage of the principal's cut, thus making their interests more aligned)
- Principals' more tenuous control of the process
- Principals who unnecessarily hamstring their agents by not leveling with them
- Agents may not get sufficient information from their principals to most effectively discuss certain options
- Principals' comfort level in personally understanding the negotiation dynamic
- Principals' more distant relationship with each other

The issue—to hire or not to hire an agent—is complex. In most negotiations there's no simple answer.

You might feel embarrassed to hire an agent to negotiate for you. Don't. It doesn't reflect negatively on your negotiating ability. To the contrary, it often illustrates your sophistication in managing the negotiation process.

To Bluff or Not to Bluff

In *The Negotiator,* actor Samuel L. Jackson plays a police hostage negotiator who takes his own hostages to prove his fellow officers framed him for murder.

During an incredibly tense scene, Jackson drags one of his hostages from view while screaming into the phone. We then hear a gunshot followed by dead silence.

Everyone, especially the police barricaded outside, believes Jackson murdered the hostage. This is critical.

Why?

Because Jackson—in what we later found out was a bluff—just established his credibility. If the police didn't believe Jackson would harm a hostage, then little would prevent them from storming the place.

Without credibility your negotiations will be exponentially more difficult, protracted, and less effective. Yet many consider bluffing, especially during the offer-concession stage, a staple of effective negotiating.

How can you establish and maintain your credibility *and* effectively bluff? Should you?

Here are some tips to help you navigate the credibility maze and to evaluate if, when, and how to bluff.

Negotiation Credibility Must Be Earned

Many people approach negotiations with some skepticism about their counterparts' credibility. They should. At least until their counterpart has provided evidence of credibility.

As discussed earlier, credibility in the offer-concession stage can be earned by: a) making consistent, specific statements throughout the negotiation, especially concerning issues you consider Blue Chips, versus Bargaining Chips; b) restricting the number of Blue Chip issues to a relative few; and c) ensuring your actions support your statements by following through on commitments.

Such actions collectively help determine your reputation, which hopefully will provide future counterparts with a reason to trust you.

Let's say I want to hire a computer consultant, and he justifies his "standard rate" by telling me he has "clients nationwide who pay it." But when I ask for references, he provides me, a week late, with the names of three local businesses. He tells me his rates for them are confidential. Credibility lost.

The More Likely a Statement Provides Its Speaker with a Strategic Advantage, the More Likely the Listener Should Independently Confirm Its Veracity

Check out the truthfulness of your counterparts' statements if the statements provide them with a strategic advantage. Likewise, providing independently verifiable information as to the validity of *your* strategically helpful statements will increase their believability. And if you can't verify the accuracy or truthfulness of these statements, consider them a possible if not probable bluff.

In 2001 I negotiated a six-week rate for a lake cabin in Big Bear, California. In my negotiations I told my counterpart the name and rate of another cabin I was considering. Its rate, not coincidentally, was significantly less than my counterpart was asking.

By sharing this information I increased the likelihood he would believe me and lower his rate accordingly. He did.

Bluffing Carries Significant Risks

I'm not a big fan of bluffing on significant issues at the end of negotiations, especially with weak leverage. As Freund notes in *Smart Negotiating,* the odds are usually stacked against you.

Let's say I offer Tracy, a Web site designer, $9,500 to revamp my Web site. I tell her I need it in a month, and she's the only top designer available at this rate. After some dickering, I say "$9,500 is it." But I'm *really* willing to pay $11,000.

Three things can happen in this classic bluff. Two have negative consequences for the bluffer. One, Tracy believes me and I save $1,500. Two, Tracy calls my bluff, says she won't move off $11,000, and I ultimately acquiesce. While I get the deal, I lose credibility. Or, three, Tracy believes my bluff and doesn't respond. I then call several days later and find she is now fully booked by another new client, who paid her $11,000 for the same amount of work. I'm now without an affordable redesigned site.

With weak leverage, the risk-reward ratio is usually just not worth it for me. The stronger your leverage, though, the less risky your bluff. But it's still risky.

Some perceive bluffing, by the way, to be straight-out lying. I discuss different people's approach to bluffing in chapter 7 on negotiation ethics.

Ways to Effectively Bluff

Of course, your capacity for risk may be greater than mine. If so, here are some tips on effective bluffing suggested by James Freund, most of which apply during the offer-concession stage.

- Only bluff on significant issues. Don't risk your credibility on minor ones.
- Support your bluff with a plausible reason why you won't move.
- Couple your bluff with flexibility on another issue. The contrast will make it more believable.
- Try to ensure you will have an opportunity to back down if your counterpart believes your bluff and starts to walk.
- Have a "circumstances have changed" explanation ready if you're forced to back down. This will help mitigate the harm to your credibility.

Jackson had to bluff in *The Negotiator*. His alternatives to bluffing? Kill an innocent man or accept defeat in his effort to prove his innocence. Fortunately, we're not often faced with such harsh choices.

Closing Strategies

The final tactic you should use in maximizing your offer-concession effectiveness occurs at the close. The end appears near. You've been at the table for hours. You're tired, hungry, and nervous. You're right near your goal. Then your counterpart digs in. "No more," she says. "I've gone as far as I can go. I would love to do the deal, but you can only push me so far. Leave me a little bit of ego, will you? This is really good for you. In fact, it's fair for both of us. Let's just ink it and move forward. What do you say? Shake on it?"

Should you push for that little bit more? You're pretty sure you can get it. Is it worth it? Or will it push her over the edge? To what extent will asking for more turn the process adversarial? Should you care? What's happening psychologically at this point? What about her ego? Do you want her walking away feeling satisfied, or feeling like she got the raw end of the deal?

What about *your* ego? What role is it playing at this point? Do you care who makes the last concession? The last offer? What's the leverage situation now? What about the parties' alternatives? Have they changed? How do you decide these issues?

The negotiation close—what you do as the negotiation nears completion—is crucial. Done right, you will walk away with a signed agreement. Done wrong, and the deal may unnecessarily blow up.

Here's how you can become an effective closer. To do so, we will address:

- The substantive analysis you should undertake at this point
- The psychological tendencies of people approaching the end
- The stages of the close (initial and final) and what you should do in each
- A few closing tactics you may face and what to do about them

The Substance at the Close

At the close, always take a step back and substantively analyze: a) your leverage and expectations; b) the detailed elements involved; c) the parties' egos; and d) possible independent procedures to close the final gap.

Whether You Close Depends on Your Leverage and Expectations

Whether or not you ultimately ink the deal should depend on your leverage. Be analytical. Take a moment to step back and determine whether or not the deal at that point is better than your best likely alternative. Also consider whether that deal is better than *your counterpart's* best likely alternative. Don't lose sight of this crucial element. Reanalyzing your leverage here should provide you with the confidence and knowledge to make more informed decisions about what to do at or near the close.

Plus, reevaluate your expectations here, in light of everything you have learned—your leverage, independent standards, and how far both sides have moved and why. Based on these factors, you may need to stretch your goal, or you might not: Reevaluate everything. Then move forward knowing you did everything you could to get what you wanted.

Pay Attention to Detail—Don't Broad-Brush It Now

The close is not the time to get lazy. Often, you have developed a good working relationship with your counterpart as the negotiation appears close to ending. Don't relax now. Pay careful attention to every detail, especially how your oral agreement gets reflected in a written document, if this is the end point. I can't tell you how many times I've reached an oral agreement with my counterpart, only to find that the written agreement they propose doesn't reflect my understanding of our agreement. Sometimes it's a misunderstanding. Other times it's a conscious effort to gain an advantage, based on others' failure to focus on the details. Many lawsuits arise out of such "misunderstandings." Don't allow yourself to be a party to one.

Be careful you don't fall into the "ambiguity trap," either. It can be tempting to agree to ambiguous language as a way to resolve conflicts near the close. Be wary of these "solutions," especially if they appear minor, but could become more serious. It's risky to leave unresolved issues at the end, even though the other side might suggest, "It's not a big deal. We will never have to deal with that anyway."

If you notice an unresolved issue at the end, and your counterpart, in an off-handed way, says, "Don't worry about it," *worry about it*. Better to face it now than face each other in a lawsuit down the road.

Beware of Ego Issues—Leave Yours at the Door

Egos mess up negotiations, especially at the close, by undermining parties' rational decision-making and causing them to ignore strategically solid agreements. Egos can cause individuals to take irrational actions in the short-term that they regret in the long-term. It's amazing how many deals go south due to egos alone. Watch otherwise rational individuals throw their expectations and leverage out the window, or ignore their carefully selected independent standards. Parties will even disregard their offer-concession strategy, the one that brought both parties so near a deal.

Why does this happen? Some people can't stand the perception that someone else beat them. When someone talks about "winning" the negotiation, look for the ego. Their goal is more to "win" than to reach an agreement that satisfies their interests. Also, when someone excessively focuses on the amount they "conceded" relative to their counterpart, look for their ego, too. The amount "conceded" was not theirs to begin with, although sometimes it feels that way. Egos, in short, have ruined many potentially great deals. Egos, as you know from chapter 1, especially rear up in auction situations where the sellers try to get the potential buyers to pay more than their leverage and realistic expectations warrant. (If you're a buyer, watch out. And if you're a seller, good luck.)

In 1973 ABC's president of prime-time programming, Barry Diller, paid $3.3 million for a single television showing of the movie *The Poseidon Adventure*. The highest amount previously paid for a movie was $2 million for *Patton*. This $3.3 million payment was so huge ABC expected to lose $1 million on it. How did this happen? According to Robert Cialdini in *Influence*, the need to win in an open-bid auction for a scarce resource played a large role in this decision.

How does Cialdini know? Listen to the participants' comments after the auction:

> *ABC's Barry Diller*: "ABC has decided, regarding its policy for the future, that it would never again enter into an auction situation."

Remember, Diller "won." Contrast this with the postauction comments of his competitor, NBC's Robert Wood, who "lost" the auction.

> *NBC's Robert Wood*: "We were very rational at the start. We priced the movie out, in terms of what it could bring in for us, then allowed a certain value on top of that for exploitation. But then the bidding started. ABC opened with two million. I came back with two point four. ABC went to two point eight. And the fever of the thing caught us. Like a guy who had lost his mind, I kept bidding. Finally I went to three point two; and there came a moment when I said to myself, 'Good grief, if I get it, what the heck am I going to do with it?' When ABC finally topped me, my main feeling was relief. It's been very educational."

Beware of your ego, especially as you approach the close. Egos have led to successful bidders' feelings of regret so often that many call it "The Winner's Curse." Don't let this curse afflict you.

Instead, take a step back near the close and make sure the last offer on the table is better than your BATNA. If it's better grab it. But if that offer appears worse than your best alternative—that is, you would lose money if you accepted it—then take a walk. Your ego may have inadvertently made an appearance.

Also, listen carefully to your counterparts near the close, and take note if they appear highly competitive or talk openly about "winning" and "losing." If these occur, keep a close eye on their egos.

Don't second-guess yourself, either. Thinking and acting strategically will lead to more effective negotiations and agreements that satisfy your fundamental interests. Success is defined by whether you have satisfied your fundamental interests. Don't lose sight of this at the close.

Let's face it—everyone has an ego. The critical question, though, relates to its size, its visibility to others, and its impact on the negotiation process. Especially the latter. If you want a rule of thumb on egos, here it is: Check your ego at the door, especially at the close. I'm sure Diller wished he had done this back in 1973.

Close the Gap with Independent Procedures
One cut, then the other choose. Take turns, draw lots, flip a coin. Pick a fair, independent party to decide. When you're down to the end and the difference between the parties is relatively minimal, consider a fair, independent procedure to close the final gap. Better yet, ask your counterpart to suggest a fair way to resolve the remaining issues.

Watch Your Psychological Level of Commitment
In addition to analyzing the substance at the close, also evaluate the psychology involved.

Ever spent a great deal of time in a negotiation and, as you near the end, feel increasingly reluctant to walk away? You think, "If I walk away I will have wasted all this time. I don't want that, so I will just concede a little more and see what happens. We're so close, it would be horrible not to reach agreement."

What are you doing? You are recognizing that parties' psychological commitment to a deal increases with the length and effort put into it. The longer the negotiation, the more likely both sides will want to finish the deal.

Understand this, recognize it, and be comfortable with it. And don't just concede to avoid "wasting" your time. As discussed above, focus on your expectations and leverage. Then decide what makes sense strategically, not psychologically.

Closing Stages

"I sent them the settlement agreement weeks ago," a commercial real estate executive once told me. "I haven't heard anything since. Everyone agreed to the terms, including them paying us $300,000. Now they won't call me back. What's the problem?"

"Tell me how the negotiation ended," I responded.

"Well, we first reached agreement. Then, since we had an arbitration date closely approaching, we canceled that date. We didn't set a new date, since that would have required a deposit of several hundred dollars."

"There's your problem," I said. "There's no incentive for your counterpart to promptly sign the agreement. In fact, they benefit by delaying. You need an effective deadline to wrap this up and get your money. Set a new arbitration date, make the deposit, and see how fast they execute the agreement. Take back control of the process."

There are two critical closing stages, each of which requires special negotiation tactics. As you read about these different stages, the initial close and the final close, evaluate how the real estate executive above successfully completed one stage, then blew it in the next.

The Initial Close

How and when should you make what will likely be your final offer?

You generally know you're approaching the end when a true deadline exists and/or the parties become increasingly rigid in their offer-concession rhetoric and behavior. Parties' offers and concessions often take place here in relatively quick succession, leading to a progressively tenser atmosphere.

It's especially critical at this closing stage—the Initial Close—in addition to substantively and psychologically analyzing the issues discussed above, to:

- Appear patient
- Confirm you have a comprehensive knowledge of the other side's interests and issues, especially those that might prevent a final agreement
- Create an appropriate sense of urgency regarding the completion of the negotiation, so that you maintain some control over the closing process

In 1999 Jennifer made a proposal to a large company to provide it with a significant-size service contract.

At that point they had been negotiating for more than a year. Jennifer knew it was nearing the end, however, as the company wanted to allocate substantial funds to the proposed contract from that year's budget—and it was mid-November.

What did Jennifer do before she made her last offer?

She reviewed her file to make sure she had a thorough understanding of any possible last-minute roadblocks.

She then reevaluated her leverage by looking at the parties' mutual need for an agreement and exploring her best alternative to an agreement with it—and the company's best alternative to an agreement with her.

Next she discussed the specific elements of a "preliminary" proposal with her counterpart over the phone and made sure she offered a low-cost, face-saving concession. She did this so her counterpart could say the company got a great deal.

Jennifer then sent over a formal written proposal that included a set time within which to respond. Finally, she restrained herself from following up too quickly.

It paid off for her, and taking similar steps will pay off for you, too.

The Final Close

Jennifer's tactics, however, did not *immediately* pay off. Why? Like the real estate executive above, she failed to adequately control the postoral commitment stage: the Final Close. She had some nail-biting time.

Here are the keys to this stage that takes place just after the Initial Close:

- Confirm all oral commitments in writing as soon as they have been made, perhaps by e-mail or fax.
- Get a ready-to-be-signed written agreement over to your counterpart ASAP—one that includes a reasonable deadline for his or her signature and some incentive to sign it by the deadline. These days, significant deals also should be reduced to enforceable written contracts. And you (or your lawyer) should draft them. *You almost always want first shot at drafting negotiated agreements.* That way your first draft becomes the template from which all subsequent negotiations proceed. Even in an era of easily revised and shared documents, it's still an advantage to start with your draft and your standard terms. Make your counterpart offer up suggested changes. Then you're in the power position, with the ability to get credit for being reasonable and accepting the changes he or she might request. You can then ensure the changes accurately reflect your agreements. It's also likely you will think of issues you didn't originally negotiate during the drafting process. If you're doing the writing, you will have first crack at them.

- Finally, don't adversely affect your leverage, such as setting aside an arbitration date, until you have a signed, sealed, and delivered deal. Done deals can unravel in a hurry if you aren't careful.

What was Jennifer's strategic error during the Final Close? She did not confirm in writing the oral commitments made to her during this stage. Fortunately, it was not a fatal error.

Closing Tactics

There are few feelings worse in business than failing to close a closeable deal. Don't let it happen to you. To prevent this, consider the following rules of thumb to get you that last mile to closure:

- Focus on the other side's gains, not losses
- Watch out for the "Nibble"
- Don't narrow it down to only one issue; keep a trade-off
- Beware of the "Take Away"
- Make the last concession and shake on it
- Watch for the "Silent Close"

Focus on the Other Side's Gains, Not Losses

Most decision makers tend to be fairly risk-averse when faced with a choice between an absolutely certain gain or a chance of getting an even greater gain. In fact, in a study on this subject described in Robert Mnookin's *Beyond Winning,* 80 percent of respondents selected the certain gain of $240, not the chance of an even greater gain (a 25 percent chance of gaining $1,000, and a 75 percent chance of getting zero). This was true, even though the expected value of the latter selection (0.25 x $1,000 = $250 and 0.75 x $0 = 0) was $10 greater than the $240 in the first choice. This gives new meaning to the phrase "bird in the hand versus two in the bush."

By contrast, decision makers tend to *seek risk* and be *loss*-averse when the tables are turned and they face either a certain loss or a significant chance of losing even more.

What does this mean in terms of your behavior near the close? If you want your counterpart to accept your last offer, *focus on what they will certainly gain from the agreement and avoid discussing their costs or losses associated with the agreement.* Gains might include: resolution of the matter; avoiding additional costs; achieving certainty; that brand-new car or house; or a 5 percent salary raise. Losses to *avoid* discussing include: any out-of-pocket payment, such as the down payment for that new house; or the potential additional gain you lose by agreeing to the offer on the table, like what you could do with an *additional* 5 percent salary raise.

The insurance industry does this in attempting to convince potential customers to buy insurance. They emphasize the protection gained from the insurance, in light of a very uncertain future (the sure gain) versus the certain loss you will suffer in the form of insurance premiums. When was the last time a car salesman emphasized the vehicle's cost versus its beautiful looks and stellar performance? *Sell the gain, not the loss.*

On the other hand, if you want to explain why you won't accept an offer, focus on what you will lose versus what you will gain. When you're sitting with the insurance agent, focus on the monthly premiums and your certain loss. See if he will reduce them even further. Or discuss the traditionally high maintenance costs for that car you're considering. Regarding our loss-averse nature, if you want your last offer accepted, and it includes a payment from the other side, with a possibility that the payment will never have to be made, then focus on the chance it will never have to be paid. We're more willing to accept risk if it includes a chance we will suffer no loss at all.

Watch Out for the "Nibble"

How many times have you reached an agreement—perhaps even shaken hands on it—when your counterpart, perhaps a day later, asks for an additional concession? The deal appeared done, but now your counterpart wants more. What should you do with the "Nibble"?

Don't be taken hostage. If you concede at the end, they'll keep on nibbling away until you put your foot down. Don't let them get away with it. Avoid it by first finding out if your counterpart has a reputation as a "nibbler." Most know the nibblers in their profession. If they're known to nibble, or if you just can't find out, make a point of asking several times during the negotiation if all the issues are on the table. When your counterpart says yes, make an obvious note of it and write it down. This lessens the likelihood your counterpart will want to appear inconsistent by nibbling later. Second, don't forget the reciprocity principle. In effect, nibble back. If your counterpart wants another concession at the end, require one in return, preferably of greater value.

Don't Narrow It Down to Only One Issue; Keep a Trade-Off

In 2001 I received a detailed proposal from a consultant to provide my company with assistance in a variety of technological areas. This proposal, which I solicited after a two-hour lunch meeting and a one-hour follow-up call, included the elements we had discussed, the number of estimated hours it would take to complete, and a "standard" hourly rate. The consultant characterized the proposal as an "agreement" ready for signing. Except that I wasn't prepared to pay his "standard" hourly rate. The rest of the proposal/agreement appeared fine.

I originally considered waiting several days, researching some independent standards underlying similar consultants' rates, and then telling him everything looked great but his rate. This would have been a mistake. I would have created a situation where, no matter what happened, there would have been a perceived winner and loser on the rate issue. I would have set up a competitive zero-sum negotiation. Sometimes this is inevitable. Often, however, you can avoid a situation where there's only one issue left by keeping at least two issues alive, so you can trade them off for each other in the end. Allow your counterpart, at the least, to save face and not walk away feeling like he won or lost on that one remaining issue.

What did I do with this consultant? I reanalyzed his proposal and found several other issues to keep on the table. It was then easier to find common ground, as several areas remained where we could each give and take and still feel satisfied with the outcome.

Beware of the "Take Away"

Remember my friend who pulled out of her condominium deal after finding out it had termites? After pulling out she had to decide whether to resign her apartment lease, which expired in just over four weeks. Ideally, she wanted to go month-to-month. This would have maximized her flexibility once she found a place to buy. When she asked about a month-to-month lease her apartment manager quoted her $960 a month, $180 more per month than her current annual lease. However, her manager said he would keep her at the $780-per-month rate if she would sign a three-month lease with a two-month notice provision.

I suggested she contact her manager and counter with $780 on a month-to-month basis, suggesting this was "fair," given the security problems recently experienced in her complex.

A day later, before she had gotten in touch with her manager to counter, she got home to find a notice on her door indicating that her month-to-month rate would be $1,020, not the $960 promised.

Shocked, she immediately contacted her manager to find out what happened. He told her his boss had just raised the rates. However, he said he would talk to him to see if he could get him to honor the $960 rate (notice the good cop/bad cop tactic, a tactic addressed in chapter 9). Not surprisingly, he "convinced" his boss to honor the $960 rate. My friend, relieved, signed that day. She never even countered with the $780 on a month-to-month basis.

What happened?

The apartment manager pulled the "take away," a tactic also used by con men in other contexts. By withdrawing his $960 offer and substituting the more expensive $1,020, my friend's manager focused her on her weak leverage (she had no other place to live at this point, and her manager knew it). Withdrawing his previous offer and substituting a more expensive one also made his $960 offer appear more reasonable by comparison. Remember the contrast principle? My friend, while not happy, was relieved to get the $960, and never even asked for the $780 rate.

You may have experienced this same strategy while looking at large appliances. Let's say you go over the features with the salesperson and get a price quote based on the store's "advertised special." You then ask for an additional discount, due to the nick on the refrigerator door. The salesperson says he would love to give you the additional discount, but he must check with his boss. He then comes back five minutes later and says, "Boy, am I embarrassed. I just spoke to my supervisor, and he told me the advertised sale ended yesterday. But he gave me the authorization to give you the advertised sale price today. I can't help you on the nick, though." In most cases you will feel relieved just to get the sale price and forget about the additional discount for the nick.

This ploy can also be used by withdrawing any element of an offer already on the table or by telling someone that, if they don't accept the offer by a certain point, the offer will get progressively worse.

Let me be clear: I don't recommend this. In most cases it leaves a bad taste in the mouth of the person on whom it is being used. But be aware of it. It's not uncommon in a number of contexts, especially as a ploy to keep parties from countering.

Make the Last Concession and Shake on It
I almost always want my counterpart to walk away satisfied, even if we don't reach an agreement. Satisfied negotiators will be much more likely to stick with the agreement, regardless of its enforceability. And dissatisfied negotiators—agreement or no agreement—will bad-mouth you to their friends and your reputation will suffer.

How can you ensure your counterparts walk away satisfied, and still get all that you want? Make the last concession, even if it's a small one. As we discussed in the context of splitting the difference, making the last concession will give your counterparts the psychological impression that they "won," or at the least equaled you. Depending on their ego, this can be significant.

Plus, always shake hands with your counterpart at the end, look her in the eye, and congratulate her on a well-done negotiation. If that's not true, congratulate her on a "hard-fought contest" or something similarly ambiguous. Taking these actions will help preserve your relationship with them and within the greater community. I am constantly amazed at our small world and the connections between seemingly unrelated individuals. Your reputation will get around, one way or the other. Take these small steps at the end. They have large ramifications.

Watch for the "Silent Close"

The final closing tactic is what salespeople call the "Silent Close." Make your offer and be silent. Let the power of silence, which works in gathering information, work for you at the close. But be careful of this, too. Too much silence—even at the end—can create an overly awkward and competitive atmosphere. At that point, though, you may not care that much. After all, you can focus on the relationship after your counterpart says yes to end the silence.

Conclusion

Here's a summary of how to design the most effective offer-concession strategy.

CHAPTER 4 REVIEW

Golden Rule Four: Design an Offer-Concession Strategy

Know Your Offer-Concession Patterns
  - Most negotiators enter the offer-concession stage too soon—so beware of the premature offer
  - The longer you wait, the less eager you appear, and vice versa—the timing pattern
  - Early concessions include relatively larger moves—the size pattern

Whether and Where to Start (First-Offer Issues)
  - First offers—to start or not to start
    — Advantages to making first offers
      - Set expectations
      - Elicit genuine reaction
      - Strategic advantages—leverage timing, information, etc.

- — Disadvantages to making first offers
  - Lack of information to appropriately set it
  - Other side gains important information
  - Bracketing

- Situations where you should make the first offer
  - — Situations involving sophisticated parties with substantial access to information
  - — Situations involving complex nonprice issues and technically detailed agreements
  - — Situations where you have more information, defined standards, and strong leverage

- Where to start
  - — First-offer expectations peculiar to your industry or context
  - — Your original goal
  - — Your most aggressive, yet reasonable, independent standard
  - — The "room to move" psychological gamesmanship dynamic

    - Get into your counterpart's head
    - Game it out
    - Use round numbers
    - Throw an anchor

  - — Special factors underlying first counters

Psychological Expectations Underlying Offer-Concession Behavior
- Play the negotiation expectation game

- Ways to counter expectations
  - — A well-known reputation may counter expectations
  - — Aggressively stick to independent standards

- The reciprocity principle
  - — The rejection-then-retreat technique

- The contrast principle

- The commitment and consistency principle

The Nuts and Bolts of Making Offers and Concessions
- Language to use in making offers and concessions
  - — Be specific and detailed
  - — Explain the offer's rationale and tie it to standards *before* introducing numbers

- Promote an air of finality and increasing rigidity
  — Point out consequences (leverage)
  — Put it in writing
    - The written offer or counter
    - The written standard
    - Leverage-related documents

  — Avoid ranges
  — Be ready to react

- Carefully communicate your priorities and order of issues
  — Prioritize issues before the offer-concession stage
  — Put a numerical value on your nonmonetary issues
  — Tips for determining the order of issues

- Learn when, how, and under what circumstances to use agents
  — Consider your ability to objectively negotiate for yourself and factor in the value of your future relationship with the other side
  — Consider your potential agent's substantive issue-related expertise
  — Evaluate your own negotiation ability vis-à-vis your potential agent's
  — Assess the strategic and structural advantages and disadvantages of the principal-agent relationship

- To bluff or not to bluff
  — Negotiation credibility must be earned
  — The more likely a statement provides its speaker with a strategic advantage, the more likely the listener should independently confirm its veracity
  — Bluffing carries significant risks
  — Ways to effectively bluff

- Closing strategies
  — The substance at the close
    - Whether you close depends on your leverage and expectations
    - Pay attention to detail—don't broad-brush it now
    - Beware of ego issues—leave yours at the door
  — Watch your psychological level of commitment

  — Closing stages
    - The initial close
    - The final close

— Closing tactics
  - Focus on other side's *gains*, not losses
  - Watch out for the "Nibble"
  - Don't narrow it down to only one issue; keep a trade-off
  - Beware of the "Take Away"
  - Make the last concession and shake on it
  - Watch for the "Silent Close"

GOLDEN RULE FIVE:
CONTROL THE AGENDA

What's your price?" Maureen asked shortly after Charlie arrived. "Cut to the chase. I'm running late, so just tell me what you've got and your bottom line."

"Wait a second," Charlie responded. "Before we discuss price, why don't you tell me a bit about what you want, why and how you think we might be able to help each other? Then we can discuss the value our company will add, which provides the basis for our fees. If we run out of time I will be happy to come back, or put together a written proposal for you, based on your needs, what we've discussed, and including our fees. Make sense?"

"Sure," Maureen said.

The issue? Controlling the agenda.

Maureen wanted to talk price. Charlie wanted to ask questions and get information.

They thus started by negotiating over the agenda—the substantive one regarding the concrete issues on the table, and the atmospheric one dealing with issues like tone, style, trust, and feelings.

Agenda control constitutes a critical element in all negotiations. *If, when, where, how,* and *how long* we address issues affects our results. So does setting the appropriate atmosphere in which to most effectively explore the substantive issues.

Charlie knew that starting their discussion with zero-sum issues like price often leads to a more adversarial, less collaborative atmosphere. After all, most parties expect to competitively butt heads on zero-sum issues.

Charlie thus wanted to first establish a problem-solving atmosphere, develop a relationship, and substantively explore Maureen's needs and interests. This meant deferring their price conversation, if possible, to the end.

How can you control the agenda? Follow these steps:

- Prepare a substantive and atmospheric agenda to start
- Negotiate the agenda
- Manage the deadlines
- Apply these agenda control tips and tactics

Prepare a Substantive and Atmospheric Agenda to Start

Think strategically about which issues you want to address first, second, and so on. Prioritize them. Then figure out what atmosphere—during the beginning, middle, and end of the negotiation—will be most likely to get you what you want. For instance, figure out how you can start with the "big shmooze," collaboratively work together to find shared and compatible interests, and aggressively compete in a businesslike but friendly way over conflicting interests. In short, don't wing it.

And don't forget to analyze why it also makes sense for your counterpart to adopt this agenda. It takes two to tango.

Setting the Agenda for Short-Term Negotiations

In the early 1990s I represented a company being sued for allegedly stealing some trade secrets from another company. The other company said my client illegally took them. My client said it developed them on its own and, anyway, the information was publicly known, so the other company had no legally protectible right in it. After litigating the matter for months, we scheduled a one-day negotiation session to try to resolve the case without going to trial.

Since my clients were not based in Arizona, they flew in for the session. I recommended that they come in a day early to prepare. When they arrived for our preparation session I gave them a written agenda that detailed our goals for the day and what we needed to accomplish. In many ways our preparation session was itself a negotiation. We analyzed our information and what we needed to get in order to aggressively set our goals and expectations, discussed how to maximize our leverage, evaluated our objective criteria, designed an offer-concession strategy and, of course, planned how to control the agenda the next day. Our short-term preparation and focus on the agenda-control process helped us immeasurably the next day in the negotiation.

What should you do before you jump into similar short-term negotiations? Explore Golden Rules One through Four and their application to your situation. Then prepare to strategically implement them once the parties engage.

Setting the Long-Term Agenda

The value of controlling the agenda applies with equal force to longer-term negotiations played out over months or even years. In fact, the more parties that are involved and the longer the expected negotiation, the more crucial it is to control the agenda. One example of effective long-term agenda control occurred during the National Basketball Association's 1998–1999 players' lockout.

"This NBA strike is ridiculous," my friend told me at the time. "The players are already making tons. Why don't they just quit whining and play?"

I can't say I disagreed. Only one problem: *The NBA players never went on strike.*

Instead, the owners created and publicly defined the issues in their lockout, forced the issues by setting the deadline, and—according to conventional wisdom—successfully achieved their major goals at the players' expense. In basketball terms, the owners got the jump, controlled the ball, ran down the clock, and slam-dunked a last-second shot to win.

What happened, and how can we learn from this negotiation?

First, I have no inside information. I only know what I've read, heard, and discussed with friends, none of whom were directly involved.

But much was played out in the public arena. And it's obvious who played this game most effectively. The owners.

Of course, they started with a lead and the players started in foul trouble, so to speak. Public perception of the players before the lockout was relatively unsympathetic. Gentlemen players like Michael Jordan seemed on the way out, with less gentlemanly players seemingly entering the fray and representing the future. It's tough to be sympathetic to players when their union defends coach-choking players like Latrell Sprewell.

So the players started behind and promptly fell even further back. From the beginning the owners set the long-term agenda and drove the process. They prepared for the lockout. They warned of the lockout. They started the lockout. And they seemed willing to cancel the season.

They could do this in part because they recognized and maximized their leverage, especially their BATNA.

The owners' alternative? A canceled season. But the owners made sure a canceled season would not devastate them financially. Sure, they would lose significant revenue from canceled ticket sales. But they minimized the financial damage this alternative would inflict. They ensured, before the lockout, that they would receive TV money during a lockout and by giving themselves a good legal shot at not having to pay player salaries during the conflict. They thus had the power and the will to set the agenda and follow through on their promise to cancel the season.

By contrast, the players' BATNA wasn't strong. They were not getting paid, and some could not comfortably write off a year's salary. And even if they could, they didn't appear willing. Unlike the owners, they hadn't improved their BATNA *before* the lockout. So their "canceled season" kitty was running near empty.

Of course, other factors also impacted the negotiations. The players never presented a united front nor refocused public attention on the owners' actions. My friend thought the players actually had gone on strike. Plus, player representative and superstar Patrick Ewing was not truly representative of many players. And public perception mattered. After all, the public ultimately was providing the revenue for the players *and* the owners by purchasing tickets and watching the NBA on television.

Bottom line: The owners controlled the long-term agenda by strategically planning for the lockout and carrying out their plan when it occurred. They got much of what they wanted as a result.

You can too.

Negotiate the Agenda

What issues do you want to address first and what should you prioritize agendawise? To make this decision, consider the agenda-control dynamic to be a mini-negotiation. What do I mean? Apply Golden Rule One (Information Is Power—So Get It) to the agenda context. Find out your and your counterparts' agendas and time interests and aggressively explore *what* you and they want to address, *when, why,* and *in what order*. Gather the information about each parties' interests concerning the agenda and explore various agenda options. Then go through Golden Rules Two through Four to determine what agenda to set, control and, if necessary, negotiate. Applying Golden Rule Two (Maximize Your Leverage), find out how much your counterpart wants a certain agenda, and if he or she is willing to walk away without it. Applying Golden Rule Three (Employ "Fair" Objective Criteria), find out what type of agendas have been used in similar negotiations in the past (precedent) or what an expert might suggest (in some international negotiations, diplomatic experts script out everything based on tradition).

Applying Golden Rule Four (Design an Offer-Concession Strategy), incorporate your offer-concession strategy into your agenda control effort. Put it into practice by applying your closing strategies.

At the end of this book there's a worksheet detailing each stage of the Five Golden Rules. It's called the *"Gain the Edge!* Strategic Guide to Effective Negotiations." Use this practical strategic template in setting your agenda. Then negotiate your agenda, applying all these strategies to the agenda context.

Also keep the following psychological tendencies in mind in tactically developing and/or negotiating an agenda:

- Listeners remember the beginning and end of a presentation more than the middle.
- Repetition of a message leads to learning and acceptance. The more you repeat, within reason, the more likely it will be accepted as true. Especially keep this in mind if you have strong leverage.
- Stressing the similarity of positions and interests will be more likely to lead to acceptance than focusing on differences.
- You will be more likely to reach agreement on conflicting issues if you link them to issues on which agreement can be more easily reached.
- You can often generate positive momentum by starting with issues on which all sides can agree relatively easily and by leaving the more competitive, difficult, and conflict-oriented issues to the end. Develop a good, trusting working relationship first. Then use this to tackle the hardest issues. (This contrasts with those individuals who want to start negotiations with the "deal-breakers," saying that "if we can't reach agreement on this issue, why waste our time?" While this latter strategy has the advantage of raising important issues early on and consistently emphasizing their true value, I have found this largely counterproductive in complex negotiations involving multiple issues and the potential for long-term relationships between the parties. In certain highly competitive contexts, however, it can be effective, especially in situations involving significant time constraints, overt conflict over zero-sum issues, and a minimal likelihood of a future relationship between the parties.)

Manage the Deadlines

"If we only had a little more time I'm sure we could have reached a deal. We were so close."

I can't tell you how many times I have heard a variation of this "we were so close" statement. Every time the speakers sound sincere. And almost every time they're wrong. As you will see, we tend to behave in certain predictable ways when faced with deadlines, a crucial element of the agenda in almost all negotiations and one you want to manage.

To illustrate this I often model deadlines' impact in my seminars. As part of most of my seminars the participants engage in a one-on-one negotiation. At the start I tell them that "this negotiation shall only last thirty minutes. This is an inflexible deadline. If you do not resolve this dispute in the next thirty minutes there will be no resolution. No deal."

Twenty-five minutes later I start the countdown. "Five minutes remaining," I announce. I later announce a two-minute warning, and finally give them one-minute and thirty-second warnings.

How does this make everyone behave, and what should we do when dealing with deadlines? Follow my Four Steps to Use Deadlines to Your Advantage:

- Determine what, if any, deadlines already exist
- Evaluate the deadlines' impact (Deadline Dynamics)
- Decide what type of deadlines you want
- Take the initiative and set or negotiate the deadlines

Step 1: Determine What, If Any, Deadlines Already Exist

The first step is finding out what deadlines already exist for you and your counterpart. If you're in sales, do you have a month-end, quarter-end or year-end deadline? If you're a trial lawyer, has your trial date been set? If you want to sell your company, what advantages exist if you close by December 31?

Likewise, what deadlines exist for your counterpart? If you're selling your house, does the potential purchaser already live in your area, or are they planning to move from another city? If they're moving, when will they arrive? Do they already have the down payment, or will they get it from the sale of their current house?

Don't just look on the surface for obvious deadlines, either. Sometimes a party's personal deadline, like an upcoming vacation, can have a substantial impact.

Finally, find out what deadlines have existed in similar negotiations in the past. Research the deadline precedents. They may crop up again.

Once you know the deadlines, chart them. They won't help you if you don't keep track of them.

Step 2: Evaluate the Deadlines' Impact (Deadline Dynamics)

In 1999 a friend in Chicago bought what he calls the Daddy Warbucks house, a house once owned by the creator of *Annie*. When he first offered to buy the house it had only been available a short time. Since he felt the house was priced below market, he worried that someone else might come in shortly after his offer and start a bidding war.

What did he do? He told the seller his offer would only remain valid to the end of the day. If not accepted within that time period, he said, he would withdraw it and offer less for the house. In other words, he used a variation of the "take away."

If you're the seller here, your first step after identifying the deadline should be to evaluate its potential impact. To do so, analyze the types of impacts that deadlines almost always create, at least to some degree. I call them Deadline Dynamics. Each occurred in this house negotiation.

Urgency Impact

Deadlines often create an increasing sense of urgency and pressure for all the parties, especially for those with weaker leverage. Deadlines tend to focus us on our weak leverage. Here the seller had weak leverage, with a need to sell quickly and no good alternative offer at the time.

My friend, by contrast, had no real need to buy, and he had a decent alternative. By imposing a deadline and combining it with the take-away he emphasized the transitory nature of his offer, increased the seller's sense of urgency, and focused the seller on her weak leverage.

Psychologically, deadlines also focus us on our tendency to want things more when the supply appears to be diminishing. After all, the supply, or the deal, disappears if the parties reach the deadline without an agreement. As we discussed in regard to leverage, walkouts, and bluffing, psychologist Robert Cialdini calls this the scarcity effect. This feeling increases even more with short deadlines imposed by independent outside factors. Deadlines also increase the competitive nature of the process and create an increasingly tense atmosphere.

Of course, sometimes setting a deadline can backfire by unnecessarily ratcheting up the tension. Certain deadlines will be counterproductive if success depends upon the parties creatively working together to resolve mutual problems. Pressure and tension can short circuit the creative process and lead to hard feelings, especially if one party attempts to impose a deadline on the other.

Understand and evaluate this urgency impact. It will help you manage it in the end.

Timing Impact

As you know, the passage of time usually helps or hurts you from a leverage perspective. Deadlines, of course, cut this time short. How can you take advantage of this? If delay and the passage of time hurts you set short deadlines. If delay and the passage of time helps you, set long or no deadlines.

In my friend's house negotiation he felt that time would help the seller by presenting alternative buyers. This hurt him. He thus imposed a short deadline to minimize this possibility. It worked. He received a signed contract back before his deadline expired.

Concession Impact

As discussed in chapter 4, the closer you get to the end of the negotiation, the faster the concessions flow and the smaller they get. Deadlines greatly affect offer-concession strategies and behavior. Since deadlines often represent the end of the negotiation, always reconsider your offer-concession strategies with the addition or removal of deadlines.

Organizational Impact

Deadlines also often increase the likelihood that the negotiations will move along at a more organized and controlled pace. Creating a set time frame within which the negotiation is to conclude, or within which certain activities are to take place, often causes parties to behave in a way consistent with the deadline.

Deadlines impact the negotiation process in fairly predictable ways. Learn and recognize these patterns, and you will be able to use them to gain an advantage.

Step 3: Decide What Type of Deadlines You Want

Different types of deadlines impact negotiations in different ways. Here are a few common types of deadlines, and when and where you should use them:

Short Deadlines

As discussed earlier, short deadlines increase pressure and tension. As a result, they are often used by those hurt by the passage of time and with little interest in a future relationship with their counterparts. The shorter the deadline, the more pressure both sides will feel. The longer the deadline (or having no deadline at all), the less pressure.

Short deadlines also create more competitive atmospheres. This may be good or bad. If the parties want a future relationship short deadlines can be quite harmful. However, if the parties have no interest in a future relationship short deadlines can be very productive.

My Chicago friend wanted pressure, tension, competition, and had no interest in a future relationship with the seller. Setting a short deadline made sense for him.

Long Deadlines

Long deadlines, or even no deadlines at all, decrease pressure and tension. As a result, they are often used by those helped by the passage of time and/or those who want a future relationship with their counterparts. Longer deadlines also help those creatively working together to resolve mutual problems.

If delay helps you and you're interested in a future relationship with your counterpart, push for longer deadlines or no deadlines at all. Do the same if you tend to shy away from overt conflict and feel overly stressed by deadlines.

In some civil lawsuits defendants benefit from delays. After all, they may be forced, at the end, to cough up some money if a judge or jury finds that they damaged the plaintiffs. The longer such defendants can delay that possible result, the better. Memories also fade with time, and plaintiffs usually must prove the defendant did something wrong. Without that evidence plaintiffs will lose. (Of course, while seeking to delay they will also aggressively attempt to defend themselves and strengthen their cases, thus simultaneously getting ready for trial and maximizing their leverage.)

Many defense lawyers thus generally try to avoid short deadlines and often seek to delay. Plaintiffs lawyers, on the other hand, typically tend to push forward as aggressively as possible. The sooner they can get to trial, within reason, the better.

Flexible Deadlines

In *You Can Negotiate Anything*, Herb Cohen describes a negotiation that illustrates the critical nature of evaluating deadlines' flexibility. It was

Cohen's first big negotiation as a young executive, and his company sent him to Japan to negotiate with his Japanese counterparts. Here's how Cohen describes it:

> When the plane landed in Tokyo I was the first passenger to trot down the ramp, raring to go. At the bottom of the ramp two Japanese gentlemen awaited me, bowing politely. I liked that.
>
> The two Japanese helped me through customs, then escorted me to a large limousine . . . [On the ride in, one of my Japanese counterparts] asked, "Are you concerned about getting back to your plane on time?" (Up to that moment I had not been concerned.) "We can schedule this limousine to transport you back to the airport."
>
> I thought to myself, "How considerate."
>
> Reaching into my pocket, I handed them my return flight ticket so the limousine would know when to get me. I didn't realize it then, but they knew my deadline [fourteen days], whereas I didn't know theirs.

For the next eleven days, Cohen's Japanese hosts entertained him and made sure he experienced, firsthand, Japanese hospitality and culture. Every time Cohen inquired about starting the negotiations, they would say "Plenty of time! Plenty of time!"

According to Cohen, "On the twelfth day, we began the negotiations, finishing early so we could play golf. On the thirteenth day we began again, and ended early because of the farewell dinner. Finally, on the morning of the fourteenth day, we resumed our negotiations in earnest. Just as we were getting to the crux of things, the limousine pulled up to take me to the airport. We all piled in and continued hashing out the terms. Just as the limousine's brakes were applied at the terminal, we consummated the deal."

How well do you think Cohen did?

He says that for "many years [his] superiors referred to it as 'The first great Japanese victory since Pearl Harbor.'"

Was Cohen's flight the last flight from Japan to the United States? Of course not. But Cohen felt his deadline was real. He felt he needed to go back to the United States with a deal. Critically, he communicated this need to his Japanese counterparts. As Cohen notes, they "correctly anticipated that I wouldn't go home empty-handed."

His deadline, like many, was flexible. It could be changed. Cohen's negotiation would have been different had he found out what, if any, time pressure or deadlines might be affecting his Japanese counterparts and overtly changed his ticket to an open return.

Many deadlines appear inflexible. Yet, they often can be changed. Find out and evaluate the flexibility of your deadlines. Have similar deadlines been inflexible in the past, or were your counterparts bluffing? Do the deadlines make sense? Always consider the advantages and disadvantages of flexible versus inflexible deadlines. Then decide when and where to use them, and when to disclose them, too.

Other types of deadlines include legally required deadlines, interim deadlines, and many others. The key: Determine what types of deadlines provide you with a strategic advantage, then decide how to effectively use them.

Step 4: Take the Initiative and Set or Negotiate the Deadlines

What should you do, once you have identified the deadlines, evaluated their impact, and determined which, if any, you want to implement? Manage and control them. Take the initiative and set or negotiate them.

Go through Golden Rules One through Four, applying them to the deadline issues. Applying Golden Rule One (Information Is Power—So Get It), find out what your counterpart wants in terms of deadlines. Do they care? If so, why and to what extent? What options exist regarding various deadlines? Applying Golden Rule Two (Maximize Your Leverage), how much do the parties need a deadline? What are the alternatives if there is no deadline? Applying Golden Rule Three (Employ "Fair" Objective Criteria), what standards or procedures apply to your deadlines? To what extent are the deadlines tied to external factors or standards over which the parties have little or no control? What do the experts say about how long this type of negotiation takes? How long would be "fair and reasonable?" What about precedents deadlinewise? Applying Golden Rule Four (Design an Offer-Concession Strategy), evaluate whether to make the first offer of a deadline, or try to elicit a first offer from your counterpart. Do you want to bracket them?

And as you approach the final deadline *don't let them see you sweat*. They will perceive your sweating as communicating impatience and desperation. As you know, you don't want the other side to *perceive* your desperation. The moment they perceive it your leverage weakens. Always appear patient.

This "perception of patience" issue arose during some political negotiations many years ago. Seven political candidates were slated to debate each other on television, and the candidates' representatives negotiated a number of issues, including what substantive issues to address, the length of each candidate's response, and whether they could ask each other questions.

The negotiation also involved the intensity of the lights. Why do candidates care about the lights? Because some people sweat more than others at higher temperatures. If the lights were turned up certain candidates would sweat more. The "nonsweaters" would have the advantage. The television audience would perceive the "sweaters" as nervous, impatient, and less able to handle the stressful job each desperately wanted.

A variation of this "perception of patience" principle also occurred during the first John F. Kennedy–Richard M. Nixon presidential debate in 1960. During this debate Kennedy appeared calm, cool, and collected. Nixon, on the other hand, sweated up a storm. Most *listening* to the debate on radio felt Nixon won. Most *watching* it on television felt Kennedy won. Many attribute Kennedy's narrow victory in November to his appearance in this first debate.

You don't have to *be* patient, but you should *appear* patient. The perception of patience pays.

All these considerations will help you effectively manage and control your deadlines. Don't leave your deadlines to chance or the other party. Those who control the deadlines often achieve the best results.

Hopefully, then, you won't soon say, "If we only had more time."

Apply These Agenda-Control Tips and Tactics

In addition to managing the deadlines, how should you control the agenda and take the initiative? Here are six effective agenda-control tactics:

- Use the power of the pen
- Preview, agree, and focus
- Just do it
- The subtle control
- Control the turf
- To phone or not to phone

You cannot effectively control the agenda, however, unless you have sufficiently prepared. This preparation should include an analysis of what, if any, agenda-control tactics your counterparts might want to use or have used in the past. Preparation pays off.

Use the Power of the Pen

He who holds the pen holds the power. Printed or written words, as discussed in chapter 4, also appear more powerful than spoken words.

Prepare a written agenda. It's one of the most efficient and effective agenda-control techniques ever devised.

How long does it take to prepare a written agenda? Sometimes just a few minutes. Try it. Prepare one. Pass out copies at your next negotiation or e-mail it ahead of time. See what happens. At best, the other side will examine it, evaluate it, and agree to follow it. In my seminars I regularly ask my attendees how often their counterparts follow their written agenda when they bring one. The majority indicate their counterparts usually just agree to follow it without giving it much thought. Even if your counterpart wants to negotiate the agenda, you will likely have organized the issues in ways you find productive. This alone is an advantage.

At worst, what can happen? Your counterpart will see you as organized, prepared, thorough, and thinking strategically about the process. In short, there's little downside to preparing a written agenda, other than your time in putting it together. It's almost always time well spent. (And if your counterpart also presents *you* with his or her written agenda, negotiate it.)

As an alternative to a written agenda, you can also capture the power of the pen by using a blackboard, whiteboard, flipchart, PowerPoint presentation, or a combination of the above.

Preview, Agree, and Focus

Sometimes your counterpart might be skeptical of a written agenda. Or a written agenda might appear too formal. In these cases, try this:

> I've given this issue a great deal of thought and think it would be very productive for all of us if we first address . . . Second, let's focus on . . . Finally, let's conclude by . . . How does that sound?

If they agree, you're off. And if they divert later after having agreed, suggest that going in their new direction is inconsistent with what they had already agreed to. In other words, first preview your agenda. Second, get their oral commitment to follow it. Finally, maintain your focus on that agenda.

Of course, your counterparts might reject your agenda and suggest their own. No problem. If this happens, evaluate the importance of the issues contained in the exchange of agendas. Those issues will contain strategic information about each side's priorities and interests.

Just Do It

In 1999 I met with Arizona Diamondbacks and Phoenix Suns chairman and CEO Jerry Colangelo to discuss his most effective negotiation strategies. For the first twenty minutes of our conversation he used those strategies on me. He started by asking me questions and developing rapport. He asked questions about my personal background (where I grew up, where I went to college, what sports I followed), my professional background (where I went to law school, how I became interested in the negotiation field), and what I wanted to accomplish in our meeting.

For the rest of the meeting I asked him questions. But he initially controlled the agenda by knowing what he wanted to do and then just doing it. He wanted to establish rapport, find out about me, and see how it went. I acquiesced. I was happy to let the meeting proceed at his direction, because it satisfied my interests, too. At the end of the meeting we both got what we wanted.

The Subtle Control

Some people control the agenda by letting others *appear* to control the agenda. Let me explain. Ego issues often appear front and center when dealing with agenda-control issues. Some people love to control and appear to be in control. Other people feel more comfortable taking a less visible, but no less effective, role. Both types of individuals can control agendas in effective ways.

Those people wishing to overtly control the process often just attempt to take control. They "just do it." In other circumstances, however, operating more subtly will be more effective. In such instances you can control the agenda by making low-key but strategic moves.

Simply asking questions or raising issues at certain strategic times can be an incredibly effective way to change the subject to your issue. Or, in a multiparty negotiation you might form an alliance with another entity that has similar interests and let your partner take the more overt role. You also might decide not to even physically show up, but simply send your representatives with instructions as to how to proceed.

Some negotiators just do it. Other negotiators take a more subtle approach. The key is to determine when and where to use each approach.

Control the Turf

At the end of the day I was escorted into his corner office. He was the managing partner of the law firm and he sat behind a large desk, in the power position. It was my last interview. If it went well, I hoped to receive a job offer.

So began our negotiation. Many negotiators would say I was already at a disadvantage. I was on his turf, in his office, at the mercy of his schedule, and he controlled the environment. I'm not so sure. While these factors can provide a leg up, I learned some crucial information about him from sitting in his office and soaking up his surroundings. For instance, I did not notice many family or personal pictures, and the environment was very businesslike. This information proved indispensable in the later stages of our negotiation.

Many negotiations begin with the turf battle: your place, my place, or a neutral ground. In some cases the home court provides a significant advantage. Other times it can work to your detriment. Neutral sites, of course, eliminate much of the bias.

What factors impact this turf issue? When deciding or negotiating where to meet, consider your control of the environment, the parties' psychological tendencies, information you want to share, efficiency and logistics, and the parties' expectations about the turf.

Control the Environment

In my office I control the environment. While some limitations exist, I largely control the seating and the office support functions that parties require. I might even control who attends, if this has not already been explicitly addressed. This control can provide a substantial advantage.

In 2002 I consulted with a large manufacturing company after it experienced a particularly challenging negotiation with one of its biggest customers. The prior year it was asked to send its team to negotiate at its customer's headquarters in the Midwest. Unexpectedly, when the company's negotiating team arrived they were told their biggest competitor was in the adjoining conference room. A bidding war ensued for the customer's business. This could not have happened without the customer's home-court advantage.

The company's mistake? They failed to address the question of who would be at the table before they traveled to their customer's turf.

Psychological Tendencies

A big reason to negotiate on your home front relates to the psychological comfort many derive from their most familiar environment. If you're psychologically at ease you will be better able to make the moves necessary to maximize your negotiation effectiveness. Plus, we psychologically tend to fight harder for what we want on our home front than elsewhere.

Sports teams know this well. These psychological factors work in the reverse if you're heading to their place.

Some experienced negotiators downplay the relevance of this factor, saying it's no big deal. It may very well be true for them. If you're an extremely confident negotiator, you may be equally comfortable in many different environments. But your counterpart may not. Take this into consideration.

Information Exchange

At your office you inevitably provide strategic information to your counterpart concerning who you are and how you approach situations. One of the first things I do when I meet someone in their office is analyze that individual's personal and business environment. Are they ego-driven, with awards and other exhibitions of their alleged expertise prominently displayed? Are they family- and relationship-oriented, with family pictures all over? Are they risk-takers, with skydiving pictures on the wall? What does it tell you if they have an organized, neat desk with sharpened pencils lined up on top? The list goes on.

You may or may not want to share this information. Evaluate this. Of course, you can always meet in a relatively sterile conference room, although your counterparts will still get a sense of the personality of your work environment.

Efficiency and Logistics

There's no travel cost in time or money if you're negotiating from your place. Plus, you can often deal more effectively with unexpected issues or emergencies. Your resources are right at hand. But if your office doesn't satisfy the parties' logistical needs, you may be forced to meet at your counterparts' place or at a neutral site. Efficiency and logistics are often critical factors to consider in deciding where to meet.

Expectations

Finally, consider what expectations exist regarding the site. Tradition may drive this decision. Be wary of conceding on the location front, though, if you believe your counterpart will consider it a sign of weakness and reflective of your negotiating style.

Consider these factors when negotiating where to meet. Turf makes a difference.

To Phone or Not to Phone

When should you negotiate in person and when over the phone? What about e-mail versus letter? Fax versus video conference? When should you start by letter, continue by phone and e-mail, and finish in person? Or use some other order? Given the pace of technological change these days, who knows when the next communication device will reach out and touch us?

These various options require that we set up a strategic framework for this decision. Here's what I suggest. Determine what you want to accomplish with *each* communication. Then decide which method most appropriately accomplishes this goal. Map it out.

For instance, consider what you want to accomplish with your first communication. Often, as discussed in chapter 1, parties want to start by establishing some rapport and a relationship with their counterpart. This obviously helps with information gathering and sharing. If so, consider all the ways you can start. Examples include, from the most personal to the least personal:

- Face-to-face meeting
- Video conference
- Telephone (landline)
- Telephone (cell)
- Telephone (speaker phone)
- Telephone (conference call)
- Handwritten note
- Facsimile
- Letter (hand-delivered)
- Letter (overnight package)
- Letter (post)

In making your decision, take into account the following three factors as they relate to your goal: relationship, efficiency, and a written record.

Relationship

The more your goal includes a long-term relationship, the more likely you should use the more personal communication methods (face-to-face, telephone, handwritten note, etc.), at least to start. You don't want to negotiate with your business partner by constantly exchanging letters. That ultimately would harm the relationship. For most people, it's also harder to establish a strong personal relationship over the phone or e-mail than it is in person.

Likewise, in buying a computer or a large appliance you may do it all over the Internet because you don't care much about a relationship.

Consider also how the forum substantively helps or hurts you. It's easier to say no on the telephone than in person. It's even easier by letter. The less personal and weaker the relationship, the easier to say no. It's also easier to be more competitive when you use less personal methods of communicating. I used to get some of the most adversarial letters I've ever seen from the opposing lawyers in some of my cases. Yet, they were entirely different in their in-person communications. (Of course, some were very adversarial in person, too.) While inconsistent, it's easier to be adversarial in writing than in person.

My recommendation? If your proposal requires a significant change, making a personal oral presentation or setting up a meeting will increase its likelihood of acceptance.

Face-to-face negotiations also lessen the likelihood of misunderstanding and provide parties with the opportunity to observe body language, facial expressions, and behavioral cues. As discussed in chapter 1, accurately reading nonverbal signals can prevent crucial long-term problems. These can be substantial advantages or disadvantages, depending on your in-person skills.

Telephone negotiations also have advantages and disadvantages. Evaluate them. For instance, you can interpret verbal signals and inflections over the telephone, but not in a written document, yet you can't view your counterpart's facial expressions or other body language.

In short, take into account your interest in a future relationship with your counterpart when deciding how to communicate.

Efficiency

Efficiency often plays the largest role in how we communicate. That's one of e-mail's greatest advantages. It's incredibly efficient. Sometimes, though, it's more efficient to meet in person, especially if the negotiation involves multiple parties. Back when I was a new lawyer, and e-mail first hit the scene, a partner in my firm used to send me half a dozen e-mails a day asking me to do various legal projects and research. His office was twenty feet from mine!

I thought it was ridiculous. It would have taken two seconds for him to pop his head in my door and ask me in person. I could then have explored with him, in depth, what he wanted and made sure I fully understood his assignment.

From his standpoint, meeting in person seemed inefficient. He could crank out e-mails without ever leaving his desk. If I had questions, I could e-mail him back or stop in to see him. Consider efficiency in deciding how to communicate. E-mail is more efficient than the phone. The phone is often more efficient than face-to-face. Efficiency sometimes comes with a cost, though. Take all these considerations into account.

Written Record

In some negotiations you want to create a paper trail and you want written commitments. As noted in chapter 4, there are many advantages to putting offers in writing. If you represent a client, for instance, you can simply copy your client on your letters and keep him or her in the loop. These should also be considered in making this decision. And even if you don't make the offer in writing, and do it over the phone, take detailed notes of your conversation and consider a confirming letter or e-mail. Memories fade—some faster than others. Thorough and accurate notes and files, however, will be relied upon by everyone.

Conclusion

Controlling the agenda can make a huge difference. In early 2003 the United States and North Korea were locked in an acrimonious standoff involving North Korea's nuclear weapons program. For months they were deadlocked over a critical agenda-control issue—who would participate in the negotiation. The United States wanted multilateral negotiations, with five countries present and participating. North Korea wanted bilateral negotiations solely between North Korea and the United States. Ultimately the parties compromised for a first meeting with three countries at the table (North Korea, the United States, and China), but not before many months of sending signals back and forth regarding what might initially appear to be a minor issue. Who sat at that table was a major issue.

Controlling the agenda is easy to discuss and hard to do. Here's my agenda-control template. Read it. Understand it. Apply it to your negotiations. Then finish reading, digesting, and implementing the strategies in this book. That's *my* agenda.

CHAPTER 5 REVIEW

Golden Rule Five: Control the Agenda

Prepare a Substantive and Atmospheric Agenda to Start
- Setting the agenda for short-term negotiations
- Setting the long-term agenda

Negotiate the Agenda

Manage the Deadlines
- Determine what, if any, deadlines already exist
- Evaluate the deadlines' impact (Deadline Dynamics: urgency, timing, concession, and organization)
- Decide what type of deadlines you want (short, long, or flexible)
- Take the initiative and set or negotiate the deadlines (and don't let them see you sweat)

Apply These Agenda Control Tips and Tactics
- Use the power of the pen
- Preview, agree, and focus
- Just do it
- The subtle control
- Control the turf
- To phone or not to phone (consider effect on relationship, efficiency, and written record)

PART TWO

MAKING THE
GOLDEN RULES
WORK FOR YOU

The Five Golden Rules provide the essential building blocks for every negotiation. In every negotiation, you want to: 1) acquire power by getting information; 2) maximize your leverage; 3) employ "fair" objective criteria; 4) design an offer-concession strategy; and 5) control the agenda.

But there's more. You also have to evaluate your own and your counterparts' negotiation styles and analyze how they interact. These styles impact how you apply the Five Golden Rules in a variety of contexts. In some situations you should share more information. In others you should aggressively exercise your leverage with walkouts and similar tactics. But these will be counterproductive in other contexts. How you negotiate with a corporate vice president should vastly differ from how you handle a curfew with your teenage son.

In Part Two we will explore why and how to negotiate differently in various contexts, and provide a blueprint for determining when and where to use the most effective strategies. First we will examine parties' personal negotiating styles. Then we will look at various approaches to negotiation ethics and discuss how to negotiate with those who lie. Next, we will address the overall strategies—Competitive versus Problem-Solving—that we generally use in different contexts.

Finally, we will discuss some tough negotiation problems, including negotiation "games," impasse-breaking strategies, dealing with overly emotional counterparts, and figuring out what to do when you're uncomfortable with the whole negotiation process. We will also focus on the multiparty negotiation and evaluate its unique challenges.

These problems require different applications of the Five Golden Rules, applications we will address so they don't undermine your effectiveness.

PERSONALITY TENDENCIES—STYLE ISSUES

You know the type: supercompetitive, hard-nosed, adversarial, big ego, risk-taker, overtly controlling, always out to "win." Can't win without beating the other side, right?

You also know the type at the opposite end of the spectrum: conflict-avoiders. They dislike any conflict, especially the interpersonal kind. They dislike activities with designated winners and losers. They value peace above most everything and go to considerable lengths to prevent open conflict.

How we naturally approach conflict impacts our ability to effectively negotiate. Effective negotiators also share certain traits and qualities.

I have found that most individuals can generally identify and learn to more effectively negotiate with those often characterized in the psychological research as, personality-wise, a) competitors, b) accommodators, and c) conflict avoiders. In categorizing individuals and evaluating its impact on negotiations, however, it's important to keep the following in mind.

One, each individual generally falls into one category or another but exhibits elements of each in their personality. Some tendencies dominate more than others. Two, different situations bring out different characteristics. We might be comfortable dealing with conflict in professional settings but avoid it in our personal lives. These are also general tendencies, not set characteristics. Individuals, especially with more self-awareness, can modify them. At the least self-awareness can help us learn to react more effectively in certain settings.

One final caveat: Do not stray too far from your own natural comfort zone. While the following tactics will help mitigate the disadvantages of some personality tendencies in certain settings, they are not a panacea. Moving too far away from your natural personality style will diminish your effectiveness. Those who passionately dislike conflict should not become trial lawyers. Those who love to compete should not teach elementary school.

So, how can you identify your and your counterparts' personality styles, and what should you do about them? And what traits and qualities do most effective negotiators share?

To answer these questions, you should understand how to:

- Recognize everyone's negotiation styles (competitors, accommodators, and conflict avoiders)
- Negotiate stylewise in the most effective way

Recognize Everyone's Negotiation Styles

Start by looking internally and asking a few colleagues to evaluate your personal style. Become more sensitized to your tendencies and evaluate how they manifest themselves. Then find out your counterpart's style. Contact others with whom they have negotiated: Past experience is a good predictor of future action.

In all your negotiations, identify if your counterpart exhibits one or more of the following constellations of traits:

Competitors

Competitors generally exhibit the following characteristics:

- High comfort level with conflict and competition
- Enjoy debating substantive issues
- Not great listeners, due at times to significant egos
- Direct, sometimes adversarial tone, words, and body language
- Relatively impatient to engage in the offer-concession stage of the process, and often aggressive in this process
- Enjoy openly controlling and framing issues
- Strong desire to win and not lose
- Enthusiastic attitude toward negotiations
- Style can appear stubborn, arrogant, and/or untrustworthy
- Often at ease with risk and pressurized environments

- Comfortable using relatively risky leverage tactics like walkouts, threats, ultimatums, bluffing, and other ways to focus the parties on the leverage and power elements in the negotiation

How Should You Negotiate with "Competitors"?

First, recognize that the overall strategic elements of negotiation universally apply to different personality styles. Apply the Five Golden Rules. With different styles, however, emphasize some elements more than others. With competitors, emphasize the following:

Ask and Listen

Competitors love to talk and persuade. Let them. In fact, encourage them. Even paraphrase and repeat their arguments to them as you actively listen. The more they try to persuade you they have a better case, the more power you're getting. Find out their critical issues. Then negotiate them.

Play to their ego, too. Competitors enjoy winning, and want others to know it. Use this to your advantage. Let them think they're winning. At the same time, get information.

Once you have gained this information, determine its applicability and effectiveness within your negotiation situation. Use it to help you get what you want.

Stick to Your Principles

Gain their respect. Competitors respect strength. But don't necessarily do it in an adversarial way, although this might be needed at times. Instead, emphasize Golden Rule Three (Employ "Fair" Objective Criteria). Find out what standards underlie their offers. Compare them to your own. And stick to your guns. Don't let them steamroll you. Don't unnecessarily concede. If you do, competitors will come at you again and again. Instead, require a reasonable rationale that makes sense before you move. Insist on reciprocity.

Frankly Emphasize Your Leverage

Competitors will not be offended by direct language about your leverage. In fact, frankly discussing leverage often will effectively focus competitors on the strategic elements of the negotiation. If your counterpart has a bad alternative to doing a deal with you, emphasize it in a direct and straightforward fashion. Lower your voice, look them in the eye, and just lay out the facts about both sides' needs and alternatives.

I will bet you can already identify many of your previous counterparts as competitors. One of my former bosses is a classic competitor. He loves to mix it up and isn't afraid to take on anyone. Not surprisingly, he's a trial lawyer.

Accommodators

Accommodators generally exhibit many of the following characteristics:

- Highly value good relationships
- Love to be liked and are often quite likeable
- Attitude reflects concern, compassion, and understanding
- Fairly accurately show nonjudgmental understanding of others' concerns
- Effective listening skills
- Tend to be viewed as trustworthy, due in part to their superior listening skills
- Dislike open conflict, especially when it might harm the relationship
- Extended conflicts make them uncomfortable, and they often try to smooth over conflicts
- Typical relationships with others lack open conflict
- Adept at creating relatively stress-free atmospheres
- Relationship concerns can overshadow substantive issues

How Should You Negotiate with "Accommodators"?

Resist the Temptation to Just Talk. Ask Back.
Accommodators are master information gatherers. They will sincerely express interest in you and it will be tempting to share a great deal of information with them. Resist the urge, at least initially. Determine early on what information to strategically share and what to not to share. Then keep to your plan.

Also, aggressively probe accommodators' interests and get *them* to share information with *you*. Ask lots of questions. It will be easy to share with them. Make sure they share back.

Recognize the Value in Relationship Issues
Be sensitive to the interpersonal dynamic that often develops with accommodators. Accommodators largely view the negotiation dynamic through its impact on relationships. Often they will shy away from choices they perceive as harmful to the relationship. This can be positive or negative. They might unnecessarily concede, to preserve the relationship.

Say an accommodator is buying a new car from a competitive salesperson. After spending a significant amount of time getting to know one another the salesperson offers to sell the car at $1,000 over invoice. He explains that his commission share of the $1,000 dealership profit will be around $300. Even though this appears to be a relatively isolated transaction where neither party anticipates a significant future relationship, the accommodator might just accept instead of countering. An accommodator may feel that the salesperson will perceive a counter as a personal slight. In effect, the accommodator would rather pay more than be perceived as indicating the salesperson did not earn his $300 commission. This would harm the relationship, the crucial factor to accommodators. (By contrast, if a competitor were purchasing the car, he would aggressively counter at or below invoice.)

Accommodators value relationships, even where others do not. As a result, parties negotiating with accommodators should be especially sensitive to the value inherent in the relationship. Act accordingly.

Focus on Objective Criteria

Accommodators love independent objective standards and procedures, because focusing on standards or procedures can take the focal point away from competing personal opinions. In this way, they find their own win-win, a "fair and reasonable" way to agree and still grow the relationship. Using objective criteria can have a greater than normal impact with accommodators.

Where you emphasize leverage with competitors, focus on objective criteria with accommodators.

Conflict Avoiders

Conflict avoiders generally exhibit the following characteristics:

- Strong need to avoid conflict, especially open conflict
- Belief that almost all conflict is unproductive
- Extremely uncomfortable with emotional conflict
- High skill level at avoiding answering questions and addressing undesirable issues
- Rarely overtly control the agenda
- Can appear aloof and uninterested as they rarely engage in negotiations involving conflict

How Should You Negotiate with "Conflict Avoiders"?

Be Patient

Your patience will pay off with conflict avoiders because it will take a great deal of time and effort to fully explore conflict-related issues. If you don't have the patience, either you will look elsewhere or you will become frustrated with the constant deflection of issues. Conflict avoiders often can creatively find ways to satisfy interests without open conflict. Sometimes anticipated contentious issues resolve themselves with the passage of time.

Focus on Your Long-Term Goal

It's easy to get off track when your counterpart can skillfully avoid issues. Keep a laser-like focus on your goal. Persevere when necessary.

Aggressively Probe Their Interests

Like you would do in dealing with accommodators, aggressively probe conflict avoiders' interests and find out what they need and want. They will try to hide these, if they believe discussing them will lead to conflict. Your likelihood of success will increase the more you find out what they truly want and need.

Negotiate Stylewise in the Most Effective Way

Marquette University law professor Andrea Kupfer Schneider completed a 2002 study that evaluated lawyers' negotiating styles and concluded that the most effective negotiators were generally not overtly adversarial and they were viewed by their colleagues as having the following qualities:

Qualities of the Most Effective Negotiators

1. Ethical	11. Dignified
2. Experienced	12. Self-controlled
3. Personable	13. Accommodating
4. Rational	14. Astute about the law
5. Trustworthy	15. Agreeable
6. Realistic	16. Sociable
7. Confident	17. Adaptable
8. Perceptive	18. Poised
9. Communicative	19. Careful
10. Fair-minded	20. Wise

Regardless of your personal approach to conflict, strive to negotiate in this way. Your effectiveness will improve.

Overall, Schneider describes effective negotiators as those who are "both assertive (experienced, realistic, fair, astute, careful, wise) and empathetic (perceptive, communicative, accommodating, agreeable, adaptable). . . . Furthermore, [the effective negotiator] is good (ethical and trustworthy) and offers enjoyable company (personable, sociable, poised)."

All negotiators should strive to exhibit these qualities.

Competitors. Accommodators. Avoiders. What are the parties in your negotiations? Our personal styles and qualities affect everything we do. Knowing and effectively managing them, and exhibiting the most effective negotiating characteristics will help you navigate the most challenging negotiations.

CHAPTER 6 REVIEW

Personality Tendencies—Style Issues

Recognize Everyone's Negotiation Styles
- How to deal with "Competitors"
  — Ask and listen
  — Stick to your principles
  — Frankly emphasize your leverage
- How to deal with "Accommodators"
  — Resist the temptation to just talk. Ask back.
  — Recognize the value in relationship issues
  — Focus on objective criteria
- How to deal with "Conflict Avoiders"
  — Be patient
  — Focus on your long-term goal
  — Aggressively probe their interests

Negotiate Stylewise in the Most Effective Way
- Be assertive, empathetic, and enjoyable, and exhibit ethical, personable, rational, and trustworthy traits

ETHICS MAKE A BOTTOM-LINE DIFFERENCE

In early 2003 a client sent me a list of negotiation "games" its counterparts regularly use. The list ranged from lying about certain facts to falsely pretending not to understand critical issues. After we discussed how to counter these "games," a subject addressed in chapter 9, my client asked me which "games" I would recommend that they use in turn. Fair is fair, right?

Wrong. I would never recommend or use unethical negotiation "games." Yet, parties should not unilaterally disarm.

So, how and where should you draw the line in deciding what "games" to play and in answering the tough ethics issues? Here's what you should do:

- Find out the questionable tactic's legality
- Evaluate what will happen in the negotiation and to your reputation if you use the questionable tactic
- Determine how you and others view the tactic's morality
- Use these tactics in negotiating with the unethical and untrustworthy

Find Out the Questionable Tactic's Legality

To start, make sure the tactic is legal. If it will or may subject you to legal liability, don't do it.

Note, however, that this legal baseline only provides the floor. Your sense of right and wrong and your evaluation of the tactic's effectiveness should further limit your conduct.

What's legal? In most negotiations, as noted by Shell in *Bargaining for Advantage,* the legality of the conduct will revolve around whether it's fraudulent. (Of course, one might be liable under other legal theories. But those are more rare.)

Most states consider conduct fraudulent if it includes: (1) a knowing (2) misrepresentation (3) of a material (4) fact (5) that is reasonably relied upon by your counterpart, and (6) causes damages. Kate the art seller will be liable for fraud if she intentionally lied about the originality of a painting and a buyer reasonably relied on her statement, thus paying more for the painting.

Knowing this, what rules of thumb can you use to stay on the right side of the law?

Honorable Intentions Make a Difference

If John says his car has never been in an accident—but later discovers a previous owner crashed it—he probably will not be liable for fraud. He did not *intend* to defraud.

Silence Is Usually Golden

Fraud generally involves affirmative lies and misrepresentations. You usually will be safe if you don't make positive misrepresentations. Expert negotiators thus are silent and avoid lying or making misrepresentations on critical harmful issues. This practice gave rise to the phrase "buyer beware."

Of course, silence will not always keep you safe. Sometimes parties have an affirmative duty to disclose. This is true in some real estate and environmental contexts and for those in fiduciary relationships, like partnerships. Also avoid statements that, while possibly technically accurate, become misleading when viewed in the overall context. Kate should not talk about the rapid appreciation of Jean Artiste's original paintings if she knows the painting under discussion is a fake.

Bluffing About Your Bottom Line and Your Interests Is Usually Legally Acceptable

If you bluff by saying you "cannot pay more than $250,000 for the house"—when in truth you can pay $275,000—you generally will not be liable for fraud. Likewise, you can bluff by saying you're extremely interested in one thing, while you really want something else.

These types of statements are generally not "material." Irrelevant "little white lies" are also generally safe. You won't be liable if you say you're feeling fine even if you feel horrible.

What about a bluff in which you make up a better alternative? In negotiating for a mattress, you say, "I can get it cheaper at ABC Mattress," even though this is untrue.

Are these statements fraudulent? It depends. Shell largely concludes that such statements will more likely be fraudulent if a) the "victims (are) small businesses (or) consumers . . . pressured unfairly by professionals," and b) the "made-up offers (are) . . . specific, factual, coupled with ultimatums, and impossible to investigate."

Bottom line: Don't make up a good, specific alternative and use it to get a better deal from a less powerful party.

"Puffery" Couched as Opinions and Statements About the Future Most Often Don't Cross the Legal Line

Fraud applies to statements of fact. Generally, you're pretty safe if you limit your puffery and exaggeration to statements of opinion or statements about the future, like predictions or intentions. Kate could say, "I consider Jean Artiste the most brilliant desert painter in the West." This is opinion. Don't overreach, though. There must be a sufficient factual basis for your statement. If your statement substantially masks the true situation, you may be in trouble.

The More Sophisticated Your Counterpart, the Better Your Position

Fraud requires that the damaged party reasonably relied on his or her counterpart's statement. If Ellen Expert knows that Kate the art seller is lying about the originality of a painting, Kate will not be liable for fraud. Ellen cannot reasonably rely on Kate's statement, given Ellen's own expertise.

No Harm, No Foul

Finally, if no damages are caused by the alleged fraudulent statement, there effectively is no problem on the legal fraud front. (Technically, it might be fraudulent. But with no damages, any legal action would be unlikely.)

Be careful, though, as parties' questionable conduct often falls into unclear legal areas. If in doubt, seek legal advice.

This constitutes your legal limits. This should be your floor. The next level of analysis should include, in addition to its legality, the tactic's potential impact on the negotiation and on your reputation.

Evaluate What Will Happen in the Negotiation and to Your Reputation if You Use the Questionable Tactic

"I don't really care much about the job security and health benefits of my soon-to-be-ex-employees," this business owner told her chief negotiator. "My financial bottom line is far more important to me. But John (our potential purchaser) doesn't know this. So tell him I really do care a great deal about the job security and benefits issues. Then we can trade these off for a more favorable financial deal."

Would this statement subject the soon-to-be-ex-business owner to legal liability for fraud? Probably not. The six elements of fraud are not satisfied.

The statement would not have been a (1) knowing (2) misrepresentation of a (3) material (4) fact (5) that is reasonably relied upon by her counterpart, thus (6) causing damage.

Did the owner and her chief negotiator knowingly misrepresent a fact, and was it relied upon by their counterpart, thus causing damage? Yes.

Was it a "material" fact "reasonably" relied on by their counterpart? Most courts would likely interpret this, in a legal sense, as expected bluffing. The owner effectively said she was extremely interested in one thing, but really wanted something else.

Yet, despite its legality, it was an intentional misrepresentation, right? Absolutely. This is why we should evaluate tactics, based on more than their legality in determining if, when, and where to use them.

Assess the Tactic's Short- and Long-Term Impact

I will never consciously use a negotiation tactic that does not have a decent chance of helping me achieve my substantive goals, might harm my relationship goal with my counterpart, assuming I want a future relationship, and/or may ultimately harm my personal reputation as an honest, straightforward, and professional negotiator.

A seminar participant once sent me an e-mail describing how one of his counterparts sawed off a portion of the legs of their chairs before they arrived to make them feel as if they were in an inferior position. Was this legal? Yes. Was it effective in accomplishing any substantive goals? No. And would doing it harm the "cutter's" reputation? Of course.

This is an easy call. The more difficult question relates to the potential impact of bluffing and other "games" that have a greater chance of helping parties achieve their substantive goals, yet likely would harm their relationships and/or reputations if their use of such tactics came to light.

If you were a union negotiator, would you tell the company representative that your members were "willing to strike" when you pretty much know this to be untrue? If the company representative asks you point-blank—how should you respond?

If you answer completely truthfully you will weaken your leverage. Yet, if you don't you may later lose some credibility. And you might try to block the question; but what if your counterpart pushes?

Bottom line: Consider how your counterpart would view you if he or she later learned that you used the tactic under consideration. Is the potential benefit worth it, or will such disclosure embarrass or harm you or your reputation? That's the key question. Answer it *before* you use the tactic.

Determine How You and Others View the Tactic's Morality

Please, don't use a tactic if you find it morally objectionable or just plain wrong. If you consider all bluffing to be unacceptable lying, don't bluff. You will have to live with yourself after the negotiation concludes. Don't compromise your moral beliefs. That just would not be right. It's not worth it.

But what about your counterpart's morality. Should that be a factor? Yes. You might consider a tactic perfectly appropriate and moral. But if your counterpart disagrees and bad-mouths you after the negotiation has concluded, your reputation may take a major hit.

Consider the ramifications of the following leverage-related tactic.

"Gary, you're going to have to do better than that if you want this company," the New York investment banker said. "We've got a higher offer from one of your competitors."

"How much better, and who made it?" Gary responded.

"I can't say, as we have a confidentiality agreement with them. But I can tell you it's much better than yours."

Gary later significantly increased his offer, which was then accepted.

And no wonder. The investment banker had made up the existence of the other buyer. Pure fiction.

Was it worth it? He thought so.

This is not simply an academic question. Negotiators must constantly evaluate their counterparts' ethical beliefs—what they will or won't do or say—in order to most effectively achieve their own goals.

How can you evaluate this?

Answer this question: Do you believe the investment banker was right or wrong?

Some of you undoubtedly believe this is an easy call. He lied. It's morally wrong to lie. Therefore, he shouldn't have done it.

Others will disagree.

"He bluffed," you might say. "People bluff all the time. Here the purchaser was a sophisticated business person who chose to believe the investment banker. No one forced him to raise his offer. Plus, he probably walked away from the deal pleased with the price."

Others may not see this in black-and-white terms. Here they might say it's a borderline issue that rests on practical considerations. They might feel uncomfortable doing it, but they don't morally condemn it—especially if such "bluffing" appears to be the norm in certain settings, and most everyone knows it occurs.

Why should we care? Because individuals, as noted by Shell in *Bargaining for Advantage,* generally approach issues like this from one of three schools of belief: the Idealist School, the Poker School, and the Pragmatist School. You will be less effective if you don't know where your counterpart resides.

How can you find out this information?

Research your counterparts' ethical reputations and analyze their language and actions in your negotiation. Get specific. Ask others who have negotiated with them the following questions, and evaluate these issues during your negotiation:

How candid, honest, and trusting are they? Did they ever tell you something detrimental to their position just because they felt it was the right thing to do?

The more trusting, candid, and honest they are, the more likely they will feel personally betrayed and draw bright moral lines if they perceive you to "lie." Shell calls these individuals "Idealists."

How did they respond when you asked them direct questions? How "slippery" were they? How much did you trust them? To what extent did you feel they treated the negotiation as a game? How competitive and focused on winning were they? If they played golf, would they be scrupulously honest scorers?

The more your counterparts treat the negotiation as a game and the more slippery they appear, the more likely they will fall into camp two, which Shell calls the "It's a Game" Poker School.

These individuals want to win and feel no qualms about bluffing, especially if it occurs in situations where individuals commonly bluff. They will walk all the way up to the legal limit. If it's legal and likely not fraudulent, it's fair game.

How practical were they? Would you describe their approach as problem-solving or competitive? To what extent did you develop a good working relationship with them, even if you were adverse?

Those in Shell's "What Goes Around Comes Around" Pragmatist School take a practical approach to these issues. If everyone "bluffs" in this industry and most everyone knows it, no problem. They will do it, too, with few qualms. And they will be unlikely to share information adverse to their interests, even if this might appear somewhat misleading.

But if there is a legal or ethical question about it they will be forthright. Their long-term focus is on their reputation and credibility. They will avoid doing anything that might tarnish it.

Most negotiators have a bit of themselves in all three schools. For some it depends on the issue. But overall, most tend toward one school or the other. You need to find this out about your counterpart to most effectively negotiate.

If you don't, beware. Beware of the Idealists—who will walk away on principle if they perceive you as untrustworthy.

Beware of those in the Poker School—who will use every tactic in the book as long as it's legal and, in their minds, likely to be effective.

Finally, beware also of the Pragmatists. They're the toughest to spot. They will draw some bright ethical and moral lines. But they will also bluff and use similar tactics in select situations, especially when the risk/reward payoff appears high enough.

The New York investment banker took a calculated risk and didn't feel he did anything wrong.

I disagree. To me his "bluff" smells bad. I don't believe it will pay off in the end, as he will get a reputation commensurate with these tactics. Then his negotiations will become exponentially more difficult.

Next time find out in which camp your counterparts reside. Evaluate their ethical thought processes. The signals you receive will make you a more effective negotiator.

And if you find they have a reputation as unethical or untrustworthy, and they're across the table from you, use the following tactics to protect yourself and ensure they do not take advantage of you.

Use These Tactics in Negotiating with the Unethical and Untrustworthy

"I don't trust him," he told me. "He's lied in the past and will do it again. But I have to deal with him. What should I do?"

First remember the role that trust plays in negotiations, an issue discussed in chapter 1. The more you blindly trust, the more you put yourself at risk. The less you trust, the less you risk. If you have spent your life building a company, and want to sell it and retire, you should not accept a handshake deal with a stranger. You will want the commitments in a legally enforceable written document. Otherwise, the risk is too great that you will end up with less than what was agreed. Likewise, you probably don't get legally binding commitments in many everyday negotiations. It's not worth the effort, and the risk is minimal if either side reneges.

In determining when and how much to trust others, first assess the risk of noncompliance and your comfort level with it. If you naturally start by trusting others, understand the possible ramifications of misplaced trust as the stakes increase. If you're more cynical, realize this also comes with costs.

What should you do if you distrust your counterparts? Most importantly, analyze *why* you distrust them and determine what incentives they have to lie. While some may be inveterate liars, most lie because they perceive it to be in their self-interest. They believe they will gain some advantage from such behavior. Take that advantage away. Make it in their self-interest to be trustworthy. If your counterparts believe they will suffer negative consequences from lying they will be less likely to do so.

Say you're having a garage sale and your new neighbor offers you $1,000 for your couch. However, he says he won't have the cash for two weeks. Should you put a sold sign on it and trust he will pay you later? I would probably ask for a nonrefundable deposit of $250. That way he will forfeit the $250 if he doesn't honor his commitment. He now has a $250 incentive to be trustworthy.

Overall, take away the other party's incentive to lie or breach an agreement. This is especially critical in dealing with those you know or suspect from past experience or from reputation to be untrustworthy. In such instances, in addition to ensuring significant consequences for any breach, take the following steps:

- Independently confirm all statements that may provide your counterpart with leverage or power, especially if they involve the existence of an alternative deal (like the New York investment banker's other "buyer")
- Discount the relevance of statements that cannot be confirmed
- Document and confirm in writing the party's commitments
- Consider recording the negotiation
- Aggressively explore your potential alternatives
- Be wary of vague and ambiguous statements
- Build mechanisms into the agreement that independently ensure each party fulfills its commitments

- Understand that such negotiations take more time and effort than others, and recognize this as a cost of dealing with this person or entity
- Pay attention to the details and don't leave ambiguous issues unresolved
- Consider bringing in an independent third party to help
- Define what constitutes a breach
- Provide for a fair and efficient way to resolve disputes that may arise from a potential breach

Finally, *don't lower yourself to their level*. Your reputation is too important to risk. Trust is a critical element in all negotiations. Trust me on this, and protect yourself.

Legality. Negotiation impact. Reputation. Morality. Trust and credibility. These factors apply in *all* negotiations. Don't forget them. Ethics make a bottom-line difference.

CHAPTER 7 REVIEW

Ethics Make a Bottom-Line Difference

Find Out the Questionable Tactic's Legality
- Honorable intentions make a difference
- Silence is usually golden
- Bluffing about your bottom line and your interests is usually legally acceptable
- "Puffery" couched as opinions and statements about the future most often don't cross the legal line
- The more sophisticated your counterpart, the better your position
- No harm, no foul

Evaluate What Will Happen—in the Negotiation and to Your Reputation—If You Use the Questionable Tactic
- Assess the tactic's short- and long-term impact

Determine How You and Others View the Tactic's Morality
- Research your counterparts' ethical reputations, analyze their language and actions during your negotiation, and determine if they reside in the Idealist, Poker, or Pragmatist School

Use These Tactics in Negotiating with the Unethical and Untrustworthy
- Understand the risks of trust
- Take away the incentives to lie by ensuring negative consequences for lying
- Don't lower yourself to their level

USE A SITUATION-SPECIFIC STRATEGY

I t's Thursday night and you have just finished a hard twelve-hour workday. It's been stressful, and you just want to eat a relaxing dinner and catch up on some reading and sleep. Unfortunately, your spouse wants you to meet your new neighbors tonight and attend a play you really don't want to see.

So begins one of the most difficult negotiations many of us face on a daily basis. Negotiating with loved ones and/or with long-term business partners and friends can pose our most challenging negotiations. Certainly, this dynamic requires strategies quite different than negotiating with a stranger over the price of an allegedly rare artifact in a foreign market.

What are these different negotiation strategies, and when and where should we apply them? While an unlimited number of negotiation strategies exist, two overall strategies tend to be the most dominant in practice and in the negotiation literature: Problem-Solving Strategies and Competitive Strategies.

Each occupies opposite ends of the spectrum and requires that we implement the Five Golden Rules in different ways. Let's first describe and analyze each overall strategy. Then we will discuss where, when, and how they and the myriad of strategies in between should be used. Here's what we will cover:

- Problem-Solving Strategies
- Competitive Strategies
- Four Factors in Deciding Whether to Problem-Solve or Compete

- Tactics to Implement the Most Effective Strategy
- Selectively Apply Your Strategy to Certain Issues and Not Others

Problem-Solving Strategies

Let's first examine the spousal negotiation over what to do Thursday night. The tired and stressed spouse should use a Problem-Solving Strategy—one characterized by strategies and tactics focused on building trust, strengthening relationships, and promoting an atmosphere where the parties can work together to find a mutually satisfactory solution.

While many situations exist in which parties should use Problem-Solving Strategies, family negotiations serve as the prototype. They represent one end of the strategic spectrum, so the strategies tend to be straightforward. Analyzing family negotiations will thus provide us with the best understanding of Problem-Solving Strategies. For those interested in business-related Problem-Solving Strategies, apply the following discussion to negotiations between long-term business partners. Better yet, think of negotiations within a family business.

How do you use Problem-Solving Strategies to negotiate within the family, and what characteristics apply? Our analysis will be based on the premise that we implement the Five Golden Rules in opposite ways in using Problem-Solving Strategies versus Competitive Strategies. Here we will apply the Five Golden Rules in the problem-solving family context.

Golden Rule One: Information Is Power—So Get It

When you negotiate with your spouse or significant other do you hide information on your true feelings and interests? Should you? What about the atmosphere in such negotiations? Adversarial or collaborative?

Mutually Share Critical Information Openly and Liberally

With Problem-Solving Strategies, parties share more information, rather than less, and hide less rather than more. Parties openly and honestly share information about their true goals, issues, and fundamental interests and priorities. They ensure this information sharing is also mutual.

**Actions and Atmosphere Confirm Trust
and a Valued Relationship**

Atmospherewise, Problem-Solving strategies are characterized by a trusting environment in which the parties value the relationship and feel comfortable sharing critical information. They don't fear it will be used against them. The spouse, in the above family context, might share his or her true feelings about meeting the neighbors, going to the theater, and do it in a productive, "let's work together to resolve this" fashion.

Parties also will often explore reasonable, principled options that might satisfy their mutual interests. Here, for example, one spouse might agree to meet the neighbors and see the show if it's really important to the other. However, either spouse might suggest it would be more enjoyable for all if they could reschedule it for the following Tuesday.

Golden Rule Two: Maximize Your Leverage

How often should you walk out on or threaten your spouse, significant other, or long-term business partner? Most individuals try to avoid such overt leverage-related tactics in family negotiations. Such tactics harm the type of stable long-term relationship we want. In fact, while this might help us "win" in the short-term, we may lose big in the long-term.

Leverage Downplayed, but Still There

Parties using Problem-Solving Strategies avoid the brinksmanship that accompanies high-pressure leverage-related tactics. Instead, they openly and honestly share information about the first element of leverage—their wants and needs—and often shy away from explicitly discussing their alternatives to an agreement with their counterpart. Parties avoid discussing their alternatives because to some this introduces a competitive, "I can do this without you" element. Sometimes even discussing alternatives can harm parties' relationships.

At times, however, it makes sense to discuss alternatives. When it does, parties discuss them in straightforward terms. They lay out in a plain and factual way the alternatives that exist if they cannot find a way to mutually satisfy their interests.

In short, while leverage still occupies an important part of the process, the parties downplay it and rarely exercise it in an overt and aggressive fashion.

Golden Rule Three: Employ "Fair" Objective Criteria

Parties frequently focus on independent standards and procedures in using Problem-Solving Strategies. This focus lets both sides accept the result as "fair and reasonable" based on the mutually agreeable standard or procedure.

Frequently Rely on Independent Standards and Procedures

Parties also often *rely* on independent standards and procedures to explain the inherent fairness of suggested solutions. They don't just mention it. They rely on it as the basis for their solution. This is key. The spouse in our example might *rely* on the principle of reciprocity by noting that last week a similar situation occurred and he or she then compromised.

I bought my first car in 1987. It was the shortest negotiation in my life. My dad offered to sell me his 1981 Datsun 280ZX for its Blue Book value. I said "Okay." End of negotiation. He told me it was a fair price because its Blue Book value reflected its market value. Sounded fair to me. We both relied on the market value standard as the basis for our Problem-Solving Strategy.

Golden Rule Four: Design an Offer-Concession Strategy

Should I have been more aggressive in my offer-concession strategy with my dad? Do you lowball a family member or longtime business partner when buying something from them? What about giving myself enough room to concede with my dad and building that into my offer-concession strategy? Wasn't that my dad's first offer? Didn't I note in chapter 4 that parties should almost always counter first offers, as they always include room to move? The key word here, of course, is "almost."

Least Aggressive Offer-Concession Moves and Tactics

Problem-solving offer-concession strategies are characterized by the most reasonable and least aggressive-appearing moves. With my dad, either side might have started with a first offer. And the timing and size of the subsequent moves in these contexts will be relatively minimal. My dad's offer to sell me his Datsun based on its Blue Book value fell squarely into this category, as did my quick acceptance.

Here's another example of a problem-solving, offer-concession strategy. In 2002 Larry's "significant other" Ellie found out last-minute that her close college friend was getting married in Chicago and wanted her to stand up at her wedding. Given the short notice, round-trip Phoenix-to-Chicago airline tickets were prohibitively expensive, around $1,200. Larry, who travels a fair amount on business, offered Ellie a frequent flyer ticket at half what he considered its market value. Market value, he figured, was about 2.5 cents per frequent flyer mile used. He derived this figure from what airlines charge for extra miles in their frequent flyer programs and the price of a ticket if he used his miles on a cross-country flight. He had previously used this process to exchange tickets within his family, and it had worked to the mutual satisfaction of everyone (recognize the precedent used here as it was "fair" to others in the past). He thus offered to give her the ticket in exchange for $250, figuring it's effectively a gift to her of $250 and a very reasonable offer.

To Larry's surprise Ellie was outraged. Ellie's expectation, based upon her "negotiations" for frequent flyer tickets with her family and close friends, was that he should give her the ticket for free. That was what she regularly did with family members and close friends (her precedent). She felt that if he cared about her he would have gladly given her a ticket. Note the market value versus precedent criteria used here.

Imagine Ellie's response if Larry had, as a first offer, started at $500, what he considered the ticket's "true" market value. Or started at $1,100, figuring he was still saving her $100 off her BATNA (purchasing an airline ticket). They might not still be together! (Ellie, by the way, ultimately received a "free" ticket from a longtime family friend who travels well over a hundred thousand miles a year on business.)

My point? Problem-Solving Strategies on this end of the continuum involve the least aggressive offer-concession behavior. In large part, this is because your offer-concession behavior will likely be reciprocated in your next family or long-term business partner negotiation.

Golden Rule Five: Control the Agenda

Overtly controlling the agenda for most family negotiations seems like overkill. It is. Instead, parties using Problem-Solving Strategies usually rely on mutually agreeable agendas and agenda control tactics. And they stay away from tension-increasing tactics like short deadlines and one-sided written agendas.

Mutually Agreeable Agenda and Agenda-Control Tactics

One way to accomplish this is to be up front about the issues on the table and negotiate an agenda to start. "What's on your mind?" you may ask. Then carefully listen. "What else is bothering you?" you may then ask if you believe additional issues might be involved.

Often, finding the right time and place to discuss the issue may be your most difficult challenge.

I travel a lot for work and tend to work until 10 P.M. or later the night before I leave. I guess I have never gotten over the last-minute procrastination habits I formed years ago. With me, the worst time to address family issues is the night before I leave. At that time I'm usually tired and focused on my work and travel. As a result, it's critical to ensure important issues don't get addressed then.

Growing up, my family had "council meetings" every Sunday. The six of us—two parents and four kids—would arrange our schedules so we could all spend this time together each week. In these meetings we discussed what happened to us that week and addressed any family issues that needed to be resolved. My dad ran the meetings and ensured everyone had their say. Of course, he was fond of saying it was a "dictatorship, not a democracy." But, in truth, we all had input, and Dad only exercised his "dictatorship rights" when we couldn't reach consensus. It was an effective forum in which to collaboratively, and in a problem-solving fashion, address family issues.

Here's a chart that summarizes the characteristics of the "end of the spectrum" Problem-Solving Strategies. Family and long-term business partnership negotiations serve as the prototype here.

PROBLEM-SOLVING STRATEGIES

Golden Rule	Characteristics of Strategy
1. Information Is Power— So Get It	*Mutually share critical information openly and liberally* *Actions and atmosphere confirm trust and a valued relationship*
2. Maximize Your Leverage	*Leverage downplayed, but still there*
3. Employ "Fair" Objective Criteria	*Frequently **rely** on independent standards and procedures*
4. Design an Offer-Concession Strategy	*Least aggressive offer-concession moves and tactics*
5. Control the Agenda	*Mutually agreeable agenda and agenda-control tactics*

Competitive Strategies

Try using Problem-Solving Strategies in another context, however, and watch your lunch get eaten. Ineffective would be a charitable description of the result. Imagine using a Problem-Solving Strategy in negotiating to purchase that allegedly rare artifact in a foreign market.

Let's see how Bob does as he uses an admittedly extreme Problem-Solving Strategy in that situation. Bob walks into the foreign shop dressed as an American tourist and spots an artifact he especially likes. He walks over to the artifact and admires it for a few minutes, expressing his interest in an obvious way. After five minutes, the shop owner comes over and tells Bob the artifact is rare and unique. As he speaks, Bob becomes more and more interested, and—in problem-solving mode—relatively freely shares his substantial interest with the shop owner.

Bob also asks questions. How was it made and with what? Who is the artist? What kind of market exists for it? How rare is it? Bob has some knowledge of the market, but should have more. Effective problem-solving negotiators extensively research and rely on standards and criteria.

Invariably, of course, the owner tells Bob it is unique. One of a kind. Nothing comparable out there. And no real market for it.

Bob, naively and in extreme problem-solving mode, trusts the shop owner. Bob thus believes he has weak leverage. It's unique, right? No real alternative or market. As Bob learns more, he wants it more. It would look great in his office.

Bob finally gets around to asking its price. The owner names a figure and it's high. Bob asks, "Is this a fixed price?" But Bob doesn't want to offend the owner. Those using Problem-Solving Strategies are interested in a relationship. So he doesn't say it with much conviction. It's a store, right? In the United States, item prices are largely fixed. Bob goes with that assumption. Ultimately, while he haggles some, he ends up paying close to the owner's asking price.

What was Bob's mistake? Everything. Bob first gave up strategically critical information by the way he dressed and by expressing substantial interest in just one item. Bob also weakened his leverage by showing too much interest, and he believed the item was unique. Regarding objective criteria, Bob accepted the owner's word that no real market existed, and didn't do his homework. In the offer-concession stage, Bob was not nearly aggressive enough. Finally, the owner set the entire agenda. Bob just accepted it. It was a recipe in how not to negotiate *in that setting*. If Bob was buying a piece of art from his identical twin, however, this extreme Problem-Solving Strategy could have been effective. Here, it was a mistake.

Problem-Solving Strategies do not work well in certain situations. Instead, in these circumstances—effectively the opposite end of the spectrum from Problem-Solving Strategies—use Competitive Strategies. Competitive Strategies should be used where you want to undermine the other negotiator's confidence in his or her bargaining position and strengthen his or her perception of your bargaining position.

How do you use Competitive Strategies to negotiate the purchase of that allegedly rare artifact, where else should you use them, and what strategies and tactics characterize them? Let's describe the strategic characteristics of Competitive Strategies within the framework of the Five Golden Rules. Then, we will see how Bob's friend Jill effectively applies them in the competitive foreign market context. That's our prototypical Competitive Strategies situation. As we go along, think about other circumstances with similar characteristics.

Golden Rule One: Information Is Power—So Get It

To start, how much information should Bob's friend Jill share with the foreign shop owner? The minimum amount sufficient to accomplish her goal—finding out as much as she can about the true nature of the artifact and, assuming she still wants it, purchasing it for the lowest possible price.

Substantial Information Bargaining— Share a Little and Get a Lot

Jill should not convey the impression that she's a wealthy American businesswoman. Nor should she express too much interest in the artifact. She should, instead, play her information cards close to her vest. This does not mean, however, that Jill wants to create an overtly adversarial atmosphere or use an aggressive style. In fact, Jill initially will want to create an atmosphere conducive to getting information. This may call for a collaborative style. Later Jill may want to become more competitive. Importantly, some Competitive Strategies call for a competitive atmosphere. Others require more collaborative styles. Here, a more collaborative "schmoozing" style works best to start, given Jill's interest in more information. But it will likely become competitive later.

Jill also will want to confirm all the information she receives from the shop owner. In some contexts involving Competitive Strategies, little trust exists between the parties. Parties overcome this by independently investigating the information disclosed by their counterparts.

Competitive Strategies are marked by a great deal of negotiating and bargaining over information. Little is shared. Much is sought.

Golden Rule Two: Maximize Your Leverage

The full range of leverage-related tactics will be on display in negotiating for this artifact. Several walkouts by Jill may dominate the process. What message is Jill communicating with these aggressive leverage-related tactics? She doesn't have a great need or interest in the artifact and has excellent alternatives. The shopkeeper, by contrast, will strive to convince Jill of the artifact's unique qualities. He will focus on the item's scarcity, and thus hopefully spike Jill's interest and need to purchase the artifact. He will also likely tell Jill that no real alternative exists, there or elsewhere. If Jill shops around, though, she might find this to be untrue.

Open Conflict on Leverage

Competitive Strategies often revolve around leverage and the parties' open conflict over it. Parties in these contexts also continually seek to change the perception of the other side about its leverage. Threats. Walkouts. Bluffing. "Take it or leave it" offers. All may be used here, and many should. Both sides—if they are relatively sophisticated negotiators—will know and expect it.

Golden Rule Three: Employ "Fair" Objective Criteria

Independent standards like market value, precedent, policy, and others constantly crop up with those using Competitive Strategies. And they can be persuasive. But they rarely will supplant leverage as the dominant negotiation element. In Problem-Solving Strategies, independent standards and procedures often form the basis for resolving the negotiation. Parties *rely* on them to satisfy their interests. In Competitive Strategies, parties largely use independent standards and procedures as tools to try to change the other side's perception of their leverage. The only exception might be their reliance on certain independent procedures to resolve impasses. Impasses, of course, tend to arise more often when using Competitive than Problem-Solving Strategies.

Minimal Reliance on Independent Standards and Procedures

In our example, Jill might tell the shopkeeper that she recently bought a similar artifact for half the owner's asking price at a shop down the street. The owner will likely respond by aggressively defending the artifact's uniqueness and challenging Jill to find this exact same one elsewhere. But, while the owner may concede some, due to Jill's precedent, it will pale in comparison to his moves if he believes Jill will walk out of his shop without buying that artifact. Then, and only then, will he make significant concessions.

Make no mistake: The language of the Competitive Strategies negotiation may revolve around the parties articulating "fair and reasonable" standards and suggesting moves due to these standards. Many negotiations share this trait. But for those using Competitive Strategies, parties' *behavior* and *actions* will be largely driven by the parties' *perception* of their leverage, not by the standards used.

Golden Rule Four: Design an Offer-Concession Strategy

The full range of offer-concession tactics will be on display in situations involving Competitive Strategies.

Most Aggressive Offer-Concession Moves and Tactics

Parties will use very aggressive offer-concession behavior when using Competitive Strategies. To start, this might include either a first offer outside the range of any reasonable, standard-based result, or a long negotiation over which party even *makes* the first offer. Regarding the timing and size of subsequent moves, the number of back-and-forth moves will tend to be high, as will the size of the moves relative to the starting point. Some describe those who regularly use these offer-concession tactics as "hagglers."

For example, if no tradition exists regarding who will make the first offer, expect to negotiate it. In our example, though, the shopkeeper traditionally makes the first offer, and we would expect him to start extremely high. Jill should start extremely low. And Jill should taper, bracket, and appear extremely reluctant to concede. Then she should only concede when given a reason to do so. Highly aggressive offer-concession strategies by all parties characterize Competitive Strategies. Prepare to go back and forth a number of times. Make sure, too, that you get as good as you give. If you don't or won't play this game, your interests are at risk.

We bought a new house in December 2002. That negotiation involved a number of back-and-forth offers and concessions before we signed. Radically different offer-concession dynamics characterized that negotiation, versus my first car purchase from my dad. Both were appropriate, given their respective situations.

Golden Rule Five: Control the Agenda

The agenda will be hotly contested in situations involving Competitive Strategies: Be strategic about it. In situations involving Problem-Solving Strategies, it's easier to agree on agenda-related issues. In contexts featuring Competitive Strategies, both sides will try to use the agenda to gain an advantage.

Overt and Biased Agenda-Control Tactics

For instance, timing and deadlines may dominate Jill's negotiation with the shopkeeper. If Jill has a flight leaving Friday, and they're negotiating Thursday afternoon, that deadline will drive the process. In fact, Jill might say she only has until 4 P.M. to shop. That's it. If so, Jill should expect to go all the way to 3:59 P.M. to get the shopkeeper's best deal. Of course, this assumes the shopkeeper believes her deadline is real and inflexible.

Another example of agenda control in the Competitive Strategies context was the United States–North Korea negotiations in 2003 over North Korea's nuclear weapons program, discussed earlier. That negotiation focused for months almost solely on agenda items, who would sit at the table.

The following chart summarizes the characteristics of "end of the spectrum" Competitive Strategies.

COMPETITIVE STRATEGIES

Golden Rules	Characteristics of Strategy
1. Information Is Power— So Get It	*Substantial information bargaining— share a little and get a lot*
2. Maximize Your Leverage	*Open conflict on leverage*
3. Employ "Fair" Objective Criteria	*Minimal reliance on independent standards and procedures*
4. Design an Offer-Concession Strategy	*Most aggressive offer-concession moves and tactics*
5. Control the Agenda	*Overt and biased agenda-control tactics*

Now you know how to recognize and use Problem-Solving Strategies and Competitive Strategies. But where should you use each? And what about the vast majority of negotiations that occur between the extreme problem-solving situation of a family negotiation and the extreme competitive strategy of the foreign open-air market? What factors should impact your approach, and how should you decide? Use these four factors:

- The relationship factor
- The number factor
- The zero-sum factor
- The mutuality factor

Four Factors in Deciding Whether
to Problem-Solve or Compete

The Relationship Factor

Your strategy should fundamentally change, based on whether and to what extent you want or expect to have a future relationship with your counterpart. The more you see your potential interests and long-term goals satisfied with a future relationship, the more likely you should use Problem-Solving Strategies. If you want a future relationship, then share information relatively liberally; be matter-of-fact about your leverage; rely on independent standards and procedures; use less aggressive offer-concession strategies; and jointly negotiate an agenda.

Conversely, the *less* you see your potential interests and long-term goals satisfied with a future relationship, the more likely you should use Competitive Strategies. If you will never have any contact with your counterpart again, or don't care, then bargain over all strategically important information; use powerful leverage-related moves; negotiate over the most "fair" objective criteria; aggressively engage in offer-concession tactics; and be especially sensitive to agenda items, especially deadlines.

Understand, however, that using Problem-Solving Strategies does not simply mean trying to find the quickest solution that minimizes the conflict between the parties. Shell, in *Bargaining for Advantage,* described a study illustrating that dating couples—those with a strong interest in a future relationship—were "much less successful than were the strangers at uncovering hidden, mutually rewarding trade-offs . . . [b]ecause they focused on simple, equal compromises on all the issues, and engaged in less problem-solving and probing of priorities than did the more competitively minded strangers."

If your major goal is to develop, continue, maintain, and strengthen a close relationship, engage in Problem-Solving Strategies. But don't just pick a standard that appears at first glance to resolve the situation (the simple, equal compromises Shell notes above). Dig deeper into both parties' interests and be assertive about exploring the *best* possible solutions that might satisfy your goals.

Let's take a look at how to incorporate this relationship factor into our negotiation strategy by exploring two scenarios:

- A Problem-Solving Strategy: Strong future relationship
- A Competitive Strategy: No future relationship

To start, let's see how to use a Problem-Solving Strategy in negotiating with a future potential client.

A Problem-Solving Strategy: Strong Future Relationship

When I started my business I did a seminar for a nonprofit leadership organization in Phoenix called Valley Leadership. Dr. Jerry Eisen, a business consultant specializing in human resource management issues, attended my seminar. After my seminar Jerry asked if I wanted to get together for breakfast to explore some ideas that might be mutually beneficial. A few weeks later we did.

Our breakfast started with an extensive rapport-building period in which we found out about each other's backgrounds. I found out Jerry had been in human resource consulting, either within companies or on his own, for over thirty years. Jerry found out about my background as a lawyer and teacher, and how I started my business. It also turns out we shared some mutual friends and common interests. In short, we hit it off.

Some time into breakfast Jerry told me he had a commercial general contractor client who might be interested in some negotiation training. Project managers at such firms, he told me, negotiate every day. And they negotiate over significant sums of money, so improved negotiation skills can have an ongoing impact.

Jerry wanted to explore the possibility of my putting together a customized, hands-on training program for his client's upcoming annual management retreat. While Jerry was organizing and facilitating the retreat, his client would be the ultimate decision-maker on whether to hire me. Needless to say, I was interested. There are numerous commercial general contractors in Arizona, and construction represents a significant part of Arizona's economy. If I could sign up this client it could jumpstart my training business among other Arizona contractors.

So, what negotiation strategy should I use with Jerry and, later, with his general contractor client? Let's analyze the relationship issues. To what extent do I want a future business relationship with Jerry and his client? And how can such a relationship satisfy my long-term goals? Here's what happened.

First I needed Jerry to decide he wanted to hire me for his client's retreat. Initially, then, I needed a working relationship with Jerry sufficient to accomplish this goal. Jerry also had other clients that probably needed negotiation-skills training. I foresaw a productive business relationship for both of us. Of course, additional programs and consulting with this particular general contractor client were also possible.

I thus used Problem-Solving Strategies from the start. I liberally shared information about what I do, about my previous clients, and brain-stormed ways I could satisfy Jerry's and his client's interests. I also spent substantial time finding out information about Jerry *and* his client. In a relaxed setting, we mutually shared information about our interests and ways we could help each other. Much of this information-sharing ulti-mately took place over an additional breakfast, after Jerry had initially discussed the possibility of my program with his client.

We also discussed leverage issues, but in a professional and straight-forward fashion. I found out Jerry was interested in my services and that he had shared this enthusiasm with his client. I also found out the re-treat was several months off, so Jerry and his client had other available alternatives if things didn't work out with me.

And, while I told Jerry I'm busy (I had other alternatives), I also told him I was very interested in working with him and his client on this program and that I had that time slot available. Neither of us used aggressive lever-age tactics like walking out, bluffing, or presenting "take it or leave it" of-fers. Nor did we use blunt language about the leverage issues. We couched everything in "soft" relationship-oriented language, and the negotiation proceeded in a series of informal environments, including over meals.

We also spoke a great deal about standards. While Jerry had already attended one of my seminars, he also wanted to check my references, which I readily provided. The standard here? Precedent. If I've done great programs for others, I will likely do a great program for his client. Plus, he could use this to find out more about my programs. He might even find out what I had charged others for similar services.

Jerry also is a human-relations expert himself, so his recommendation on my behalf would carry great weight. It's another independent stan-dard. As such an expert, Jerry is well aware of the market value of full-day training programs. In fact, he himself provides human-relations seminars to his clients and belongs to a management-consultant association that shares such information with each other.

I also shared how negotiation training could increase his client's nego-tiation efficiency and profitability. Given the large sums involved in his client's negotiations, I emphasized that if each project manager imple-mented just one new negotiation tactic the training program would pay off many times over, both financially and organizationally.

Our offer-concession stage was thus well-buttressed by our extensive focus on independent standards: precedent, expert opinion, market value, efficiency, profitability, and costs. This is typical of Problem-Solving Strategies.

When I finally shared my "standard fee," based on these and other independent standards, Jerry agreed to take it to his client. What did I do offer-concessionwise? I put on my reasonable hat, started at a place that appeared credible, based on numerous legitimate standards, and looked to quickly find a final result with a minimum of moves.

Jerry then set up a breakfast meeting to introduce me to his client. His client wanted to eyeball me before spending a significant amount of money on my negotiation-training services. We met with Jerry present, and I negotiated with his client directly, again using Problem-Solving Strategies. But here it was slightly more competitive. Jerry's client wanted to test my skills. If I couldn't effectively negotiate with him, how could I teach these skills to his project managers? We sparred some over my fees, and I kept returning to the independent standards.

At this point, regarding our mutual agenda, we were about two months away from his retreat. And the hotel and other arrangements were already set. So the deadline for his decision was approaching, and his alternative did not appear great to me. But the deadline was also approaching for me, as I had tentatively reserved this date on my calendar. The closer we got to that date, the less likely I could replace him with another client if he didn't hire me.

Ultimately we reached a fair agreement that satisfied our mutual interests, largely based on the independent standards. The most influential standard? Jerry's expert recommendation. He told his client I would be well worth my standard fee.

My negotiation strategy worked out well with both Jerry *and* his client. Jerry has become a client and a friend, and we continue to do business together. I also have continued to work with Jerry's client and his general contracting company on additional training programs and consulting. Plus, Jerry and his client (now mine also) have provided me with continuing referrals as I develop work with other general contractors.

A Competitive Strategy: No Future Relationship

What if you don't care much about the relationship? How should these negotiations proceed?

I once helped a lawyer negotiate a multimillion-dollar settlement involving financial fraud allegations against a series of defendants, including a large accounting firm's foreign office, several lawyers and law firms, numerous individuals, and some investment advisors. The plaintiffs were over a hundred elderly individuals who had been sold a series of "guaranteed" high-return investments. In effect, they were victims of a type of Ponzi scheme.

This matter called for Competitive Strategies. The parties had no interest in any type of a future relationship. The plaintiffs were ripped off and had lost millions. They just wanted to get back as much as possible.

How did the negotiation proceed? By the time I got involved the facts were well known to everyone. The discovery process, the legal mechanism in which parties to a lawsuit gain information from the other parties, had concluded. That process, however, was marked by highly competitive and adversarial interaction between the lawyers and parties. This is to be expected. The defendants fought to keep private as much strategically valuable information as possible. They ultimately produced what the court forced them to produce. This was appropriate.

The biggest issue in the negotiation revolved around the parties' leverage. Here, it involved two matters: 1) the parties' evaluation of what would happen at trial; and 2) how much the plaintiffs could collect on that trial judgment. Interestingly, the defendants did not really dispute the likelihood of the plaintiffs' success at trial. Nor did they dispute the plaintiffs' likelihood of getting a multimillion-dollar judgment. The bigger issue, and the issue on which the negotiations centered, related to how much plaintiffs could collect. One of the masterminds of the fraud was a foreign citizen with strong political connections in his native country. Enforcing a judgment against him in his country and getting money from him appeared unlikely. Plus, the accounting firm's foreign office could just go bankrupt if the judgment was large enough. Not much to gain there.

On the other hand, a trial would publicly highlight the accounting firm's culpability. Even though it might not legally have to pay much if its foreign office declared bankruptcy, its other offices would suffer reputationwise. These leverage issues became the focal point of the negotiations, and open conflict occurred. This is a hallmark of Competitive Strategies.

Certain standards did, however, come into play. These included the size of earlier settlements with other defendants, defendants' fines, litigation costs, the efficiency of a settlement, the accounting firm's profitability, and the money illegitimately made by the wrongdoers. But these standards took a backseat to the leverage issues. The parties raised the standards as reflective of a "fair and reasonable" settlement, but they did not ultimately rely on them to form the basis of the final settlement. Leverage trumped the standards.

The offer-concession strategies also differed substantially from those in my negotiations with Jerry and his client. Here both parties engaged in very aggressive offers and concessions, and it was exponentially tougher to get any movement.

Agenda control and deadlines also played a more prominent role here. The parties' settlement occurred just prior to one of the case's deadlines, relatively close to the trial date. The deadline, in part, presented the parties with more incentive to settle.

Did the parties have any interest in a future relationship? No. As a result, they appropriately engaged in Competitive Strategies.

The Number Factor

The second factor affecting your choice of negotiation strategy—the number factor—relates to the number of issues on the table. The more issues, the more likely you should use Problem-Solving Strategies. The fewer issues, the more likely you should use Competitive Strategies.

A Problem-Solving Strategy:
Future Relationship + Many Issues

Typical problem-solving-strategies negotiations here involve complex disputes between business partners or coworkers, or even a large merger between two companies where the parties need a future working relationship to ensure the merged company succeeds. In all these instances the parties want and need a future working relationship *and* the number of issues to be negotiated is significant and, often, ongoing.

For instance, multinational pharmaceutical companies will sometimes seek out partnerships with local pharmaceutical companies in other countries in order to increase their products' market share in that country, build their products' brand names, and reduce the probability that others will copy their products and compete against them. Under these agreements, called co-promotion agreements, the local pharmaceutical company agrees to sell and promote the multinational's product under the multinational's product name. In return, the multinational pays the local company, based on the incremental increase in the products' net sales over a baseline amount (what the multinational would anticipate selling, absent an agreement).

These deals involve parties with a potential long-term future relationship and a significant number of issues on the table. After all, the local pharmaceutical company must perform, in effect, as the multinational's sales and marketing arm in that country. Success for both parties depends on a strong working relationship and the efficient and effective resolution of ongoing negotiations involving a wide variety of sales and marketing issues.

Individuals negotiating co-promotion agreements on both sides know that success cannot occur without: a) significant information sharing from each side; b) a reasoned discussion of leverage and an absence of extremely competitive leverage tactics; c) reliance on varied independent standards and procedures; d) medium-aggressive offers and concessions; and e) a mutually acceptable agenda. In short, they want to use Problem-Solving Strategies. The future relationship is critical, and the number of issues is high.

A Competitive Strategy:
No Future Relationship + Few Issues

The largest purchase most individuals make in their lives is a house. How many issues are usually involved? Not many. The biggest and most likely issue to dominate the negotiation is the price. It should. And do the seller and potential buyer have an interest in a personal or business relationship after the sale? Usually not. Minor relationship interest plus few issues equals Competitive Strategies.

The buyer *and* seller will want to: 1) reluctantly share critical strategic information; 2) mask their levels of need and openly discuss their strongest alternative; 3) aggressively use standards to their advantage; 4) appear relatively uncompromising in their offers and concessions; and 5) consciously and perhaps overtly control the agenda and deadlines. Remember my Chicago friend who bought the Daddy Warbucks house with a version of the "take away" offer? He used a Competitive Strategy.

Another negotiation situation involving a minor relationship interest and relatively few issues involves a business purchase of large manufacturing equipment. Assume you are the new vice president of technical services at Brown Brick, one of the world's largest brick manufacturers. Brown Brick is a division of Brown Industries, a multinational building and construction materials company headquartered in Chicago, Illinois, that has over 10,000 employees and over $2 billion in annual sales.

As vice president of Technical Services you were asked to generate some options to increase Brown's brick-manufacturing capacity, including possibly building a new brick plant, a relatively rare occurrence. Assume that the two most reputable companies in the world that build brick plants are Sand Manufacturing and PaveCo.

What negotiation strategy should you use with Sand and PaveCo? Competitive Strategies. Since building a brick plant is a rare event, you want a working relationship, but you're not overly concerned about it. Relationship importance: relatively low. And while there may be a fair number of technical issues to resolve, three major issues will dominate the negotiation: price, capacity, and time to completion. Number of issues: relatively few.

The Middle Road:
Future Relationship + Few Issues; or,
No Future Relationship Likely + Many Issues

So far we have addressed situations at the end of the spectrum of Problem-Solving and Competitive Strategies. It's an easy call when there's a future relationship and many issues. Both strategy factors—relationship and number of issues—suggest Problem-Solving Strategies. Likewise, it's an easy call when there's no future relationship and relatively few issues. There both factors point to Competitive Strategies. The greatest strategic challenge, then, arises with situations in the middle, when the factors point to different strategies. For instance, what strategy should you use when you want a future relationship—suggesting Problem-Solving Strategies—but only one issue exists—suggesting Competitive Strategies? And what about when you don't care about a future relationship—thus suggesting Competitive Strategies—but many issues exist—suggesting Problem-Solving Strategies?

Since a continuum of strategies exist—with Problem-Solving on one end and Competitive on the other—these scenarios fall in the middle. But not exactly in the middle. Not all strategy factors are created equal. When the relationship factor conflicts with the number of issues factor, the relationship factor carries the most weight. So, when the relationship factor suggests Problem-Solving Strategies (significant future relationship) and the number factor suggests Competitive Strategies (few issues), use a better Problem-Solving Strategy.

Future Relationship + Few Issues

Say you and your business partner of twenty-five years have decided to terminate your business relationship. Your partner wants to retire, while you still love working. You have decided to buy out your partner's share of your manufacturing business. But you intend to remain good friends. Assume the issues in the business are few and straightforward. Here you have a future relationship with few issues. On the continuum of strategies, this falls much closer to the problem-solving end than the competitive end. What does this mean? You share more information rather than less; avoid tough leverage tactics like walkouts and bluffing; liberally use and perhaps rely on independent standards and procedures; do not make overly aggressive offer-concession moves; and mutually control the agenda, without short deadlines.

No Future Relationship Likely + Many Issues

And when the relationship factor suggests Competitive Strategies (no future relationship) and the number factor suggests Problem-Solving Strategies (many issues), use a more Competitive Strategy.

Remember *Pretty Woman,* with Richard Gere and Julia Roberts? Richard Gere played the ruthless corporate raider who bought companies and immediately turned around and sold off their various parts. No future relationship existed between the corporate parties—Gere didn't need or want the old executives, as he sold off their assets. But the number of issues involved in purchasing a large corporation is significant. On the continuum of strategies, this falls closer to the Competitive end of the spectrum than the Problem-Solving end. This means you should: share less information rather than more; directly engage on leverage issues; use objective criteria to buttress your leverage strategies, but don't rely on it; be very aggressive with your offer-concession moves; and make sure you control the agenda, fully utilizing timing and deadline strategies.

Of course, at the end of *Pretty Woman* Gere decided to create even more value by not selling off his target company but running it himself. We will deal with this value-creating situation—where we ultimately should use more Problem-Solving Strategies—in the next section.

Here's a chart of the continuum of strategies so far.

	"Most" Problem-Solving Strategy		**"Most" Competitive Strategy**	
	←---→			
The Relationship Factor	Strongest future relationship	Future relationship	No future relationship likely	No possible future relationship
	+	+	+	+
The Number Factor	Many issues	Few issues	Many issues	One issue

The Zero-Sum Factor

Creativity sets apart some of the greatest negotiators in the world. Yet, even the most creative negotiators can't add value to a transaction if the negotiation only involves zero-sum issues—where more for one side necessarily means less for the other. The nature of the issues involved is the third factor impacting your negotiation strategy decision. The more zero-sum-type issues exist, the more likely you should use Competitive Strategies. The less zero-sum-type issues—with greater opportunities for creativity and finding nontraditional solutions—the more likely you should use Problem-Solving Strategies.

How do you evaluate this? Two keys govern this decision.

The Interest Key

The most important key involves the nature of the parties' fundamental interests. In chapter 1 we explored whether the parties' interests were shared, compatible, or conflicting. Shared interests were interests both sides wanted. Members of a sales team all want to increase the team's efficiency, as they all benefit when the team wins. They share that efficiency interest.

Other negotiations involve compatible interests. Landlords often want the security long-term tenants provide. Tenants often want a quiet, well-maintained apartment complex and a permanent address. They have different—but compatible—interests.

Parties also have conflicting interests. The person injured in the car accident wants to maximize his financial recovery to compensate him for his pain and suffering. The other driver's insurance company wants to keep the money it pays the injured person within a relatively minimum range and wants to fairly represent its insured.

The more the parties' interests are shared or compatible, the more likely they can creatively develop options that satisfy those interests. Thus, the more likely they should use Problem-Solving Strategies.

The more the parties' interests conflict and involve zero-sum issues, the more likely they should use Competitive Strategies.

The Timing Key

The second key involves the timing of the parties' overall strategy decision. At times the issues may initially appear zero-sum in nature. So the parties use Competitive Strategies and reluctantly share strategically critical information—including information about their fundamental interests. But their initial assumption and strategy may be wrong. If so, and if some creative options exist that would provide value to both parties, they will likely leave this on the table by using Competitive Strategies.

Why? Using Competitive Strategies will not create the right environment in which to find their compatible or shared interests, nor will it create the atmosphere that would allow them to explore value-added situations. This is the classic "expand the pie" scenario, and they will go hungry.

In all negotiations, then, find out as much as you can about the parties' fundamental interests *before* deciding which strategy to use. This may be tricky, of course, as many will only reluctantly share such information. But that's a key part of the process.

Let's see how this works. In 1999 I was contacted by Karen, an account executive at a Phoenix television station. She asked if I would speak on impasse-breaking strategies for thirty minutes at their monthly sales meeting. Only one catch—she had no budget for it. Since I'm in the profit-making business, my initial reaction—which I kept to myself—was "thanks, but no thanks." Instead of saying this, though, I told her that speaking to such groups was a part of my business. I then asked her how she could make it worth my time.

This is how she generally responded: "First, we just got bought out by a national media company. Assuming you do a great job in our thirty-minute session, this would give you a foot in the door for profitable future training programs. Second, while I can't offer you cash, we often get sporting and entertainment tickets to events we sponsor. I might be able to get you some excellent tickets to some of these events."

In essence, she felt we might have some compatible interests: I had an interest in future business with her and a business-development interest in taking clients to sporting events or concerts; and she had an interest in having her team learn to more effectively negotiate.

She was right, and she found a way to creatively satisfy both our interests. If I had gone with my first thought—to just say no—we would never have even explored these options. I would have left a significant value on the table. Eventually I spoke at her monthly meeting in exchange for four Phoenix Suns tickets and two Arizona Cardinals tickets.

Here's a chart of the continuum of strategies, now taking into account the zero-sum factor.

	"Most" Problem-Solving Strategy		"Most" Competitive Strategy	
	◄------------------------------		------------------------------►	
The Relationship Factor	Strongest future relationship	Future relationship	No future relationship likely	No possible future relationship
	+	+	+	+
The Number Factor	Many issues	Few issues	Many issues	One issue
	+	+	+	+
The Zero-Sum Factor	Creative possibilities with many shared and/or compatible interests	Creative possibilities more important than zero-sum issues	Zero-sum issues more important than creative possibilities	Zero-sum issues only, with directly conflicting interests

The Mutuality Factor: Will They Problem-Solve?

The final factor involved in deciding what strategy to use is whether *both* sides will use Problem-Solving Strategies. Does mutuality exist? Let's say you have extensively analyzed the negotiation and believe: 1) both sides want a future business relationship; 2) many issues need to be resolved; and 3) few zero-sum issues exist, as more interests appear to be shared and/or compatible than conflicting, thus indicating substantial value may be added through creatively exploring options. All three strategy factors point to Problem-Solving Strategies. You decide to use Problem-Solving Strategies, right?

Wrong. At this point, it's still premature to make this decision. To effectively use Problem-Solving Strategies, *all* parties must be willing to use them. It doesn't work if only one party wants to use Problem-Solving Strategies.

Remember Bob in the foreign open-air market? For starters, if you share strategic information and your counterpart doesn't reciprocate you have lost power. And if your counterpart engages in leverage games designed to make you feel defeated, and you don't highlight your strengths, you will be perceived as weak. Since leverage is based on perception, you have lost power here, too. Regarding independent standards, you may focus on a reasonable standard that appears fair to both sides. Your counterpart, by contrast, will likely ignore it or counter it with a standard strongly supporting its position. No gain here. Regarding offers and concessions, if you start in the mid-range and move in big chunks and they start aggressively and move in tiny chunks you will be bracketed and at a major disadvantage. Finally, you will likely face significant timing and deadline issues created by your counterpart.

In short, if you use Problem-Solving Strategies and your counterpart uses Competitive Strategies you will be on the wrong end of a win-lose negotiation.

The solution? Start by using Problem-Solving Strategies in small increments. Share a little strategic information and see if they reciprocate. If they don't, and you can't get them to join you in using Problem-Solving Strategies, match their Competitive Strategies until they realize both sides will lose with this approach.

William Ury, author of *Getting Past No: Negotiating Your Way from Confrontation to Cooperation,* has also detailed steps you can take if you believe Problem-Solving Strategies will be the most effective way to negotiate— but your counterpart appears to be using Competitive Strategies. In other words, he explains how you can help show your counterpart that it should also use Problem-Solving Strategies. Some of these strategies have been used effectively in many contexts. I describe these in chapter 9, as they also form the basis for how to effectively deal with overly emotional negotiators.

Tactics to Implement the Most Effective Strategy

In addition to evaluating the relationship, number, zero-sum, and mutuality factors to determine whether and to what extent to use Problem-Solving or Competitive Strategies, keep the following tactics in mind to help maintain your overall strategic focus and to ensure you achieve the maximum benefit from the strategy you choose:

- Determine your strategy based on initial goals
- Continually evaluate your counterpart's strategy
- Don't choose too early
- Remain flexible

Determine Your Strategy Based on *Initial* Goals

Remember our discussion in chapter 1 about initially evaluating whether your goals include a continuing relationship with your counterpart? At the start of your negotiation evaluate what strategy—Problem-Solving or Competitive—will be most likely to accomplish your goals. Tie your strategy to your goals. From the beginning every signal you send will be evaluated as a strategic move. Make sure you intend to send those signals.

Continually Evaluate Your *Counterpart's* Strategy

Making the right strategic decision will help you get what you want. But the appropriateness of your decision may change as you continually seek to ascertain your counterparts' strategy.

Here are some tips to help you determine your counterpart's strategic approach.

Research Their Reputation, Style, and Strategy

Some negotiators use the same approach in almost all their professional negotiations. Research it. Ask your colleagues to describe your counterparts' strategic moves.

To what extent do they freely share information?

How do they discuss leverage, and how often do they walk out or bluff?

How persuasive do they find independent standards, or do they use them more as trading pieces?

How aggressively do they engage in the offer-concession process?

How much do they attempt to overtly control the process?

Answers to these questions will help you evaluate your counterparts' strategy. But make your own decision. Expert negotiators use different strategies in different situations.

Find out your counterpart's style, too. Those with competitive personal styles will be more likely to use Competitive Strategies. Those with accommodative styles will be more likely to use Problem-Solving Strategies. Conflict avoiders usually won't use Competitive Strategies.

Of course, some negotiators using Competitive Strategies may come across as nonadversarial. Stylewise, they may appear collaborative. Strategically, though, they're using Competitive Strategies. Carefully analyze your counterparts' *strategic* moves on information, leverage, objective criteria, offer-concession strategies, and agenda-control issues. Don't be taken in by their style.

Be Sensitive to Trust and Atmosphere Issues
Your initial atmosphere will provide you with a good idea as to your counterpart's approach. Open your senses at this critical juncture. Be aware of trust issues, too. If your counterpart appears less than trustworthy, this suggests a Competitive Strategy. Be on guard.

Constantly Evaluate Willingness to Share Strategic Information
Keep your eye on your counterparts' willingness to share strategically important information. Those using Competitive Strategies may *appear* to be using Problem-Solving Strategies. Make them walk the walk. If you share some strategic information that puts you at risk and they don't reciprocate, watch out. It's a competitor in sheep's clothing. Insist on reciprocal information exchange. Otherwise, put on your competitor's hat. Don't get taken.

Evaluate the Extent of Competitive Tactics and Games
It's an obvious point, but worth making. When you see overtly competitive games and tactics as described in chapter 9, highly Competitive Strategies are at work. If you don't feel comfortable playing these games ask a friend to help or even negotiate for you. A successful marketing director I know hates negotiating for a new car. She knows she's ineffective

in that competitive context. Her solution? Her dad loves it, so she asks her dad to negotiate for her. Auto brokers, for a fee, will do the same. My friend knows her limitations. It's critical to her success.

Don't Choose Too Early

Don't choose a strategy too early and become unnecessarily locked in. It may take time to obtain sufficient information to determine your most effective strategy. Take the time. Get the information, especially about shared, compatible, and conflicting interests. Evaluate the information's potential to generate creative options. Then decide.

Remain Flexible

Stay nimble. You may need to switch from Problem-Solving to Competitive Strategies, based on your counterpart's changing actions. Flexibility is key. Your leverage may change during your negotiation as may the type of interests involved. You may not care about a relationship to start. But you may learn during the negotiation that a future relationship could be productive. Remain open to these possibilities and choose your strategy accordingly.

Strategies can change. Atmospheres can change. So, constantly analyze your counterparts' moves. Then make your moves with this in mind.

Selectively Apply Your Strategy to Certain Issues and Not Others

Finally, you can apply Competitive Strategies to some issues within a negotiation and Problem-Solving Strategies to others. You may determine that some zero-sum issues, where the parties' interests significantly conflict, require that you use mostly Competitive Strategies. On other issues, perhaps addressed in a different context and/or a different forum, Problem-Solving Strategies may be more effective. If you see the potential down the line for a switch, however, it's more difficult to start with Competitive Strategies and transition to Problem-Solving Strategies than the other way around.

In other words, apply a situation-specific strategy to your negotiations and to certain negotiations within negotiations.

Let's put all this together and analyze this in the context of the 2002 baseball negotiations.

The 2002 Baseball Negotiations

Thousands of fans sat on pins and needles as negotiators met late into the night trying to avert the ninth work stoppage in baseball history. And they succeeded. "Who succeeded?" you ask. The owners? The players? Neither? Or both?

Before I go further I must note that I was not involved in these negotiations and have no knowledge of what occurred, other than what I saw and read in the media.

But it's clear what happened negotiationwise. First the situation seemed ripe for Problem-Solving Strategies. The parties had a long-term relationship and could not succeed without each other. The relationship factor pointed to Problem-Solving Strategies. Plus, many issues continually arise between the owners and players that must be resolved by working together. The number factor also pointed to Problem-Solving Strategies. And while substantial zero-sum issues existed, thus pointing to Competitive Strategies, the relationship factor should have trumped the zero-sum factor.

Yet both sides used highly Competitive Strategies. Why? History, styles, and money. Neither side trusted the other, due to their acrimonious history and strained relationships. Highly competitive individuals knocked heads against other highly competitive individuals, many of whom had healthy egos and a strong desire to "win" and beat the other side. And zero-sum financial and salary issues characterized the central element of the negotiation.

What happened? Leverage dominated the negotiations. Rhetoric notwithstanding, both sides *really* needed a deal. And neither side appeared willing to risk another strike and the devastation likely to occur in its aftermath. This was both sides' BATNA. Baseball, after all, generated $3.5 billion in revenue in 2001, and players' salaries averaged $2.38 million. That's a significant amount of money at stake.

Wait a second, you might say. This is easy enough to analyze *after* they settled. Isn't this the ultimate Monday-morning quarterbacking?

Yes, except that one overriding leverage-related fact was also clear at the time: Baseball attendance still had not fully recovered from the players' 232-day 1994 strike and the first cancellation of the World Series in ninety years. This was the real leverage pushing both sides to a deal, and the fans held these cards. What do I mean?

The fans, increasingly vocal as the strike date approached, voiced their opinion that a 2002 baseball strike would drive them away in droves. This alternative to an agreement and the damage to the owners and players that would result from it proved extraordinarily powerful.

Philadelphia Phillies Manager Larry Bowa perhaps stated this best. As someone who had lived through all eight work stoppages as a player, coach, and manager, he said, "There's definitely public pressure (to get a deal done)—more than I've ever seen." Texas Rangers pitcher Jeff Zimmerman also put this in stark terms, stating "We've lost enough fans over the last seven, eight years. We can't afford to lose any more." This leverage was the big reason the players' union finally made significant concessions.

But the negotiation wasn't all about leverage. The owners, and especially commissioner Bud Selig, engineered an effective public relations effort that largely turned the public against the players and helped the public sympathize with the owners. Of course, this is relative. I'm not suggesting that the public largely agreed with the owners. I don't know if this is true or not. But I do know that public opinion in these negotiations appeared more sympathetic to the owners than the players.

This form of objective criteria, possible loss of reputation and fan support, put additional pressure on the players to compromise. They did.

Agendawise, both sides used overt agenda-control tactics to attempt to gain the strategic advantage. The players set a strike date of August 30 in order to create a sense of urgency and ratchet up the pressure. It did. It's no coincidence that concessions on both sides increased as the strike date approached. Nor is it a coincidence that the parties reached an agreement right around the deadline.

Here, both parties used Competitive Strategies, even though it appeared that Problem-Solving Strategies would have been more effective. The lesson: Analyze the situation, research the history, and use a situation-specific strategy.

Conclusion

If your tired and stressed spouse comes home, plops down on the couch, grabs a beer, flips on the TV, and says that he or she's in for the night, using Competitive Strategies will be unsuccessful in the long-run for both parties.

And if you tell the used-car seller you have been unsuccessfully looking for this make, style, year, and color car for six months, you're going to pay more than necessary for it.

Use a situation-specific strategy in your negotiations. It will pay off in the end.

CHAPTER 8 REVIEW

Use a Situation-Specific Strategy

Problem-Solving Strategies or Competitive Strategies

Golden Rules	Problem-Solving	Competitive
1. Information Is Power—So Get It	Mutually share critical information openly and liberally Actions and atmosphere confirm trust and a valued relationship	Substantial information bargaining— share a little and get a lot
2. Maximize Your Leverage	Leverage downplayed, but still there	Open conflict on leverage
3. Employ "Fair" Standards	Frequently *rely* on independent standards and procedures	Minimal reliance on independent standards and procedures
4. Design an Offer-Concession Strategy	Least aggressive offer-concession moves and tactics	Most aggressive offer-concession moves and tactics
5. Control the Agenda	Mutually agreeable agenda and agenda-control tactics	Overt and biased agenda-control tactics

Factors in Determining Whether to Problem-Solve or Compete

	"Most" Problem-Solving Strategies		**"Most" Competitive Strategies**	
	◄ ---------------		--------------- ►	
The Relationship Factor	Strongest future relationship	Future relationship	No future relationship likely	No possible future relationship
	+	+	+	+
The Number Factor	Many issues	Few issues	Many issues	One issue
	+	+	+	+
The Zero-Sum Factor	Creative possibilities with many shared and/or compatible interests	Creative possibilities more important than zero-sum issues	Zero-sum issues more important than creative possibilities	Zero-sum issues only, with directly conflicting interests

The Mutuality Factor: Will They Problem-Solve?
- If yes, use Problem-Solving Strategies.
- If no, use Competitive Strategies.

Tactics to Implement the Most Effective Strategy
- Determine your strategy based on *initial* goals
- Continually evaluate your counterpart's strategy
- Don't choose too early
- Remain flexible

Selectively Apply Your Strategy to Some Issues and Not Others

COMMON NEGOTIATION PROBLEMS
AND THEIR SOLUTIONS

S ome of the most common questions I get asked include:

- What should do I do about the negotiation games people play?
- How can I break through impasses?
- What are the most effective strategies to use with emotional counterparts?
- I don't like the process and it limits my effectiveness. How can I get over it?
- How can I effectively negotiate in multiparty environments?

Here are my suggestions.

Foiling Common Negotiation "Games"

Here's a list of negotiation games you might see and some effective countermeasures:

- Good Cop/Bad Cop
- The Nibbler
- The Blowup or Verbal Attack
- The Flinch
- The Higher or Limited Authority
- The Context Manipulator

- Power in Numbers
- Feigned Irrationality

Good Cop/Bad Cop

Tactic: One negotiator is tough, the other feigns being nice.

Here's how the good cop/bad cop routine usually goes down. The prisoner is sitting alone in a locked room when two police officers enter. One's the good cop. The other's the bad cop. Officer Toughguy starts by banging his hand on the table and pointing out the horrible situation in which the prisoner finds himself. "If you don't tell us what you know about that murder," he yells, "who knows what'll happen? We've got you on several charges. You may think they're minor, but Judge Hangem will put you away for sure. But I don't really care. Someone's going to pay and it might as well be you."

After more theatrics, Officer Toughguy storms out. Officer Niceguy then sidles up to the prisoner as if he's the prisoner's only friend in the world. "Look," he says, "my partner's crazy. But he's right about your situation. If you cooperate we can help. If not, you've got a serious problem."

Business negotiators also see this tactic frequently. "I would love to help you," your counterpart might say, "but my partner will never agree. I will see what I can do." He then returns later, saying he really worked hard but his partner wouldn't budge. "The next move," he says, "is up to you."

Response: In most cases, I just ignore it. Alternatively, explicitly recognize the tactic. Say the following: "You know, it's funny, last week I noticed two guys using the same tactic you're using now: good cop/bad cop." I doubt your counterparts will continue using the tactic after this statement. Saying this will put them on notice that it's not working. The important part is to recognize its use and not allow it to impact your behavior.

The Nibbler

Tactic: One side asks for or demands an additional concession after the deal appears done. (As you will recall, this was also discussed in chapter 4, as it relates to closing tactics.)

Response: Don't be taken hostage at the end. Don't just give in. If you do they will keep nibbling. Avoid this situation by asking several times during the negotiation if all the issues are on the table. When your counterpart says yes make a note of it. This lessens the likelihood your counterpart will want to appear inconsistent by nibbling away later. You should also find out if your counterpart has a reputation as a nibbler. Many do. If they do, plan for it. Then don't forget the reciprocity principle. If your counterpart wants another concession from you at the end require at least one in return—preferably of greater value. Nibble back.

The Blowup or Verbal Attack

Tactic: Someone truly loses his cool or gets overtly angry and aggressively adversarial.

Response: Take a break. The length of the break, however, should vary with the extent of the blowup. At the least, take a twenty-minute break. In my experience, it takes most individuals twenty minutes, at a minimum, to come back down after an outburst. Of course, you may want to take a day, a week, or an even longer break.

You might also use the tactics described more fully later in this chapter under "Dealing with Emotional Counterparts" (page 292). These include: not reacting and thus avoiding a situation where the anger and emotions may spiral even more out of control; putting yourself in their shoes and asking questions in a calm and rational way in an effort to find the underlying feelings and interests behind the outburst or verbal attack, and then addressing those fundamental feelings; and depersonalizing the situation through the liberal use of powerful fair and independent standards.

And if you believe it's an act or a show just to appear "tough," ignore it and possibly even smile slightly in response. Let them know it's not having any impact on your negotiation behavior.

The Flinch

Tactic: A visible negative reaction to any offer or concession by the other side, as recommended by Roger Dawson.

Response: Ignore it or smile a bit in response when the other side uses it—subtly acknowledging that you understand what they're doing and why they're doing it.

The Higher or Limited Authority

Tactic: One side constantly defers to a "higher authority" to make any substantive move and says they just "don't have the authority."

Response: Explore the extent of your counterpart's authority early in the negotiation. Get him to state his level of authority, if you can. At the least, evaluate the authority similarly situated individuals on his side—those with the same title or position—have had in the past. Research it. Then you can generally match that level of authority or use this move yourself. Don't be caught with authority if the other side doesn't have it. If that happens, while you might initially consider yourself more powerful as the decision-maker, you're actually at a negotiation disadvantage. You can concede. Your counterpart can't. The less authority you have, the less you will concede.

The Context Manipulator

Tactic: One party manipulates the time, location, and/or setting of the negotiation to attempt to make you *feel* less powerful. This might include making you wait in his lobby for an hour after the scheduled negotiation start time, consciously sitting you in a lower chair than his, and/or setting up the conference room so the sun is shining in your eyes.

Response: Negotiate the context. If he keeps you waiting, leave and set up a new session at your office. If you're sitting in a lower chair, move. If the sun is in your eyes, lower the shade. These tactics don't change the substantive negotiation elements. Instead, they prey on your feelings and attempt to get you to feel less powerful. Don't let these tactics get to you. And let your counterparts know they're not working.

Power in Numbers

Tactic: You show up and you're outnumbered three to one. In addition to its regional vice president, the other side's team includes a technical expert (a walking independent standard) and a secretary (whose sole purpose is to take notes). You have less power here because you lack an expert and will end up with a less detailed written record of the commitments made during the session. It's no coincidence that the arms control negotiations between the United States and the former Soviet Union almost always included the exact same number of individuals on each side of the table.

Response: Find out *before* you show up who will attend. Negotiate this element of the agenda. If this isn't realistic, suggest to the decision-maker on the other side that the two of you go into a conference room nearby and see if you can reach a deal. Say: "You don't really need your entire team with you, right?"

Feigned Irrationality

Tactic: Your counterpart appears to act irrationally, thus undermining all the strategies and tactics discussed in this book, which are based on parties acting rationally.

Response: Determine if your counterpart is *seemingly* irrational or *truly* irrational. If he's truly irrational, consider whether you even want a deal. The strength of any deal, once completed, is based on your counterpart deciding to stick with it, rather than go with his alternative. That's a rational decision. If he's truly irrational, who knows if he will stick with your deal? It's better to just walk—if you can—if he's truly irrational. If he's only *acting* irrationally in an attempt to gain a strategic advantage, though, that's another situation. There you might want to strike a deal.

The tough part here is determining if he's truly irrational or just acting that way. My suggestion? Evaluate if he *consistently* acts irrationally only on issues that help him (like by "irrationally" stating that he would be more than happy to go with his weak alternative). If he consistently acts irrationally only on issues that help him, he's probably just trying to gain a strategic advantage. If this happens, just ignore his behavior and proceed as in any other highly competitive negotiation.

We've all seen these tactics, and many of us have used them. Interestingly enough, one thing works to counter all of them. Find out your counterparts' reputation for using these tactics. If you know their reputation, you can anticipate these tactics and foil them. *Knowledge is power.* Use it to your advantage.

Top Ten Impasse-Breaking Strategies

Former Chrysler president Lee Iacocca overcame a formidable impasse with congress in 1979, as described by William Ury in *Getting Past No,* when Chrysler sought to avoid bankruptcy by negotiating with congress for a $1.5-billion-loan guarantee. At the time most lawmakers believed government should not bail out private enterprises.

What did Iacocca do when faced with this seeming impasse and his company on the line? He asked congress reality-testing questions that highlighted the consequences of congress not helping out.

"Do you want to pay the $2.7 billion now (the Treasury Department's estimate of the first-year cost in unemployment insurance and welfare payments if Chrysler went under) or do you want to guarantee half that amount with a good chance of getting it all back?"

Congress guaranteed the loan, largely because—as Iacocca later wrote—when each member of congress "realized how many people in his constituency depended upon Chrysler for their living, it was farewell ideology."

A big challenge in many negotiations revolves around how to break impasses. While unlimited options exist, here are my Top Ten Impasse-Breaking Strategies:

Get or Share More Information

Many negotiations break down because the parties have not gathered sufficient information to accurately evaluate either side's alternative to a negotiated agreement or failed to learn where they might have shared and/or compatible interests. So, get or share more information. As you know, information is power. Ask reality-testing questions. And recognize the value in possibly answering your counterpart's questions, too.

Switch Objective Criteria

As you know, negotiators often substantiate their positions as "fair and reasonable" by pointing to objective criteria such as expert opinions, precedent, market value, efficiency, costs/profits, or tradition. When impasses occur switching justifications can break the logjam. For example, a home-buyer might switch from focusing on a home's market value to the seller's profits.

Prioritize Needs and Interests

Parties negotiate to satisfy their needs and interests. The negotiation dynamic, however, can distract parties and focus energies on inconsequential issues. As discussed above, individuals' egos and desire to "win" can get in the way of satisfying fundamental needs and interests. Explicitly prioritizing the parties' needs and interests can get parties back on track, especially when egos get involved. Make a list of your needs and interests. Then do the same for your counterpart. Even consider doing this jointly with your counterpart. It will help both parties focus on what they really want and need and why they decided to talk in the first place.

Brainstorm Options

Creative solutions escape many negotiators when they don't sufficiently explore ways to satisfy both parties' interests. Impasses disappear when brainstorming parties find unexpected ways both can get what they want.

Set Deadlines

As you know, fast, furious concessions increasingly occur as parties approach deadlines. Lawyers often talk of "settling on the courthouse steps." This occurs because it's their last opportunity to reach agreement. Agreeing to deadlines increases the likelihood parties will act and move, and ratchets up the urgency felt by both sides. Remember the 2002 baseball dispute and how the players set a deadline to get the process moving.

Temporarily Put Aside the Issue

Sometimes parties negotiating multiple-issue deals can't seem to get past one important issue. Set it aside and revisit it later, after you have gained some momentum by agreeing on minor issues. Momentum can be a powerful force.

Take a Break

Impasses can form when parties get tired, nervous, emotional, scared, or lose sight of what they're trying to accomplish. Take a break. Time away from the table can allow parties to regain composure and reassess the issues. Concessions often occur after breaks.

Move up the Chain

Sometimes counterparts don't have the authority to concede any more, refuse to negotiate in good faith, or your personalities just clash. Ask to speak to their boss. You have usually got nothing to lose, and flexibility often increases as you move up the chain of command. This can be particularly effective in situations involving customer-focused industries with seemingly inflexible policies. The higher up the chain you go, the more likely your counterpart will concede in an effort to preserve the customer relationship.

Pick a Fair Alternative Process

Flipping coins, taking turns, drawing lots, or asking independent third parties to mediate or arbitrate represent fair independent procedures to break impasses. Parties also often agree to "split the difference" when the numbers reach relatively inconsequential amounts. Of course, don't *offer* to split it (as discussed in chapter 4).

Concede

Conceding provides an almost surefire way to break impasses. While possibly your last choice, it may still be in your interest to concede if your alternative—no deal—leaves you worse off than you'd be after your concession.

Next time you reach a negotiation impasse, check these suggestions. If none work, consider the possibility that the deal was not meant to happen. Sometimes your best strategy is to walk, or even run. At the least, you will be in better shape for your next negotiation.

Dealing with Emotional Counterparts

At stake was $150 million. AT&T was pitching its new telecommunications system. Boeing wanted to purchase it. Early in the negotiation AT&T described its reliable service, its prompt response rate, and the speed with which it would fix possible problems.

Boeing then requested that AT&T put its promises in writing and guarantee its problems would be immediately fixed, with 100-percent liability for damages.

The AT&T's salesman balked, stating, "We will make our best efforts, but we can't be held liable for all the things that can go wrong. Lightning can strike."

"You're fooling with us," the Boeing negotiator then interrupted, losing his temper. "First you tell us about your services. Now you're not willing to commit yourself to what you promised. . . . You're not negotiating in good faith. We can't deal with you." Boeing walked.

Have you ever dealt with similar emotions in negotiations—be it anger, fear, defensiveness, suspicion, or even hostility? I suspect everyone has.

What should you do, and how did AT&T get this back on track?

William Ury, in *Getting Past No*, describes the effective framework that AT&T used here, and that you can use in negotiations involving a high degree of emotion. These strategies also can help if your counterparts are using Competitive Strategies and you believe—based on the strategy factors discussed in chapter 8—both sides should use Problem-Solving

Strategies. Using these may help them see the problem-solving light. Here's what Ury suggests, plus a few thoughts of my own.

Don't React: Go to the Balcony

Start by not reacting. Reacting will often lead to an emotional escalation that can spiral out of control. To prevent this, Ury suggests you figuratively detach yourself by imagining you are on a balcony, overlooking the negotiation. Then take the time on the balcony, perhaps in a formal break, to focus on what you fundamentally want. Devise a strategy to attack the problem, not your counterpart. Thomas Jefferson once said, "When angry, count ten before you speak; if very angry, an hundred."

Perhaps simply be silent and let your counterpart vent. Silence can be an effective counter in highly emotional situations.

Don't Argue: Step to Their Side

Ury also suggests you must defuse their emotions and understand the reasons underlying their actions *before* you can effectively address the problem. Attempting to convince your counterpart you're right rarely sheds light on the issue. Listening respectfully and acknowledging the legitimacy of their points and feelings, without agreeing, will be far more productive.

Show them you understand by actively listening and asking questions—especially open-ended ones like "why," "how," "what," "tell me about," and "explain."

Don't interrupt, either. Interrupting often is perceived as signaling that you believe your thoughts are more important than theirs.

Above all, imagine yourself in their position. Figure out what's *really* going on. Then search for a solution.

Depersonalize the Situation with Independent Standards

Solutions in highly emotional negotiations often revolve around the parties finding some way to resolve their differences without appearing to give in. How can you do this? Focus on Golden Rule Three: Employ "Fair" Objective Criteria. Find an independent standard or procedure that both sides will accept as leading to a fair result.

Let's say you want to purchase your sibling's interest in some property once owned by your grandparents. Substantial emotions are involved, given your family's long connection with this property. How can you reduce the emotion? Propose that both sides agree to be bound by an independent appraiser's valuation of the property.

An expert's opinion, similar to standards like market value, precedent, and costs, can depersonalize negotiations by focusing the parties' attention on objective standards. Otherwise, it's your opinion versus theirs, and this can lead to unnecessarily adversarial situations.

In the AT&T/Boeing dispute, the AT&T representative used all these strategies to get its negotiation back on track. First, he went "to the balcony" by letting time pass before requesting another meeting with Boeing. Second, he "stepped to their side" by initially stating that he wanted to ensure he understood why Boeing walked. He then stated *Boeing's* position (a form of active listening), which Boeing confirmed.

The AT&T representative then said he would feel the same way if he were in Boeing's shoes. As he understood it, airline manufacturers put promises and safety specifications in writing and include significant liability provisions to minimize the risk that mistakes will be made. This is especially critical when lives are at stake.

Importantly, AT&T came to better understand this by asking questions and studying Boeing and its precedents, an independent standard. AT&T, by contrast, was largely in the service business and approached these issues differently. Up to that point, AT&T only rarely had to reduce all its promises to writing with comprehensive liability provisions. After all, it enjoyed a reputation as a company that took excellent care of its customers.

The conflict and the emotion arose because of the companies' different perspectives on the same issues.

They ultimately reached a deal, and so can you. Don't let emotions control you or the deal.

Overcoming a Fear of the Negotiation Process

"I don't like negotiating," my friend said. "Especially when it involves me personally. In that case I hate it. I especially hate negotiating for a raise. And I really hate negotiating with my neighbor over his constantly yelping dog when I'm by my pool."

Do you dislike negotiating in certain contexts? What about those "conversations" with your significant other that always seem to degenerate?

Everyone dislikes certain negotiations. Many even go to elaborate lengths to avoid them. But almost everyone has to face some unpleasant negotiations.

Here's my advice regarding how to most effectively address these situations:

- Explore your feelings and what's really at stake
- Minimize the likelihood your fears will come true
- Research "fair and reasonable" standards
- Assess whether you're the right person at the table

Explore Your Feelings and What's Really at Stake

Few individuals enjoy asking for a raise. We're scared of what we might hear. After all, we largely perceive the response to reflect our employers' true evaluation of us. Our self-worth, financial security, and even emotional health frequently are involved, although often overstated in our own minds. The existence of important personal relationships also raises the ante. These are substantial and fundamental interests. So there's often a great deal at stake.

And if we lack knowledge about the process or the individuals involved, these interests appear even more at risk. Here's the deal: The more the negotiation matters, the more we fear its possible negative consequences. And vice versa.

Exploring these feelings and fundamental interests, and researching the process and individuals involved, will lessen your anxiety. You can then more objectively analyze your capacity for risk and take appropriate action.

By contrast, walking into a negotiation with a vague fear of the unknown—especially when you perceive much at stake personally or professionally—can be paralyzing.

Minimize the Likelihood Your Fears Will Come True

What's the worst that will happen if you mess up the negotiation? Answer this question. Then take practical steps to improve the value of your alternative. Strengthen your leverage.

Let's say you find the new car–buying process frustrating because you dislike pressure and assume the salesperson wants to gouge you.

Yet, you drive a lot for work and it makes financial sense to get a new car every five years, given the repair bills that invariably occur around the five-year mark. Your worst likely alternative to getting a new car (your

WATNA)? Continuing to drive your five-year-old car and paying high repair bills. What should you do?

Minimize the likelihood of paying high repair bills on your car and thus lessen your perceived pressure and need by purchasing a new car *earlier* than normal.

Also, investigate your area car dealerships and avoid those with hard-sell, high-pressure reputations. Taking these steps will minimize the likelihood your worst fear will occur, and will increase your comfort level and leverage.

Research "Fair and Reasonable" Standards

A big fear in many negotiations involves the evaluation of whether an offer is truly "fair and reasonable." Many are comfortable accepting an offer if they believe it's fair. But how do you decide?

Remember Golden Rule Three: Employ "Fair" Objective Criteria? Comprehensively research applicable independent standards like market value, precedent, tradition, expert opinions, costs, and professional/industry standards.

If you're evaluating the fairness of a raise, find out the market value of your services, or determine the average percent raise received by your colleagues.

If you dislike buying cars, find out the dealer's cost. Figuring their profit margin, you can then evaluate the fairness of their offer.

Also, research these standards with others. As discussed in chapter 1 in the context of setting goals, brainstorm. If your friends agree a certain standard or price is fair, you will be more likely to agree and remain comfortably firm on the issue. This will increase your confidence and decrease your anxiety.

Assess Whether You're the Right Person at the Table

Some individuals simply are not well suited for particular negotiations.

While these individuals can become more effective, they should consider involving a negotiation coach in special circumstances.

For instance, as discussed in chapter 6 on personality styles, some intensely dislike interpersonal conflict, even with strangers. Such conflict avoiders might use an agent to negotiate for them. This especially makes sense in tough, competitive zero-sum negotiations with strangers. These negotiations often involve significant conflict.

Fear can overwhelm many negotiations. But effective planning, research, and analysis can help you conquer this fear. Especially when fear is involved, preparation and a more comprehensive knowledge of the process will make a world of difference.

Negotiating in Multiparty Environments

In the original hit CBS series *Survivor,* sixteen participants started out on an island together and, one by one, they voted off their colleagues until only one remained. That "survivor" won, taking home the $1 million prize. How did he win? His strategy largely revolved around building a coalition with three other participants. These four participants initially banded together and agreed to vote as a bloc. It worked. They all made it to the final four, when the rules of the game broke up the coalition.

Coalitions form a crucial element in almost every multiparty negotiation. Whether you have countries ganging up on each other in the United Nations or three people forming a partnership, coalitions make a huge difference. So, how can you effectively negotiate in multiparty contexts?

First, understand that multiparty negotiations, while unique in many ways, do not change the fundamental strategies you should use in all contexts. In fact, it makes those strategies, and your preparation of them, even more critical. In every negotiation, and especially in multiparty negotiations, go through the Five Golden Rules and then determine if Problem-Solving or Competitive Strategies make the most sense. Apply them, though, to *all* the parties involved. Here's how this works.

Golden Rule One: Information Is Power—So Get It

In multiparty negotiations get as much information as possible about everything and everyone. Ascertain *each party's* goals and interests and figure out whose goals and interests conflict and whose are shared or compatible. This may be your key to success. Your allies or coalition partners will be those with whom you share and/or have compatible goals and interests. And they will be your allies as long as those interests remain aligned.

After September 11, 2001, the United States aggressively solicited allies from around the world by emphasizing a critical shared interest—the risk every country faced from terrorism.

Golden Rule Two: Maximize Your Leverage

You maximize your leverage in multiparty negotiations by a) evaluating how much each party needs a deal relative to the others, b) finding out each party's best alternatives to a deal, and c) taking practical steps to increase the value of your own alternatives if the deal falls apart. Holdouts in multiparty negotiations know this well.

Here's an example: In real estate, as noted earlier, developers sometimes set up dummy corporations to separately buy the parcels of land they need for each project. They do this because, if a seller finds out a developer is buying all the land in his area, that seller could hold out until the end, when he would likely get a much greater price. If you own that last parcel and know the developer really needs it because he can't complete his development without it, you have strong leverage.

Golden Rule Three: Employ "Fair" Objective Criteria

Objective criteria such as independent standards take on added importance in multiparty negotiations. Why? Peer pressure and precedent. If you can get just one of your counterparts to accept the validity of your standard (like a market-value analysis of the product you're selling or your expert's opinion in a lawsuit), it will be easier to get the rest to fall into line.

At that point peer pressure will come to bear on the rest, based on the precedent just set. I once advised a plaintiff's lawyer involved in a negotiation with multiple defendants. In it one of the defendants had settled early for a substantial sum. The plaintiff's lawyer used this precedent—set by the defendants' former colleague—to justify his fair and reasonable settlement offers to the other defendants.

Golden Rule Four: Design an Offer-Concession Strategy

Multiparty offer-concession dynamics are complex. As such, first find out what offer-concession behavior has characterized similar multiparty negotiations in the past, including who has historically made the first offer, why, and how far the parties have moved from start to finish. Then brainstorm what might occur when the real negotiation begins.

Golden Rule Five: Control the Agenda

It's hard to emphasize enough the importance of controlling the agenda in multiparty negotiations. As the number of parties increases, so does the importance of controlling the agenda. Of course, this does not necessarily mean you should try to overtly control the agenda. Subtlety and silence can work effectively too.

I was once involved in a seven-party negotiation in which I said virtually nothing. Another party took control of the agenda, and it was a great agenda for me, too. I just sat back and enjoyed it.

I've only watched *Survivor* a few times. Each time I watch it, though, I see the participants forming or breaking coalitions. The question thus arises: Will the coalition last? It depends on the parties' personal interests and trustworthiness.

A prize of $1 million rides on this answer.

CHAPTER 9 REVIEW

Common Negotiation Problems and Their Solutions

Foiling Common Negotiation "Games"
- Good Cop/Bad Cop
- The Nibbler
- The Blowup or Verbal Attack
- The Flinch
- The Higher or Limited Authority
- The Context Manipulator
- Power in Numbers
- Feigned Irrationality

Top Ten Impasse-Breaking Strategies
- Get or share more information
- Switch objective criteria
- Prioritize needs and interests
- Brainstorm options
- Set deadlines
- Temporarily put aside the issue
- Take a break
- Move up the chain
- Pick a fair alternative process
- Concede

Dealing with Emotional Counterparts
- Don't react—go to the "balcony"
- Don't argue—step to their side
- Depersonalize the situation with independent standards

Overcoming a Fear of the Negotiation Process
- Explore your feelings and what's really at stake
- Minimize the likelihood your fears will come true
- Research "fair and reasonable" standards
- Assess whether you're the right person at the table

Negotiating in Multiparty Environments
- Apply the Five Golden Rules to every party and build coalitions

PART THREE

APPLYING THESE STRATEGIES TO REAL-LIFE SITUATIONS

Now you know the Five Golden Rules. You understand negotiating styles, Problem-Solving and Competitive Strategies, and you're familiar with the "games" and problems you will likely encounter. These are critical. But there's one more piece. You still need to apply this knowledge to your daily negotiations. Here's how to do it in five typical business and life situations.

Whether you're in business, law, academics, or work in the nonprofit community, you regularly face business-related negotiations. When was the last time you bought computer equipment? Or entered into a partnership with a friend? Or had a dispute with one of your co-workers? It happens everyday. In chapter 10 we apply your negotiation knowledge to garden-variety business negotiations.

The most expensive word in the English language is "okay." Why? It's how most of us respond when our boss offers us a raise. Yet, it may not be "fair," based on what our colleagues in the industry make or based on the profit you generated for the company last year. What should you do? Chapter 11 is about salary negotiations, and it explains what to do and how to get more of what you want and deserve.

Family negotiations between spouses and/or with children can present your most rewarding *and* challenging ongoing negotiations. In chapter 12, I describe my top ten family negotiation strategies.

The car-buying process may be the most feared negotiation of any. But it doesn't need to be. Understanding the games some car dealers play is often half the battle. The rest is doing your homework. You don't have to battle on their turf and under their rules, but you do need to have your weapons available with the key information at your fingertips. Chapter 13 will illustrate how you can do this and drive off the lot comfortable because you got a good car at a fair price.

Buying a house may be the single largest purchase you will ever make. The stakes are high, the money significant. In chapter 14 we will analyze the home-buying and -selling process and lay out the negotiation rules you should follow to ensure you buy or sell the right home at the right price.

Each of these situations present unique challenges. Each also requires the application of specialized negotiation strategies and skills.

10

GARDEN-VARIETY BUSINESS NEGOTIATIONS

Assume you're a senior vice president of ABC Mattress Corporation, one of the world's largest mattress manufacturing companies. Recently ABC became involved in a dispute with a relatively new bedspring supplier, Sleepwell Bedspring Corporation. The dispute, and your subsequent negotiation, involves Sleepwell's delivery to ABC of 10,000 nonconforming bedsprings. According to your investigation ABC's purchasing director ordered 10,000 regular-size bedsprings when it needed a rush order it could not complete in its own plants. Unfortunately, Sleepwell delivered 10,000 *extra-long* bedsprings. Since ABC has a written contract with Sleepwell specifying regular-size bedsprings, your lawyer told you ABC will likely win at trial if you sue to recover ABC's damages and lost profits of $1.5 million.

Sleepwell contends it did not make a mistake. It says your purchasing director, despite the written contract, *orally* ordered the extra-long mattresses. Sleepwell also contends your alleged $1.5 million in damages and lost profits is unproven and speculative.

This negotiation appears, at first glance, like a straightforward contract dispute. A contract was allegedly breached. Damages were incurred. The only question is how much Sleepwell will have to pay to resolve it.

There's a catch, though. While ABC's legal claim is strong and Sleepwell's weak, Sleepwell is in a precarious financial situation with little cash on hand. A $1.5-million judgment against it, the expected result if the case goes through trial, would probably throw it into bankruptcy. Both sides know this.

What should you do? Go through the Five Golden Rules. Preliminarily identify:

1. Your goals, interests, and possible options that might satisfy your interests
2. How to maximize your leverage
3. What "fair and reasonable" objective criteria you might employ
4. Expected offer-concession dynamics
5. How to control the agenda

Then determine if you want to use a Problem-Solving or a Competitive Strategy.

Golden Rule One: Information Is Power—So Get It

First get sufficient information to set aggressive, realistic long-term strategic and short-term tactical goals. Here's some information you need to help set those goals.

Information About ABC

- ABC Mattress, a Phoenix, Arizona–based company, is one of the largest mattress producers in the United States. It manufactures most of its mattresses in Phoenix, although it also has a Tucson plant where it manufactures bedsprings.
- ABC plans to replace its Tucson plant in the next five years at a cost of $10 million. This is because it has experienced decreasing output in its Tucson plant in the last five years (150,000 bedsprings were manufactured in Tucson this past year).
- It costs ABC $30 per unit to manufacture each bedspring at its Tucson plant. This is fairly high compared to the industry, largely due to the plant's aging equipment and the high labor costs from the experienced workers required to run the equipment.
- ABC's projected new plant in Tucson will have the capacity to manufacture 300,000 bedsprings per year, which is needed for its current and projected customer base.

Information About Sleepwell

- Sleepwell Bedspring is also based in Phoenix. It is a two-year-old company with a brand-new manufacturing plant in Phoenix.

- Sleepwell has a good reputation, but has been rumored to have marketing and salesforce challenges since its start. Most in the industry believe it has substantial unused capacity in its plant, due to these challenges.
- Sleepwell's labor costs are low compared with the industry average. Its new plant has efficient high-speed equipment and does not require as many experienced workers as older plants.

Information Step 1: Brainstorm to Determine Goals and Interests

ABC's Goals and Interests

What does ABC want to achieve in this negotiation? From a strategic long-term perspective, ABC wants to maximize its overall profitability by increasing its market share and profit margins. From a tactical short-term perspective, it wants to satisfy its following interests, in general priority order:

- Grow its market share and satisfy its customers' demands
- Increase its efficiency by lowering its plant and labor costs
- Ensure a long-term, reliable supply of low-cost bedsprings
- Improve its reputation and recapture customers' goodwill lost due to Sleepwell's delivery of nonconforming goods
- Take care of its employees' health and welfare
- Improve its financial condition by recovering its $1.5 million in damages and lost profits
- Minimize its litigation costs, including the time spent on the possible litigation by its employees

Sleepwell's Goals and Interests

Now you know what ABC wants. What about Sleepwell? It's fair, at the start, to make some assumptions. For instance, Sleepwell also likely wants to maximize its long-term profitability. It likely has other short-term goals and interests, too. Most importantly, it probably wants to stay in business by improving its cash position and financial stability and protect its reputation as an efficient and reliable supplier of quality bedsprings. Sleepwell also has some shared interests with ABC. For instance, it wants to minimize its litigation costs, too, including the time and effort spent on it by its employees.

Given these assumptions, should you as ABC's senior vice president now set ABC's negotiation goals? Do you now have enough information? Probably not. What should you do? Find out more about Sleepwell by doing more research on Sleepwell and setting up a face-to-face meeting with a Sleepwell representative. The goal for this meeting? Get sufficient information, both substantive and strategic, to set an aggressive yet realistic goal for this negotiation. Plus, find out about other interests—shared, conflicting, and/or compatible.

Also evaluate what ABC or Sleepwell interests might be satisfied with a continuing relationship between the parties. Consider the possible value of future relationship.

Before meeting, then, brainstorm and go through the Five Golden Rules in preparation for this critical first negotiation session. In going through those rules, list the information you still need to get to effectively implement each Rule.

Information Step 2: Brainstorm Options That Might Satisfy ABC's Interests

You now know some of ABC's and Sleepwell's general goals and interests. The next step is to brainstorm to find some options that might satisfy ABC's short- and long-term interests. This way you can better determine what information to get in the meeting to help evaluate the options that most effectively satisfy ABC's interests.

Here are some options that might result from a brainstorming session with your colleagues, along with the ABC interests possibly satisfied. The options are not yet prioritized. The asterisks represent ABC's more critical interests.

Options	ABC interest(s) satisfied
Cash settlement now, possibly paid over time	Improve financial condition Minimize litigation cost—especially time of executives involved
Litigate and cash settlement later, possibly paid over time	Improve financial condition
Sleepwell admission of liability	* Recapture customers' goodwill lost due to Sleepwell's delivery of nonconforming goods Deter future suppliers from similar actions
Long-term supply contract at a "below-market" rate for a certain number of bedsprings (This assumes	* Long-term reliable supply of low-cost bedsprings Minimize litigation

Sleepwell can show how its order problem has been resolved for the future)	cost—especially time of executives involved
Find creative uses for the nonconforming bedsprings, perhaps partner with Tall Clubs International	* Sleepwell recovers some of its costs at no cost to ABC Possible new relationship with new partner
Type of joint venture, including long-term, reliable supply of low-cost bedsprings	* Long-term reliable supply of low-cost bedsprings Minimize litigation cost—especially time of executives involved
Purchase or merge with Sleepwell	* Long-term reliable supply of low-cost bedsprings Minimize litigation cost—especially time of executives involved
Various combinations of the above	Various combinations of the above

Now that you've identified some options that might satisfy ABC's interests and have generally prioritized those interests, list the substantive information you want to get that would help you evaluate the feasibility of your various options. Here's a list, along with the reason the information might be helpful:

Substantive Information to Get	Reason
Sleepwell's overall plant capacity	To determine if its plant could satisfy ABC's short- and long-term bedspring needs
Sleepwell's unused plant capacity	To determine if its plant could satisfy ABC's short- and long-term bedspring needs
Sleepwell's per unit manufacturing cost	If Sleepwell's cost is lower than ABC's, this could provide a basis for a long-term, "below-market" bedspring supply deal

Sleepwell's cash and financial condition	To evaluate if Sleepwell has the financial capacity to enter into a long-term deal, to enter into a cash settlement, or to finance the litigation To possibly form the basis for a merger or purchase decision
Sleepwell's customer base and market share, current and future	To evaluate if Sleepwell can satisfy ABC's short- and/or long-term bedspring needs
Steps Sleepwell has taken to prevent similar disputes in the future	To ensure no future order problems
Cost of Sleepwell's manufacturing plant	To compare to ABC's proposed plant's cost and possibly provide a basis for merger or purchase discussions

Information Step 3: Find Out *Strategic* Information About Sleepwell, Including Its Negotiation Styles and Strategies

Here's the substantive information you have obtained so far in preparation for your meeting with a Sleepwell representative:

- The basic facts about each party and the nature of the negotiation
- The parties' goals and interests, with some interests prioritized
- Possible options that satisfy interests
- A list of information needs and the possible benefits of obtaining the information

What additional information do you need before you meet with a Sleepwell representative? Let's say Sleepwell has decided to send CEO Kelly Johnson to meet with you. You should find out, before the meeting, the following *strategic* information: Sleepwell's reputation in its negotiations with others in the industry; Kelly's reputation; Kelly's personal likes and dislikes; ways to develop some rapport with Kelly; habits, like whether she consistently walks out of negotiations and then comes back; her personal approach to conflict, be it as a Competitor, an Accommodator, or a Conflict Avoider? And the list goes on.

Find out this critical strategic information, if you can, before the meeting.

Golden Rule Two: Maximize Your Leverage

Find Both Sides' Ongoing Leverage

Now that you have explored both parties' goals, interests, and options and researched your counterpart's styles and strategies, turn to the leverage situation. Assume you have assessed and quantified the leverage in the following fashion, based on the information you possess. Also assume both sides perceive this to be accurate at the time.

The Parties' Level of Need

Your Need Level (ABC):	Low (+1)
Sleepwell Need Level:	Very High (+2)
Your Need Score:	+3

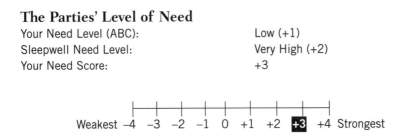

Weakest –4 –3 –2 –1 0 +1 +2 **+3** +4 Strongest

Alternatives and BATNAs

What about ABC's and Sleepwell's alternatives and BATNAs? Consider the following possible ABC alternatives in determining your BATNA:

ABC's Alternatives:

1. Litigate dispute, lose, and build new $10-million plant
2. Don't litigate dispute (ignore breach), and build $10-million plant
3. Litigate dispute and win, forcing Sleepwell into bankruptcy. Then purchase Sleepwell plant and equipment 2–3 years down the road at fire-sale prices in bankruptcy. Possibly no need for a new plant.
4. Litigate dispute and win, forcing Sleepwell into bankruptcy. Then get into bidding war with ABC's competitors for Sleepwell's plant and equipment 2–3 years down the road in bankruptcy. May or may not build a new plant, depending on the delay and success in acquiring Sleepwell's plant and equipment.

At this point what is ABC's Best Alternative to a Negotiated Agreement with Sleepwell? Option 3, although it may not be particularly attractive or likely, given the timeframe for getting Sleepwell's plant and equipment and the risk of a bidding war with ABC's competitors. The most likely alternative? Option 3 or 4.

Sleepwell's Alternatives:

1. Litigate dispute, lose, go bankrupt.
2. Litigate dispute, win, attempt to grow business. Unlikely to do much future business with ABC.
3. Find corporate "white knight" or investor to shore up financial condition or do long-term bedspring deal.

At this point what is Sleepwell's Best Alternative to a Negotiated Agreement with ABC? Option 3, although the likelihood of this may not be great. The most likely best alternative? Option 1. Obviously, this is not an appealing alternative. But it's not a good alternative for ABC either. In fact, it's so bad for ABC that if I represented Sleepwell I would play the "bankruptcy card" in the negotiation. "Go ahead. Sue us. At the end of the day you will spend thousands and realize nothing. That's not good for you, is it?" Potential bankruptcy can translate to strong leverage. Just look at the concessions several major airlines extracted from their unions in 2002 and 2003 when they experienced substantial financial problems. Or think about the leverage highly indebted real estate investors exercise with their banks when the real estate market slumps and they raise the possibility of defaulting on millions of dollars in loans. The banks, facing huge losses if these investors go bankrupt, often restructure their loans and repayment terms.

Quantified, the parties' BATNAs might look like this:

Your BATNA Value (ABC):	Poor (–2)
Sleepwell's BATNA Value:	Very Poor (+3)
Your BATNA Score:	+1

Your BATNA Score: +1

Weakest –6 –5 –4 –3 –2 –1   0 **+1** +2 +3 +4 +5 +6 Strongest

What is your overall leverage? Your Need Score (+3) plus Your BATNA Score (+1) equals +4.

Overall Leverage: +4

Weakest –10 –9 –8 –7 –6 –5 –4 –3 –2 –1 0 +1 +2 +3 **+4** +5 +6 +7 +8 +9 +10 Strongest

Overall leverage advantage here goes to ABC, although perhaps not as clearly as it initially seemed. And remember, leverage is fluid and can change.

Improve Your Alternatives and
Limit the Attractiveness of Your Counterparts'

How can you improve ABC's alternatives and limit the attractiveness of Sleepwell's alternatives? Improve your alternatives by directing your lawyer to draft a complaint and prepare a lawsuit against Sleepwell for the damages and lost profits resulting from its breach. You will then be able to present this alternative as more likely and realistic when it becomes necessary to engage on the leverage front.

At the same time limit the attractiveness of Sleepwell's alternatives by finding out who else, if anyone, might be interested in acquiring Sleepwell's plant and equipment, or business. Then consider what steps can be taken to minimize the likelihood of that acquisition. However, recognize that time may work against you. ABC does not want to give Sleepwell the opportunity to seek out alternative buyers if ABC decides it wants to purchase Sleepwell.

Plus, remember your leverage-related-information needs for your upcoming meeting with Sleepwell's CEO. Specifically, if you can, find out if Sleepwell has had any communications with ABC's competitors or others about the possibility of a sale or long-term deal. If so, find out as much as you can about these communications. Of course, this might be challenging, as you don't want to tip off Sleepwell to this alternative if they haven't thought of it themselves.

Golden Rule Three: Employ "Fair" Objective Criteria

What standards and procedures might you and Sleepwell use to support the "fairness and reasonableness" of a deal? We've already listed several, but there are more. Investigate each prior to and during the meeting with Sleepwell's CEO. They include:

- *Market value* of regular and extra-long bedsprings
- *Precedent*—terms of the previous deal and other deals with similar counterparts
- *Costs*
  — Sleepwell's plant, equipment, and other assets
  — Sleepwell's per-unit bedspring-manufacturing cost
  — ABC's cost to build a new plant
  — ABC's per-unit bedspring-manufacturing cost
- *Financial strength*—how close is Sleepwell to bankruptcy?

- *Expert opinions*—appraisal of Sleepwell plant and equipment and possibly overall business; detailed financial analysis of Sleepwell's condition
- *Industry standards* for sale or merger of similar businesses
- *Efficiency*—cost savings in event of merger/buyout/long-term supply contract, etc.

Try to find out what standards Sleepwell has previously used—experts it may have used in the past or terms of other long-term supply contracts. Then prepare to negotiate over the most "fair" standard and do the "standards dance."

Golden Rule Four:
Design an Offer-Concession Strategy

At this point it's premature to design a full-blown offer-concession strategy. However, you should find out the offer-concession patterns that exist in this context. For instance, who would traditionally make the first offer if ABC decided to explore purchasing Sleepwell? Do parties in these situations generally move toward the center of the two opening positions?

You will also have a strategic advantage in your meeting, as you will be meeting with Sleepwell's CEO. Before the meeting, consider having ABC's CEO limit your authority to answer certain questions and explore certain issues. Kelly Johnson may find it more difficult to plead limited authority given her position, although she may have to "run certain issues by [her] board."

Your offer-concession strategies should be more fully explored after the meeting and before you present any offers or concessions.

Golden Rule Five: Control the Agenda

Finally, how can you control the agenda—short-term for the meeting and long-term for the entire negotiation? Short-term, try preview, agree, and focus. In this context, have your representative contact Kelly Johnson and indicate that the purpose of this meeting is purely to meet and exchange information. Once that understanding has been reached, stick to it. It's critical that this meeting not lose that focus, especially from ABC's standpoint.

However, the passage of time likely favors Sleepwell. So plan to set another meeting in the near future to continue these discussions.

After this meeting, among other things, set a goal and evaluate whether Problem-Solving or Competitive Strategies would be most effective.

Problem-Solving or Competitive Strategy?

Does ABC want to pursue a Problem-Solving or a Competitive Strategy? Unsure at this point. Your choice of strategy depends on information you don't yet know for certain about Sleepwell, including its leverage, "fair" objective criteria, offer-concession strategy, and agenda control. Once you get this information consider each of the following four factors, indicating for each if it leans toward using Problem-Solving or Competitive Strategies:

Factors	Decision	Strategy
1. Relationship Factor: Expected future relationship?	Yes ——————> No ——————>	Problem-Solving (PS) Competitive (C)
2. Number Factor: Number of issues?	Many issues ————> Few issues ————>	PS C
3. Zero-Sum Factor	Creative options possible Zero-sum in nature —>	PS C
4. Mutuality Factor	Yes —————> No (overrides Factors 1–3) —————>	PS C

Based on the information you learn in your meeting with Kelly Johnson, you may decide to litigate. If so, direct your lawyers to largely use Competitive Strategies in any possible settlement discussions. There's little likelihood of a future relationship. There are relatively few issues at the core of the dispute, and the critical issues are zero-sum in nature. If you decide after your meeting to seriously explore a long-term contract, merger, or buyout, Problem-Solving Strategies make more sense. Overall, get the information, then decide the most effective strategy.

This is a general step-by-step strategic template to give you a flavor of how to implement these strategies in your business negotiations. For a more comprehensive and detailed template for use here and in other negotiation situations, see *"Gain the Edge!* Strategic Guide to Effective Negotiations" on page 347.

Business negotiations dominate many of our lives. Whether you work within an ABC or Sleepwell-type corporation, or another business, these steps will provide you with the crucial building blocks to negotiate your way to success. Use them.

11

SALARY NEGOTIATIONS

A law student of mine in 1996 asked me for help in negotiating a salary with a law firm for which he had worked the previous summer. He told me he loved the firm and wanted to accept its offer, but thought its starting salary was low.

So he asked if he should interview with other firms, even though he was pretty sure he would ultimately accept the first firm's offer? Here's the overall strategy I recommended. Many of these same principles apply to those requesting raises.

Of course, as you know by now, we start by going through the Five Golden Rules. Here, however, we apply them to the salary and work context and highlight the elements to emphasize in this environment.

Golden Rule One: Information Is Power—So Get It

I first asked my student a number of questions to help him focus. Could the firm satisfy his fundamental financial and nonfinancial short- and long-term strategic goals and interests? And what other compensation-related issues might be on the table? We identified areas where he needed to get more information, and preliminarily set his goals and expectations, based largely on this information.

In this context, don't be afraid to explore or introduce nonmonetary interests and options. As mentioned earlier in chapter 1, consider how you can "expand the pie" with perks, different kinds of benefits, title changes, office space, working arrangements and flex time, agreement for future raises, and—the list goes on.

Golden Rule Two:
Maximize Your Leverage

Once he completed his research I suggested he evaluate his level of need versus the firm's level of need. He also needed to explore and improve his alternatives and his BATNA. Interview away, I told him. Find out what alternatives exist if, for whatever reason, he decided not to accept the firm's offer. Then take steps—such as interviewing with others—to turn those *likely* alternatives into *viable* alternatives.

The benefit? Assuming he got other offers, and he did, he would feel and act stronger and strengthen his leverage for when he enters the salary negotiation with the firm he really wants.

I also suggested he find out the law firm's alternatives to hiring him. What is its BATNA? Who else had they interviewed? How much additional time and money would it have to spend finding someone else, if he declined its offer?

For most seeking a raise, their short-term leverage is relatively weak. In most circumstances, the individual seeking a raise does not interview and seek alternative employment with other firms or companies. As a result, they don't have a good choice in the short-term but to accept what they are offered. Longer term, of course, they will strengthen their leverage by interviewing and finding better alternatives if they do not find that their current position satisfies their financial or other interests. To get what you want, even from your current employer, it's critical to have or create good alternatives.

Golden Rule Three: Employ
"Fair" Objective Criteria

Ascertain your value using fair independent standards. If your leverage is weak in the short-term, focus on your best standards. Find out the going market salary for similarly situated persons, i.e., similar corporate level, industry, geographic area, professional background and experience, etc.

Look to precedent (what they paid you the past year and your raise in past years) for another standard.

How can you find this information? Ask peers in your field. Contact industry associations. Ask a human-resources consultant or headhunter for an expert opinion. Check salary surveys (e.g., JobStar.org). If you want a raise, also find out what your boss considers the most "fair" standards and how he or she values your contributions. Perhaps you should document a list of your achievements during the past year, or evaluate the amount of money you saved the company. How much has the company profited from your efforts? What has the company traditionally given in raises? Is inflation part of its raise calculation?

Prepare to negotiate over the most "fair" salary or raise.

Golden Rule Four: Design an Offer-Concession Strategy

Find out what offer-concession patterns apply in your industry and context. Some law firms traditionally give lockstep raises in lawyers' first few years according to a fairly rigid formula based on hours billed. After that it becomes more individualized, based on the quality of the lawyer's work and many other factors, including their profitability and ability to bring in new clients. Research the patterns. They will tell you a lot.

Then go through the advantages and disadvantages of making a first offer. Often your boss will have more information than you on the patterns and standards involved. In that case, if you can, consider getting your boss to make the first offer. As a general rule, avoid making the first offer, as you may undervalue your services or contributions. And practice your response, making sure you choose your words carefully.

If you're extremely uncomfortable asking for a raise—and many are—practice with a tape recorder. Consider using phrases like: "I'm interested in asking for a raise. How would you do that if you were me?" Or "I feel like I'm doing a good job here, and yet I understand I'm making less than my coworkers. What do I need to do to earn more?"

Then prepare a response to their offer or counters. As noted above, most simply respond with two letters: OK. If it's an exceedingly fair offer, based on your knowledge of independent standards, this might be the best response. On the other hand, "OK" might be two very expensive letters. Try this instead: Repeat their offer and then go "hmmm." Consider

the offer in silence. Then wait a bit and see what happens. You will probably be pleasantly surprised.

Finally, make sure you carefully present your offer or counter in the most
effective fashion possible, taking into consideration the offer-concession
tactics discussed in chapter 4.

Golden Rule Five:
Control the Agenda

Just do it. This usually isn't the place for a formal written agenda or written offer, unless this negotiation comes during an annual performance review and the company requests your input in writing. Plus, informal is
usually best in these circumstances. But do it in person. As you know, it's
more difficult to say no to someone's face than in writing or on the phone.

But have an agenda in mind. You will want to relatively openly and
honestly share the information you have found about the market value for
someone in your position, especially if it's good. And you will want to
show how it's in the company's best interests to provide you with what
you want.

When and where should you hold this conversation? That depends on
your relationship with your boss. But don't just cede the agenda and the
time, place and manner of the discussion. Do your research on when,
where, and how your colleagues received raises. Then evaluate if that
makes sense for you.

Also consider the order in which you want to raise the compensation
issues. For instance, should you raise the salary issue—often a zero-sum
issue—early in the negotiation or later? I usually recommend raising it
near the end, especially if there are a number of significant nonmonetary
issues on the table.

Problem-Solving or
Competitive Strategy?

Problem-Solving or Competitive Strategies in salary negotiations? Let's go
through our four factors.

This scenario most often heavily favors the use of Problem-Solving
Strategies. There's a long-term relationship, many ongoing issues (in this
negotiation and the future), significant creative option possibilities (albeit

Factors	Decision	Strategy
1. Relationship Factor: Expected future relationship?	Yes ————————> No ————————>	Problem-Solving (PS) Competitive (C)
2. Number Factor: Number of issues?	Many issues ————> Few issues ————>	PS C
3. Zero-Sum Factor	Creative options possible Zero-Sum in nature —>	PS C
4. Mutuality Factor	Yes ————————> No (overrides factors 1–3) ————————>	PS C

with some zero-sum issues), and often your counterpart will reciprocate with Problem-Solving Strategies as well. Four of our five factors suggest Problem-Solving Strategies would be most effective. This is why most should use Problem-Solving Strategies in the compensation arena.

Of course, this assumes both you and your boss usually use Problem-Solving Strategies. If so, use Problem-Solving Strategies here. Shy away from anger, threats, warnings, games, direct confrontation, and extreme offers unsupported by facts and standards.

Instead, promote an atmosphere of trust consistent with valued long-term relationships. Be cool, calm, respectful, and go through the Five Golden Rules in the problem-solving context.

Let's face it. No one likes to ask their boss for more money. It's commonly viewed as one of our toughest negotiations. That's why many don't even ask. They just accept, even though they likely deserve more. Next time, at the least, ask. My law student did. He's now better off. You can be, too.

12

FAMILY NEGOTIATIONS

Linda and I got married on March 16, 2003. At that point a whole new type of negotiations began—spousal negotiations. Family negotiations occupy a pretty unique place in the negotiation world. How should you negotiate in these situations? As the prototypical environment in which to use Problem-Solving Strategies, we've already extensively addressed this in chapter 8. But here's some more targeted advice, in the form of my top ten family negotiation strategies:

- Remember the long-term relationship involved
- Listen and understand
- Dig deep for the true issues and interests involved
- Identify the feelings and emotions involved
- Consider its impact on you and your identity
- Put yourself in their shoes
- Find and use objective standards
- If the temperature gets too hot, institute a cooling-off period
- Men and women communicate differently
- Don't always try to do it yourself

Remember the Long-Term
Relationship Involved

Avoid the competitive, hard-nosed, brinksmanship negotiations that you might utilize with a used-car salesman. Instead, remember that you want to spend the rest of your life in very close proximity with this person. Use Problem-Solving Strategies at all times. Keep this in mind as you deal with the inevitable conflicts that arise. If you think you might later regret taking a certain position or making a certain statement, don't do it. That's your relationship conscience talking.

Listen and Understand

Don't underestimate the value of just listening and understanding. A friend of mine is a great problem-solver. In many ways his business success is based on his excellent skills in this area. The biggest challenge in his marriage? Whenever his wife shares a problem with him he tries to solve it for her. But often that's not what she wants or needs. She just wants him to listen and empathize. He's had to learn to do this.

Dig Deep for the True Issues
and Interests Involved

In *Difficult Conversations: How to Discuss What Matters Most* by Douglas Stone, Bruce Patton, and Sheila Heen, the authors distinguish between three "conversations" within every difficult communication: the What Happened Conversation, the Feelings Conversation, and the Identity Conversation. In the What Happened Conversation parties often focus on what happened and discuss it in terms of "who's right, who meant what, and who's to blame."

The problem is that focusing on right and wrong, assuming what someone "really" intended, and playing the blame game, frequently leads everyone down a negative path. Alternatively the authors suggest we explore our perceptions, interpretations, and values underlying the issues, stop assuming we know the other's intentions, and focus on how to avoid similar future problems. Dig deep to find the true interests and issues involved. Then change how you discuss them and positively focus on the future, not negatively on the past.

Identify the Feelings
and Emotions Involved

How many of your most difficult discussions with a family member were really about anger, disappointment, shame, or some other feeling or emotion? Sometimes this is the core problem. In *Difficult Conversations*, the authors suggest you explicitly address the feelings question by identifying everyone's feelings and seeking to better understand them. Perhaps discuss them openly, then manage them if you can. This can be tough. But it's worth it. In your next disagreement with your spouse ask yourself, "How do I feel about this, and why?" Then ask your spouse how he or she feels and why. That will get you started.

Consider Its Impact
on You and Your Identity

Major disagreements with loved ones often involve at a deep level our sense of identity and self-worth. Called the "identity conversation" in *Difficult Conversations*, this can be the hardest area to explore, because our self-esteem appears to be at stake. How can you identify this, and what can you do about it? As noted in *Difficult Conversations*, the "biggest factor that contributes to a vulnerable identity (and that signals the presence of an identity issue), is all-or-nothing thinking: I'm either competent or incompetent, good or evil, worthy of love or not." When you see this in others, or when you recognize it in yourself, put the issues into some long-term perspective and find the right balance. All-or-nothing thinking, especially about identity issues, often presents a false choice. Avoid it.

Put Yourself in Their Shoes

My wife had been dreaming of her wedding day for her entire life. Frankly, I hadn't really thought about the details (an inside or outside ceremony, a long or short aisle, etc.) until we got engaged. As we began to discuss these details and evaluated their financial impacts, I consciously tried to see these issues through her eyes. It made a big difference.

Find and Use Objective Standards

A great way to lower the emotional level of many negotiations, as you know from our discussion in chapter 3, is to find an objective standard that can lead to a mutually acceptable solution. Since family negotiations often generate high emotions, objective standards can be great problem-solvers. Standards that work well here, especially with kids, include precedent (your older brother received the same allowance), policy (everyone must finish their vegetables before leaving the table), and expert opinion (the dentist told you to brush your teeth after every meal, if you want healthy teeth). Of course, expect your kids to start using these with you, too. They generally love to appeal to the market. "John can cross the street alone, Mom, so why can't I?" your son might say.

If the Temperature Gets Too Hot, Institute a Cooling-Off Period

Almost everyone has lost their temper at one point and said something to a loved one that they regret. If you see this coming take a break. It's easy to say, but often tough to do. Yet, it can make or break a relationship.

Men and Women Communicate Differently

John Gray has had great success with his bestseller *Men are from Mars, Women are from Venus*. While I was skeptical at first, I now am convinced that most men and women tend to process information differently. It's worth your time to explore these differences in Gray's books or in others.

Don't Always Try to Do It Yourself

Finally, some seemingly intractable family negotiation issues may require outside help. Don't be embarrassed to ask for help from friends, parents, or the professionals who have helped countless others in similar situations.

One more thing. Don't forget to say "I love you" at least every day. After all, that's why you're in the relationship in the first place.

13

CAR NEGOTIATIONS

We arrived at the dealership on December 28. Our goal? Find out as much as possible about the new sports car I had been eyeing. Two hours later, goal accomplished, we walked out. But I was hooked. The car cornered like a dream. And I needed safe, reliable, and fun transportation.

So began my 2002 car purchase. It's a negotiation many dread. But you shouldn't. A new car purchase shares many characteristics with negotiations everyone regularly faces, at work and at home, negotiations we've already reviewed.

Golden Rule One:
Information Is Power—So Get It

As you know, the first step in every negotiation, including buying a new car, involves obtaining critical information. In the car context, look inward and figure out what you want and need. Prioritize your interests, e.g., safety, reliability, appearance and styling, price and affordability, energy efficiency, comfort, practicality, and, of course, enjoyment value.

Then find a vehicle that satisfies your interests. These days, hit the Internet. Hundreds of Web sites are devoted to model-by-model comparisons, safety, features, financing and more. A good place to start is ConsumerReports.org or Edmunds.com.

After you have narrowed your choice to several vehicles, get some firsthand information. Ask friends with these vehicles what they like and dislike. Go for a test drive. Kick the tires. See how it feels. Then set a preliminary goal. Write it down.

And research the dealer's style and reputation for negotiating. Some dealers have a well-deserved reputation for pulling every competitive trick in the book, like nibbling, flinching, lowballing, and on and on. Others hope to establish a long-term relationship with their customers and take a far more low-key, low-pressure style. Find out their reputation. Evaluate their relationship goal.

Golden Rule Two:
Maximize Your Leverage

At the same time you're information-gathering at the dealership, take steps to maximize your leverage. If you like it, express some interest. But don't ooh and aah. If you show too much interest you lose leverage, and your perceived need level increases.

From the dealer's standpoint, find out how they are doing saleswise that month. How busy are they? How good are their alternatives? On my trip I found out the dealership had several versions of the car I liked due to arrive within one to two months. This told me it would likely deal to move the car I liked off the lot to make room.

Don't get sucked into a price discussion, either. A high-pressure salesperson will try to push you to start the offer-concession stage. "Tell me what we need to do so you can drive out of here today," he will say.

Resist the urge. Use your first trip simply to gather information and send some preliminary signals regarding your leverage. Wait until you're fully armed to talk price.

Golden Rule Three:
Employ "Fair" Objective Criteria

The most "fair" standard in new car sales: dealer's cost. Find it. *Consumer Reports* will provide you with a detailed statement of the dealers' vehicle cost, including current rebates, unadvertised incentives, and holdbacks (a hidden financial incentive from the manufacturer to the dealer when the vehicle is sold that can increase the dealer's profit on the vehicle). You can order this relatively inexpensive report on its Web site.

You now can figure out dealers' anticipated profits, as you now know the vehicle's invoice price (manufacturer's price to the dealer), sticker price (what the dealer wants you to pay), and the invoice and sticker prices for that vehicle's options and packages. The report on "my" sports car ran twenty-nine pages.

Now you're ready to hit the offer-concession stage.

Golden Rule Four:
Design an Offer-Concession Strategy

Design an offer-concession strategy based largely on your goal and leverage, and on potentially working various dealers off against each other. Once you have decided on a vehicle, contact some dealers and find out how many have "your" vehicle on their lot. Consider setting up a competitive bidding situation, like an auction in reverse. Get them to bid for your business.

Golden Rule Five: Control the Agenda

You will get a better deal if the vehicle is physically on their lot and they want to move it. You will get an even better deal if it's year-end and they need space for their new models. It's no coincidence I made my first trip to the dealer on December 28.

Once you have found "your" vehicle at two or more dealers, comparison shop by calling and telling each dealer:

- You're a serious buyer and will likely buy "your" vehicle in the next few days
- You're a very price-sensitive consumer
- You have done your homework and know the dealer's costs (and holdbacks, dealer incentives, and rebates, if applicable)
- You're getting price quotes from a number of dealers for that vehicle
- You want a breakdown of the charges in their quote
- You want their absolute best price, and you will not even consider them unless their price is practically the lowest

Do this by phone, too, if you can. It puts you in control, not the dealer, and is the most efficient use of your time. This also will save you the aggravation involved in many of the negotiation games some dealers play. And if a dealer resists giving you a phone quote push him. If they want your business they will talk. Of course, if this doesn't work you may have to visit them.

One cautionary note on getting quotes over the phone: Some dealers will give you a low-ball phone quote in an effort to get you to then visit their dealership. But then they won't honor it when you show up. While obviously unethical, protect yourself here by using the tactics discussed in chapter 7 in dealing with unethical negotiators.

You can also obtain price quotes online from CarsDirect, CarOrder, and InvoiceDealers, all dot-com Web sites. Or you might solicit on-line bids from dealers through car referral services such as Autobytel or Carpoint.com.

Finally, use these additional agenda-related tactics to get what you want:

- Negotiate up from the dealer's cost, not down from the sticker price. Frame your discussion around the dealer's profit, not the discount off the sticker price.
- Don't discuss leasing, financing options, or your possible trade-in until after you have agreed to a purchase price. Negotiate these separately.
- Beware of prices "good only today." Legitimate quotes today should be equally good tomorrow (unless rebates or special promotions have specific cutoff dates). Remember to evaluate these deadlines' flexibility.
- Leave if you get a firm price that the manager subsequently rejects.

Problem-Solving or Competitive Strategy?

Let's go through the four factors in determining what strategy to pursue.

This scenario often points to the use of Competitive Strategies. Overall, there is usually little value to a future relationship, relatively few issues (price and maybe some terms), hardly any creative options, and a price-dominant zero-sum issue, and many dealers will use very Competitive Strategies. With these four factors all pointing to Competitive Strategies, it's often extremely competitive from the start.

Your next step? Assuming an extremely competitive environment, work these dealers off against each other. They're competitive and usually don't want to lose your business. So don't just accept their first offer as their last. Take the low dealer's price to the second lowest and get him to beat it. Then go back to the original low dealer and get him to beat your new lowest price. Don't stop until they do.

Overall, experts suggest you should be able to negotiate a price of 4 to

Factors	Decision	Strategy
1. Relationship Factor: Expected future relationship?	Yes ————————> No ————————>	Problem-Solving (PS) Competitive (C)
2. Number Factor: Number of issues?	Many issues ———> Few issues ————>	PS C
3. Zero-Sum Factor	Creative options possible Zero-Sum in nature —>	PS C
4. Mutuality Factor	Yes ————————> No (overrides factors 1–3)	PS C

8 percent over the dealer's cost. If vehicle demand is unusually high, though, you may have to pay more. Vice versa, too.

Car negotiations tend to be extremely competitive for the reasons stated above. Yet some sales personnel and dealerships strongly object to this characterization. They take a different approach—very relationship-oriented, customer-focused, and friendly. And they freely share strategic information, have no hard-sell leverage tactics or games, and they rely on independent standards, reasonable offer-concession strategies, and low-pressure agenda-control tactics. Here, the defining difference relates to the extent that the dealership or salesperson *truly* values a long-term future relationship with you and if you anticipate or want a long-term relationship with them. This is especially true if the dealership where you purchase the vehicle will also be providing the service on that vehicle.

So, evaluate your goals and interests and proceed accordingly in these situations by using more Problem-Solving Strategies.

Here's an example. My dad has bought a half-dozen cars from one salesman at a Minneapolis-area dealership over the last thirty years. They have an excellent business relationship, and both have benefited greatly.

Some dealerships also have substantial repair facilities and many dealers of lower priced, mass production vehicles have a much higher profit margin on repairs than sales. They may take a smaller profit margin on the sale to get your ongoing repair work. This, of course, would require a future relationship. (By contrast, dealers in higher-end vehicles generally make the majority of their profit from sales and not service.) Keep this in mind also when looking for a car and researching dealers' and salespersons' reputations. You might find that special salesperson or dealership.

14

HOUSE NEGOTIATIONS

She wouldn't budge. Despite our concerted efforts to illustrate the unreasonableness of her position, she had dug in her heels.

The negotiation? The sale of a house. The participants? The seller, the seller's real estate agent, the potential buyer (me), and my agent. The sticking point? Some significant repairs to the pool identified during the home-inspection period. What did I do? I dug in my heels, too. I felt my purchase offer—which the seller had accepted prior to the inspection period—included a fully functioning, self-cleaning pool.

Plus, despite the seller's claims to the contrary, I was convinced the repairs were needed. The independent pool inspection company was told up front they would not get any potential repair work. So it had no incentive to do anything other than point out whatever repairs truly were needed.

Yet the seller wouldn't budge. It looked like this might sink the whole deal. After all, we held two inflexible positions, and a firm deadline approached.

We reached a deal.

How? Our real estate agents pitched in and paid for the pool repair out of their commissions.

What negotiation lessons can we learn from this?

House negotiations involve multiple parties, including agents. The agency dynamic in house negotiations is critical for you to understand for two reasons. First, almost all your strategic communications with your counterpart go through your respective agents. This can often add complexity to the communication process. It also puts a premium on finding an agent with effective negotiation experience. Remember, experience does not equal expertise. Take the list of effective negotiator qualities from chapter 6, on personality styles, and find an agent who fits the bill. Take the time at the start to make the right choice, it will pay off in the end. Even then you may need to coordinate some of your agent's communications. There were three negotiations in my pool-repair situation, and each required different strategies. In addition to the negotiation between the buyer and seller, both the buyer and seller were independently negotiating with their respective real estate agents. These latter two negotiations occur on a not-infrequent basis, and should be factored into the situation even though some agents bristle at this.

Second, it's critical to understand this agency dynamic because real estate agents have built-in conflicts of interest. Most agents work on commission. Once a potential home or buyer has been found, most real estate agents have a strong interest in closing the sale, collecting their commission, and moving on to new clients. Understandably, they don't want to start over. For them time equals money. The more time they spend with you finding and closing on a house (or helping you sell one), the less profit for them. (In dollar terms, their actual take-home sum may not change. But the more time they spend with you, the less time they spend finding and representing other paying clients.) This isn't a criticism of agents. It's just how the incentives work within their compensation system. From the sale perspective, agents also have an incentive to price houses on the lower end of the "reasonable" scale. While they might receive a slightly lower commission, the house may sell far more quickly. The more houses they sell, the more they make.

Long-term, most successful agents ignore this conflict. They must. After all, they grow their careers by helping you satisfy *your* interests, and you represent their future referral network. Agents' conflict of interest doesn't always work against you, either. Once a contract has been signed, most agents will work extremely hard and creatively to close the deal. And if you as a seller interview several agents before selecting one, each agent has an incentive to suggest your house should be listed *higher* rather than lower. Why? The higher the price Agent A suggests, within a reasonable range, the more likely you as the seller will view Agent A favorably. After all, the higher the sale price, the more in your pocket, if that's the price at which it sells. Agents call this "buying a listing."

What does this mean for you? Keep agents' interests in the back of your mind, as you ensure your agent aggressively represents *your* interests.

Let's see how this works. Assume you have decided to sell your house, as you have been transferred out of state to a city with a higher cost of living. How should you begin?

Golden Rule One:
Information Is Power—So Get It

Get Information to Set Your Long-Term
Strategic and Short-Term Tactical Goals

First gather sufficient information to set your long-term strategic and short-term tactical goals. A comprehensive, internal information-gathering stage, especially in selling a house, is crucial. Let's take this goal-setting process step-by-step. To start, evaluate the advantages and disadvantages of hiring a real estate agent (see chapter 4 on agents). Most sellers ultimately decide to hire one: In 2002, the National Association of Realtors estimated 87 percent of sellers used agents. So you interview three agents, all of whom were recommended by individuals you trust. You then hire an experienced and successful agent named Joe. How much should you involve Joe in the information-gathering process? As much as you can. Joe is your expert. Listen to his advice. Joe also will be directly engaging any potential buyer. Joe should thus intimately know your thinking, not only what you want, but also why you want it. But remember, make your own decision.

Also consider involving a neighbor who knows the area well. I listed my house in May 2003. My neighbor, a retired commercial appraiser, had lived in the area for over thirty years and knew almost everyone. He also knew the market and the condition of many of the houses. When I got ready to list my house I asked for his advice. He was a great source of information and insight.

Brainstorm with Joe and your neighbor to set and prioritize your goals. As you're moving to a location with a higher cost of living, you likely will primarily want to maximize the money you will receive from selling your house. You can then use these funds to purchase a new house. The more you get from this sale, the nicer the house you can buy. Regarding your specific goal and original asking price, wait to decide on one until after you have analyzed potential buyers' goals, and the importance, if any, of a relationship with the buyer. *Goal/interest #1: financial.*

Parties also often have a time interest involved in the sale of their house. The sooner your house sells, the better. However, this isn't always true. I bought a house and closed on it in mid-December 2002 (a different house than the one I listed in May 2003). The seller's wife, according to the seller's agent, wanted to stay in the house through the holiday season. Their new house wasn't ready, and closing in mid-December meant they would spend the holidays in a temporary house. The seller's husband, however, wanted to close as soon as possible. Perhaps he had a cash-flow interest and wanted the money sooner rather than later. The seller's husband prevailed. Time can be an important factor. Sometimes it will even cause parties to accept less financially. *Goal/interest #2: timing*.

Another goal often involved is emotional closure. Selling a house can be an emotional event, especially if you have lived in it for years. In 1992 my parents downsized and sold the house where we grew up. They had lived there since 1967. It was tough. In emotionally laden cases it's particularly important to use an agent. Agents can provide the appropriate amount of dispassion that will allow you to most effectively achieve your goals. *Goal/interest #3: emotional closure*.

Of course, sellers may have many other goals and interests involved. But these are usually the most critical.

Determine and Prioritize Buyer's Goals

What do potential buyers want? While you may be unable to know for sure, and will want to confirm this, most buyers want to pay the least amount possible for the house. Other buyers' goals may include a cash-flow interest, the timing of the closing, and a host of interests related to the quality and features of the neighborhood and home.

Evaluate the Power of Your Relationship with the Buyer

How much do you value a relationship with the potential buyer? At this point it's probably not a priority, unless you know the potential buyer in another context. (In one law firm where I practiced, one partner sold his summer home to another partner. There the partners' relationship meant a great deal and substantially affected the process.)

Knowing this, let's set your asking price and your financial goal. In doing this: a) set an aggressive and specific goal; b) tie your goal to a realistic standard—don't just "do the best you can"; c) *expect* to succeed; and d) commit to your goal.

Fortunately, your agent Joe has researched the "comps"—comparable houses recently sold in the area and those on the market—and your neighbor knows the condition of these houses when sold. Here's more helpful information you will need to comprehensively set the most appropriate goal and list price. While this information is not exhaustive, rarely will you have all the information you want. As you will see, this list also doubles as independent standards:

- You bought your house five years ago for $150,000 and, while it has been updated, you haven't replaced anything major, like tile or carpet.
- The average annual appreciation in home prices in your neighborhood in the last five years has been 5 percent.
- In the last year the following four houses in your neighborhood have sold. Each sold within three weeks of listing, was built by the same builder in 1990, and had roughly the same features and square footage as your house. No other homes in your neighborhood are currently for sale.

House	List Price / Sale Price	Sale Date	Distinguishing Element
Comp #1	$200,000/$195,000	Two weeks ago.	Completely renovated with new pool surface and new tile and carpets. The seller put about $10,000 into the house shortly before listing it.
Comp #2	$175,000/$170,000	Nine months ago.	Run-down interior due to hard usage by kids.
Comp #3	$170,000/$170,000	Three months ago.	Sold by the bank after it had been repossessed.
Comp #4	$183,000/$175,000	One year ago.	Similar to yours.

What's an aggressive enough goal? $200,000? $195,000? $190,000?

In this case, list the house at $194,000 and expect to realize $190,000, not including the agents' commissions and closing costs. Only tentatively select your goal, though, as you cannot yet fully evaluate your leverage.

That cannot occur until you have engaged with a potential buyer and can find out their level of need and alternatives. Still, write this $190,000 goal down, put the note in a visible place, and commit by telling your agent and your neighbor.

How did I arrive at this $190,000 goal? First look at Comp #4, the most similar, recently sold house in the neighborhood, and a great standard. Evaluating its estimated present market value will help set our price and goal. Assuming Comp #4 appreciated at the normal 5-percent rate this past year (it sold a year ago for $175,000), we arrive at $183,750. Then look at another standard: The present value of your house, based on a five-year appreciation rate of 5 percent per year. Starting at $150,000, and figuring it appreciated 5 percent per year, we come to $182,326.

Then analyze the other comps and the traditional offer-concession patterns in your market and figure out the highest listing price you can reasonably justify. Your agent should know the offer-concession patterns well. Understand, of course, once you set the list price, it's rare to get more. (In some extremely strong sellers' markets, however, buyers have been known to get into bidding wars and pay over the list price.) In any event, the highest neighborhood comp—Comp #1—sold two weeks ago for $195,000. Even though it had a new pool surface and new tile and carpeting, it's still similar enough to consider its sale price as a standard. Since it listed for $200,000 and sold for $195,000, it's reasonable to select $194,000 as your listing price. I would not list your house at or above $195,000, because it's tough to justify, given the new features of Comp #1 (which cost about $10,000). It helps if your house is not the most expensive in the neighborhood. This is important if the potential buyer has an investment interest in your house.

"All right," you say, "but if you think the most reasonable standards suggest a value around $183,000, why expect $190,000, and why list it at $194,000? Aren't you setting yourself up to fail? And, isn't it true that most individuals tend to have an unrealistic expectation as to the worth of *their* house?"

While many sellers may have an unrealistic expectation to start, $190,000 is not "unreasonable." Remember, two standards suggest a value around $183,000, but standards don't set the value of your house. Your negotiations with potential buyers set the value. And the negotiations have not yet begun. Plus, a number of intangible factors may affect the value of your house, or may have affected the price of the comps. For one, you don't know the negotiation ability of the other house buyers or sellers in the neighborhood. Your previous neighbors/sellers may not have been as effective as you. Or, they may have had weaker leverage and were forced to sell their houses in a short period of time. In your case, perhaps you will find a potential buyer who absolutely loves the neighborhood. In addition, the average time from listing to sale is three weeks, a fairly brief period of time. This suggests significant demand for homes in your neighborhood. This strengthens your leverage. Finally, you should be able to find something about your house—even if it's not a big deal—to justify the additional amount. Effective agents can often help with this.

Overall be aggressive, but give yourself sufficient flexibility to move. Setting a lower goal is giving up before you have even begun. Don't do it. We haven't even explored your leverage yet.

Golden Rule Two: Maximize Your Leverage

The Seller's Need Level Relative to the Buyer's Need Level

How much do you need to sell, relative to the potential buyer's need to buy? I listed my house in May 2003, five months after buying a new house. At the time I needed to sell. I was paying for two homes, but only living in one. In effect, I was losing money each month my old house sat empty. The sooner I sold it, the better.

Importantly, I tried to keep this level of need to myself. Remember, leverage is based on perception. On our level of need scale, I would rate my need as High (−1).

What about potential *buyers'* level of need? Sellers should find out as much as they can, through their agent or on their own, concerning the potential buyer. This especially includes why potential buyers want their house. Every time a potential buyer says, "I want, I like, I am interested because . . ." in the presence of the seller or the seller's agent, the seller gains leverage. If Shari, a potential buyer, was just relocated to Phoenix by her company and she's moving in four weeks, Shari probably has a significant need. On our need scale, put Shari's need at High (+1). Overall, then, your Need Score here would be 0, with no need advantage to either party.

If Shari looks at your house, the $ 194,000 list price may make a great deal of sense. It makes even more sense if she's moving to Phoenix from Los Angeles or New York City, because getting a 2,100-square-foot house with a pool in a nice neighborhood would likely cost a lot more in those markets. Remember the contrast principle? A house like this for $194,000 may seem like a super deal *by comparison*. This is especially true if Shari just sold a house in Los Angeles or New York City.

Here's someone else with a significant need and thus weaker leverage. One potential buyer told me in late April 2003, before I even listed my house, that he just sold his current house and would close on June 2. At that time, he said, he and his wife and baby need to be in a new house. He had a significant need, one I would rate as Very High (+2). Unfortunately, he needed a four-bedroom house. Mine only had three.

Whether you're a buyer or seller evaluate both sides' level of need. Then decide how to communicate it. This is crucial, as most of this communication will occur through your agent. Make sure your agent strengthens, and doesn't weaken, your leverage.

Sellers' Alternatives and BATNA

As a seller, I want at least two buyers bidding on my house, preferably at the same time. The more, the better. Without any other offers, as the seller, my BATNA is keeping the house on the market, usually an unattractive alternative. To improve your alternatives as the seller, generate as much traffic through the house as possible. Make your house available to all qualified buyers. The more potential buyers see the house, the more likely you will generate offers. The more offers, the higher the likelihood you will maximize your leverage and achieve your goal.

When my wife and I first toured our present house, the seller's agent, Greg, was with us when he received a cell phone call. After the conversation, Greg told us it was another potential buyer interested in seeing the house. This seemed too convenient to us, because, if true, it might have strengthened the seller's leverage.

As a buyer, how can you find out the seller's alternatives, or evaluate if they're making it up to gain leverage?

First ask, probe, and evaluate the truth of any seller statement indicating the existence of an alternative buyer. Have your agent probe, too. Be curious. What did I do? I immediately asked Greg enough questions to see if he was making up the alternative buyer. Later, I asked our agent about his reputation. It turned out he actually did speak with another potential buyer.

Second, analyze the length of time the house has been on the market at the same price. Generally, the longer its availability, the weaker the seller's leverage and the more suspect a seller's statement that they have several potential buyers simultaneously making offers.

Third, find out if the house has been previously listed at a higher price. If so, find out how long and at what price. This will help you evaluate the seller's need. In our case, the sellers had just dropped their price. As a result, more potential buyers became interested.

Finally, find out as much as you can about any previous offers made for the house, including their terms, timing, and if, when, and where the sellers countered. For the house we bought in December 2002, we learned that the sellers had previously entered into a contract at a higher price. The buyers, however, had pulled out during the inspection period. The sellers later dropped their asking price. This provided us with crucial information concerning the seller's level of need.

Buyers' Alternatives and BATNA

Of course, leverage is relative. The sellers might have a significant level of need and a poor BATNA, but this means little until compared with potential buyers' level of need and BATNA. I spent almost eight months looking before I bought my first house. I didn't have a high need at the time, but I had a fairly poor BATNA. While I liked my apartment, my alternative to purchasing any particular house was to keep looking. That took time. And I wasn't finding much I liked in my price range.

What did I do? I expanded the geographic boundaries of my target area to increase the number of potential houses. Leveragewise, this increased my possible alternatives once I bid on any one house. As a buyer, what's your BATNA? What will happen if you don't get your target house? You will likely keep looking. And that's what you should do when you engage a seller. Engage, but keep looking. At least instruct your agent to continue to pull up new listings in your target area in your price range.

Buyers also should maintain the right amount of dispassion, analytically evaluating houses' strengths and weaknesses and the extent to which any given house will satisfy their interests. The more emotional, passionate, and committed you or your spouse become to any one house, and the more your agent communicates this, the weaker your leverage. There's nothing wrong with these emotions. In fact, they're natural. But recognize their impact. As you increase your interest, you weaken your leverage, as your BATNA will appear less suitable by comparison. Express interest, but not too much.

What if you find your absolute dream house and can afford it? While you may have weak leverage, keep your eyes on the prize: *Don't lose the house.* We almost lost the house we bought in December 2002 during the inspection period. As my wife told me at the time, losing it over a relatively small amount of money was a bad alternative.

Golden Rule Three:
Employ "Fair" Objective Criteria

Powerful independent standards abound in the house-buying and -selling context. In fact, we used two of the most dominant in setting our goals above. We extensively analyzed the house's market value, based on the comps and appreciation, and also evaluated its original cost. Other powerful standards commonly involved include expert opinions from real estate agents and appraisers and industry standards in the form of the real estate contract involved.

Also analyze how long houses generally remain unsold in your particular market conditions. The faster the homes sell, the stronger the sellers' market. The slower the homes sell, the stronger the buyers' market.

Make sure you and your agent exhaustively research the "most fair" standard to start—either as a buyer or a seller. Explicitly use it to justify your moves. And since many moves in this context traditionally occur in writing, ask your agent to communicate in a written letter the principled basis for your offer and whatever other messages you want to communicate to the seller (that you're prequalified for the loan amount, etc.).

Prepare your agents for the "standards dance." Maybe even practice it.

Golden Rule Four:
Design an Offer-Concession Strategy

Let's say Michael has looked at your house, listed at $194,000, and wants to make an offer. What should he offer? Now it's time for Michael and his agent to get as much information as he can. Like you, Michael now needs to go through the Five Golden Rules. First he needs to set his goals and find out as much as he can about you and the house. Second, he needs to maximize his leverage. Find out why you're moving and when. Is anyone else interested in the house or seen it recently? What about his level of need and alternatives? Third, he needs to employ "fair" objective criteria. Research the comps and the market appreciation. Have his agent contact the agents for the comps and find out their condition when sold. Find out your cost. It's public information. Fourth, he needs to design his offer-concession strategy.

How should Michael design the most effective offer-concession strategy? First, he needs to know the following regarding his goals, leverage, and standards. Assume the following:

- Your house has been on the market for three weeks.
- Michael has strong leverage. He started looking last week, likes several other listed homes, has no urgency to buy, and knows no other buyers have recently looked at the house.
- A good standard for Michael is Comp #3, which the bank sold for $170,000 three months ago. This comp suggests the market value of your house is around $172,125 (factoring in the appreciation rate). However, the leverage was substantially different for Comp #3, as the seller lost it to the bank and the bank sold it.
- Another good standard for Michael is Comp #2, a run-down house that sold for $170,000 nine months ago. It would come in at $176,375, factoring in the market appreciation.
- Based on all the standards, and especially the most applicable comp, Comp #4, the house appears to have a market value of $183,750.

With this information, Michael might set an aggressive goal at $180,000. It's lower than the most applicable comp, but he has strong leverage. (If he had weak leverage, by comparison, he should set $185,000 as a goal. And if he has extremely weak leverage, $190,000.) Having set his goal, he should design an offer-concession strategy based on ending up at $180,000. How should he start? Meet with his agent and find out what offer-concession patterns exist in the area. How many times do parties usually move after the start? How aggressively do potential buyers usually begin? Does the center-moving dynamic often occur? What's the average concession from the list price to the sale price in this house's price range?

Regional patterns also exist, so research the patterns in your geographic area. The best source for these patterns is your agent. Push your agent to quantify them, too. Then incorporate the patterns and other negotiation elements into your goal-setting process and determine where to start and where to move in order to end up at your goal.

According to the four comps, the average concession off the seller's list price is roughly 3 to 4 percent. Applied to your $194,000 list price, this would put the sale price at $186,000–188,000. But this takes its starting point off the list price, an amount set by the seller.

Traditionally, sellers make the first offer by listing the house at a specific price. They usually have more information about the house, and they want to set the mindset and range for the negotiation. Remember the concept of anchoring? It applies here.

However, sellers don't always make the first offer. Two months after we closed on our new house in December 2002 we received a flyer from a real estate agent stating that she had a "qualified buyer who wants to purchase a home in your area." If interested, the flyer suggested we contact the agent. If we had any interest in selling, we could have gotten the "qualified buyer" to make the first offer. That would have been to our advantage, because that buyer had already expressed a significant need. We could have used that leverage to get more for our house than by using any "fair and reasonable" standard. If we made the first offer in that context, and incorporated this leverage into our list price, a potential buyer might consider it overreaching. By getting the buyer to make the first offer, though, we can avoid sending this message. And we can still hold out. But we didn't have any interest in selling.

So where should Michael start, if he wants to end up at $180,000? In the low-to-mid-170s. At that price he's sending the message that he thinks the house is overpriced, but he's still interested. Plus, he has several comps that underscore the "fairness and reasonableness" of his offer. It passes the straight-face test, barely. He might have his agent tell or write to your agent, Joe, when giving him the offer, that his offer still gives you a healthy profit of over $20,000 more than you paid, and that he feels it's overpriced, given Comps 1, 2, and 3. This communicates to you that he's done his homework. The next move is up to you.

You are likely getting nervous at this point. The house has been listed for three weeks and no one other than Michael has expressed serious interest. No one has made an offer. Your leverage now appears weaker than when you initially evaluated the situation. Perhaps the market is changing. Plus, you had Joe find out how much Michael needs or wants the house, and it's a low level of need. Assume on our level of need scale Michael has a Low Need (−1) Meanwhile, *your* level of need is increasing, as you will soon be relocating. When you do, the house will be empty. That will make it more difficult to sell and weaken your leverage further. Empty houses don't appeal as much as fully furnished homes, largely because they're less likely to generate an emotional "I love this house" feeling by potential purchasers.

How far should you move off your asking price? Given your weakening leverage, reset your ultimate goal to $185,000. Then move $5,000 off your $194,000 list price in your first move, bringing you to $189,000. There's a psychological barrier at $190,000, and moving under it will communicate to Michael that you're serious about his offer, even though you consider it low. In your counter, also have Joe tell Michael's agent that you're moving a significant amount, $5,000, in part due to Joe's expert recommendation (which, of course, should be true).

Where will you end up? Assuming relatively normal offer-concession patterns, you will probably end up around $184,000. How long will it take to get there? It depends on who is controlling the agenda.

Golden Rule Five: Control the Agenda

Ask your agent how to control the agenda in buying or selling your house, and whether you should put a deadline on your offers or counters. If you don't use an agent, research it. Local customs and practices regarding agenda control and deadlines play a significant role in the process. In Phoenix, parties regularly put 24- to 48-hour deadlines on offers and counters. If the other side doesn't respond within that time frame, the original offer or counter expires. Parties impose this deadline to give the other side sufficient time to properly evaluate the offer, but not so much time as to change their leverage (by finding another house or another potential buyer). Parties also want create a relative sense of urgency from the other side, and to keep the emotionally laden process moving.

By contrast, in Ann Arbor, Michigan, placing a deadline on your offer or counter is often perceived as rude. But most people expect that parties will respond within a reasonable time period. You need to know this local expectation in evaluating what deadline to set, if any. Of course, nothing prevents a party from countering after a deadline has passed, and many do. These deadlines often are flexible.

Agenda-control devices often have a significant impact in house negotiations. Remember my friend in Chicago who bought the Daddy Warbucks house? He bought it at a great price, largely because he controlled the agenda. How aggressively should you attempt to control the agenda? It largely depends on whether you want to use a Problem-Solving or a Competitive Strategy.

Problem-Solving or Competitive Strategy?

Let's go through the four factors in determining what strategy to pursue.

Competitive Strategies usually work best in house negotiations, especially while negotiating price. Unless you live in a small, close-knit community where everyone knows everyone, the parties: 1) generally have no current or future relationship; 2) one issue—price—dominates the process; 3) price is zero-sum in nature, and relatively few ways exist to creatively "expand the pie" (except during the inspection period); and 4) many

Factors	Decision	Strategy
1. Relationship Factor: Expected future relationship?	Yes ————————> No ————————>	Problem-Solving (PS) Competitive (C)
2. Number Factor: Number of issues?	Many issues ————> Few issues ————>	PS C
3. Zero-Sum Factor	Creative options possible Zero-sum in nature —>	PS C
4. Mutuality Factor	Yes ————————> No (overrides factors 1–3) ————————>	PS C

agents recommend competitive-type strategies. Using Problem-Solving Strategies also comes with a substantial downside risk on the price issue.

Of course, you should still try to find ways to creatively satisfy both parties' interests. Often, this can occur on nonprice issues, like the timing of the closing date or whether to include certain appliances in the sale. When I moved from an apartment to my first house I didn't own any appliances. Given my cash-flow situation, I didn't want to buy new appliances either. As a result, my offer included the refrigerator, washer, and dryer. That way I ended up with less expensive appliances and financed these into the purchase price. The seller, of course, got more take-home cash for the house, probably her most important consideration.

By the way, use Problem-Solving Strategies with your agent. Hopefully you will be able to establish a good working relationship and use him or her in the future. It's not easy to find a top-notch agent who knows how to effectively negotiate. But it's probably the most critical decision you will make in this process. Make sure it's the right one.

CONCLUSION

Adam now works for a great architectural firm in San Francisco and loves his job. He also did pretty well in his salary negotiation with his new managing director. How well?

Did he find out as much information as he could before going into the negotiation, and then set a specific, aggressive, and realistic goal? Yes.

Did he turn that goal into an expectation of success? Yes.

Did he establish rapport with his managing director by finding some common interests and building on them? Yes.

Did he get a substantial amount of substantive and strategic information by doing his research and asking a ton of questions, both open-ended and close-ended? Yes.

Did he maximize his leverage by evaluating his level of need relative to the managing director's, and then improve his BATNA and lessen the attractiveness of the firm's BATNA? Yes.

Did he employ "fair" objective criteria and find some independent standards that helped him? Yes.

Did he design an offer-concession strategy based on the patterns in that industry, and get the firm to make him the first offer? Yes.

Did he control the agenda? Yes.

You can too. You're now armed with the knowledge to effectively negotiate in a wide variety of business and personal contexts. The next step—put it into practice. Practice what you've learned. Do it. And do it strategically, not instinctively.

But don't worry. You don't have to remember everything. I have a *"Gain the Edge!* Strategic Guide to Effective Negotiations" for you. It's on the next four pages, and it includes a comprehensive practical outline summarizing the strategic steps you can take to become a more effective negotiator. Use it to prepare and negotiate. You will do better. Guaranteed. That's my goal and my expectation.

Do it and you will—absolutely—Gain the Edge!

GAIN THE EDGE! STRATEGIC GUIDE TO EFFECTIVE NEGOTIATIONS

LATZ'S FIVE GOLDEN RULES OF NEGOTIATION*

Rule 1 Information Is Power—So Get It	Rule 2 Maximize Your Leverage	Rule 3 Employ "Fair" Objective Criteria	Rule 4 Design an Offer-Concession Strategy	Rule 5 Control the Agenda
Get the Info to Set Your Goals • Set and prioritize your goals • Determine and prioritize your counterpart's goals • Evaluate the power of relationships ***Practical Tactics for Goal-Setting*** • Brainstorm to set your goals • Be aggressive and specific • Tie your goals to realistic standards • *Expect* to succeed • Commit to them **Develop an Information Bargaining Strategy** • Get *substantive* information — Find facts, issues, opinions — Uncover interests, not positions — Brainstorm options • Get *strategic* information — Obtain sooner, not later — Negotiate with right person — Learn counter's past tactics	**Evaluate Initial Leverage** • Find each side's need level • Determine Best Alternative to a Negotiated Agreement (BATNA) **Leverage Is Fluid** **Strike While Leverage Is Hot** **Leverage-Enhancing Tactics** 1. Quantify all sides' initial leverage ***Need Level Chart*** |	Yours	Counterpart's | |---|---|---| | Very high | −2 | +2 | | High | −1 | +1 | | Medium | 0 | 0 | | Low | +1 | −1 | | Very low | +2 | −2 | Yours + Counterpart's = Your Need Score *Weakest* ◀——▶ *Strongest* −4 −3 −2 −1 0 +1 +2 +3 +4	**The Power of Standards and Procedures** • Creates the perception of independence and objectivity • The more independent and objective, the more power **Powerful Standards** • Market Value Power • Precedent Power • Tradition Power • Expert- and Scientific-Judgment Power • Efficiency Power • Costs and Profit Power • Policy Power • Reciprocity Power • Status Power: Title and Position • Professional or Industry Standards Power **Powerful Procedures** • One cut, the other choose • Take turns, draw lots, or flip a coin • Use an independent third party, e.g., arbitrator or mediator	**Know Your Offer-Concession Patterns** • Beware of the premature offer • The longer you wait, the less eager you appear—timing pattern • Early concessions include relatively larger moves—the size pattern **First-Offer Issues** • Advantages to first offers — Set expectations — Elicit genuine reaction — Strategic advantages—leverage timing, information . . . • Disadvantages to first offers — Lack of information to appropriately set it — Other side gains information — Bracketing • Where to start — First-offer expectations — Your original goal — Your most aggressive, yet reasonable, independent standard — "Room to move" psychology	**Prepare a Substantive and Atmospheric Agenda to Start** • Setting the agenda for short-term negotiations • Setting the long-term agenda **Negotiate the Agenda** **Manage the Deadlines** • Determine what, if any, deadlines already exist • Evaluate the deadlines' impact (deadline dynamics: urgency, timing, concession, and organization) • Decide what type of deadlines you want (short, long, or flexible) • Take the initiative—and set or negotiate the deadlines *Don't let them see you sweat* **Apply These Agenda-Control Tips and Tactics** • Use the "power of the pen" • Preview, agree, and focus • Just do it

(Continued)

LATZ'S FIVE GOLDEN RULES OF NEGOTIATION* (Continued)

Rule 1 Information Is Power—So Get It	Rule 2 Maximize Your Leverage	Rule 3 Employ "Fair" Objective Criteria	Rule 4 Design an Offer-Concession Strategy	Rule 5 Control the Agenda
Ten Information-Gathering Tactics		**Harness the Power by Using These Four Critical Tactics**	**Psychological Expectations**	• The subtle control • Control the turf • To phone or not to phone—consider effect on: — Relationship — Efficiency — Written record
1. Leave your ego at the door 2. Be sincere 3. Establish trust 4. List your information needs 5. Do the "big shmooze" 6. Ask questions 7. Use the funnel—open- to close-ended questions 8. Actively listen and use the "power of silence" 9. Ask "why"—get to interests, not positions 10. Evaluate and use nonverbals/ body language	*BATNA Chart*	1. Find your most powerful standards and procedures *at the start* 2. Research standards and procedures your counterpart previously used 3. Do the "standards dance" 4. Never forget: Leverage trumps objective criteria	• Play the expectation game	

BATNA Chart

	Yours	Counterpart's
Excellent	+3	−3
Very Good	+2	−2
Good	+1	−1
Okay	0	0
Fair	−1	+1
Poor	−2	+2
Very Poor	−3	+3

Yours + Counterpart's = Your BATNA Score

Weakest ←————→ *Strongest*
−6 −4 −2 0 +2 +4 +6

Your Need Score + Your BATNA Score = Your Overall Leverage

Weakest ←————→ *Strongest*
−10 −8 −6 −4 −2 0 +2 +4 +6 +8 +10

Rule 4 – Offer-Concession Nuts & Bolts

• Use specific, detailed language, explain the offer's rationale, and tie to standards
• Promote an air of finality and rigidity
• Carefully communicate your priorities and order of issues
• Learn when, how, and under what circumstances to use agents
• To bluff or not to bluff
• Closing strategies

Rule 2 (continued)

Prepare Blocking Techniques

Reevaluate Your Goals

2. Improve your alternatives and limit their alternatives
3. Tactically share your leverage-related information
4. Communicate your leverage credibly and confidently
5. Selectively use risky tactics like walkouts and threats

MAKING LATZ'S GOLDEN RULES WORK

| Personality Tendencies (Style Issues) | Ethics Make a Bottom-Line Difference | Use a Situation-Specific Strategy | | Common Negotiation Problems and Their Solutions |

Personality Tendencies (Style Issues)

Recognize Parties' Styles

- **Competitors**
  - Characteristics
    - Enjoy debating substantive issues
    - Not great listeners
    - Direct, sometimes adversarial, tone, words, and body language
  - Tactics to use with them
    - Ask and listen
    - Stick to your principles
    - Frankly emphasize your leverage
- **Accommodators**
  - Characteristics
    - Highly value good relationships
    - Effective listening skills
    - Attitude reflects concern, compassion, and understanding
  - Tactics to use with them
    - Resist just talking; ask back
    - Recognize value in relationship issues
    - Focus on objective criteria
- **Conflict Avoiders**
  - Characteristics
    - Belief that almost all conflict is unproductive
    - Highly skilled at avoiding questions and undesirable issues
    - Can appear aloof and uninterested
  - Tactics to use with them
    - Be patient
    - Focus on your long-term goal
    - Aggressively probe their interests

Ethics Make a Bottom-Line Difference

Find out the Questionable Tactic's Legality

- Honorable intentions make a difference
- Silence is usually golden
- Bluffing about your bottom line and your interests is usually legally acceptable
- "Puffery" couched as opinions and statements about the future rarely cross the legal line
- The more sophisticated your counterpart, the better your position
- No harm, no foul

Evaluate What Will Happen in the Negotiation and to Your Reputation If You Use the Questionable Tactic

- Assess the tactic's short and long-term impacts

Determine How You and Others View the Tactic's Morality

- Research their ethical reputation
- Analyze their language and actions during your negotiation
- Determine if they are:
  - Idealists
  - Poker Players
  - Pragmatists

Use a Situation-Specific Strategy

Problem-Solving or Competitive Strategies

	Problem-Solving Strategies	Competitive Strategies
Golden Rule 1 Info Is Power	Mutually share critical information. Actions/atmosphere confirm trust and a valued relationship	Substantial information bargaining; share a little and get a lot
2 Leverage	Leverage downplayed, but still there	Open conflict on leverage
3 Criteria	Frequently rely on independent standards and procedures	Minimal reliance on independent standards and procedures
4 Offers	Least aggressive offer-concession moves/tactics	Most aggressive offer-concession moves/tactics
5 Agenda	Mutually agreeable agenda	Overt and biased agenda

Common Negotiation Problems and Their Solutions

Foiling Common Negotiation "Games"

- Good Cop/Bad Cop
- The "Nibbler"
- The Blowup or Verbal Attack
- The Flinch
- The Higher or Limited Authority
- The Context Manipulator
- Power in Numbers
- Feigned Irrationality

Top Ten Impasse-Breaking Strategies

1. Get or share more information
2. Switch objective criteria
3. Prioritize needs and interests
4. Brainstorm options
5. Set deadlines
6. Temporarily put aside the issue
7. Take a break
8. Move up the chain
9. Pick a fair alternative process
10. Concede

Dealing with Emotional Counterparts

- Don't react—go to the "balcony"
- Don't argue—step to their side
- Depersonalize with independent standards

(Continued)

MAKING LATZ'S GOLDEN RULES WORK (Continued)

Personality Tendencies (Style Issues)	Ethics Make a Bottom-Line Difference	Use a Situation-Specific Strategy	Common Negotiation Problems and Their Solutions

Negotiate Stylewise in the Most Effective Way
 	
• Be assertive, empathetic and enjoyable
• Exhibit ethical, personable, rational, and trustworthy traits
	Use These Tactics in Negotiating with the Unethical and Untrustworthy
	
	• Understand the risks of trust
	• Take away the incentives to lie by ensuring negative consequences for lying
	• Don't lower yourself to their level
		Factors in Determining Whether to Problem-Solve or Compete
		
		• The relationship factor
		• The number factor
		• The zero-sum factor
		• The mutuality factor: will they problem-solve?
		  — If yes, use Problem-Solving Strategies
		  — If no, use Competitive Strategies
		
		Tactics to Implement the Most Effective Strategy
		
		• Determine your strategy based on initial goals
		• Continually evaluate your counterpart's strategy
		• Don't choose too early
		• Remain flexible
		
		Selectively Apply Your Strategy to Some Issues and Not Others
			Overcoming a Fear of the Process
			
			• Explore your feelings and what's really at stake
			• Minimize the likelihood your fears will come true
			• Research "fair and reasonable" standards
			• Assess if you're the right person at the table
			
			Multiparty Environments
			
			• Apply the Five Golden Rules to *every party*
			• Build coalitions on shared and compatible interests

This Strategic Guide may be downloaded for free in 8 ½ × 11 format at
www.GaintheEdge.com

ACKNOWLEDGMENTS

When I began this journey into the world of negotiation, I had no idea it would result in the publication of this book. But it did, and there are many friends, family members, and colleagues to whom I owe a substantial debt of gratitude for their help along the way. All of them played a significant role in the creation and production of *Gain the Edge!*

I first became exposed to the strategic approach to the negotiation process in law school from Harvard Law Professors Roger Fisher and Frank Sander. Like many, up to that point I had largely negotiated instinctively. They taught me that negotiation can and should be a strategic process. In doing so, they inspired me to study and learn more about it. This, of course, has turned into a lifelong passion.

Arizona State University Law Professor Gary T. Lowenthal's call to me in early 1995 changed my life. In it, he offered me the opportunity to teach negotiation as an adjunct professor at the ASU College of Law. I quickly found out how much I truly loved teaching. This ultimately led me to leave my law practice to start a business teaching and training individuals how to more effectively negotiate. I will always be thankful for this opportunity.

I started writing a negotiation column for *The Business Journal of Phoenix* in 1999. That opportunity, granted to me by then editor and current publisher Don Henninger, helped me refine and grow my thoughts on negotiation over the years. Many of the ideas generated for those columns have blossomed into more extensive strategies in this book.

I would be remiss if I did not also thank the members of the Latz Negotiation Institute Advisory Board for their invaluable advice and encouragement ever since I started my business. Members have included Tom Dooley, Lanny Lahr, Greg Mischel, Mary Nesset, Todd Peterson, and Nancy Williams-Bonnett.

I would also like to thank the following negotiation experts for their careful reading of this manuscript and their insightful comments that have made it a more effective and useful guide for everyone who negotiates: Arizona State University Law Professor M. Robert Dauber, University of Texas Law Professor Kimberlee Kovach, Harvard Law Professor Frank Sander, and Marquette Law Professor Andrea Kupfer Schneider.

I would also like to thank Gary and June Beier and my parents, who painstakingly reviewed the manuscript to ensure that it accomplished my goal of providing helpful advice in a straightforward and nonacademic fashion. My dad especially has provided me with his invaluable analysis and perspective gained in more than forty years of practicing law and engaging in literally thousands of negotiations.

Two expert real estate agents, Judy Cohen and Michal Poplawski, also reviewed my chapter on house negotiations. They deserve special thanks for their helpful comments.

My agent, Frank Weimann, also deserves a great deal of credit and thanks for his support, his expertise in the world of publishing, and his top-notch negotiation skills.

My editor at St. Martin's Press, Ethan Friedman, helped immensely in a wide variety of ways. He carefully read the manuscript and made a number of very helpful suggestions, patiently walked me through the steps required to bring this book to market, and worked hard to ensure that everyone involved in this process—and it was a team effort—had their input at all the critical stages. He also strongly believed in the success of this book and effectively communicated this to all around him.

I would also like to thank my copyeditor, Art Gatti, who did a great job.

And where would I be without my dedicated assistant, Mary K. Popovich? Mary is my right hand in almost all aspects of my business, and I was very fortunate to be able to draw on her marketing and editing talents in addition to the reliable support she provides me in our daily work together.

Finally, I want to thank my wife, Linda, who has experienced first-hand all the late nights and incredible hours that have gone into this book. Linda not only supported me in this effort, but she spent many hours going through the manuscript herself, lending her critical eye and superb writing and editing skills to help make this book a success.

I have been very fortunate to associate with and draw upon the many and varied experts named above in the writing of *Gain the Edge!* To them, I say,

Thank you. I appreciate it.

Martin E. Latz

NOTES

Editor's note: Entries are keyed by page number.

Introduction

1 **Adam's salary negotiation:** This story was based on an actual negotiation that took place between a young architect looking for work in San Francisco in 2002 and his prospective employer. However, I devised the specific dialogue and strategies utilized in the story for illustrative purposes both here and at the end of the book.

3 **telephone negotiation scenario:** I first gave this example (using Bob instead of Jane as the main character) in my column "Negotiation preparedness delivers the advantage," *The Business Journal of Phoenix,* December 24,1999.

5 **Wooden quote:** I first became aware of John Wooden's quote in Richard G. Shell, *Bargaining for Advantage: Negotiation Strategies for Reasonable People* (New York: Viking, 1999), p. 131.

1. Golden Rule One: Information Is Power—So Get It.

17 **sale of Tom's software company:** The events related in this story occurred in 2000, although the name of the seller—Tom—was changed.

18 **value of goal-setting:** Richard G. Shell, *Bargaining for Advantage: Negotiation Strategies for Reasonable People* (New York: Viking, 1999), pp. 22–27. Shell cites a variety of sources for the value of goal-setting, including G. Latham and E. Locke, "Self-regulation Through Goal Setting," *Organizational Behavior and Human Decision Processes,* Vol. 50, No. 2 (1991), pp. 212–247; E. Locke and G. Latham, *A Theory of Goal Setting and Task Performance* (Englewood Cliffs, N.J.: Prentice-Hall, 1990), pp. 29–31; I.R. Gellatly and J.P. Meyer, "The Effect of Goal Difficulty on Physiological Arousal, Cognition, and Task Performance," *Journal of Applied Psychology,* Vol. 77, No. 2 (1992), pp. 694–704; Blaine L. Kyllo and Daniel M. Landers, "Goal Setting in Sport and Exercise: A Research Synthesis to Resolve the

Controversy," *Journal of Sport and Exercise Psychology*, Vol. 17, No. 2 (June 1995), pp. 117–137; and Kenneth R. Thompson, Wayne A. Hochwater, and Nicholas J. Mathys, "Stretch Targets: What Makes Them Effective?," *Academy of Management Executive*, Vol. 11, No. 3 (1997), pp. 48–61.

18 **Akio Morita:** Shell, pp. 22–24. I first related Morita's story in my column "Positive attitude and goals can make a difference," *The Business Journal of Phoenix*, June 23, 2000.

21 **$20-bill auction:** The original idea to auction money can be credited to Yale Professor of Mathematical Institutional Economics Martin Shubik, who wrote "The Dollar Auction Game: A Paradox in Noncooperative Behavior and Escalation," *Journal of Conflict Resolution*, Vol. 15, No. 1 (1971), pp. 109–111.

23 **sold bill for $204:** Max H. Bazerman and Margaret A. Neale, *Negotiating Rationally* (New York: The Free Press, 1992), p. 12.

24 **Sale of the Phoenix Suns:** I obtained the facts for this story during an interview with Phoenix Suns Chairman and CEO Jerry Colangelo in 1999. That interview formed the basis for my column "Colangelo is a seasoned negotiator," *The Business Journal of Phoenix*, September 24, 1999.

27 **Sam Walton quote:** I first became aware of Sam Walton's quote in Shell, p. 22.

27 **Siegel and Fouraker study:** Shell, p. 31, citing Sydney Siegel and Lawrence Fouraker, "The Effect of Level of Aspiration on Differential Payoff," in *Bargaining and Group Decision Making* (New York: McGraw-Hill, 1960), pp. 61–70.

28 **don't be too aggressive:** Shell, p. 32, citing Peter M. Blau, *Exchange and Power in Social Life* (New York: John Wiley & Sons, 1964), p. 145; Kurt Lewin, Tamara Dembo, Leon Festinger and Pauline S. Sears, "Level of Aspiration," in J. McV. Hunt, ed., *Personality and the Behavior Disorders*, Vol. 1 (New York: Ronald Press, 1944), pp. 337–340.

29 **passionate positive attitude:** Shell, pp. 24–33.

30 **aspiration level connected to effectiveness:** Shell, p. 31.

30 **H. Wayne Huizenga:** Shell, p. 27, citing Gail DeGeorge, *The Making of Blockbuster* (New York: John Wiley & Sons, 1996), pp. 17–43. Quote from DeGeorge, p. 42.

31 **specific goals:** Shell, p. 33–34, citing Vandra L. Huber and Margaret A. Neal, "Effects of Self- and Competitor Goals on Performance in an Interdependent Bargaining Task, *Journal of Applied Psychology*, Vol. 72, No. 2 (1987), pp. 197–203.

31 **power of commitment:** Robert B. Cialdini, *Influence: Science and Practice*, 4th ed. (Boston: Allyn & Bacon, 2001), p. 61. See also www.influenceatwork.com.

31 **Moriarty study:** Cialdini, p. 54, citing Thomas Moriarty, "Crime, Commitment, and the Responsive Bystander: Two Field Experiments," *Journal of Personality and Social Psychology*, Vol. 31, No. 2, (1975), pp. 370–376.

33 **Malcolm Jozoff quote:** This statement was made during a seminar I moderated in Phoenix, Arizona on September 28, 2001, entitled "Winning Without Selling Your Soul: A Roundtable on Ethical Negotiations," sponsored by CLE West, and quoted in my column, "Leaders share negotiation strategies anyone can use," *The Business Journal of Phoenix*, April 5, 2002.

34 **get as much information as possible:** Harvey Mackay, *Swim With the Sharks Without Being Eaten Alive* (New York: William Morrow and Company, Inc., 1988), p. 94.

34 **national intelligence budget:** Melvin A. Goodman, "U.S. Intelligence needs retooling," *The Baltimore Sun*, Aug. 20, 2002. Available on-line at www.ciponline.org/nationalsecurity/BS8-20-2002.htm.

35   **Alameda naval station:** The background of this White House Advance Team negotiation was first published in my column "Active listening is critical to successful negotiating," *The Business Journal of Phoenix*, April 28, 2000.

37   **two men quarreling in a library:** Roger Fisher, William Ury, and Bruce Patton, *Getting to Yes: Negotiating Agreement Without Giving In* (New York: Penguin, 1991), p. 40, as related by the late Harvard professor in social work Mary Parker Follett (1868–1933).

40   **Jack's annual performance review:** This story was devised for illustrative purposes.

42   **skilled negotiator more likely to focus on common ground:** Shell, p. 80, citing N. Rackham and J. Carlisle, "The Effective Negotiator—Part 1 : The Behavior of Successful Negotiators," *Journal of European Industrial Training*, Vol. 2, No. 6 (1978), pp. 6–11; N. Rackham and J. Carlisle, "The Effective Negotiator—Part 2: Planning for Negotiations," *Journal of European Industrial Training*, Vol. 2, No. 7 (1978), pp. 2–5.

42   **percentage of time spent getting and clarifying information:** Ibid.

42   **Prison Hostage exercise:** This exercise was written by University of Michigan Law School Professor James J. White and one of his students.

45   **Bill Richardson quote:** Roger Dawson, *Secrets of Power Negotiating: Inside Secrets from a Master Negotiator,* 2nd ed. (Franklin Lakes, N.J.: Career Press, 2001), p. 180, as quoted in *Fortune,* May 27, 1996.

45   **flight delay:** The events related in this story were first published in my column, "Collecting facts can get you where you need to be," *The Business Journal of Phoenix,* May 26, 2000.

49   **Oil Pricing Exercise:** Roger Fisher, Bruce Patton, and Andrew Clarkson, "Oil Pricing Exercise" (Cambridge, Mass.: Clearinghouse, Program on Negotiation at Harvard Law School, 1995).

49   **trust a matter of risk analysis:** Roger Fisher said this during a course on negotiation I took at Harvard Law School in 1991.

52   **the "big shmooze:"** I first wrote about this in my column "Advance your negotiations with the big shmooze," *The Business Journal of Phoenix,* October 27, 2000.

53   **the Liking Rule:** Cialdini, p. 144.

53   **tendency to like and agree with others similar to ourselves:** Cialdini, p. 150, citing D. Byrne, *The Attraction Paradigm* (New York: Academic Press, 1971).

53   **say yes during lunch:** Cialdini, p. 167.

54   **Steve Ross and Caesar Kimmel:** Shell, p. 136, citing Connie Bruck, *Master of the Game: Steve Ross and the Creation of Time Warner* (New York: Penguin, 1994), p. 27.

54   **Columbo:** I first wrote about Columbo's ability to ferret out information in my column "Watch out for egos when negotiating," *The Business Journal of Phoenix,* January 10, 2003.

55   **twice as many questions:** Shell, pp. 145–146, citing N. Rackham and J. Carlisle, "The Effective Negotiator—Part 1: The Behavior of Successful Negotiators," *Journal of European Industrial Training*, Vol. 2, No. 6 (1978), pp. 6–11.

55   **car accident information gathering exercise:** I adapted this exercise from materials prepared by Professor Gary Lowenthal, Arizona State University College of Law.

57   **Funnel Approach:** David A. Binder and Susan C. Price, *Legal Interviewing and Counseling* (St. Paul, Minn.: West Publishing Co., 1977), p. 92.

57   **active listening:** I first discussed this in my column "Active listening is critical to successful negotiating," *The Business Journal of Phoenix*, April 28, 2000.

58 **Parrot Approach:** Binder and Price, p. 30.

58 **list of effective listening techniques:** This list was prepared by University of Wisconsin-Madison Law School Professor Ralph M. Cagle and is included in his "Effective Negotiation Techniques—Workshop Materials," 2003. His list includes the following techniques: "Want to Listen; Stop Talking; Don't Interrupt; Pay Attention; Eliminate Distractions; Listen with Your Whole Presence; Encourage People to Tell You More; Don't Mentally Argue When Someone Is Speaking; Clarify; Defer Judgment; and Emulate Great Listeners."

60 **getting to interests, not positions—ask why:** Fisher et al., p. 44.

61 **nonverbal signals:** Cheryl Hamilton with Cordell Parker, *Communicating for Results: A Guide for Business & the Professions,* 5th Ed. (New York: Wadsworth Publishing Co., 1997), p. 13, citing R. L. Birdwistell, *Kinesics and Context: Essays on Body Motion Communication* (Philadelphia: University of Pennsylvania Press, 1970), p. 158.

61 **Judy's personal appearance:** This example is based on an actual event, and I first related this story in my column "Body language is critical to successful negotiations," *The Business Journal of Phoenix,* January 28, 2000.

62 **facial expressions:** Hamilton, p. 135, citing Birdwhistell.

63 **attractiveness and attire matter:** Hamilton, p. 140, citing J. Mills and E. Aronson, "Opinions Changes as a Function of the Communicator's Attractiveness and Desire to Influence," *Journal of Personality and Social Psychology* 1 (1965), pp. 73–77; H. Sigall, "Psychologist 'Proves' Good Looks Helpful," Associated Press Release, 1974; R. N. Widgery and B. Webster, "The Effects of Physical Attractiveness upon Perceived Initial Credibility," *Michigan Speech Journal* 4 (1969, pp. 9–15; Martin L. Hoffman, "Sex Differences in Empathy and Related Behaviors," *Psychological Bulletin* 84 (1977), pp. 712–722.

64 **blocking techniques:** I first wrote about this in my column "Truth, strategy can be tough elements to mix," *The Business Journal of Phoenix,* January 4, 2002.

2. Golden Rule Two: Maximize Your Leverage.

68 **CEO versus activist:** I first wrote about this in my column "Leverage: understanding and exercising it is key," *The Business Journal of Phoenix,* August 25, 2000.

69 **leverage elements framework:** Richard G. Shell, *Bargaining for Advantage: Negotiation Strategies for Reasonable People* (New York: Viking, 1999), p. 92, and Roger Fisher, William Ury, and Bruce Patton, *Getting to Yes: Negotiating Agreement Without Giving In* (New York: Penguin, 1991), pp. 97–106.

69 **Trump on leverage:** Shell, p. 102, citing Donald J. Trump, *The Art of the Deal* (New York: Random House, 1987), p. 37.

71 **BATNA:** Fisher et al., pp. 97–106.

74 **WATNA:** This term originated with a participant at a seminar given by Michael K. Lewis, managing partner of ADR Associates, LLC, Washington, D.C.

75 **The No-Leverage Dilemma:** A seminar participant posed this problem to me, and it became the basis of my column "Negotiation from strength, even if you don't have any," *The Business Journal of Phoenix,* April 27, 2001.

77 **Nissan repair negotiation:** I related this incident in my column "Look for realistic alternatives to any first offering," *The Business Journal of Phoenix,* May 21, 1999.

80 **Bob's insurance settlement story:** Although the facts related by the lawyer are accurately portrayed, the lawyer's name—"Bob"—has been changed.

81 **Ortega:** This statement was made during a seminar I moderated in Phoenix, Arizona, on September 28, 2001, entitled "Winning Without Selling Your Soul: A Roundtable on Ethical Negotiations," sponsored by CLE West and quoted in my column "Leaders share negotiation strategies anyone can use," *The Business Journal of Phoenix,* April 5, 2002.

81 **Plummer and stadium vote:** The facts as related were confirmed in a conversation between the author and Leigh Steinberg on December 2, 2003.

87 **The Software Sale:** I first wrote about this in my column "Hold out: timing is critical when selling companies," *The Business Journal of Phoenix,* June 7, 2002.

91 **Marlon Brando in *The Godfather*:** Francis Ford Coppola (director), and Robert Evans (producer), and Francis Ford Coppola and Mario Puzo (screenplay), *The Godfather* (Paramount Home Entertainment, 1972), from Mario Puzo, *The Godfather* (New York: Putnam, 1971).

91 **Trump Tower air rights story:** Shell, p. 103, citing Donald J. Trump, *The Art of the Deal* (New York: Random House, 1987), pp. 103–104.

94 **conveying leverage effectively:** James C. Freund, *Smart Negotiating: How to Make Good Deals in the Real World* (New York: Simon & Schuster, 1992), p. 38.

97 **walkouts:** I first wrote about walkouts in my column "Walkouts present risk in negotiation strategies," *The Business Journal of Phoenix,* November 24, 2000.

97 **Trump walkout:** Shell, p. 183, citing David Johnson, "In Taj deal Trump used an old tactic," *The Philadelphia Inquirer,* November 18,1990, p. D1.

98 **walkout signals:** Shell, pp. 183–184.

98 **Huizenga New Orleans walkout story:** Shell, p. 183, citing Gail DeGeorge, *The Making of Blockbuster* (New York: John Wiley & Sons, 1996), pp. 73–74.

98 **Huizenga Blockbuster walkout story:** Shell, citing DeGeorge, p. 282.

100 ***Jerry Maguire*, Rod Tidwell "changed man":** Cameron Crowe (director) James L. Brooks, Laurence Mark, Richard Sakaj, and Cameron Crowe (producers), and Cameron Crowe (screenplay), *Jerry Maguire* (Columbia TriStar, 1997).

101 **"No. No. No.":** Harvey Mackay, *Swim With the Sharks Without Being Eaten Alive* (New York: William Morrow and Company, Inc., 1988), p. 91.

3. Golden Rule Three: Employ "Fair" Objective Criteria.

104 **America West Airlines vs. flight attendants:** I first wrote about this negotiation in my column "America West dispute: what's fair?," *The Business Journal of Phoenix,* March 5,1999.

109 **market value countermeasures:** I first discussed these in my column "Market value may not matter if product, service is unique," *The Business Journal of Phoenix,* August 1, 2003.

124 **LBJ master horse-trader:** President Lyndon B. Johnson's reputation in this regard is a well-known historical fact, according to American Enterprise Institute congressional expert Norman J. Ornstein.

126 **status power (called "situation power" by Dawson):** Roger Dawson, *Secrets of Power Negotiating: Inside Secrets from a Master Negotiator,* 2nd ed. (Franklin Lakes, N.J.: Career Press, 2001), pp. 279–280. This element of power formed the basis for my column "Sharp negotiators are aware of status power," *The Business Journal of Phoenix,* January 26, 2001.

126 **definition of status:** *Webster's New Collegiate Dictionary* (Springfield, Mass.: G. & C. Merriam Company, 1979), p. 1128.

135   **NASD process:** NASD Rule 10308, Selection of Arbitrators.

135   **benefits of mediation:** Howard Raiffa, *The Art and Science of Negotiation: How to Resolve Conflicts and Get the Best Out of Bargaining* (Cambridge, Mass.: Harvard University Press, 1982), pp. 108–109.

137   **Bill and Kate at the art sale:** This story was devised for illustrative purposes only.

140   **consistency principle:** Robert B. Cialdini, *Influence: Science and Practice,* 4th ed. (Boston: Allyn & Bacon, 2001), p. 54.

4. Golden Rule Four: Design an Offer-Concession Strategy.

145   **Roger and the "cut to the chase" story:** The facts related are essentially true, but the client's name has been changed. Back in the mid-1990s, a very experienced family lawyer described the basic elements of this actual negotiation to me. However, I devised the specific financial and other details here for illustrative purposes.

151   **advantage of making first offer:** James C. Freund, *Smart Negotiating: How to Make Good Deals in the Real World* (New York: Simon & Schuster, 1992), pp. 114–115.

153   **The "Flinch":** Roger Dawson, *Secrets of Power Negotiating: Inside Secrets from a Master Negotiator,* 2nd ed. (Franklin Lakes, N.J.: Career Press, 2001), pp. 29.

155   **Edison's stock ticker:** I first related this story in my column "Know the value of your product to your customer," *The Business Journal of Phoenix,* June 18,1999. I found this story in Donald G. Gifford, *Legal Negotiation Theory and Applications* (St. Paul, Minn.: West Publishing Co., 1989). The story's original source is Frank Lewis Dyer and Thomas Commerford Martin, *Edison: His Life and Inventions* (New York: Harper Brothers, 1929), p. 132.

158   **Walt Disney World land purchase:** Reporter Emily Bavar Kelly (1915–2003) broke this story in the *Orlando Sentinel* on October 21,1965, in her article entitled "'Mystery' Industry Disneyland?" Further details on the land deal were obtained during a telephone conversation on December 2, 2003, with Jim Robison, journalist for the *Orlando Sentinel* and co-author of *Flashbacks: The Story of Central Florida's Past* (Orlando: Orange County Historical Society and *Orlando Sentinel,* 1995).

159   **Henry and the pizza place:** This story is fictitious and the figures used for gross revenue and sales were devised for illustrative purposes and do not reflect actual figures for small mountain community pizza/bar restaurants.

166   **preferred range:** Freund, p. 119.

167   **expectations and wheel of fortune study:** Robert H. Mnookin, Scott R. Peppet, and Andrew S. Tulumello, *Beyond Winning: Negotiating to Create value in Deals and Disputes* (Cambridge, Mass.: The Belknap Press, 2000), pp. 212–213, citing Amos Tversky and Daniel Kahneman, "Judgment Under Uncertainty: Heuristics and Biases" in Daniel Kahneman, Paul Slovic, and Amos Tversky, eds., *Judgment Under Uncertainty: Heuristics and Biases* (Cambridge: Cambridge University Press, 1982), p. 14; Lax and Sebenius, *The Manager as Negotiator,* p. 134.

167   **starting point:** Robert B. Cialdini, *Influence: The Psychology of Persuasion,* rev. ed. (New York: William Morrow, 1994), p. 40.

169   **psychological expectations:** I first wrote about this in my column "Learn to play the negotiation expectation game," *The Business Journal of Phoenix,* July 27, 2001.

173   **split the difference:** I first related this story in my column "'Split the difference' can translate as 'lose the edge,'" *The Business Journal of Phoenix,* February 23, 2001.

177   **Christmas card experiment:** Cialdini, *Influence: Science and Practice,* 4th ed. (Boston: Allyn & Bacon, 2001), p. 20.

178   **rejection-then-retreat:** ibid., p. 38.

179   *Happy Days:* Robert B. Cialdini, Ph.D., *Influence: The Psychology of Persuasion,* rev. ed. (New York: William Morrow, 1984), pp. 40–41.

180   **commitment through consistency:** ibid., p. 61.

180   **Cancer Society commitment study:** ibid., p. 62.

188   **Delaware closed story:** Herb Cohen, *You Can Negotiate Anything* (New York: Bantam Books, 1980), pp. 59–60. I first used this story in my column "Know how to proceed when talks take a write turn," *The Business Journal of Phoenix,* October 4, 2002.

191   **The "Flinch":** Dawson, p. 29.

193   **blue chip and bargaining chips:** Freund, pp. 72–74.

193   **inflexibility:** Freund, p. 70.

193   **numeric value for nonmonetary interests:** Freund, p. 160–161.

194   **The "Vise":** Dawson, p. 42.

194   **logrolling:** This term originated with early American pioneers who often helped each other out when clearing land and building cabins. The term's earliest recorded use in the congressional sense occurred in 1823.

194   **proportionate increase/decrease:** Freund, p. 139.

195   **agents concede less:** I first wrote about this in my column "Offer and concession strategies: how much to budge," *The Business Journal of Phoenix,* March 24, 2000. I subsequently generally wrote about agents in my column "Agents—learn when to use them in negotiations," in *The Business Journal of Phoenix,* June 22, 2001.

196   **advantages and disadvantages of using agents:** Freund, pp. 175–176.

197   **Samuel L. Jackson in *The Negotiator*:** F. Gary Gray (director), David Hoberman (producer), and James De Monaco and Kevin Fox (screenplay), *The Negotiator* (Warner Brothers, 1998). I first wrote about this in my column "The negotiation bluff: when, where and how to do it," *The Business Journal of Phoenix,* August 24, 2001.

199   **bluffing risks and effective tactics:** Freund, p. 74.

202   *The Poseidon Adventure*: Cialdini, *Influence: The Psychology of Persuasion,* pp. 224–226.

203   **psychological commitment:** Cohen, pp. 38–39.

204   **commercial real estate closing dilemma:** The real estate closing problem was related to me by a seminar participant. His dilemma and my response formed the basis of my column, "Close, maybe, but no cigar until final commitment," *The Business Journal of Phoenix,* October 26, 2001.

204   **Jennifer and the service contract proposal:** This story occurred as I have related it; however, "Jennifer" is a fictitious name.

206   **focus on gains, not losses:** Robert H. Mnookin, Scott R. Peppet, and Andrew S. Tulumello, *Beyond Winning: Negotiating to Create Value in Deals and Disputes* (Cambridge, Mass.: The Belknap Press, 2000), p. 161.

5. Golden Rule Five: Control the Agenda.

214   **"cut to the chase":** I first wrote about this in my column "Agenda control aids negotiation success," *The Business Journal of Phoenix,* May 25, 2001.

216 **NBA lockout:** I first wrote about this in my column "NBA owners take players to negotiation school," *The Business Journal of Phoenix,* February 5, 1999.

219 **managing deadlines:** I first wrote about this in my column "How to use imposed deadlines to your advantage," *The Business Journal of Phoenix,* March 7, 2003.

220 **time limits and "scarcity effect":** Robert B. Cialdini, *Influence: Science and Practice,* 4th ed. (Boston: Allyn & Bacon, 2001), p. 207.

222 **Cohen and the Japanese:** Herb Cohen, *You Can Negotiate Anything* (New York: Bantam Books, 1980), pp. 93–95.

227 **Colangelo interview:** This interview took place on August 30, 1999.

227 **employment interview and "turf":** I first wrote about controlling turf in my column "Does turf matter? Negotiating place can impact deal," *The Business Journal of Phoenix,* May 2, 2003.

228 **psychological role of turf:** James C. Freund, *Smart Negotiating: How to Make Good Deals in the Real World* (New York: Simon & Schuster, 1992), p. 208.

232 **North Korea negotiations deadlock:** Philip P. Pan and Glenn Kessler, "U.S. and N. Korea agree to bilateral meeting set in multilateral form," *Washington Post,* picked up by *Pittsburgh Post-Gazette,* Aug. 2, 2003. Available on-line at www.postgazette.com/pg/03214/208122.stm.

6. Personality Tendencies—Style Issues.

239 **personal styles:** I first wrote about personal styles in my column "Personal styles can make or break a negotiation," *The Business Journal of Phoenix,* August 2, 2002.

239 **personality types:** Robert H. Mnookin, Scott R. Peppet and Andrew S. Tulumello, *Beyond Winning: Negotiating to Create Value in Deals and Disputes* (Cambridge, Mass.: The Belknap Press, 2000), pp. 9–12. Much of the psychological research is derived from the Thomas-Kilmann Conflict Mode Instrument that was developed in the 1970s by psychologists Kenneth W. Thomas of UCLA and Ralph H. Kilmann of the University of Pittsburgh.

240 **competitor characteristics:** Mnookin et al., pp. 51–52.

242 **accommodator characteristics:** Mnookin et al., p. 52.

243 **conflict avoider characteristics:** Mnookin et al., pp. 52–53.

244 **effective negotiator traits:** Andrea Kupfer Schneider, "Shattering Negotiation Myths: Empirical Evidence on the Effectiveness of Negotiation Style, *Harvard Negotiation Law Review,* Vol. 7 (Spring 2002), p. 143.

7. Ethics Make a Bottom-Line Difference.

247 **fraud as basis for determining ethics from legal standpoint:** Richard G. Shell, *Bargaining for Advantage: Negotiation Strategies for Reasonable People* (New York: Viking, 1999), p. 206.

247 **legal limits:** For a good analysis of the legal limits, especially those pertaining to lawyers, see Robert H. Mnookin, Scott R. Peppet, and Andrew S. Tulumello, *Beyond Winning: Negotiating to Create Value in Deals and Disputes* (Cambridge, Mass.: The Belknap Press, 2000), pp. 274–281. See also Shell, pp. 201–222.

249 **job security and health benefits misrepresentation:** I first wrote about this, a fictitious story, in my column "Negotiations should be based on truth, moral terms," *The Business Journal of Phoenix,* June 13, 2003.

250 **Gary and investment banker:** I first wrote about this true story in my column "Know who you're dealing with: ethics do matter," *The Business Journal of Phoenix,* March 1, 2002. The name of the investment banker has been changed.

251 **schools of belief:** Shell, p. 215

251 **"Poker School":** Shell, pp. 215–217

251 **"Idealist School":** Shell, pp. 217–219

252 **"Pragmatist School":** Shell, pp. 219–20

252 **"I don't trust him":** I first wrote about this in my column "Trust's boundaries best marked in units of risk," *The Business Journal of Phoenix,* May 3, 2002.

8. Use a Situation-Specific Strategy.

255 **spousal negotiation example:** I first wrote about this in my column "When closing deals one size doesn't fit all," *The Business Journal of Phoenix,* July 28, 2000.

258 **Datsun purchase story:** I first wrote about this in my column "Offer/concession strategy must reflect ultimate goal," *The Business Journal of Phoenix,* February 7, 2003.

258 **Larry and Ellie airline tickets story:** The facts stated in this story are true, but the names have been changed.

266 **"soft" style carries a cost:** Richard G. Shell, *Bargaining for Advantage: Negotiation Strategies for Reasonable People* (New York: Viking, 1999), pp. 66–67, citing William R. Fry, Ira J. Firestone, and David L. Williams, "Negotiation Process and Outcome of Stranger Dyads and Dating Couples: Do Lovers Lose?" *Basic and Applied Social Psychology,* Vol. 4, No. 1 (1983), pp. 1–16.

274 ***Pretty Woman***: Garry Marshall (director), Arnon Milchan, Steven Reuter, and Nancy Gross (producers), J.F. Lawton (screenplay), *Pretty Woman* (Disney Studios, 1990).

277 **Ury's problem-solving strategies:** William Ury, *Getting Past No: Negotiating Your Way From Confrontation To Cooperation* (New York: Bantam Books, 1991).

281 **The 2002 Baseball Negotiations:** I first wrote about this in my column "Fans' squeeze play led to baseball deal," *The Business Journal of Phoenix,* September 6, 2002.

9. Common Negotiation Problems and Their Solutions.

286 **Officer Toughguy:** I first wrote about common negotiation "games" in my column "Prepare yourself to parry common negotiation ploys," *The Business Journal of Phoenix,* April 6, 2001.

287 **The "Flinch":** Dawson, p. 29.

289 **top ten impasse-breaking strategies:** I first wrote about these in my column "Here are 10 ways to break through a late impasse," *The Business Journal of Phoenix,* August 27, 1999.

289 **Lee Iacocca:** William Ury, *Getting Past No: Negotiating Your Way From Confrontation To Cooperation* (New York: Bantam Books, 1991), pp. 134–135.

292 **AT&T and Boeing:** Ury, pp. 52–53, 73–75. The headings "Don't React: Go to the Balcony" and "Don't Argue: Step to Their Side" came directly from Ury's *Getting Past No.* I first wrote about this in my column "When emotions stop the talks, it's time to step back," *The Business Journal of Phoenix,* November 23, 2001.

293 **Jefferson quote on anger:** Ury, p. 45. The original source of this quote is an 1825 letter from Thomas Jefferson to his grandson, Thomas Jefferson Smith, found in Thomas Jefferson, *Jefferson the Man: In His Own Words,* Robert A. Baron, ed. (Golden, Colo.: Fulcrum Publishing, 1998).

294 **overcoming fear in negotiation:** I first wrote about overcoming fear in negotiation in my column "Knowledge a key to overcoming fear in negotiation," *The Business Journal of Phoenix,* September 28, 2001.

297 *Survivor:* Mark Burnett, executive producer (CBS Network, 2000). I first wrote about this in my column "The more the merrier in negotiations, if you're ready," *The Business Journal of Phoenix,* November 1, 2002.

11. Salary Negotiations.

317 **law student salary negotiation:** I first related this story in my column "Don't by shy, learn how to negotiate, ask for raise," *The Business Journal of Phoenix,* February 25, 2000.

12. Family Negotiations.

322 **spousal negotiations:** I first wrote about this in my column "Take softer approach when negotiating with family," *The Business Journal of Phoenix,* April 4, 2003.

323 **blame game:** Douglas Stone, Bruce Patton, and Sheila Heen, *Difficult Conversations: How to Discuss What Matters Most* (New York, N. Y.: Penguin Books, 1999), p. 59.

324 **express feelings:** Stone et al., p. 86.

324 **identity conversation:** Stone et al., pp. 7–8.

325 **gender communication differences:** John Gray, *Men are from Mars, Women are from Venus* (New York: HarperCollins, 1993).

13. Car Negotiations.

326 **car negotiation 2002:** I first wrote about this in my column "Lowering your dream car's price means raising your knowledge," *The Business Journal of Phoenix,* February 1, 2002.

14. House Negotiations.

331 **"she wouldn't budge":** I first wrote about this in my column "Flexibility and timing are critical in negotiations," *The Business Journal of Phoenix,* September 22, 2000.

343 **offer/counteroffer deadline in Phoenix market:** This was confirmed by Michal Poplawski, a long-time Phoenix-area real estate agent.

343 **offer/counteroffer deadline in Ann Arbor market:** This was confirmed by Judy Cohen, a long-time Ann Arbor–area real estate agent.

Conclusion.

345 **Adam's story conclusion:** As noted above, this story was based on an actual negotiation that took place between a young architect looking for work in San Francisco in 2002 and his prospective employer. However, I devised the specific dialogue and strategies for illustrative purposes here and at the beginning of the book.

INDEX